Matthew Parker

MONTE CASSINO

Matthew Parker is the author of *The Battle of Britain*. He is a writer and editor specializing in modern history, and lives in London, England.

MONTE CASSINO

The Hardest-Fought Battle
of World War II

Matthew Parker

ANCHOR BOOKS
A Division of Random House, Inc.
New York

For Hannah

Love conquers all

FIRST ANCHOR BOOKS EDITION, MAY 2005

Copyright © 2004 by Matthew Parker

All rights reserved under International and Pan-American Copyright Conventions. Published in the United States by Anchor Books, a division of Random House, Inc., New York, and simultaneously in Canada by Random House of Canada Limited, Toronto. Originally published in hardcover in Great Britain by Headline, London, in 2003, and subsequently in the United States by Doubleday, a division of Random House, Inc., New York, in 2004.

Anchor Books and colophon are registered trademarks of Random House, Inc.

The Library of Congress has cataloged the Doubleday edition as follows:
Parker, Matthew.
Monte Cassino: the hardest-fought battle of World War II / Matthew Parker.—1st ed.
p.   cm.
Originally published: London: Headline, 2003.
Includes bibliographical references and index.
1. Cassino, Battle of, Cassino, Italy, 1944.   I. Title.
D763.I82M657   2004
940.54'215622—dc22   2003068778

Anchor ISBN: 1-4000-3375-6

Author photograph © Angus Muir

www.anchorbooks.com

Printed in the United States of America
10   9   8   7   6   5   4   3   2   1

CONTENTS

PART THREE
The Second Battle

PART FOUR
The Third Battle

PART FIVE
The Fourth Battle

FOREWORD

They are saying, "The Generals learnt their lesson in the last war.
There are going to be no wholesale slaughters." I ask, how is
victory possible except by wholesale slaughters?
—EVELYN WAUGH, OCTOBER 1939

War makes sense only in black-and-white. The Second World War has a unique position in popular memory as a "good war," particularly when compared with the First World War. Fought by the United Nations (as the Allies referred to themselves) against the tyranny of Nazism and the aggression of the Japanese, the victorious conclusion of the fighting ended many appalling crimes against humanity and justified all the sacrifices made by the men on the right side. Now, whenever the morality of a war is discussed, it is always measured against the yardstick of the Second World War. It has become the war that justifies war.

To a large extent, the Second World War has been written by its victors as a heroic narrative. For every *Catch-22* or *Slaughterhouse-Five*, there have been hundreds of novels, histories, and films celebrating the unshakeable moral certainties of the fighting. For my generation, growing up in the 1970s, the war films we were shown and the comics that seemed to be everywhere were all about the Second World War. It is impossible to imagine the popular conception of the First World War making an appropriate backdrop for such straightforward stories, just as war games played by young boys never involved the trenches or more recent, even more morally ambiguous conflicts. It was always us against the Nazis, good versus evil.

The First World War, as well as contributing to the causes of the Second, also shaped people's responses to it. At the beginning of the Second World War, it was hoped that new technologies would prevent the appalling attrition of infantrymen that occurred in the First. Interwar advances in aircraft, guns, tanks, submarines, and bombs led people to believe that, this time, the fighting would be fast-moving, mechanized, dominated by air power, somehow "remote-controlled," or carried out by a few experts. The popular story of the Battle of Britain—with scores of downed planes being chalked up on blackboards as if it were a cricket match—to an extent conforms to this pattern, and this view of the Second World War, at least in the West, as somehow "cleaner" than the First, has survived both the subsequent fighting and the postwar period.

The Battle of Monte Cassino throws all of this into question. Instead of fighting a battle of rapid movement, the men found themselves in scenes straight out of the Western Front in 1916–17. The terrain at Cassino sent the fighting back to a premechanized age. The mountains of central Italy and winter weather conspired to make technology such as armor useless. One hard-working mule was more prized than a dozen tanks, and the Allies' huge numerical advantage in artillery and aircraft was seldom decisive and often a hindrance. For one thing, such firepower had its risks. It has been estimated that a third of Allied casualties in Italy were caused by "friendly fire"; one American artilleryman at Cassino bemoaned that American bombers killed more of his division than did the Luftwaffe.

Nor was there much nationalistic certainty or unity of purpose driving the forces in Italy. With so many different national and ethnic groups from such radically different societies, it would have been an impossibility. As well as American and British soldiers, the Allied ranks included New Zealanders, Canadians, Nepalese, Indians, French, Belgians, South Africans, Tunisians, Algerians, Moroccans, Senegalese, Poles, Italians, and even Brazilians. Within these groups were units made up of Native Americans, Japanese-Americans, and Maoris. They were all there for different reasons. The result was a coalition riddled at the highest level with distrust and jealousy, with the inevitable consequences of misunderstandings and mistakes. In large part badly led and poorly equipped, the Allied soldiers who fought at Cassino could see from the way they were downgraded in the press at home that they were fighting battles of enormous scale and cost that were, at best, of secondary strategic importance, with the scant resources in reserves to match.

The Germans were even worse off. For every shell that Krupps sent over, General Motors sent back five. As well as artillery ammunition, the Germans were desperately short of basic food and clothing for the frontline troops guarding icy mountaintops in mid-winter. Many froze to death for lack of a greatcoat.

Between these opposing groups of men, in some places facing each other over just twenty or thirty yards of open ground, there was a shared suffering of the fighting and the elements, and surprisingly often the war would be stopped in local areas so that teams of stretcher bearers from both sides could work together to rescue the numerous wounded. Many record the bafflement of then resuming efforts to kill one another once the time of the truce was up.

From firsthand accounts, contemporary diaries and letters, and through listening to hundreds of veterans, a picture emerges of most people's experience of war that is different from the black-and-white image of popular conception. The men's descriptions of their times in action are dominated by confusion, fear, blunders, and accidents; they also talk about the times of boredom, of longing for home, the "chickenshit" or "bull" of the army as well as of the companionship with friends, many lost. They discuss how the experience changed them, and their feelings now about what happened.

While aiming to explain the strategic and tactical compromises and fudges that led to the battles, this book focuses on the human experience of the men there at the time, rather than playing "what if?" games or "weighing" the performance of the generals. To this end, I have tried as much as possible to let the eyewitnesses tell the story in their own words.

MAPS

INTRODUCTION

The Monastery and the Gustav Line

Only the bloodbaths of Verdun and Passchendaele or the very worst of the Second World War fighting on the Eastern Front can compare to Monte Cassino. The largest land battle in Europe, Cassino was the bitterest and bloodiest of the Western Allies' struggles against the German Wehrmacht on any front of the Second World War. On the German side, many compared it unfavorably with Stalingrad.

After the conquest of Sicily, the invasion of Italy in 1943 saw Allied troops facing the German army in a lengthy campaign on the mainland of Europe for the first time for three years. By the beginning of 1944, Italy was still the Western Allies' only active front against Nazi-controlled Europe, and progress had been painfully slow. The campaign was becoming an embarrassment, and tensions between the Allies were rising.

It was not an easy task the Allies had set themselves. Not since Belisarius in A.D. 536 had anyone successfully taken Rome from the south. Hannibal even traversed the Alps rather than taking the direct route from Carthage. Napoleon is credited with saying, "Italy is a boot. You have to enter it from the top." The reason is the geography south of Rome. High mountains are bisected by fast-flowing rivers. The only possible route to the Italian capital from the south is up the old Via Casilina, now known as Route 6. Eighty miles south of Rome, this road passes up the valley of the Liri River. This was where the German commander, Kesselring, chose to make his stand. Towering over the entrance to the valley was the monastery of Monte Cassino.

It is one of Christianity's most sacred sites. Reportedly founded by the Roman nobleman Saint Benedict in 529, the abbey became the blueprint for monasteries in Western Europe. From Monte Cassino, Benedictine monks set out to establish monasteries throughout the Christian world. Meanwhile, the monastery's great library saw the preservation and copying of writings from antiquity onward, the safeguarding of the heritage of early civilization. The monastery was largely destroyed during an earthquake in 1349, but rebuilding started straightaway with the support of Pope Urban V. The new abbey was massive, a vast complex of buildings around five courtyards. It had walls twenty feet thick at their base; from below, the huge building, with its grim rows of cell windows, looked like a fortress. During the Renaissance the abbey became a favorite destination for pilgrims. The Benedictine monks, as was their custom, washed the travelers' feet and served them at the table. During one year in the early seventeenth century there were eighty thousand visitors. Generations of Italians labored to beautify the buildings. During the eighteenth century, in the hands of several of Italy's finest artists, the monastery became a baroque masterpiece and a center for the fine arts. In 1868 the abbey became Italian national property, but the library remained one of the most important in the world: By 1943 it contained over forty thousand manuscripts and much of the writings of Tacitus, Cicero, Horace, Virgil, Ovid, and many others. Over the gate of the monastery was carved one word: *Pax.*

But Benedict had chosen his site at a time when Christianity, based on Rome, was at its lowest ebb. To protect his new community, he had built his monastery on the top of more than five hundred meters of solid rock at the end of a mountain spur that rises almost vertically above the valleys beneath. From its high windows, one can see for miles around; all the approaches to the mountain are laid out to view like a map.

At the end of 1943 it was already considered one of the finest defensive positions in Europe and had been studied as such in Italian staff colleges for years. As well as benefiting from its commanding position, it was protected by the Rapido and Garigliano Rivers, which form a natural moat in front of it. Its flanks are guarded by jagged, trackless mountains: from the Liri valley almost to the coast stretch the Aurunci Mountains; behind the monastery the Cassino Massif rises into the forbidding Abruzzi Range.

North of Cassino there is no series of river barriers, as on the Adriatic coast. Beyond the Rapido valley, the rivers run south and north, the Tiber leading up to the Lake Trasimeno area whence the Arno leads to Florence. So Cassino was the last natural defensive position before Rome, and the fall of Rome would mean the fall of central Italy.

The Cassino Massif on which the abbey stood was the key position on the Gustav Line, a system of interlocking German defenses that ran all the way across the narrowest part of Italy between Gaeta and Ortona. It was an awesome piece of military engineering, the most formidable defensive system encountered by the British or Americans during the war. Much of the line overlooked rivers with steep banks, in particular the Garigliano and the Rapido, or was in either coastal marshland or on high mountaintops. The natural defensive advantages of the mountainous terrain had been accentuated by the Germans by removing buildings and trees to create fields of fire. Elsewhere, the natural caves of the area had been extended and defensive positions reinforced with railway girders and concrete. Dugouts were created, linked by underground passages. Rather than a single line, the defenses were multilayered, with positions planned from which to launch instant counterattacks on frontline areas lost. From November 1943, Hitler took a personal interest in the Gustav Line, ordering that it be upgraded to "fortress strength." A system of antipersonnel minefields interlocked with barbedwire entanglements, was set up to cover the flats before the hills to a depth of up to four hundred yards beyond the riverbanks. A dam on the Rapido was blown to divert the river; the entire plain in front of the monastery, already soggy from winter rain, had become a quagmire. The Germans had the time to survey every possible route of attack and take countermeasures. Everywhere there were nasty surprises—any seeming cover for attackers was mined or booby-trapped.

On 24 January 1944, British and American bombers dropped leaflets on the defenders of Monte Cassino offering them "Stalingrad or Tunis"—encirclement and destruction or honorable surrender. But in a grim echo of the orders to hold the city on the Volga, Hitler decreed that there would be no more retreat in Italy. In the same month the German leader issued the following order: "Within the next few days the 'Battle for Rome' will begin. It will be decisive for the defense of Central Italy and for the fate of the 10th Army . . . All officers and men . . . must be penetrated by a fanatical will to end this battle victoriously, and never to relax until the last enemy soldier has been destroyed . . . The battle must be fought in a spirit of holy hatred for an enemy who is conducting a pitiless war of extermination against the German people . . . The fight must be hard and merciless, not only against the enemy, but against all officers and units who fail in this decisive hour."

The Allies by now dominated the sea and the air. They also had superiority in tanks and armored vehicles. But a combination of the Italian geography and winter weather often nullified such advantages. The line could be broken only by infantry. The battle, then, was man to man, to be fought with grenades, bayonets, and at times bare hands, and the outcome would be decided by the caliber and determination of the soldiers involved.

As the Allied troops neared the Gustav Line, they could see what they were up against. A Scots Guards lieutenant, D. H. Deane, remembers arriving on the other side of the Rapido River, and, along with everyone else, taking in the battlefield to come: "Impregnable mountains, obviously with armies of Boche," he noted. "Vast mountains lie in front, bleak and sinister."

Lieutenant Deane's premonitions were correct. The battles to take Monte Cassino were some of the hardest fought of the war in any theater. Between Deane's first sight of Monte Cassino and the triumphant moment when Polish soldiers raised their pennant on the shattered walls of the ancient monastery lies an extraordinary story of ordinary soldiers tested to the limits under conditions more typical of the horrors of the First World War. As the battle progressed, it became increasingly political, symbolic, and personal. As the stakes were raised, more and more men were asked to throw themselves at the virtually impregnable German defenses. Monte Cassino is a story of incompetence, hubris, and politics redeemed at dreadful cost by the bravery, sacrifice, and humanity of the ordinary soldiers.

We're the D-Day Dodgers, out in Italy,
Always on the vino, always on the spree,
Eighth Army skivers and the Yanks.
We go to war, in ties like swanks,
We are the D-Day Dodgers, in sunny Italy.

We landed at Salerno, a holiday with pay,
Jerry brought his bands out, to cheer us on our way.
Showed us all the sights and gave us tea,
We all sang songs and the beer was free.
We are the D-Day Dodgers, the lads that D-Day dodged.

Salerno and Cassino were taken in our stride,
We did not go to fight there, we just went for the ride,
Anzio and Sangro are just names,
We only went to look for dames.
We are the D-Day Dodgers, in sunny Italy.

Looking round the hillsides, through the mist and rain,
See the scattered crosses, some that bear no name.
Heartbreak and toil and suffering gone,
The boys beneath, they slumber on.
They are the D-Day Dodgers, who'll stay in Italy.

PART ONE

Sicily to Cassino

We heard all through the war that the army was "eager to be led against the enemy." It must have been so, for truthful correspondents said so, and editors confirmed it. But when you came to hunt for this particular itch, it was always the next regiment that had it. The truth is, when bullets are whacking against tree-trunks and solid shot are cracking skulls like eggshells, the consuming passion in the heart of the average man is to get out of the way. Between the physical fear of going forward and the moral fear of turning back, there is a predicament of exceptional awkwardness from which a hidden hole in the ground would be a wonderfully welcome outlet.

—David L. Thompson, *Battles and Leaders of the Civil War*

PART ONE

1

The Casablanca Conference and the Invasion of Sicily

On 14 January 1943, Roosevelt and Churchill met in the newly liberated city of Casablanca in Morocco. In the East, the ring had closed around Stalingrad, and the Western Allied leaders now debated their next steps. With Churchill in the lavish surroundings of the Villa Mirador on the outskirts of the city was Gen. Sir Harold Alexander, later to be overall Allied commander at Cassino, whose "easy, smiling grace," Churchill wrote, "won all hearts." Harold Macmillan, then the British resident minister in North Africa, wrote of Churchill, "I have never seen him in finer form. He ate and drank enormously all the time, settled huge problems . . ." Officially, all were in agreement: With the campaign in Tunisia taking longer than expected, the cross-Channel invasion would be delayed until 1944. Once German resistance in North Africa had been ended, an invasion of Sicily would follow. If successful, this would give the Allies control of the Mediterranean, reopen the Gibraltar–Suez shipping lane and, they hoped, knock Italy out of the war.

Behind the outward shows of unity, however, lurked serious disagreements about strategy. In fact, the Casablanca Conference saw the stormiest negotiations ever to occur between the Western Allies. The Americans, observing the military dictum that an attacker should go the shortest route to his objective with the greatest strength he can muster, were deeply suspicious of further delays to the invasion of France. The staunchest holder of this line was Gen. George Marshall, the US Army chief of staff and Roosevelt's right-hand man as far as running the war was concerned. In his view the Mediterranean was a sideshow and an unnecessary drain on manpower and resources that could be better employed by returning immediately to England and then heading via the shortest route to Berlin. Churchill though, like all the British, haunted by the ghosts of the Western Front a generation earlier, was determined to delay the battle in northern France until success was far more assured. He didn't think that moment had come, and also had other motives for pushing forward in the Mediterranean. Traditionally a British concern because of the route to India, Churchill was also intent on "setting the Balkans alight"—exploiting the resistance to Nazi occupation that had already tied down vital German divisions and aiming to cut supplies of oil and other products essential to Germany's war machine. He was even far-sighted enough to wish to get Western Allied soldiers into Central Europe and especially Greece before the Red Army arrived.

Exasperated by British reluctance to proceed full-steam-ahead with plans for the cross-Channel invasion, the Americans were suspicious that Churchill's Mediterranean ambitions were motivated by imperial interests. There had been tension between Britain and America between the wars, including fierce exchanges over Britain's economic policy of Imperial Preference, which damaged US trade, and the American leadership could be absolutely sure of its people's deeply held anticolonialism. For Churchill, though, the empire was not up for discussion.

But at Casablanca the British, much to their surprise, got their way, and after ten days of heated negotiation a compromise was reached that prepared the invasion of Sicily. This, as will be seen, led almost inadvertently to the major struggle in Italy, and the Americans retained the impression that they had been duped, or "led down the garden path" as far as Southern Europe was concerned.

The ramifications of the Casablanca Conference were to affect the whole of the Italian campaign. To a great extent, at the highest level the Americans were unwilling participants in Churchill's "Mediterranean adventure." This made the southern theater a low priority for supplies and manpower, and also fed the distrust and dislike between the two principal allies, which was to reach its grim conclusion at Monte Cassino.

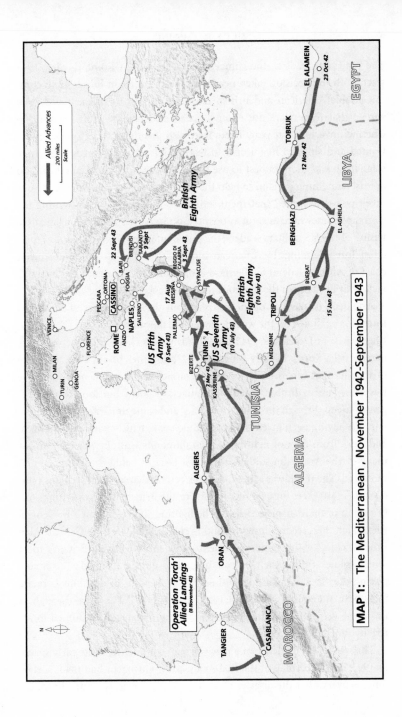

MAP 1: The Mediterranean, November 1942-September 1943

The road that leads to the climactic battles south of Rome in early 1944 starts with the decision taken nearly two years earlier in July 1942 to commit sizable American and British resources to North Africa. It had been agreed that there were not enough specialized landing craft for a cross-Channel invasion that year. There were also insufficient US forces already trained and shipped to Europe. Instead of letting what forces there were stagnate, it was thought best to use them to clear North Africa and thus do at least something on land to help the hard-pressed Soviets. President Roosevelt was determined that there should be American troops fighting the Germans somewhere as soon as possible. So in November 1942, against the wishes of the US military leaders, the president gave the go-ahead for Operation Torch; landings by American and British troops along the northwest coast of Africa. General Sir Bernard Montgomery's 8th Army, following its victory at El Alamein the previous month, attacked from the east.

The deep misgivings of the British about the unreadiness of the Allied forces for an attack on the well-defended northern French coast proved justified when in December 1942 the 8th Army was checked by the outnumbered Afrika Korps. In early February 1943, Rommel, briefly back in charge of the German forces in Africa, counterattacked American units near the Kasserine Pass in Tunisia. Initially the attack was held, but soon rumors began to sweep through the American ranks, and some units started retreating without having been given the order to do so. Exhausted and demoralized, and weak from days of fighting in the mountains without water, it was for many of the American soldiers their first taste of being dive-bombed and mortared. The result was a panic-stricken retreat that saw the Germans push back their attackers for over fifty miles. For the British, it was upsetting confirmation of their suspicions about the fighting ability of their ally. General Alexander, then second-in-command in the theater, wrote to Gen. Sir Alan Brooke, chief of the Imperial General Staff and effectively Britain's most senior soldier, calling the GIs "soft, green and quite untrained . . . is it surprising they lack the will to fight? . . . If this handful of divisions here are their best, the value of the rest may be imagined." The breakthrough at Kasserine was not exploited, but German reinforcements continued to arrive in Tunisia.

This move was evidence of a new German confidence in the early spring of 1943. To the dismay of the Red Army, the Wehrmacht had made a startling recovery after the disaster of Stalingrad the previous winter. In March

1943 the Soviets were driven back in places by a hundred miles when the Germans counterattacked around Kharkov in the Ukraine. In addition to this success, new weapons were coming through, including Tiger heavy tanks and Panther heavy-medium tanks. A massive manpower mobilization using slave labor had freed thousands of Germans for military service, and the Wehrmacht was now close to its size of two years earlier in spite of the enormous losses on the Eastern Front. Germany's increasingly unwilling allies—Italy, Finland, Hungary, and Romania—had been kept in the war, and another great offensive was planned for May around Kursk. Submarine production was up and it was hoped that offensives against the West at sea and the East on land would see Germany through until the unlikely alliance between the United States/Britain and the Soviet Union fell apart.

Furthermore, even relations between the United States and Britain were strained. After the Casablanca Conference and the setback in the Kasserine Pass, the Americans persisted in their suspicions that they had been hoodwinked into an expensive sideshow, and the British remained fearful that their ally would pull the plug on the Mediterranean theater, or, even worse, go back on the Germany First policy and transfer the bulk of their forces to fight Japan. Events on the ground had also led to distrust on one side matched by resentment on the other. President Roosevelt himself complained that the British had relegated American units to supporting roles, unwilling to trust them with anything else. In fact, the performance of the American II Corps in Africa improved markedly as the soldiers and commanders gained experience and received training from British troops. As Gen. Omar Bradley, II Corps' commander, commented after the war, Tunisia was an important testing ground. "In Africa," he wrote, "we learned to crawl, to walk—then run." By 3 March, the ground lost in Rommel's February counterattack had been recaptured, and at the end of the month General Patton's American divisions met up with Montgomery's 8th Army, which had at last broken through the German defensive lines in southern Tunisia. Alexander then reorganized the Allied armies and ordered a general offensive to start on 4 May. By then German supply lines to their army in Tunisia were under constant attack, and it was decided in Berlin to abandon the Afrika Korps, now commanded by Gen. Jurgen von Arnim. Three days later Bizerte and Tunis were captured, and on 12 May a message was intercepted by the Allies from von Arnim: "We have fired our last cartridge. We are closing down for ever." By the next day, all Axis forces in North Africa had surrendered. In all, some 130,000 German and 120,000 Italian prisoners were taken. Notes made by an Allied cameraman recording the capitulation maintain that the lines of prisoners stretched for twenty-two kilometers. By any standards, it was a spectacular victory for the Allies.

The front line was now the Sicilian Channel, and, as agreed at Casablanca, preparations started for an assault on the island. There was considerable nervousness about what was to be the Allies' first major amphibious landing on an enemy-held coast, and Britain's first return to Europe since its ignominious expulsion from Greece and Crete in 1941. Unlike the North African landings, when the invaders had faced Vichy French troops, this time they would be up against German divisions; and, also in contrast to North Africa, they did not possess a network of agents and informers to provide intelligence information.

As the Tunisian campaign was nearing its conclusion, the Allied leaders met in Washington for the Trident Conference. Again, the arguments were dominated by the question of priorities, with the Americans still deeply suspicious of the "distraction" of the Mediterranean theater and the British, to General Marshall's continuing frustration, doing their utmost to delay the cross-Channel invasion. Repeatedly throughout 1943, Churchill would return to his worries about this operation, fearing that the Germans' excellent transport links to northern France would enable them to assemble "an overwhelming force against us and to inflict on us a greater military disaster than Dunkirk. Such a disaster would result in the resuscitation of Hitler and the Nazi regime." Already desperately short of manpower, the British, having been driven off the continent three times already—from Norway, France, and Greece—simply could not afford another such loss. Instead, and in keeping with Britain's traditional role as a maritime power, the prime minister still pushed for opportunistic attacks around the periphery, what he called the "soft underbelly" of Europe: the Balkans, the Dodecanese, and Italy. At the conference Brooke, Marshall's opposite number in the British high command, argued in favor of an invasion of Italy, pointing out that it would be much more difficult than northern France for the Germans to reinforce. To knock Germany's principal ally out of the war, suggested Churchill, would bring many benefits: as well as being a huge boost to opponents and unwilling allies of Germany everywhere, it would force the Germans to take over the garrison duties of the Italian army in the Balkans and the Aegean, and the British Mediterranean Fleet would be free to sail against the Japanese. More than anything, he insisted, it would mean that British and American armies remained in contact with the enemy, reminding the conference that the Russians were now facing 185 German divisions in the East.

There were disagreements, too, among the commanders of the various service arms, both between and within the two Allied camps. The US Army chief of staff General Marshall, together with the air commanders of both sides, wanted Mediterranean operations scaled down in favor of the cross-Channel invasion; British sea and land commanders wanted to concentrate on knocking Italy out of the war.

The outcome was compromise and indecision. Eisenhower's staff was told to prepare plans for invasions of Sardinia and Corsica as well as of southern Italy, but the Mediterranean force was to lose most of its assault shipping and seven experienced divisions by November 1943, to return to England for the cross-Channel invasion. Then called Roundup, this was set for May 1944. So the question of the next step after Sicily—should the operation be a success—was left unresolved at the highest strategic level. Eisenhower himself felt that the resources available for any operation post-Sicily were "very slender indeed." It was an inauspicious start, and it would be events in Rome, rather than a clear and united "grand plan," that would precipitate the Italian campaign to come.

As the invasion fleet of nearly 2,600 Allied vessels left Africa for Sicily, neither side at the talks in Washington was fully satisfied. Marshall, who had been against even the Africa offensive as a dispersion of effort, predicted that the outcome would be that neither the Mediterranean nor the forthcoming cross-Channel invasion would be properly equipped. Brooke, writing in his diary on 24 July 1943, despaired that the American general could be so blind: "Marshall absolutely fails to realize what strategic treasures lie at our feet in the Mediterranean, and always hankers after cross Channel operations. He admits that our object must be to eliminate Italy and yet is always afraid of facing the consequences of doing so. He cannot see beyond the tip of his nose and is maddening."

<hr />

After successful bombing attacks had destroyed the Italian and seriously weakened the German air forces in Sicily, the landings on 10 July went better than anyone had dared expect. There were counterattacks on one of the

American beaches, but by 12 July both Allied armies were marching inland. Not so the airborne landings, which fell foul of high winds and sustained "friendly fire" from Allied ships and suffered very heavy losses. Nevertheless, Syracuse and its nearby airfields were captured after just two days, and a rapid advance was started.

Although the two German divisions fought hard from the outset, the loss of so many men and so much material in Tunisia had seriously compromised the Italian defenders of Sicily. They were chronically short of transport for their nine weak divisions, and morale among the fighting men was in freefall. The Italians had had enough. When Patton's troops entered Palermo on 21 July, they were greeted by its inhabitants not as enemies but as liberators, an ominous sign for Mussolini and Italy's Fascist leadership.

Presented with this early progress and the evidence that Italy's collapse might be imminent, the Allied planners began to add detail to their outline for an invasion of the mainland. Five days before the Sicily invasion the Germans had launched their Kursk offensive against a huge bulge in the Soviet line, using nearly three-quarters of their available strength on the Eastern Front. There were very real concerns that Russia would be knocked out of the war and might make a separate peace with Germany—it was known that there had been contacts between the Soviet Union and Germany through Sweden.

It was now felt that operations in Italy would tie down the most enemy troops, and an amphibious assault on Naples, which had good landing beaches nearby, was planned as the main attack. This was as far north as land-based fighter aircraft could provide cover for the beaches. The assault would be supported by a smaller, preliminary landing right at the toe of the country. As the planners, British and American but working separately, mulled over the possibilities, greater ambitions always loomed for them over the horizon. If the attack on Naples failed to knock Italy out of the war, why not head on for Rome? That would trap the German divisions left in the south and provide a priceless symbolic victory.

Mussolini had boasted that the attack on Sicily would be smashed "at the water's edge." By the end of July 1943, when there could be no mistaking the news from the south, the king and the vast majority of the Italian army and people were united in their desire to get rid of the dictator and end Italy's participation in the war. Even senior Fascist leaders, led by Dino Grandi, the head of Mussolini's Grand Council, were planning *il Duce's* overthrow. The plotting came to a head on the evening of 24 July when the Grand Council met for the first time since the beginning of the war. Earlier that same day, Mussolini "still felt himself firmly in the saddle," a view shared by the German commander in the Mediterranean, Field Marshal Albert Kesselring. One of the very few senior German army commanders not to fall out with Hitler at some point, Kesselring was a committed Nazi and friend of Hermann Göring. In his memoirs, Kesselring admits that none of the German army commanders or diplomats in Rome "believed in an immediate danger for the regime." However, German plans were already in place in the event of an Italian collapse. As early as 1 April 1943, even before the fall of Tunisia, the German embassy in Rome had been ordered to send home sensitive papers as a precaution.

Mussolini had tried to act as a restraining influence on Hitler, urging a more conciliatory policy toward the conquered peoples. Along with the Japanese, he had advised that Germany should make peace with the Soviet Union in order to concentrate on defeating the West. But he overestimated his influence on Hitler as much as he deluded himself about the capabilities of his army and the loyalty of his followers. Kesselring tells of how, just before the Grand Council met, he had gone to see the Italian leader. The German field marshal was kept waiting for half an hour, having been told that Mussolini had an important political meeting. When he went in to see him, he found the Italian's face "wreathed in smiles."

" 'Do you know Grandi?' [Mussolini] said. 'He has just left me. We had a heart-to-heart talk, our views are identical. He is loyally devoted to me.' "

"I understood his spontaneous delight," says Kesselring, "but when I learned the very next day that this same Grandi had led the revolt against Mussolini in the Fascist Grand Council I had to ask myself which was the more astonishing: Mussolini's credulity or Grandi's wiliness."

Mussolini refused to accept his Grand Council's vote of no-confidence and appealed to the elderly king for support. The king had him arrested and appointed Marshal Pietro Badoglio, a former head of the armed forces and longtime opponent of Mussolini, to head the Italian government. On 26 July Kesselring went to see Badoglio. During a "chilly, reticent and insincere" interview, the new Italian leader assured Kesselring that his government would fully respect its obligations under the treaty of alliance. *Il Duce*, Badoglio said, was in custody for his own protection. When Kesselring asked where, Badoglio said only the king knew.

Kesselring then went to visit the king. There was a marked difference in tone. "My audience at the palace lasted almost an hour and was conducted with striking affability," Kesselring later wrote. "His Majesty assured me that there would be no change as to the prosecution of the war; on the contrary, it would be intensified . . . He said he had made the decision [to dismiss Mussolini] with great reluctance. He did not know where Mussolini was, but assured me he felt personally responsible for his well-being and proper treatment. Only Badoglio knew where the Duce was (!)."

In fact, Badoglio was keen to take Italy out of the war altogether, and the Germans suspected as much. "They say they'll fight, but that's treachery!" Hitler jeered. "We must be quite clear: it's pure treachery! . . . Does that man imagine that I'll believe him?" As soon as Mussolini was deposed, German divisions and staff began pouring into northern Italy, to the deepening gloom of the Italians. On 31 July, distinguished Italian civilians approached the British embassy in Madrid and the British consul in Tangier to start peace negotiations, but when those approaches got nowhere, a high-ranking officer of the Italian army was sent to Madrid in disguise. Talks broke down when the representatives of the Allies insisted on unconditional surrender, a policy announced at the end of the Casablanca conference back in January.

On Sicily, Italian troops started disappearing to the mainland as soon as the news arrived of Mussolini's fall. By then, however, the offensive had stalled. Montgomery had split his forces and his thrust toward Messina weakened and then became bogged down. The Germans, reinforced with part of the elite 1st Parachute Division from the end of July, fought delaying actions with great skill in successive defensive positions around Mount Etna. In a foretaste of what was to come in Italy, clever use of the mountainous terrain enabled some 60,000 German troops to hold off 450,000 Allied soldiers for thirty-eight days. The upshot was that although over 100,000 Italian soldiers were captured (nearly 35,000 deserted during the campaign), the Germans were pushed off the island rather than destroyed. Because of the strategic uncertainties about an invasion of Italy, there was no operation to close down the ports opposite Messina, and nearly 40,000 German troops and over 10,000 vehicles were successfully evacuated. Had these been captured or destroyed, the story of what followed in Italy would have been very different.

Some of the problems that had delayed the successful conclusion of the campaign can be laid at the door of Gen. Harold Alexander, the immediate superior of the generals in the field, Patton and Montgomery. Harrow and Sandhurst-educated, modest and unassuming, Alexander was a favorite of Winston Churchill throughout the war. He had led with distinction at Dunkirk and in Burma and had replaced Gen. Claude Auchinleck as commander in chief for the Middle East in August 1942, some two months before El Alamein. In Sicily he failed to prevent bickering between the British and American generals, or to display sufficient "grip" and decisiveness to exploit the swift early successes. A skilled diplomat, he would later handle his multinational force at Cassino with great tact, but out of necessity in a coalition force, he led by consensus rather than decree, which allowed the rivalries and jealousies between the British and the Americans to fester.

The Sicilian campaign had also seen the disgrace of "Old Blood and Guts" Gen. George Patton, who had been so influential in restoring American morale after the Kasserine Pass disaster. Visiting a hospital near Palermo on 3 August, the American general had stopped at the bed of a young soldier who had no apparent injury. "What's wrong with you, soldier?" Patton asked. The man replied that he was a psychiatric casualty. Patton then slapped him across the face with his glove, saying, "You're just a goddamned coward." A week later, at another hospital, Patton threatened a soldier with his pistol and then punched him in the head. He was forced to issue an apology and was relieved of his command. These incidents did, however, highlight the growing problem of psychiatric breakdown among the Allied soldiers that was to become such an important part of the Cassino story.

But the Allies had much to be pleased about with the capture of Sicily. The success of a major amphibious landing to a certain extent laid to rest the ghosts of Gallipoli; the Germans realized that the Italians would not be effective at defending their homeland, so, just as the Battle of Kursk reached its climax, Hitler was forced to withdraw units to Italy. For the Germans it was the end of all offensive operations on the Eastern Front. Troops and aircraft had to be sent not only to Italy itself, but to those parts of conquered Europe garrisoned by Italian troops. At this time there were five Italian divisions in France and no fewer than twenty-nine in the troublesome Balkans.

Now there was a change of heart among the Allied air leaders, who came down firmly in favor of an invasion of Italy, with a view to using the airfields at Foggia, southeast of Rome, to bomb important targets in southern Germany and the Balkans. Not only would new areas come within range, but attacks would be able to avoid the belt of fighter and antiaircraft defenses guarding the northern and western approaches to Germany that had taken such a toll on the bomber crews. A consensus for the invasion of Italy was now in place.

The new Italian leadership found that they were now trusted by neither the Germans nor the Allies. But another emissary, accompanied as a sign of good faith by a high-ranking British general who had been a POW, made contact with the Allied high command, and armistice talks started at last at the end of August. While these continued, plans progressed to invade Italy in early September. The Italians were reluctant to join the Allies' side, but the USA and Britain insisted that Italian neutrality was impossible. The end result was more mistrust, and although a secret armistice was signed on 3 September, the Allied leadership refused to let the Italians know any of their invasion plans. The Italians, fearful of German reprisals, pleaded with the Allies to hold off announcing the armistice until there were significant American and British forces ashore. Eisenhower kept the secret for five days, but on 8 September, worried that the numerous Italian units on the mainland might resist an invasion, proclaimed the end of the war against Italy at 6:30 P.M. from Radio Algiers, saying he hoped that "all Italians" would now "help eject the German aggressor from Italian soil." By then, the main fleet was approaching the beaches of Salerno, some thirty miles south of Naples. The British and American troops on board, to whom the news of the armistice, broadcast over loudspeakers, came as a complete surprise, cheered lustily. "I never again expect to witness such scenes of sheer joy," an American officer reported. "Speculation was rampant and it was all good . . . we would dock in Naples harbor unopposed, with an olive branch in one hand and an opera ticket in the other."

2

The Invasion of Italy

In the last weeks of August 1943, Allied warships had sailed, guns blazing, through the Straits of Messina, and artillery batteries had been moved up to face the coast of Italy on the western shore of the straits. The bombardment of the beaches north of Reggio di Calabria started at 4:30 A.M. on 3 September. The artillery alone fired four hundred tons of ammunition. The writer Alan Moorehead watched the bombardment: "It was night, and we could see little except the yellow flame," he reports. "Here we sat in the Sicilian hills above Messina, and the guns fired out of the olive groves. We fired out of Italian farms on this side of the Straits and the shells made the short passage of a mile or two across the sea and landed on other Italian farms on the mainland." Then three brigades of Canadian and British infantry of Montgomery's 8th Army crossed the three-and-a-half-mile-wide strait and landed. There was hardly any resistance from the two German divisions in the "toe" of Italy. Their artillery positions were quickly silenced by air attack, and they moved back into the mountainous terrain of Calabria, leaving the fight to the Italian coastal defense divisions. These quickly surrendered, faced as they were by so many threats from the sea and the air, and even supplied eager hands to unload the landing craft. On the same day as the landings, Montgomery himself, accompanied by journalists, took a landing craft to the beach. In the back were ten thousand cigarettes, which he handed out at every stop.

The retreating Germans left behind a web of demolitions—all road junctions and bridges were destroyed with a precision and thoroughness that would mark the entire Italian campaign. For five days, units of the 8th Army struggled northward, but on 8 September, Montgomery ordered a halt as the engineers had already run out of the crucial bridging materials.

The announcement of the surrender that evening left the men of the Italian Army bereft of instructions. Badoglio and the king fled Rome the same day, leaving only cryptic instructions that the army should "resist the enemy." In the Rome area, landings from the air were expected at any moment. In the city, Italian forces matched the Germans in numbers, and, had the Italians been able to hold the capital against their former allies, the German troops south of Rome would have been trapped. But lacking high-level direction or plans, landing strips were not secured and a highly risky plan by Eisenhower to land an American airborne division near the capital was canceled. In the end the Italians were able to resist for only a day.

The Germans, too, had been thrown off balance, albeit not for long. At midday on 8 September, Kesselring survived a near miss when his headquarters in Frascati, just south of Rome, was bombed. "The raid was illuminating," he later wrote, "because we found on a map in one of the bombers shot down the house in which I and von Richtofen had our headquarters exactly marked, indicating some excellent lackey work on the part of the Italians." In fact, there were over a thousand civilian casualties from the raid. Kesselring heard the news of Eisenhower's announcement regarding the Italian surrender from German army headquarters, but when he telephoned his contacts in the Italian military, he was told it was a hoax. However, by the time the news was confirmed, the Italian army had begun surrendering to the Germans, and prior plans were put into action to secure the country.

Even before the Italian capitulation, which the Allied high command had convinced themselves would lead to the Germans abandoning southern Italy, if not the whole country, confidence was running high among the men of the Salerno invasion force. Yorkshireman Geoffrey Smith, who was soon to celebrate his nineteenth birthday, was an artillery signaller with the British 46th Division. In his "first and only encounter with a general" he had been told, "We're going somewhere to do an invasion. You have nothing to worry about. It will be a piece of cake. You'll land in ankle-deep water and wade ashore. It'll be a holiday really, in the sun. We'll have wonderful air cover. There's nothing to worry about." Most of the men in the invasion force were happy to be leaving behind the dirt, the months of training, the boiling days and freezing nights of Africa. The sea was calm and there was very little sickness. Maj. Gen. Fred L. Walker wrote in his diary: "The sea is like a mill pond. I hope we have as calm and peaceful a day tomorrow for our work in Salerno Bay . . . At first light this morning I looked out the port hole of my stateroom . . . and could see ships in all directions . . . an inspiring sight . . . Our plans are complete and it is only a matter of executing them. Everyone is cheerful and full of confidence. I expect the division to do well."

Walker was in command of the American 36th "Texas" Division. A National Guard outfit, the division had originally been earmarked for the Sicily operation but had been considered too inexperienced and was therefore free for the Salerno landings. The 36th still contained a high proportion of its original Texan volunteer makeup, along with conscripts from all over the United States. If his men were "green," Walker was one of the United States' most experienced serving commanders. Fifty-six years old, he had been wounded and decorated in the First World War when he had been a captain in command of an infantry battalion. Between the wars he had worked as an instructor at the Command and General Staff School and the Army War College, and served a tour of duty in China. Toward the end of 1941, Walker had been given the command of 36th Division, and soon after, in common with other US infantry divisions, it was reduced to 16,000 men of whom the frontline contingent was organized into three regiments of 3,600 men each. The regiments were subdivided into battalions of about 800 men, further split into companies, platoons, then sections. At each level there would be specialist machine gun and mortar operators as well as signals and engineer personnel. The rest of the number was made up of headquarters staff, drivers, mechanics, medics, and other "support" staff. The 36th Division, which was to find itself at the center of perhaps the worst fighting at Cassino, had arrived in Africa in April 1943, but this landing was to be their first taste of combat.

The rest of the initial landing force was made up by two British divisions—the 46th "Oak Tree" and the 56th London "Black Cat"—organized as British X Corps under the command of Gen. Richard McCreery. All were part of US 5th Army, in charge of which was Lt. Gen. Mark Clark, the US commander around whom revolves so much of the controversy of the Cassino battles. Considered a good planner, and called by some the cleverest general in the southern theater, Clark had enjoyed a meteoric rise through the ranks after an ordinary record in the First World War. At one point he had been Fred Walker's pupil at Infantry School, but now, having never commanded an army in the field, he found himself the latter's superior. The speed of his promotion had provoked concern as well as jealousy among other US generals. One who had reservations about Clark's appointment was General Bradley. "I was not certain that Mark Clark was the best choice for this rather bold leap into Italy," he wrote, citing Clark's inexperience. "Moreover, I had serious reservations about him personally. He seemed false, somehow, too eager to impress, too hungry for the limelight, promotions and personal publicity." Nor did General Patton trust Clark, finding him "too damned slick" and more preoccupied with bettering his own future than in winning the war. Sometimes veterans speak fondly of their commanding officers, but it has been impossible to find anyone who was part of the 5th Army, whether British or American, who has a good word for Clark.

The first troops started landing on the beaches of Salerno in darkness at four-thirty in the morning of 9 September. For Geoffrey Smith of the British 46th Division, it was not quite as it had been described to him: "When we arrived we were neck deep in water, it was really cold. A lad who'd been behind me on the landing craft—I never knew his name—when we got on to the shore at last, said to me, 'When the sun comes up this will be "sunny Italy," ' and he immediately trod on a land mine; the next thing he's dead."

Landing alongside the 46th Division was the British 56th Black Cat Division, and further south, some distance from the British X Corps, the US 36th Texas Division went ashore with the best part of another US division, the 45th, in reserve. In the first wave of landings was twenty-one-year-old Clare Cunningham from Iona County, Michigan, the son of an Irish immigrant. He remembers that when they heard the "surprising" news of the Italian surrender they thought it was "going to be a kind of walk in." But about half a mile out from the beaches, the Germans started "sending shells" over, "throwing up geysers all around us." Soon most were of the opinion that it would be safer on land, where they could at least spread out. As they neared the beaches, they came under machine gun fire, and Cunningham, from his position in the middle of the landing craft, could see "the tracers bounce off the ramp." On his boat a heavy machine gun returned the fire, silencing the position, and the ramp came down about fifty yards from the beach. Cunningham and his fellow assault troops jumped into the waist-deep water, waded ashore, scrambled across the beach, and dug in about fifty yards from the water's edge.

In theory, Cunningham's company was supposed to land at H hour plus seventy minutes. "But there were no footprints on the sand other than ours," he says. "I heard many years later that the marines in the Pacific were told before landings, 'Oh, yes, you're the third wave, you'll just walk in.' Well, when they got there they were first. So that was just to build up their morale." Cunningham suspects the same trick may have been played on his unit. There followed, he remembers, a day of "playing hide and seek," which mainly involved staying out of the way of German tanks and 88mm guns until Allied artillery support could be landed. By the end of a momentous day he had lost some of his friends, had taken German prisoners and had, he believes, killed someone for the first time. He remembers having a reaction "in his gut": "I went through a Catholic school and was taught the Ten Commandments—thou shalt not kill and all that—and three years later that's what I was doing."

In charge of the German defenses south of Rome was Gen. Heinrich von Vietinghoff, 10th Army commander, described by a subordinate as "an old Prussian infantryman of the Guards, competent, sure of himself." Kesselring himself was for the moment concerned with events in Rome. The long coastline of Italy continued to cause the Germans worry throughout the campaign, and by 9 September, von Vietinghoff's forces were thinly spread along the southwest coast of Italy. The presence of a huge invasion armada off this coast was unmistakable, and although Salerno had been spotted as a possible landing place, this was far from certain.

In spite of the inevitable confusion of a landing in the dark, the first day of the attack was a success for Clark's 5th Army. To the north of the Bay of Salerno, elite British Commando and American Ranger units landed and set about securing the high passes between Salerno and Naples. British X Corps established a shallow bridgehead and to their right, the US 36th Division could begin landing their artillery and antitank weapons.

The Germans, still in the process of disarming the Italian army, were beset by organizational, communications, and logistical problems. In particular, the hasty demolition of a gasoline depot south of Salerno had left them critically short of fuel. For the next two days, as troops from the south, unpressured by the delayed Montgomery, rushed north to Salerno, all von Vietinghoff could launch were small, local, and uncoordinated counterattacks by his single, thinly spread Panzer division on the spot. To the Germans' great surprise, these were often startling successes, despite the inexperience of many of the tank crews. On 11 September alone, 10th Army captured fifteen hundred prisoners, most of them British. Two days later, with reserves arriving faster than the Allies could disembark their own reinforcements, the Germans spotted a gap between the British and US forces right in the center of the bridgehead, and, convinced that the Allies were preparing to reembark, pushed forward quickly. Having captured more than five hundred officers and men from a single battalion of the US 36th Division, they were poised to reach the beach itself. All that stood in their way was a hastily raised company of headquarters and support staff, including cooks and drivers, and two batteries of artillery, firing at close range into the German armor. As well as threatening to split the Allied forces and then turn both flanks, the German attack was almost on top of the American headquarters, situated in a great barn hung with drying tobacco leaves. The US corps commander, Maj. Gen. Ernest Dawley, who had been considered impressive during training, started buckling under the pressure. Clark noticed him becoming increasingly nervous and twitchy, and when Alexander visited the beachhead he found Dawley "obviously under great strain," with trembling hands and a shaky voice. Clark, though, kept calm, and although he ordered preparations to be made to reembark parts of his forces, the support of the guns of the fleet helped drive off the German attack.

The moment of crisis for Clare Cunningham's unit came on the evening of the fifth day after the landing. "We got pushed back out of Altavilla," he says, "tried to retake it again and got pushed back again. We were just outnumbered. Finally we got pushed back to a hill—you could see the beach down there three or four miles away and that was the last stronghold we had. We dug in, and I remember we had General Wilbur there [second-in-command of the division]. He was right up there among us, walking around while we were hugging the ground, saying, 'No man leaves this hill but a dead man.' He was going mad and walking around under fire."

For the next few days fierce fighting continued as both sides threw their reserves into the battle. As *The Times* (London) reported on 15 September, "The battle is one of ceaseless alternation of attack and counter-attack at one point or another." By the sixteenth, however, the Allies had received substantial reinforcements and the German armor was out of fuel. On the same day, Kesselring ordered a disengagement on the coastal front to "evade the effective shelling from warships." The 8th Army was finally arriving at Salerno from the south, and the Germans, after their unexpected successes in the previous few days, reverted to their original plan to withdraw to the north.

It had been just over a week since the announcement of the armistice with Italy, and, apart from at Rome, there was only very scattered resistance to the Germans from the Italians. Where it occurred, such as in Cefalonia and Lero, there were ruthless reprisals. In all, 716,000 Italian troops were rounded up by the Germans and sent to the Reich, where they were set to work in savage conditions, denied the status of prisoners of war. They were considered "military internees" and as such were unprotected by the provisions of the Geneva Convention. Others fled to their homes in Italy or took to the mountains in the Balkans. Some units assisted their erstwhile allies, handing over to the Germans fuel and other supplies. Most, though, tried to take the opportunity to disappear to their homes as quickly as they could.

Norman Lewis, a British officer with the Field Security Service, whose book, *Naples '44*, is one of the classics of the Italian campaign, arrived at Salerno soon after the first landings. Taking over an empty farmhouse on 11 September, Lewis could see "Italian soldiers who had walked away from the war . . . plodding along the railway line in their hundreds on their way to their homes in the south. Their feet were usually in terrible shape, with blood sometimes oozing through the cracked leather of their boots." Nevertheless, at last out of the war, "they were in tremendous spirits, and we listened to the trail of their laughter and song all through the day."

Lewis also provides a vivid eyewitness report of the worst moment during the Salerno battles, when the German counterattack nearly succeeded. In his entry for 14 September he describes American officers abandoning their men, and "outright panic" among the troops left behind. "In the belief that our position had been infiltrated by German infantry they began to shoot each other, and there were blood-chilling screams from men hit by the bullets . . . Official history," he concludes, "will in due time set to work to dress this part of the action at Salerno with what dignity it can. What we saw was ineptitude and cowardice spreading down from the command, and this resulted in chaos. What I shall never understand is what stopped the Germans from finishing us off."

Four days later, he discovers the answer. On 18 September, he describes the effects of the naval shelling on a number of German tanks that had nearly broken through: "Several of these lay near, or in, tremendous craters. In one case the trapped crew had been broiled in such a way that a puddle of fat had spread from under the tank, and this was quilted with brilliant flies of all descriptions and colors."

Naval gunfire, although effective in this instance, was something of a blunt weapon. In the absence of efficient aerial or ground observation, the guns were often aimed at obvious targets such as villages, which turned out to have little military significance. Major General Walker, commander of the US 36th Division, was appalled by the destruction of the village of Altavilla, which had been attacked by artillery and planes as well as naval gunfire: "I doubt very much," he wrote in his diary, "if this bombardment of a village full of helpless civilian families, many of whom were killed or injured, contributed any real help in capturing the dominating ground in that vicinity." At Battipaglia, he was "greatly depressed at the complete destruction of this old town by our Navy and artillery. Not a single building was intact . . . one could smell the odor of dead bodies . . . such destruction of towns and civilians is brutal and unnecessary and does not assist in furthering the tactical program . . . Italian people stood about looking at their destroyed homes in bewilderment."

However, neither the Americans nor the British, but particularly the latter, were about to change their belief that overwhelming firepower could save the lives of infantrymen. Throughout the Italian campaign, there could be little squeamishness from the Allied high command about civilian "collateral" casualties, or about the destruction of ancient buildings, as demonstrated most firmly in the case of the monastery of Monte Cassino.

Although disaster had been averted at Salerno, it had been a poor start to the Italian campaign for the Allies, who, albeit on the offensive, had suffered nearly 9,000 casualties, more than twice that of the Germans. Three thousand Allied prisoners had been taken, against only 630 German. For Clare Cunningham's 36th Division, it had been a very difficult first taste of battle, and they lost nearly 4,000 men, a high proportion of those who did the fighting in the front line. "Everyone knew someone that was killed," says Cunningham. "We had one sixteen-year-old from Michigan who had lied about his age to get in. He 'fessed up after that. He got out of there."

While Kesselring was now confident that one German soldier was worth three Allied ones, recriminations between the British and Americans started straightaway. British liaison officers criticized the performance of American troops, and Clark took a virulent dislike to McCreery, the commander of the British X Corps (56th and 46th divisions), whom he called in his diary a "feather duster," a term, along with "peanut," he also used to describe Alexander. For public consumption at home, it was decided by Alexander's press unit to talk up the 8th Army's advance at the expense of the far from perfect performance of the 5th Army. The situation was made worse when Montgomery arrived and was photographed in the manner of the victor reaching down from an amphibious truck to shake Clark's hand. Montgomery, still piqued at having been given a supporting role in the invasion, and perhaps justifiably dismissive of the entire campaign as having no "grand plan," was his usual arrogant and patronizing self to Clark.

The American was incensed, and vowed not to be "cheated" again. His vanity, which he saw as a wish to receive proper "credit" (i.e., favorable domestic newspaper coverage) for his American troops, became almost obsessive. After Salerno, Clark would have nearly fifty public relations people working for him, operating the "three in one" rule: every news release was to mention Clark's name three times on the first page and at least once on all other pages. As the press descended on Salerno, Clark insisted he would be photographed only on his good side, his left. It has even been said of Clark that "his reading of Clausewitz's famous dictum was that war was the pursuit of publicity by other means."

The British high command, obsessed with morale, had their own problems to deal with. On 16 September, seven hundred British soldiers had landed on the beach and organized a sit-in, effectively a mutiny, refusing to join the units to which they had been allocated. The complaint was not that they did not want to fight but that they were joining unfamiliar regiments. In fact, these soldiers, left behind in Africa by their divisions because of illness or injury, had expected to be returning home. The incident, which sent a shiver down the spines of the British high command, was dealt with sensibly and gently. The soldiers were given the chance to change their minds, which most of them did, and the 190 who refused were shipped back to Africa and court-martialed. Most were then allowed to work their way back into favor in combat. Even so, the episode did nothing to reassure the British generals that their men were up to the tasks ahead.

The Germans, on the other hand, had been allowed to recover their poise following the confusion of the Italian surrender. After the Salerno fighting, von Vietinghoff was promoted, and Kesselring began to argue that Italy could be defended south of Rome after all. As early as the day after the landing, the German commander had drawn successive lines across the map denoting possible defensive positions. In the first instance he insisted to von Vietinghoff that his 10th Army hold a line on the Volturno River twenty-five miles north of Naples, until 15 October. After some indecision, Hitler was convinced and agreed to allow Kesselring to hold on to as much Italian territory as he could for as long as he could. By now, Mussolini had been rescued in a daring commando raid. Early on 12 September, SS units had landed by transport glider in front of the Campo Imperatore Hotel north of Rome and, with Badoglio's guards offering no resistance, seized *il Duce.* Mussolini was now installed as the leader of a Fascist North Italy. Obviously, the more territory he could be said still to govern, the better, and the surrender of Rome would have been a blow to the new "government."

One of Kesselring's lines on the map went through Mignano, about fifty miles north of Naples. This became the Reinhard Line, referred to by the Allies as the Winter Line, and was to be ready by 1 November. A dozen miles north of this, the terrain around Cassino provided even better ground for defense. Here Gen. Hans Bessel, Kesselring's chief engineer, was to create his masterpiece, the Gustav Line. "I had full confidence in this naturally very strong defensive position," Kesselring wrote of the Winter Line, "and hoped by holding it for some length of time, perhaps till the New Year, to be able to make the rear Gustav Line so strong that the British and Americans would break their teeth on it." At the center of the Gustav Line was Cassino.

Cassino was a typical central Italian town with four churches, a prison, a railway station, a high school, and a magistrate's court. Including outlying linked villages, there were about twenty-two thousand inhabitants over an area of about 160 acres. Like many Italian towns, it had its own amphitheater, a scattering of temples, and a Roman thermal bath still in use. In the valleys around were orchards and vineyards, and woods of oak, spruce, and acacia. In the foothills, extensive terracing allowed for olive groves, but on the surrounding mountains, baked in the summer and windswept in the winter, only thornbushes and small trees could survive. Saturday was market day, and the town would be full of farmers from a twenty-five-mile radius, trading cattle or selling their fruit, vegetables, or cheeses. Situated on the main road and railway line from Naples to Rome, Cassino was an affluent town with several sumptuous villas, and visitors could stay in a choice of high-class hotels. Above it towered the famous Benedictine monastery, a magnet for pilgrims.

Twelve-year-old Tony Pittaccio found himself in Cassino at the start of the war. Born there but brought up in Southampton, he had been visiting relatives of his mother, an Italian also born in the town. His father, himself half Italian, half English, had stayed at home in England. Together with his mother and two sisters, Tony became trapped in Italy when war was declared on 10 July 1940, as the family was not allowed passage through France back home to England. They were to remain in Cassino or its environs until May 1944, only able to receive news from their father two or three times a year, through the town's monastery or the Vatican.

Pittaccio describes the reaction in the town to the start of the war as "mixed." As in many Italian towns, there were a fair number of people who had relatives in France, Britain, or the United States. Pittaccio's family endured a certain amount of teasing about being English, but "Everyone treated us kindly, it was all in good fun," says Pittaccio. "Among the older people there was a knowledge from early on that Italy was not going to win the war, and people would say, 'Oh, it won't be long before you'll be able to go home again.' " One of Pittaccio's cousins—a young man of nineteen or twenty—was called away to fight. Before he left, he said to Tony, "Look, you're not going to hear from me for a while, because the first opportunity I have, I'm going to cross over to the other side."

Other young inhabitants, though, "saw heroic deeds in front of them"; it was the "older people" who "were still looking over their shoulders at the First World War." Gemma Notarianni, thirteen years old at the beginning of the war, lived with her family in nearby Valvori, a small village a few miles up the Rapido valley from Cassino. She remembers that after the declaration of war, "most people were not happy about it, but life continued pretty much as normal to start with." Those with memories of the last war, though, were fearful: "My father had lived during the First World War," she says, "so he was really scared. He knew what could happen, and eventually *did* happen."

Mussolini's Fascism had always gained more followers in the north of Italy and in the country's towns rather than its villages. Pittaccio's family was a microcosm of the political divisions within Cassino. One of his mother's brothers was a staunch Fascist, the other a Socialist. Her brother-in-law,

Agostino Sassoli, was a Christian Democrat. But "none of this bothered any-body, people could speak quite freely," Pittaccio remembers. After the sudden fall of France, some of his young schoolmates taunted him about Britain being about to lose the war, but in general "there was a respect for England" and an awareness that "invading England was not going to be an easy thing to do."

There was also an Englishwoman living in the town, and a man who had lived many years in England. "He had a beard and kids used to tease him about it, that it had English lice in it. He was a very vociferous anti-Fascist, as was my mother. One of my uncles said to my mother, 'For goodness' sake, you're going to get arrested,' but nothing happened."

Nevertheless, the Fascist Party dominated life in the town. Most Saturdays the population would have to go through the motions of dressing up in Fascist attire and "digging for the country," cultivating any spare land, including public parks. To get a job you had to be a member of the party.

Initially Pittaccio went to a religious school in the town, which was an outpost of the monastery. For special lectures and tests, he would go up the cable car to the monastery itself. But when the time came for him to go to the local town school, he had to join the Gioventù Fascista (Fascist Youth) movement in order to be allowed in. He frankly admits to rather liking it: "I had my black uniform, my imitation rifle. What kid of eleven or twelve wouldn't enjoy that sort of thing? It was just like the Boy Scouts in England: we used to sing, to march. But my mother never liked it."

Children are always the most able to adapt to new situations, and Tony Pittaccio continued to enjoy his time in Cassino. Along with his sisters, he would join the peasants to listen to their music and singing as they brought in the harvest or journeyed home after a day's work in the fields. As well as the "delicious, fresh ricotta cheese" his family would buy on market day, he loved the colorful costumes donned on feast days such as the Assumption or St. Antony, when statues of the Madonna and the saint would be carried through the town. On Easter Monday it was usual to traipse up to the monastery, and the mountain "resembled an anthill" with all the people making the climb. In May there was a feast of the Madonna Della Rocca, when the focus would be the castle just above the town, originally constructed in the ninth century as an outer defense for the monastery. In this small building, later to be one of the epicenters of the battle for Cassino, resided a statue of the Madonna, and on her feast day "the castle would glow with hundreds of lanterns or lights lit in her honor. We would make our way to the castle in procession and there attend mass. To us young boys the castle was a wonderful place where to play soldiers. We would divide into two teams, those defending and those attacking the castle. Little did we dream that a real battle would be fought there one day."

As the war dragged on into 1942, it began to have a greater effect on the people in the Cassino area. Mussolini appealed for gold wedding rings to be donated for the war effort and replaced with metal ones. "Mother gave her ring," Gemma Notarianni remembers. "She was not very happy about it, but it was a small village, and everyone had to do it." Rationing started in 1942 as well, and its effects, light at first, grew over the next twelve months. Initially the worst shortages were in salt, which had been a state monopoly, then the rationing became more severe. "God only knows what the bread was made of," says Pittaccio, "and the pasta turned out to be black. Whenever we heard there was a shipment of sugar or butter to a shop, there'd be crowds." Soon, as elsewhere, there was a flourishing black market in Cassino, especially in olive oil, meats, and wheat. Harvests were attended by a Party official, as most was purchased by the state, but the young Fascists, mainly university students, were open to bribes.

When Sicily was invaded in July 1943 and Mussolini fell, the senior Fascists disappeared from the town, soon to be replaced by an increased German presence in the area. Cassino town gradually became full of German field hospitals, three in school buildings and one in quarters previously occupied by nuns. The young of the town, though, took it in their stride. "I have no bad memories of the Germans," Pittaccio recalls. "On one occasion there was a German on a motorcycle with a sidecar and he wanted some directions. I tried to explain to him, and he said, 'Look, jump in and show me.' So there I was, in that sidecar, with this German, on top of the world. For us it was like a game. The Germans had these huge troop transporters, and we young kids always tried to get a ride to be able to wave to our friends, shouting, 'Look at me, everybody!' "

The first time the reality of war came to those living in Cassino was in mid-July 1943 when the Allies bombed the airfield at Aquino, a few miles to the northwest. "That was when we started seeing the war," says Gemma Notarianni. Tony Pittaccio's mother became concerned about stray bombs and moved the family into the countryside outside the town. There they lived in a large farmhouse with a stable. Part of the house was occupied by Germans, whom the young Pittaccio found "just ordinary . . . One German used to come along every day and spend the evening with us. He obviously missed his family. He was married with kids. We tried to share a little of what we had with him, not because he needed it, but because he wanted to be part of the family. One evening he came in beaming. The Germans had been having a party and he had his mess tin with chicken pieces and chicken soup. He came over and was so delighted that he was able to give that to us. He said, 'My ration for the kids.' "

Nevertheless, for most residents of Cassino, the fall of Mussolini had raised hopes that the unpopular war would be coming to an end for them. When the armistice was announced on 8 September, there was "genuine rejoicing in the streets," Pittaccio remembers. "We thought we were spared any further sufferings of war and that Cassino had escaped quite well."

Eighty miles south at Salerno, while the advance units tried to force their way up to Naples, Allied reinforcements poured ashore. Twenty-five-year-old Terence Milligan, later to be known to the world by his nickname, Spike, landed on 24 September with his battery of heavy artillery to join British X Corps as it tried to blast its way through the mountains that ringed the Salerno beachhead. After a journey on HMS *Boxer,* accompanied by the "merry sound of retching," and involving a submarine scare, Milligan found plenty of evidence on the beach of the recent fighting. Soon his battery was in action, and under attack from German Stuka dive bombers. After his first day in Italy, he wrote to his parents: "I'm writing this in a hole in the ground, it's convenient, because if you get killed, they just fill the hole in and sell it as a cemetery. That's all the cheery news, will write again when the situation is less fraught."

Although the bulk of the German forces were now retreating to Kesselring's defensive lines, skillful use of demolitions and rear guards made the Allied progress out of Salerno tortuously slow. All road junctions, bridges, and railways had been destroyed. To advance the first fifteen miles out of the town, the American 45th Division needed twenty-five new bridges. There were few roads, and many of these snaked up and down mountains. The destruction of a road carved out of a sheer cliff would often cause even more work for the divisional engineers than destroyed bridges. All the demolitions would be ringed by mines, and on several occasions small groups of German

riflemen and machine gunners, covering a destroyed bridge from the opposite side of a gorge, could hold up entire Allied divisions, necessitating time-
consuming and exhausting marches through the mountains to outflank the
position.

As Clark's 5th Army approached the outskirts of Naples, Montgomery's
8th Army advanced up the Adriatic coast. In between was the Apennine
mountain range, with peaks of up to six thousand feet, already tipped with
snow, effectively creating two separate fronts. On 22 September the British
78th "Battleaxe" Division landed at Bari. The Foggia airfields, one of the
prime objectives of the Italian campaign, were captured five days later.

The Engineer Corps remained the most important motor for forward
movement, having effectively to recreate from scratch an entire infrastructure to carry the huge amount of men, vehicles, and supplies up the narrow
peninsula. Each Allied division contained up to two thousand vehicles,
whose movement was largely restricted to the roads because of the mountainous terrain. Major General Lucian Truscott, the commander of the
American 3rd Division, wrote after the war: "There was no weapon more
valuable than the engineer bulldozer . . . no soldier more effective than the
engineers who moved us forward." The sappers also had to clear mines and
obstacles specially designed to make their jobs a nightmare. Road mines
were fitted with "antihandling" devices that were constantly updated. As
soon as one type became familiar to the Allied engineers, another would appear to take them by surprise. So the whole Allied advance, in effect, "depended on the nerve and skill of relatively few men engaged in this lethal
battle of wits, scrabbling about in the mud feeling for tell-tale protrusions
and wires, only too aware that a wrong guess would be punished by their being blown to bits."

Each of the British divisions contained three engineering companies of
about 250 men each, mostly drawn from prewar tradesmen such as carpen-
ters, builders, electricians, and plumbers. In American divisions there would
be a single engineering battalion of about 800 men. Twenty-three-year-old
Matthew Salmon was part of the 220th Field Company, attached to the
British 56th Black Cat Division. He had joined the Territorial Army in June
1939, at which point he was an apprentice builder working near his home in
Hackney, northeast London. Like many of those who fought at Cassino, his
father had been a soldier in the First World War. Salmon spent the early part
of the war working on the anti-invasion defenses and airfields in Britain,

and by the time he reached Italy in September 1943, his unit had journeyed from Britain to India, then to Egypt and the desert via Iraq. India, where even the lowliest sapper had a servant, had been a fairly easy time as well as an education in itself for a young man who had never before left England; but Iraq, he remembers, was so hot that while writing an airgraph home, sweat would drip on to the page and smudge the ink. His time in combat, which would come to an end in the early stages of the Cassino battle, began near Tripoli, and he was severely wounded soon after while dismantling an Italian mine.

But he survived and after a time in the hospital in Alexandria rejoined his unit just before the Salerno landings. The early stages of the Italian campaign involved, for him, a seemingly endless number of Bailey bridges to be constructed, and, of course, mines. Rescuing men trapped within a minefield was one of the most traumatic jobs Salmon was called upon to carry out. On one occasion his unit was resting behind the lines and for once everyone was warm and happy. They had found a house with a grand piano, which a corporal started playing. But then an officer came in and asked for three men. Salmon was chosen and reluctantly collected his kit and followed the officer. "We walked the final part of the way and arrived at the minefields. It was very dark and we were unable to see anyone. We called out but got no reply so we started sweeping and made our way towards the faint sound of voices. When we got to our men it was the middle of the night, and the first chap we came across was lying dead with a mine detector on his back. Many others were wounded and some of the infantrymen were crouched together, too frightened to move. Our men had gone out to rescue them earlier but it had all gone wrong for them. It was very emotional to see men we knew in such a predicament. One of our chaps had been in position for nearly three hours by the time I got to him, and when I reached him he put his arms round me and thanked me for saving his life."

The Engineer Corps was called upon for all sorts of jobs. On one occasion Salmon was ordered to go to Lt. Gen. Mark Clark's hut to install a bath and a fireplace. Unfazed by the presence of the 5th Army commander, the engineers were more struck by the differences they saw between the American and British setups. They were surprised by the informality of the American officers, and even more amazed at the food on offer to the Americans: "The grub they got compared with what we got, it was like going to the Ritz," says Salmon. "Spam, in a tray with different compartments. We were more or less hard tack, bully beef and stew. They had fruit!"

But the work never let up, and precious little of it was in the safety of the rear echelon. "The shelling never stopped," Salmon remembers. "We slept where we stood." As losses from shellfire, snipers, and mines mounted, reinforcements arrived from home. The life expectancy of the new, inexperienced men was short. "Very often these chaps had only been in the army for a matter of six weeks or so," says Salmon, "and they were under the illusion that they were going to finish the war off in no time, just as we did when we first started . . . We would advise them what to do and what not to do, but it never seemed to work. I saw men come in and be dead after just a few days. We would tell them always to keep their heads down, but inevitably they would look up and get caught by snipers. The only way they seemed to learn was by seeing their comrades die—then they knew it was no game."

Having battled as much against the terrain as the enemy, the Allied forces finally entered Naples on 1 October. Advance units moved through the outskirts of the city and advanced to the Volturno River, thus completing the original objective of the Salerno landings: the capture and securing of the port of Naples. The cost of the operation had been more than 12,000 British and American casualties, of whom approximately 2,000 were killed, 7,000 wounded, and 3,500 missing. Naples itself was destroyed. Allied bombing had accounted for much of the industrial area, and the Germans, who continued to shell the city with artillery for the next few days, had done the rest. Kesselring's orders had been very thorough—anything that could be of remote use to the Allies had to be destroyed. The port facilities were blown up and the harbor choked with sunken ships; all civic amenities—the sewer, water, and electrical systems—were wrecked; even typewriters and accounting machines were removed or destroyed. Anything valuable had been looted. Half the population of 800,000 had fled the city and the remainder were in a parlous state. Alan Moorehead accompanied the Allied troops entering the city: "On the outskirts of Naples itself it was one tumultuous mob of screaming, hysterical people, and this continued all the way into the center of the city . . . they screamed in relief and pure hysteria . . . in every direction there was a wall of emaciated, hungry, dirty faces . . . there was no question of war or enmity here. Hunger governed all."

One source of food, of a sort, was the city's aquarium. In the days leading up to the Allies' arrival, much of the collection of exotic fish had been consumed, but the prize exhibit, a baby manatee, was kept for a welcome dinner for Mark Clark, who, it had been rumored, was fond of seafood. What he made of the manatee, boiled in a garlic sauce, is not recorded, but he was sufficiently pleased with the capture of the city to cable his wife, "In the grand manner of conquerors: 'I give you Naples for your birthday.' " Outside the city, on 8 October, Norman Lewis found "hundreds, possibly thousands of Italians, most of them women and children . . . in the fields all along the roadside driven by their hunger to search for edible plants . . . all I recognized among their collections were dandelions." The Italians had had to walk for two to three hours to reach this spot, as nearer the city anything remotely edible had already been collected.

Although wrecked and containing a starving population, Naples was a great prize for the Allies, and work started immediately on repairing the port. For the soldiers, Naples had a special exotic and illicit appeal. Gunner Milligan, on hearing that Allied patrols were in the city, commented, "Cor Naples, eh? We would all like to be in Naples. It would be the first European city since we left England nearly two years ago. We've all been warned of the 'dangers.' If the brochure was telling the truth, venereal disease was walking the streets of Naples and one could contract it just by shaking hands with a priest." In fact, in order to survive, the inhabitants of Naples wasted no time in turning their city into the black market and prostitution capital of the world. One Allied soldier recorded in his diary his first impressions of arriving in the city: "The docks had suffered a great deal of damage, but 'jerry' had flown, now the Italians were trying to scrape together some kind of life. Only too willing to please the Allied troops, they would offer their daughters, some as young as twelve, to the soldiers for a few Liras. It was pathetic, but they had brought it upon themselves."

As work on the port facilities continued, the capture of the city raised confidence and expectations. On 2 October, Churchill telegraphed to Alexander: "I hope . . . by the end of the month or thereabouts . . . that we shall meet in Rome." By 4 October the first lighters were lying in the badly damaged harbor, and the following day the first of the Liberty ships was unloading. From then on a constant stream of supplies flowed in. Soon the capacity of the port was twenty thousand tons a day.

On 13 October, Italy declared war on Germany. But there was to be no mass participation by the Italian army in the fighting ahead. Lacking supplies and carrying antiquated equipment, the Italian divisions could be reactivated only by using material needed elsewhere, so it was decided that nothing more than a token force would join the Allies in the fighting during the winter. Their great contribution, though, was in providing vital porters, labor parties, and mule handlers, thus freeing up thousands of soldiers for the fighting.

For the Allied commanders on the ground, speed was of the essence. The autumn rains had swollen the rivers and created a sea of mud in the valleys, and it was felt essential to cross the defended Volturno River as quickly as possible in order to deny the Germans time to reinforce the mountains beyond, where Kesselring had ordered the creation of the Reinhard or Winter Line. But delays soon became inevitable. "Rain, rain, rain," Maj. Gen. John Lucas, Dawley's replacement as commander of the US VI Corps, wrote in his diary on 8 October. "The roads are so deep in mud that moving troops and supplies forward is a terrific job. Enemy resistance is not nearly as great as that of Mother Nature." But by 13 October, there were Allied troops across the river. The next river valleys to the north, across forty miles of mountainous terrain, were now the Garigliano and the Rapido, flowing through Cassino.

3

The Gustav Line

When the armistice between Italy and the Allies was announced on 8 September, Italian guards at the prisoner-of-war camps in the country opened the gates and handed the Allied soldiers their freedom. Many were quickly recaptured by the German troops pouring into the country, but others tried their luck at getting home. Some joined Italian resistance groups operating in the mountainous interior. Very many, though, headed for Switzerland to the north or toward the advancing Allied armies in the south. For sustenance and shelter, these men were forced to throw themselves at the mercy of the Italian civilian population.

Allied soldiers who were likely, if captured, to end up in camps in Italy were advised, should they escape, never to approach the big house in a village, but to head instead for the poorest, "because they had nothing left to lose." In fact, the Germans dealt very severely with those who sheltered Allied prisoners, but there are many stories of escaped POWs being looked after by Italian villagers for considerable periods of time.

Bhaktabahadur Limbu was captured at Tobruk in North Africa while serving with the 2/7th Gurkha Rifles. Among thousands of other Allied prisoners, Limbu was taken to Italy, where the Gurkha and Indian contingent was addressed by Subhas Chandra Bose, the pro-Nazi Indian nationalist, who tried to persuade them to join the German side. "He lectured us and said that we Nepalese knew nothing, had to rid ourselves of the British and join him. We refused, telling him that we had all taken an oath which we could not break." Soon after came the armistice. "Italy had had enough of the war and we were let out at night to escape if we wanted to. If we didn't want to, we could stay in the camp. I chose to escape and went to live in a village. I did not understand what they said but they fed me as I was hungry." After Limbu had been in the village for two months, the Germans threatened reprisals against the villagers, and the prisoners were spirited away. "I was sent up into the mountains to live with some shepherds," Limbu recalls. "It snowed heavily. One shepherd gave me goat's milk. He caught hold of the animal and told me to kneel on the ground and suck the teats, not to bite them. The goat gave me a lot to drink and my belly swelled. The shepherds looked after me well. In all I was six weeks with them. I was not far from Cassino and heard shooting and bombing. Guerrillas came to fetch me and I got back to my unit." Once back with their regiment, the escapees were given leaflets and asked to fill in the names of those Italians who had helped them.

In Cassino itself the armistice, thought to have been the end of the townsfolk's troubles, was, in fact, just the beginning. On 10 September, the day after the Salerno landing, Allied bombers appeared over the town just before nine in the morning. Tony Pittaccio, by then fifteen years old, was on his way home from school and remembers waving to "our new friends." Another Cassino resident, Guido Varlese, then nineteen, was in the piazza with a friend, "when we saw Flying Fortresses, going toward Rome from Naples . . . We were all amazed at these marvelous flying machines, then we realized what was happening." The aircraft unloaded their bombs on the outskirts of the town, and "caused enormous damage and killed many, many people," says Varlese. "We were not expecting this at all, due to the fact that the armistice was already in effect. For us, we thought that the war was over . . . I took refuge in the shop where I usually had my hair cut. While in there, in came a German soldier with his ear shot to pieces by shrapnel. I put a towel—the first thing I could see—around his head to stop the blood pouring from his ear. He certainly would have died otherwise." Later in the day the railway and the road to Rome were both bombed and, in all, sixty civilians were killed and many more injured. Tony Pittaccio's own mother was hit in the foot by a bomb fragment.

After the bombing, many residents of Cassino left the town. Some traveled north to other parts of Italy, others south to cross the Allied lines and endure a lengthy screening for spies. Over a thousand took shelter in the monastery, where they were housed in the college and the episcopal seminary. As the cable railway, which used to carry people to the monastery in just eight minutes, had been destroyed when hit by a German aircraft back in the summer, the refugees and monks alike had to haul food up the hill, an arduous journey by foot that took a good hour from the town.

Increasingly, Cassino was being cleared of all its residents as the Germans busied themselves fortifying their defensive positions. Many civilians simply took to the hills, sheltering in small cottages or in the numerous caves in the surrounding mountains.

Gemma Notarianni, now seventeen, had watched the bombing from the balcony of her family's house in Valvori. She was particularly concerned as she had a brother studying in Cassino. Soon after, her family moved to a primitive, one-up, one-down shepherd's house they owned in the mountains to the north of the village. Above all, they were concerned to protect the male members of the family from being taken away by the Germans as forced laborers. The hills around Cassino, Gemma quickly discovered, were seeing more activity than ever before. Italian soldiers were passing through on their way to their homes. Many had removed their uniforms to avoid identification, and all were fearful of being conscripted to work for the Germans. The Wehrmacht soldiers themselves were creating defensive positions and also sending out patrols to try to recapture the numerous escaped Allied prisoners of war now in the area. With these were the civilian refugees, desperately trying to survive as the winter closed in.

At the Notariannis' shack, a pair of British POWs came to eat once a week. The two men had one meal at a different house each day. Their hosts were running considerable risks. Meanwhile, one of Tony Pittaccio's Italian cousins, just short of his eighteenth birthday, came across two airmen on the run, one English, one American, and decided to try to get them some food. This was successfully accomplished on a couple of occasions, until one day he was taking water to the men as they hid in a ditch when he saw an approaching German patrol. He tried to hide up a tree, but was spotted and ordered down. At that point he decided to make a run for it. The Germans opened fire and he was hit. He managed to crawl back to where his family were sheltering. In desperation, all they could do was take him to a German field hospital, where everything possible was done to save his life, but in vain.

On the night of 10 October there was another Allied air raid on the town. Most of the civilian refugees had by now been evacuated from the monastery, but about 150 remained, and many more would use the building as an alternative refuge to their nearby caves or shacks. Most shared the hope of Tony Pittaccio, who explains what he believed at the time: "Oh, Monte Cassino will protect us. It's all right. There's nothing to worry about. They won't do anything to Monte Cassino, we thought."

Three days later, Lieutenant Colonel Schlegel, an Austrian engineer officer from the Hermann Göring Division, drove to Cassino on his own initiative. He met the abbot, Don Gregorio Diamare, to warn him that the monastery, situated at the heart of the German defenses, was in danger. The Austrian proposed that the treasures of Monte Cassino be evacuated, along with its monks. Diamare was unmoved, convinced that the Allies would never damage the famous building. Schlegel left, but returned two days later, on Saturday, 16 October, by which time the abbot had changed his mind and agreed that the evacuation of paintings and books should start without delay. Helped by the refugees in the monastery, Schlegel's engineers built cases and boxed up some seventy thousand volumes from the library and archives. These were then driven in shifts to Rome, each trip accompanied by a pair of monks. Many of the priceless paintings could not be crated and had to travel stacked in lorries protected only by sheets. Nevertheless, by the time the operation was completed on 8 December, much irreplaceable treasure had been saved, and the German propaganda machine made much of the move. Most of the eighty monks also left at this time; only the abbot, four monks, and five lay brothers remained.

The Germans were making good use of the time bought for them by the rearguard actions to the south, and progress on the Gustav Line was proceeding apace. All around the Cassino area, local Italian men were conscripted into labor gangs, building deep underground shelters or blasting buildings to clear fields of fire. Agostino Sassoli, Tony Pittaccio's uncle, who now had responsibility for a wife, an elderly mother-in-law, a wounded sister-in-law (Tony's mother), his three young children, a young nephew (Tony), and two young nieces was among those sent to work on the defenses. He was soon aware of the immense strength of the Gustav Line. "What they are doing there is extraordinary," he told his family. For the first few days they were allowed to go home for the night, but then they were kept under guard by the Germans, although the children were allowed to take them food and water. For the Germans, the Italian laborers were useful, but expendable. Sassoli, who was in his forties, remembered one incident that had a great effect on him. On one occasion his three-man team had to blow up a house, but the fuse on the explosive was so short that whoever lit it didn't stand a chance. The three Italians had to draw lots. The one who lost said to Sassoli and his companion, "Off you go," and didn't even bother to run away.

Soon after, Allied bombers came over while they were working on the defenses. Pittaccio's uncle saw his chance and in the confusion of the raid made a run for it. His path took him across a newly laid minefield, but his luck held and he made his escape.

In the mountains to the north of Cassino, construction activity in front of the Gustav Line was witnessed by Gemma Notarianni. Near their shepherd's shack, a machine gun position was built, but one day around Christmas it was sabotaged by a person or persons unknown. The Germans immediately rounded up everyone in the area. Nobody confessed, and all the men were taken away. The next day, as the Allied forces at last began to near Cassino, most of the Germans withdrew to the Gustav Line, and Gemma and her family decided to return to their home in Valvori. There they waited, effectively in no-man's-land, hoping that the arrival of the Allies would mean the end of their ordeal.

The forty miles from the Volturno River to the high ground opposite Cassino had been a very hard slog for the American and British troops. The weather had deteriorated, and by the time the Allies had fought their way to the Gustav Line, "sunny Italy" seemed a grim joke. The Italian winter had closed in. Temperatures fell far below freezing during the night, and driving rain and snow made roads and tracks impassable and greatly increased the wear and tear on frontline soldiers. Ernie Pyle, the famous US correspondent who traveled with the soldiers, wrote: "Our troops were living in almost inconceivable misery. The fertile black valleys were knee-deep in mud. Thousands of men had not been dry for weeks. Other thousands lay at night in the high mountains with the temperature below freezing and the thin snow sifting over them. They dug into the stones and slept in little chasms and behind rocks and in half-caves. They lived like men of prehistoric times." Pyle wrote vividly about the everyday life of the US combat troops, or "dogfaces," and his column in the US Army newspaper *Stars and Stripes* was hugely popular with his GI readers, as he communicated to those back home the indignities and pains of life in the line in an unadorned and down-to-earth style. By the end of 1943 his columns were appearing in more than 200 daily newspapers and 400 weeklies in the United States. He had covered the first deployment of troops to Europe in 1942 and now traveled with various US divisions fighting in the Winter Line south of Cassino. There he recorded the exasperation of the troops as mountain after mountain had to be captured, their pain when friends were killed or injured, their sickness, and, above all, the overwhelming exhaustion brought about by combat and exposure to the harsh winter conditions. Seeing men returning from two weeks in the front line, he describes them as looking "ten years older than they were . . . Soldiers became exhausted in mind and in soul as well as physically. The infantry reach a stage of exhaustion that is incomprehensible to folks back home . . . to sum it up: A man just gets damned sick of it all."

As the weather worsened and the assault troops tired, the pace of the advance from Salerno to Cassino became even slower. It had taken fourteen weeks to conquer the fifty miles from Naples to Cassino, the last seven miles before the Gustav Line accounting for nearly half of that time, at the cost of sixteen thousand casualties. Every delay gave the Germans more time to work on the Cassino defenses. Around this time the Germans printed and distributed throughout the south of Italy a poster depicting a snail climbing Italy, with the caption "It's a long way to go!" Only on the rare occasions that the Allies had been able to make use of their significant advantage in artillery or airpower had there been any decisive defeats for the Germans. Over half of the total weight of German artillery was back at home pointing at the sky, using huge quantities of ammunition trying to ward off the strategic bombing offensive over German cities. Many of their fighter planes were also kept at home for the same purpose. But this crucial advantage in the air for the Allies in Italy, which Eisenhower had thought "worth ten divisions," had been nullified by the appalling weather conditions, the worst in living memory.

Although retreating, the Germans had held the initiative and von Vietinghoff and Kesselring were able to choose where and when they fought. The endless mountains and rivers in the way of the advance had cost the Allies dear. With their superior armor trapped on the narrow, smashed roads, frontline action was confined to small groups of men battling at close quarters with machine guns, small mortars, bayonets, and, above all, grenades. In

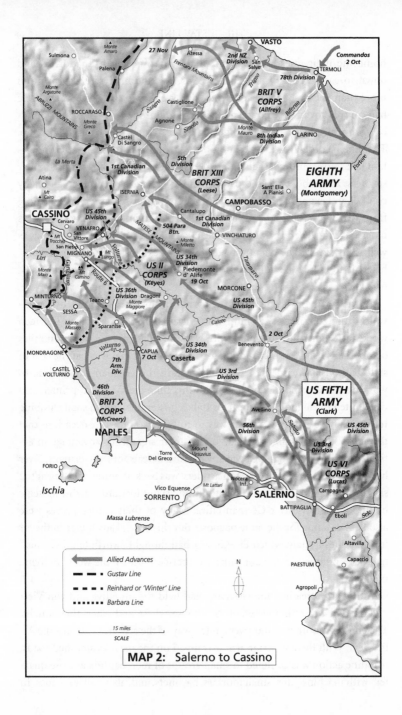

MAP 2: Salerno to Cassino

such circumstances, the fighting will and stamina of the men involved were crucial in determining the outcome of the clashes. As General Alexander put it in his memoirs, "The seemingly unending succession of mountain ranges, ravines and rivers of the Italian terrain demanded the soldierly qualities of fighting valor and endurance in a measure unsurpassed in any other theater of war."

The two sides facing each other at Christmas 1943 came from radically different cultures. There were important differences, too, between the Americans and the British. Both sets of Allied soldiers, though, came from essentially unmilitary societies. Both had been hastily raised and trained. Although the British army had picked up more experience in fighting the Germans (as they never failed to remind their American counterparts), few of those fighting in Italy had been in combat before. Neither country had had a large regular army before the war, and in both Britain and America the peacetime status of the army had been low. Most British and American soldiers saw themselves as civilians first and foremost, and their being in uniform as an unfortunate consequence of when they were born. The war was an unpleasant task to be got out of the way as quickly as possible in order to return to normal life. By the end of 1943, only 2 percent of company commanders in American infantry units were former regular soldiers. The expression "It was just a job we had to do" appears in countless interviews, letters, and memoirs of British and American veterans who, even while they were serving, considered the army a strange and alien body with its ridiculous rules and distasteful practices. Bill Mauldin, whose hugely popular *Stars and Stripes* cartoon series "Willie and Joe" featured two tired, cynical, wisecracking, and unshaven GIs, was often in trouble with the authorities for his depiction of the army as "full of blunders" and "irritations." Although his cartoons eulogize the comradeship and dry humor of the GIs, the soldiers' leaders consistently come across as distant and incomprehensible. "Not all colonels and generals and lieutenants are good," Mauldin wrote in 1944. "No organization of eight million is going to be perfect. Ours are not professional soldiers. They have recently come from a life where they could cuss and criticize their bosses and politicians at will . . . They accept orders and restrictions, but because they are fundamentally democratic the insignia on the shoulders of their officers sometimes look a hell of a lot like chips."

Everyone's first experience of the army had been the training camp, and for many it had been a dismaying shock, particularly if they were better educated or slightly older than most. J. M. Lee Harvey, a British gunner at Cassino, was thirty when he enlisted in July 1941, joining not through any patriotic or heroic motive, but "more out of loneliness. Seeing my office contemporaries joining up one by one had given me a sense of insecurity and a realization that the war might possibly be over before joining in the fray. It would have been hurtful if, after the war was over, I had been asked what I did, and to have replied that I was one that stayed at home." As he swore his oath of allegiance to King and Country, turning from "an ordinary citizen" into "Gunner 1835056," he resolved "in dangerous action" to "blend bravery with caution, with particular emphasis on the latter." Like many others, Lee Harvey found his first day deeply dispiriting. He was given a very unfriendly welcome and sat miserably alone on his allotted barracks-room bed wondering what he had let himself in for. Making for the training ground, he was chewed out for having his hands in his pockets and thereafter "played it very carefully . . . every action was considered with a view to the avoidance of any further trouble." He soon found that newcomers were welcomed to the barracks by having someone urinate in their boots, and that vicious fighting between the men was commonplace. Everywhere he found squalor and discomfort endemic, the food was revolting and unhygienic, and he was shocked when he discovered that prostitutes regularly visited the camp with the tacit approval of the authorities. The money paid to the soldiers was inadequate, and many, like Lee Harvey, were simply unused to being treated so badly. Every group of soldiers, it seems, contained a joker, in this case a young cockney from northeast London, whose "bantering philosophy" did much to help the troops unite in the face of the army's "bull" and apparent total disorganization. Nevertheless, Lee Harvey "soon resented the needless amount of 'bull,' " he wrote after the war, "the waste of materials and time, the movement from one area to another without apparent reason." Visits to the camp from higher-ups were preceded by "bulling up the site": clearing weeds, painting concrete stones and pillars. "How this was helping to win the war it was difficult to understand," he complained. Soon, he admits, he began to develop "a cynicism bordering on the misanthropic, particularly over what appeared to be incompetence in Army administration."

Born in 1921 in Rahway, New Jersey, Tom Kindre had completed his ROTC (Reserve Officer Training Corps) at Rutgers University in 1942 and entered the military at the rank of second lieutenant. After training in a series of camps, he found himself in Shenango, Pennsylvania, in charge of six hundred men and encountering regular prewar army men, mainly NCOs, for the first time. He was not impressed. "The way these guys lived was sort of appalling. All they were interested in was sex and finding a place where they could bring women in. Their language was absolutely foul and so there was a lot of tension." Other college educated recruits record being shocked by the number of men who were illiterate. After Shenango, Kindre's group was moved to another camp that acted as the "last stop" before being sent abroad. There, Kindre had to discipline many of his enlisted men, who seized the chance to go AWOL because they knew they were heading overseas. "They would take off in every direction," Kindre says, "and the MPs would drag them back. I had one guy that did it three times in the few days we were at the camp. Each time I gave him the standard company punishment, which was to dig a hole six feet deep and then I would put a fork in the hole, cover it and then [have] him fill in the hole. Then I'd ask, 'Now which way is the fork pointing?' He didn't know, so he'd have to dig it up again."

The greatest difference between the British and American armies (except perhaps for the former's rules on personal, "soldierly" appearance) was in their attitudes to conserving manpower. For the British, there was a grim determination not to repeat the mistakes and carnage of the First World War, but instead to do everything possible to minimize casualties, even at the expense of operational success. This was reinforced by the end of 1943 by a serious manpower crisis in Britain, where there were just not enough men available for all the commitments. The Americans, on the other hand, had had a less traumatic experience in the First World War, and, of course, had much greater reserves of manpower. This led their generals to be far quicker in ordering men forward to the attack, whatever the casualties. This difference fed much of the distrust that grew during the Italian campaign. To the Americans, the great reluctance of the British to sustain casualties was seen as a lack of drive and appetite for combat. Clark referred disparagingly to the "usual practice for British commanders to depend largely on air bombardment and artillery fire . . . in an effort to minimize the necessity of making infantry attacks." To the British, American commanders were profligate and callous in their use of men—to them high casualties were evidence not of aggression, but of a lack of skill or diligence on the part of the senior officers.

The experience of the First World War also shaped the British attitude to leadership. The popular interwar view of First World War generals ordering their men forward to certain death while themselves remaining far behind the front line was influential in shaping the behavior of high-ranking British officers in Italy and elsewhere. Men like Montgomery and his imitators would tour frontline areas dispensing cigarettes and encouragement, and even the theater commander, Alexander, would frequently pop up on the front line, sometimes to the great inconvenience of the soldiers there. American GIs were often surprised and impressed to find very senior British officers in dangerous frontline positions. Some US riflemen didn't even know the name of their regimental commander, and few had any love for their generals.

However, in both armies the leadership role of the junior officer, a platoon or company commander, was crucial. In the US Army, where junior officers and men often treated one another as equals, "the substitute for hierarchy, as well as for discipline and adequate training, was the old American one—inspirational leadership." This meant junior officers leading from the front and exposing themselves to even greater risks than the men they led. The result was appalling loss. A study of American combat troops in Italy showed it took a mere eighty-eight days of combat to cause 100 percent casualties among an infantry division's second lieutenants. One American second lieutenant explained what usually happened to a "green" officer arriving in a rifle company in action: "The normal tendency is to attempt to stress his ability in the attack, an attitude of 'I'll show you all I've got what it takes.' The result is generally one officer casualty—and frequently fatal." The same was true for the British Army. Eric "Birdie" Smith, who fought at Cassino as a twenty-year-old Gurkha officer, tells the story of one of his battalion's company commanders, Bill Nangle, up on the Cassino Massif at the beginning of March 1944: "His company of green, inexperienced troops were jittery, ready to run after a long and protracted barrage fired at their position. To calm the young men, the old warrior sat outside his foxhole, puffing contentedly away on his pipe while he cleaned his rifle. A single mortar bomb landed near where he was sitting, and Bill Nangle, who had survived so much, in so many battles, died without a single enemy being in sight."

Most junior officers felt they had no choice but to put themselves at greater risk than their men. As one lieutenant in the Durham Light Infantry, who fought hard battles in front of Cassino, has recorded: "Rightly or wrongly, I led from the front whenever possible. I felt more confident that way. I felt it was my duty, to tell you the truth, I really felt I couldn't send somebody else there if I wasn't prepared to do it myself." There was another factor as well, as the junior officer goes on to explain: "It was quite clear to me that unless platoon commanders led their platoons, nothing happened." An American officer who fought at Cassino concurs: "A man forgets to be afraid if you can get him to start firing." Alex Bowlby, in his classic account of his experiences as a British rifleman in Italy, tells of an incident earlier in the campaign: "The Germans fired two shots. The Company went to ground as if it had been two hundred. Only Captain Kendall remained on his feet. A Spandau [German machine gun] opened up. We clung to the ground as if it alone could save us. Captain Kendall walked slowly through the Company. 'Look at me,' he said quietly walking from man to man under fire. 'They can't hit me. Look at me.' We looked. He might have been taking a stroll in the sun. The Germans didn't hit him. His courage hit us. We got to our feet." There are numerous similar stories, and such behavior by officers even became a cliché of the campaign. Bill Mauldin satirizes it in one cartoon drawn in January 1944, which shows his two GIs cowering under cover behind a machine gun while a clean-shaven officer stands upright in front of them. One of the sheltering GIs calls out: "Sir, do ya hafta draw fire while yer inspirin' us?"

Although the German divisions had their share of young, inexperienced troops, their cultural background was utterly different to that of the "citizen" armies of Britain and the United States. Part of this difference can be traced back to the German reaction to the end of the First World War and earlier. Although 2 million Germans had died during the Great War, the carnage had a markedly different effect in Germany than it did in France and Britain. For the Allied populations, it was the "war to end all wars," but the Germans had not only suffered more; they had also gone without the consolation of victory. Even more than for the bruised victors, the war became for Germany a double tragedy. At least for the Allies all the suffering had resulted in being on the "winning" side, but for the Germans everything had been in vain. What emerged in Germany after the war, and long before the Nazis came to power, was a theory that the war had, in fact, not been lost at all. Although the home front had been devastated by the effects of the Allied blockade, German soil was never the scene of battle; and there had been an

armistice rather than an unconditional surrender. The brave men at the
front, so the growing belief went, had been betrayed by the politicians, communists, and financiers at home. The result was a flourishing of the "cult of
the soldier" and, in due course, the militarism, nationalism, and anti-
Semitism of the Nazis.

So the interwar German armed forces, or Wehrmacht, enjoyed a far
higher status than those of the Western Allies. When the Nazis came to
power in 1933, the army was seen, and viewed itself, as an "integral part of
state and society in the Third Reich," and "intentionally formed the second
pillar of the Führer state, alongside the party." Since the introduction of conscription in 1935, the army was considered an essential part of a German's
education. Conditioning young German minds was one of the Nazi regime's
priorities, great care being taken at various stages—when joining the
Jungvolk at ten, the Hitler Youth at fourteen, and the Wehrmacht or *Arbeits-
dienst* (labor service) at eighteen. By 1944 the Nazi Party had had ten years
to educate and indoctrinate its male population in martial virtues, to consider themselves not as civilians in uniform, but as soldiers first and foremost.

Robert Frettlöhr, who fought as a paratrooper at Cassino, was nine years
old when Hitler came to power in 1933. His father worked for a big steel
company in their home town of Duisburg, and Robert started his appren-
ticeship in the same firm when he was fourteen. "I was in the Hitler Youth,"
he says, "yes, there was discipline and it helped. It makes something out of
you." Frettlöhr's favorite activity was flying gliders in the hilly area around
his home town. The boys would also go camping and make model aero-
planes. "But," he adds, "we were being prepared to be soldiers . . . We saw the
men marching and we just took it as part of our lives. It was just there. You
see, you had no choice, and I didn't query the thing because I was far, far too
young." He volunteered for the Luftwaffe when he was eighteen and, having
seen a film about German paratroops, "was hooked."

Joseph Klein, another paratrooper who fought at Cassino, was a teenager
during the late 1930s. "I was—at that time—a true Nazi," he says. "Basically
it was not possible that one wasn't connected to politics . . . the entire population was caught up in this political idea, this National Socialism. It had
been chaos [in Germany]. The West had crippled Germany, through the
Treaty of Versailles, and the economy could not stand on its own. But with
Hitler in a short time the unemployment halted and it was going better for

the Germans for once. There was hardly any poverty. There were no beggars. Everyone helped one another. In the first year of the Hitler regime everyone suddenly had a Christmas—everyone had gifts and the rich had to give something to the poor. There was *Volksbewusstsein,* standing up for one another." Klein also was an enthusiastic member of the Hitler Youth and its junior version. "One was automatically in the Hitler *Jungvolk,* one could not stand apart. I was brought up as a total National Socialist. I was raised in this way from a young age. I couldn't think otherwise. Nobody could at that time. Why should I have been different? Basically, as a young man I wasn't allowed a critical ability in the sense that people have it today."

While the citizen armies of the British and Americans had to be handled with great care, there was no talk of "rights" in the Wehrmacht. A German soldier caught deserting would be shot. During the war the Germans executed over fifteen thousand of their own soldiers. The Americans did have the death penalty in theory, but executed only one man in the course of the war. The British had abandoned the firing squad as a punishment for desertion by 1930, although in March 1944, as the situation in Italy worsened, Alexander sought unsuccessfully to have it reimposed.

The extent to which these differences account for the superb battlefield performance of many Wehrmacht units in Italy is almost impossible to judge, but certainly while on the Allied side nobody expected the war to drag on into 1945, German prisoners taken at Cassino and before amazed their captors with their confidence in ultimate German victory. It was only as they made their way to the Allied rear echelon and saw the enormous material wealth there—in tanks, supplies, and ammunition—that their optimism began to fade.

For the British and American troops, victory would mean simply the end of the war and a return, at last, to civilian life. Those men who kept fighting through the terrible Italian winter of 1943–44 and into the bloodbath of Cassino did so because enough factors outweighed the rational, essential survival instinct: they did not want to let down their comrades or their families; they were more frightened of the shame of showing cowardice in front of their group; because it was kill or be killed; because they had to. In neither country had the start of the Second World War been greeted with the sort of patriotic rhetoric seen in the First. In the United States there was widespread disinterest as Germany overran first Poland and then France. Robert Koloski, from Minneapolis in the American Midwest, was a medic at

Cassino and throughout the fighting in Africa, and describes his reaction to the start of the war in September 1939: "Europe was not talked about a great deal. I think we were still pretty isolationist. So few of us understood, or thought about Europe at all." When Pearl Harbor was attacked on 7 December 1941, "the country was in absolute panic," says Koloski. "We were shuttled around various towns in the southern United States, guarding ports and things of that nature against a Japanese invasion, which of course turned out to be absolutely impossible, but they were busy cranking up everything about that time." When Germany declared war on the United States four days later, it took many Americans by surprise. "Nobody really understood why we were going to go to Europe," says Koloski. "Given our educational level and everything else, we didn't understand the circumstances particularly." Throughout the war, the motivating slogan remained "Remember Pearl Harbor." As has been pointed out, "No one [in the United States] ever shouted or sang 'Remember Poland.' " The playwright Arthur Miller worked in the Brooklyn Navy Yard during the war and noted "the near absence among the men I worked with . . . of any comprehension of what Nazism meant—we were fighting Germany essentially because she had allied herself with the Japanese who had attacked us at Pearl Harbor."

Although many joined up hoping to "do their bit," little of such idealism survived exposure to combat and the close company of a group of frontline soldiers. "By the time we got to Italy," remembers Koloski, "all that 'For God and patriotism,' that was all gone. We very quickly lost any shred of seeing it as a heroic endeavor. There was very little 'ra ra' for God and country and if you tried that they probably would have shoved a bayonet in you." Bill Mauldin agreed: "Some say morale is sky-high at the front because everybody's face is shining for the great cause. They are wrong." A Canadian soldier puts it more bluntly: "Who the hell dies for King and Country any more? That crap went out in the First World War." Englishman Charlie Framp, who served with the Black Watch and wrote about his experiences during the war and at Cassino in particular, sums up the motivation of the typical British infantryman in a passive, fatalistic way: "He was there, quite simply, because he was there." Little was known and less believed about the horrors that the Nazi regime was perpetrating across Europe; what has retrospectively led to the Second World War being labeled a "good war" was largely irrelevant to the frontline soldier in Italy at Christmas 1943.

The American GIs in particular distrusted Allied propaganda about atrocities and prison camps. Disillusioned and hardened by the rigors of the Great Depression, their generation was in general suspicious of authority and of the sort of high-minded rhetoric that they associated with the First World War. "For most of the troops, the war might just as well have been about good looks, so evanescent at times did its meaning and purpose seem," an American ex-soldier has written. "The puzzlement of the partici-pants about what was going on contrasts notably with the clarity of purpose felt, at least in the early stages, by those who fought the Great War." Hence the popularity of writers like Ernie Pyle, whose unideological, down-to-earth tone both reflected and shaped Americans' attitudes to the war, par-ticularly in Europe. Certainly Pyle could find very little evidence of any real hatred of the Germans; if anything, there was a certain amount of com-radeship felt with the fellow combat soldiers on the other side of the front line. Writing about the fighting in the mountains in front of Cassino, Pyle marvels at the prodigious weight of the Allied artillery fire on the Germans, and then goes on to add, "no matter how cold the mountains, or how wet the snow, or how sticky the mud, it was just as miserable for the German sol-dier as for the American."

The American authorities hoped to create a distinction in the soldiers' minds between Germans and Nazis, but this made little headway with the GIs, and official concern grew about the unwillingness of the frontline sol-dier deliberately to kill the enemy at close quarters. Surveys were carried out, and it was found that fewer than 10 percent said they would "really like" to kill a German soldier (nearly half did "really want" to end the life of a Japan-ese soldier). Unlike the "treacherous, Oriental" Japanese, the Germans were seen by the Americans and, perhaps to a slightly lesser extent, the British, as much like themselves. Tom Kindre had arrived in Casablanca in April 1943 with other newly trained replacements and found himself in Italy shortly af-ter the Salerno landings. When two German soldiers wandered into his po-sition with their hands up, he remembers being surprised by how ordinary he found them: "I spoke a little German but I didn't interrogate them. You weren't supposed to do that. You saved that for the people who did the offi-cial interrogation, but I did talk with them a little. The first thing, of course, was that they were hungry, so I took them to the mess tent and got the mess sergeant to give them some food. Well, my image was that of the movies: the arrogant jackbooted German SS officer. I was impressed with the fact that these men were very, very ordinary-looking people, nothing special about them at all." When he encountered his first dead Germans, his initial instinct was one of pity and sympathy. "There'd been rapid advance by our division so the graves registration people hadn't had time to catch up. We moved into a new area and I was walking out to establish a location for a latrine, and here was a little mound and two bodies, two Germans who had been in a machine gun emplacement. One had apparently just received a package from home. It was still half full of cookies. I remember being particularly impressed by the fact that there were letters. The guy had been reading a letter from home. Near by there was a little book with names and addresses in it."

Many British soldiers have recorded similar emotions. One, on taking over a dugout recently occupied by the Germans, noticed that it was still permeated with the smell of its former occupants: "The tastes and morals of the individual fighting men, on whatever side they fought, were not solely dependent on nationality. Gazing at the rubbish, the clutter, the signs of a hurried departure, one could even find it in one's heart to pity."

To kill or maim an enemy so recognizably human, as a frontline infantryman was expected to do, face-to-face with rifle, grenade, or bayonet, again required an outweighing of fundamental human instincts. Together with the fear of being killed oneself, it was the very worst aspect of the war for those involved; for many it made them feel degraded and disgusted, particularly once the immediate action was over. Such feelings have in many cases persisted for over sixty years. "You don't become a killer," wrote Bill Mauldin. "No normal man who has smelled and associated with death ever wants to see any more of it . . . the surest way to become a pacifist is to join the infantry."

For those arriving in combat for the first time, there seems to have been a shared progression of emotions from shock and horror or anger, through to a numb acceptance of the awful realities of war. Almost all soldiers vividly remember the first time their unit sustained casualties, or the first time they saw a dead body in the field, but thereafter memories become less focused. Werner Eggert, an eighteen-year-old paratrooper with the German 4th Regiment, 1st Parachute Division, was sent to the Adriatic front at the end of November 1943. The most hazardous part was the journey up to the frontline positions. "It was in the first week," he says, "that we got into a grenade-thrower assault. Every soldier knows that you can't get down fast enough in this situation. Two of our people were hit by small fragments, which could be removed later by the medic. But the young blond Lawrenz was hit crosswise in the throat. We tried to press on to his carotid artery and carried him into the protection of the next house ruins. I tried to reassure him: 'That is not so bad, we'll be able to fix it . . .' He tried to breathe, but we heard only gargling sounds. The dressing material sucked itself full of blood. My hands were sticky. Five minutes later, long before the company medic reached us, he was dead. The medic, hardly older than twenty-three or twenty-five years, could not have done anything anyway. Two men carried Lawrenz back to the village. And the rest of us four continued our way in a disturbed mood. What would they say to his parents? He died for his people and his fatherland? He died as a hero? Something along those lines. In reality he was smashed by the 'soulless' shrapnel of a grenade thrown blindly into the night. Eighteen years old. But that was just the beginning. I still remember the name of the first guy who had to bite the dust. Later, however, with the rushing events, with the continuous replacements, when everything became habit, the memory faded. And even more frightening, the sympathy for the dead faded, too." Eggert puts this down to the "emotional blunting which got to everyone in the course of time," a sentiment echoed by troops of all nationalities.

Some soldiers, however, fought to settle scores, to avenge companions or loved ones killed. Denis Beckett, who commanded a company of British infantry at Cassino, remembers one of his men putting notches on his rifle to record the number of Germans he had killed: "[He] had been living in Coventry," says Beckett. "The city was bombed by the Germans and he lost his mother, father and his girlfriend. He was always wanting to volunteer for things which would give him the chance to shoot Germans." A very small number, also, did undoubtedly enjoy war. To the majority, they were at times incomprehensible, sometimes a liability, and sometimes an inspiration. Sapper Richard Eke, who served in Italy with the 754th Field Engineering Company and wrote a brilliant memoir of his war, had a corporal who was a veteran of the Spanish civil war: "Slightly mad and brave, and a little out of place in a section that hoped to avoid being heroic at all cost. He volunteered for everything, and we had never seen him show any fear." Eke himself had long before assumed the weary fatalism most prevalent among the men. After his unit had sustained their first casualties, he writes, "We had learned our first lesson, mainly that fate, not the Germans or Italians, was our undiscriminating enemy. With the same callousness of Army orders, without fairness or judgment—'You and you, dead—The rest of you on the truck.' "

Matthew Salmon, the 56th Division British engineer who had helped install a bathroom in Clark's trailer, also had an officer who was considered "slightly mad." "Major Smith, our commanding officer, who was later killed, loved war," Salmon says. "He used to go out sniping at night with 200 rounds of ammunition . . . we used to think he was mad to be so keen, but on the other hand we all wanted the war to be over as soon as possible and it was men like him that were most likely to bring it to an early conclusion." The major, who had originally been in the Indian Army, was very strict on discipline and had little fellow-feeling for his men, but they acknowledged that he would not have asked them to do something he would not undertake himself. Nevertheless, his heroics were often treated with suspicion by his men, who felt that they merely attracted trouble.

However honestly war correspondent Ernie Pyle wrote about the conditions in central Italy in the winter of 1943–44, there were some subjects that he chose to ignore or, perhaps, that he did not think would make it past the censor. As has been pointed out, he said little about the frequent casualties from "friendly fire," the problem of mental breakdown in the troops, the racial segregation in the US Army, or the extensive looting by American soldiers. He also understated the growing disillusionment and lack of enthusiasm in the Allied armies in late 1943. He did accept, though, that there was a marked difference in performance among the frontline troops: "I don't know what it is that impels some men, either in peace or in wartime, to extend themselves beyond all expectation, or what holds other men back to do just as little as possible. In any group of soldiers you'll find both kinds." In fact, there was by now an increasing number of the latter. As one historian has commented, Italy toward the end of 1943 saw "an ever smaller number of strivers, and a growing number of skivers." Aside from anecdotal evidence, the numbers falling ill—always a good indication of morale and drive, whatever the conditions—indicate an army losing heart. Up to the end of 1943, Mark Clark's 5th Army had suffered 40,000 battle casualties, but the American contingent alone had over 50,000 men out sick.

Desertion was also becoming a real problem. Some estimates of those "on the trot" in Italy at any one time are as high as 20,000. In Africa, desertion had held few attractions, but in Italy it held many, for there were farms into which men were welcomed with open arms and warm beds for replacements for husbands and sons who were prisoners, refugees, or dead. In the cities it was not difficult to hide, and a thriving black market provided a living. The scale of the problem in the British army was such that "commanders and staff were alarmed . . . quite apart from the effect upon operations, the difficulty of providing accommodation for deserters in detention barracks was becoming acute."

Most did not desert from battle, but chose not to return to their units after being sent to the rear. They could easily lose themselves in Naples for a week. When they eventually made their way back to their units or were apprehended, they faced three to five years' penal servitude. But nearly all sentences were reviewed after six months, and, with manpower desperately short, the soldier would then find himself back in the ranks. Although there were a few "deliberate" deserters, who would rather face prison than go into combat, a report for the War Office in late 1944 found that most was "involuntary" and that the majority of deserters were simply men at the end of their rope. The British 56th Division official historian, who candidly admits that Christmas 1943 and the two months after saw "a peak period" in desertions, asserts that many "deserters" were encountered wandering around in a confused state having experienced some form of breakdown. Tom Kindre backs this up. He was working as a defense counsel on the Division Court Martial Board, and he says he "saw many men being tried for misbehavior before the enemy who in my opinion were stunned, dazed, in some ways not fully in command of themselves."

Thus the military and medical authorities found themselves "struggling to differentiate between the medical and disciplinary spheres of behavior." A number of factors, such as circumstance and prior record, would help determine whether a soldier who absented himself from the battle or his unit ended up in detention camp or in the hospital. By and large, though, the decision fell to the military psychiatrist on the spot, who on the one hand had to consider the welfare of his patient and on the other was under enormous pressure from the army authorities to return men to the fighting. Some cases of breakdown were successfully treated with a couple of days' rest at an exhaustion center not too far from the front line. Experience in Sicily and North Africa had taught the doctors that to remove the soldier from his support group of mates and routine would often exacerbate the problem, as it took away a vital prop and heightened the man's feelings of shame and worthlessness.

For many, though, it would be mental injuries that would end their time as fighting soldiers in Italy. There was nothing new in this; as a recent explanatory leaflet on post-traumatic stress disorder (PTSD) published for

American veterans puts it, "War is a life-threatening experience that involves witnessing and engaging in terrifying and gruesome acts of violence . . . It is normal for human beings to react to war's psychic trauma with feelings of fear, anger, grief, and horror, as well as emotional numbness and disbelief." There have been various names for the psychological problems that combat brings, reflecting current beliefs about their cause and possible treatment. In the American Civil War it was described as "soldier's heart"; in the First World War, it was initially known as "shell-shock," as it was at one time erroneously believed that these nervous symptoms were simply the result of concussion from shell blasts. The Second World War saw the coining of the euphemisms "battle fatigue" and "battle exhaustion," as if all the shattered men could be restored by a good night's sleep.

With hindsight, it is astonishing that even more men did not break down at Cassino. As the fighting grew more static, it was possible for young American psychiatrists to visit the front line for the first time. What they found there amazed them: nearly all the troops, even those thought to be the strongest in their unit, had most of the symptoms—the shakes, nightmares, sweats—they had been treating on the mental wards back at their base hospitals. A psychiatrist sent from Washington visited exhaustion centers around Cassino in early 1944. His report destroyed the idea that it was only the weak or cowardly who broke down, stating that there was no such thing as "getting used to combat" and that "practically all men in rifle battalions who were not otherwise disabled ultimately became psychiatric casualties." The attitude of the other men to such cases usually depended on how long they had been in combat. Veterans accepted such "casualties" as being as inevitable as the weather, and if they had "done their bit" they would be cared for by their mates; it was newcomers who "viewed the matter as an affront to their beliefs about proper soldierly behavior." But, as one much-decorated Canadian veteran warned, "Persons who are not exposed to the bullets and shells in a slit trench situation or having to advance over open ground against a determined enemy should be very careful of using the words 'cowardice,' 'yellow,' and 'malingerer.' Sooner or later, in those circumstances, we would all break down."

Soon after the Salerno landings, British gunner Spike Milligan had caught sandfly fever, a virus that caused headaches, back pain, and in some cases lethargy and mental confusion. He was hospitalized for a few days and then spent a long time in the boredom of a transit camp near Salerno. When he rejoined his unit on 20 October on the north bank of the Volturno, he was pleased to be back with his group. The X Corps was on the move. "We travel north along a tree-lined road," Milligan wrote, "ahead in the distance lie a range of mountains, some snow-capped: these are the ones we will have to cross to gain access to the Garigliano plain. Jerry has pulled back into them and is waiting."

By mid-October it had become clear to the Allies that the Germans were not going to abandon southern Italy in favor of a defensive line along the Po River, far north of Rome, as had been predicted. This then posed the question of what to do after Naples was secure. Many of the original aims of the campaign had already been achieved—Italy was out of the war, Naples and the Foggia airfields had been captured. The other purpose, to tie down as many German divisions as possible was, in tactical terms, as the American official historian complained, so "vague as to defy description."

When the Allied leaders met in Tehran in November 1943, Stalin even suggested that the armies in Italy should go on to the defensive. This may have been to stir the disagreements still raging between the British and Americans about the low priority of the Italian campaign for shipping, reinforcements, and supplies. Brooke still fumed in his diary about the "limitations of Marshall's brain" and bemoaned lost opportunities in the Mediterranean, while the Americans insisted that the transfer of seven divisions to the United Kingdom must go ahead as planned. What emerged from the meetings was a plan to use Allied troops in Italy to make a landing in southern France to support the Normandy invasion, an operation code-named Anvil. This was pushed for vigorously by Stalin, who had no wish to see Western Allied troops east of Italy. But Anvil envisaged the attackers making a "short hop" from northern Italy, which demanded that they be far north of Rome by the spring of 1944, so the painful advance had to continue, although Churchill successfully pressed for some of the landing craft earmarked for Normandy to be retained in the Mediterranean for amphibious actions around the Germans' flanks. There was another incentive, the capture of Rome itself, which Churchill in particular believed would be of great propaganda value and would keep the whole Italian campaign from "sinking." The air chiefs, who had been eyeing the airfields around Rome, also wanted the front advanced nearer their targets in southern Germany and the Balkans. The end result was a commitment to take Rome, with the implicit idea of an amphibious operation.

But in truth, the campaign on the ground had created demands and a momentum of its own. The 5th Army had to move forward as quickly as possible not only to avoid looking beaten and to keep the pressure on the Germans, but also to prevent the further fortification of places in its path. From air reconnaissance, from civilians, and from escaped POWs, they learned of the work going on along the Gustav Line based on the Rapido and Garigliano Rivers and at Monte Cassino. There had been a large-scale concentration of German troops behind the two rivers, gun pits were being blasted out of solid rock, the banks were being cleared to create fields of fire, and antitank ditches, mines, and barbed wire were being readied everywhere. If the lines in front of Cassino would be defended firmly enough, the Gustav Line, it seemed, the Germans intended to hold. All the Allies could do was try to reach this lethal killing field as quickly as possible. Effectively, they were being sucked into a tactical trap.

In the mountains between the Volturno and the Garigliano and Rapido valleys, the pattern continued of the Germans holding out and counterattacking, then withdrawing just at the moment when the Allies had established fields of fire and ranges for mortars and artillery or had laboriously outflanked the position. Village after village would be fought over and pounded to bits until at last the Americans or British threw themselves forward, only to find the target deserted by the enemy in favor of the next position, sometimes less than a mile away. For 10th Army commander von Vietinghoff, all was going to plan: "Enemy gains constituted no great threat," he wrote later, "and every step forward into the mountainous territory merely increased his difficulties."

Also increasing as the battlefield slowly moved northward was the destruction of the country being fought over. As Mauldin, no friend of the Italians, wrote: "There is no doubt that the Italians are paying a stiff price for their past sins. The country looks as if a giant rake had gone over it from end to end." Everywhere the Allies had advanced were to be found shattered olive groves, wrecked orchards, and demolished buildings. "You can usually tell what kind of fighting went on in a town," Mauldin goes on, "and how much was necessary to take it, by the wreckage that remains. If the buildings are fairly intact, with only broken windows, doors, and pocked walls, it was a quick, hand-to-hand street fight with small arms and grenades and perhaps

a mortar or two. If most of the walls are still standing, but the roofs have
gaping holes, and many rooms are shattered, then the entry was preceded by
an artillery barrage. If some of the holes are in the slopes of the roofs facing
the retreating enemy, then he gave the town a plastering after he left. But if
there isn't much town left at all, then planes have been around. Bombs sort
of lift things up in the air and drop them in a heap. Even the enormous
sheet-metal doors with which shop-owners shutter their establishments
buckle and balloon out into grotesque swollen shapes."

Spike Milligan wrote in his diary on 24 October: "Feeling very nervous.
Can't eat my food. As day came to an end I felt really exhausted. What's
wrong with me?" He was becoming increasingly depressed by the effects of
the war he was fighting and the endless trail of smashed towns and villages.
The next day his unit drove through the remains of Sparanise, which had
been "badly shelled and bombed, some buildings still smoldering. The inhabitants are in a state of shock, women and children are crying, men are
searching among the ruins for their belongings or worse, their relatives. It
was the little children that depressed me the most, that such innocence
should be put to such suffering. The adult world should forever hang its
head in shame at the terrible, unforgivable things done to the young."

Many other Allied servicemen shared Milligan's sympathy for the inno-
cent victims of the war. S. C. Brooks, a machine gunner attached to the
British 56th Division, wrote in his diary on 1 October: "We end up in village
for the night, we get crowds of kids round wanting meat and biscuits, some
bring pieces of veg, beans, tomatoes, grapes, potatoes. All these people seem
in a bad way for food, I don't know how they will go on in a month or so . . .
A lot of kiddies have disease, usually with their eyes and legs." Whenever the
soldiers ate there would be a crowd of "ragged and miserable" civilians beg-
ging for food or going through the bins looking for scraps. As Mauldin
wrote, "The doggie knows where his next meal is coming from. That makes
him a very rich man in this land where hunger is so fierce it makes animals
out of respectable old ladies." During the fighting in the desert, there had
been few civilians around, but here in Italy they were everywhere. In film
footage taken by British army cameramen, they seem ever-present, some
clearly wearing all their clothes, the women with baskets on their heads, the
children wearing German forage caps, the old men in Homburg hats, arguing or pleading with a soldier.

Artilleryman Lee Harvey, like many, was surprised by the poverty in southern Italy, even before the effects of the fighting. In 1940, Italy as a whole had less than a quarter of the GDP per head of Britain, and the south was always the poorer half. Lee Harvey visited a poor part of Naples soon after its capture: "It was without doubt the most squalid area inhabited by humanity it was possible for anyone to see," he wrote. "The people who had their homes here, if such they could be called, must have been in the lowest depths of degradation." Mauldin, who complained that the Italians stole everything he owned except "the filling in my teeth," commented, "Those of us who have spent a long time in Sicily and Italy are more amazed every day that such a run-down country could have had the audacity to declare war on anyone, even with the backing of the Krauts." Lee Harvey was typical in dividing the Italians into two types: peasants "for whom we had all so quickly developed a great respect. They were all so hard-working, warm-hearted and munificent in all respects to the Allied invaders . . . On the other hand, the town-folk consisted of shopkeepers, artisans and others who were predominantly fascist or communist and who lost no opportunity with the varying war conditions to feather their own nests under a thin guise of patriotism."

In fact, the "peasants" seem to have been equally generous to the Germans. An eighteen-year-old German infantryman wrote in his diary on 10 December, upon arriving in a village on the Adriatic coast, "Everybody is hungry here; there is no bread. Found civilians friendly and I was received by a nice family with two daughters and given dinner. They gave me a crucifix."

<hr />

The left wing of the Allied advance had made contact with the Gustav Line on the Garigliano River on 2 November at patrol strength, but it was felt that the coast road to Rome—Route 7—with numerous canals and marshes, was unsuitable for the main axis of attack, which would have to go up Route 6, Via Casilina, the road that ran past the Cassino monastery. About ten miles before Cassino, the road travels between high mountains, through what was known as the Mignano Gap, and here the Germans were determined to defend vigorously. On 5 November, General McCreery's British X Corps was ordered to capture Monte Camino, which controlled the southern side of the road. After good early progress, the attackers from 56th Division found the approaches to the top carefully mined, booby-trapped, and covered by heavy weapons in pits blasted out of solid rock. Whenever they reached a peak, they would be counterattacked off it, and ended up clinging to near-vertical slopes. An entire battalion was doing little more than carrying rations and ammunition to the men fighting, and the whole division was becoming exhausted. Two companies that had penetrated near to the summit were surrounded, and, having held out for five days on one day's supplies of food and water, were forced to break out and withdraw. It had been a defensive victory for the Germans, much to the fury of Clark, whose confidence in the British to achieve the goals he set them was now at a very low ebb.

"Armistice Day. Ha ha ha," wrote Spike Milligan in his diary on 11 November. "We hear by the grapevine that our PBI [poor bloody infantry] are suffering fifty per cent casualties. Thank God I'm not in the infantry." There were constant rumors in his battery that they would be going home to England, but in the meantime there was an outbreak of illness in the unit, as the rain and the mud seemed to take over. At one point, Milligan records, the "shit pit" flooded out and had its contents "float under the tent flaps."

It would be another three weeks before the attack on Camino was repeated. Meanwhile, Alexander ordered a halt to rest his exhausted troops. When McCreery tried again at the beginning of December, there would be no half measures, with the 56th and 46th divisions both being used as well as prodigious quantities of artillery shells. The conditions, though, were as bad as before. Milligan recorded the preparations in the artillery lines: "Ammunition is being dumped by the guns, through the day the pile of mustard-colored shells mounts up. Mud is everywhere. Are they going to attack in this weather? Up a mountain? At two in the morning?"

On 1 December, 46th Division attacked; her sister division, the 56th, jumped off the following night. Initial progress was good until a fierce counterattack drove back the British troops. They got to the top of the mountain again on the morning of 4 December, but were once more beaten back by a counterattack. Frequently the attacking troops would find themselves sheltering in the Germans' previous forward positions. Although the German workmanship was much admired, naturally the enemy knew exactly where to drop their mortar bombs. For Lance Cpl. William Virr, of the Durham Light Infantry, "It was awful. I never did like mortar shelling because they come straight down. You can be in a slit trench but it can drop right in with you, whereas a shell at least comes down at an angle. Mortar fire was worse to me. If you're under a long bombardment I think you go mad eventually,

go off your rocker. Every man has a different breaking point and some go before others. So you could never point the finger at anyone because another
half-hour and it might be you. You tend to be on the brink and it takes all
your striving to prevent yourself from going to pieces. I've been on the point
of it a few times and I suppose everybody else had. When you feel like letting everything go—gabbling and screaming, gibbering away—just letting
go. I just managed not to—till next time. You just curl up in a ball and hope
nothing comes your way." Finally, by the evening of 6 December, the highest
point of the mountain was secure, and after three days of mopping-up operations, Camino was clear of enemy troops.

Along with air operations against the German defenders, the weight of
the Allied artillery had been decisive. Monte Camino became known as
Million-Dollar Hill—so named for the cost of the artillery fire the Allies
needed to take it. According to Ernie Pyle, someone worked out that it was
costing twenty-five thousand dollars in shellfire to kill each German. Someone else wondered if it might not be simpler just to offer them the money to
surrender.

For Maj. Gen. Fridolin von Senger und Etterlin, commander of the German XIV Panzer Corps, the artillery bombardment at the outset of the second Camino battle had been "of an intensity such as I had not witnessed
since the big battles of the First World War." Von Senger would be the man
Kesselring would charge with the task of preventing the Allies from getting
past Cassino. An enigmatic figure far removed from the popular conception
of a Nazi general, he had been a Rhodes scholar to St. John's College, Oxford,
in 1912 and remained an Anglophile thereafter. Intellectual, sophisticated,
and anti-Nazi, he was also a devout Roman Catholic and as a young man
had become a lay Benedictine and visited many Benedictine monasteries in
Germany. He had been involved in the defeat of France, and after two years
near Paris was sent to the Eastern Front as part of the force that unsuccessfully tried to relieve von Paulus's trapped 6th Army at Stalingrad. His skillful direction of the defensive battles at Cassino, ignored or denigrated by
German propaganda because of his known anti-Nazi sympathies, was to
cost many thousands of Allied lives.

The end of the battle for Camino gave Spike Milligan a chance for a
much-needed breather, and he took the opportunity to have "a wayside bath
in a tin. It's so cold you keep the top half fully dressed while you do the legs,
then on with the trousers, strip the top half and do that," he wrote in his diary on 8 December. But the next day he reports that he is again depressed:

"I can't take much more of this bloody rain." The same day the body of a man is found in the regimental headquarters. "It turned out to be an engineer who had committed suicide. 'Lucky bastard,' said Nash."

The rain had also ended the offensive on the Adriatic coast, by which means Montgomery had hoped to break through and approach Rome from the east. There had been slow progress and heavy losses, and when the Sangro River flooded on 5 December, all the engineers' bridges had to be laboriously rebuilt. By the middle of the month the front was closed down, and the focus for the Allies and Germans alike would be the southern part of the Gustav Line around Cassino. Montgomery himself along with Eisenhower was recalled to Britain for Overlord and would play no more part in the Italian campaign, which he had from the first castigated as lacking overall direction.

The American 36th Texas Division, rested since Salerno, entered the fighting in front of Cassino, capturing two more mountains alongside Route 6, and then pushing on to the small village of San Pietro. Their first attack on 7 December was unsuccessful, the worst part being the effort by the small Italian contingent that had by now joined the 5th Army. Known as the Raggruppamento Italiano Motorizzato (1st Motorized Group), the regiment of about 5,500 men failed to take their objective, Monte Lungo, high ground near San Pietro, amid failures of coordination and communication with the Americans. Walker's 36th Division tried again with tanks, but incurred very heavy losses. Only when the position was eventually outflanked on 16 December did the Germans withdraw. The next day American troops entered the eerie silence of the smashed remains of the village. Over 300 civilians, who had trusted in their cellars and stayed in their homes, had been killed.

After Salerno, it was another huge bloodletting for the US 36th Division. Clare Cunningham, whose 142nd Regiment had been ordered to take the high ground overlooking the town, vividly remembers the horrors of fighting up an exposed mountainside against well-entrenched defenders: "It was very demoralizing losing so many men, and such a dumb move." Most of the casualties came from mortar fire, although occasionally an artillery shell would score a direct hit. "I remember one guy who was from here in Michigan," says Cunningham. "He had a fox-hole dug and he pulled a shelter over him. He was killed that night—a shell just landed right square on top of him. The only way we knew it was him was that he had a helmet that he boiled clothes in and the helmet had turned black. They were on him over getting that helmet repainted or replaced. When we saw it there it looked like a sieve. He never knew what struck him." Only a small minority of fatalities died instantly. Cunningham tells the story of a medic from Indiana called Harold Welch: "He'd run up after the company ahead got hit by mortars. He came back with tears streaming down his face. I didn't know what happened to him but sometime later, after we got off the front, he told us that one guy that got hit badly asked him to shoot him with his rifle. Of course, he wouldn't do it, so he just ran away. I am sure the guy died anyway but that was just too much for Welch to take. Pretty shattering, really." Some of the reaction of horror channeled itself into anger at the enemy. "We had one GI that said he would never take a prisoner and he didn't," Cunningham continues. "I remember on Monte Lungo a German coming out holding a white handkerchief. Maybe he got within five yards of him before he blasted him, killing the German. Having seen that, the Germans to a man just opened up with everything they had on us. Most of us didn't like it, most didn't believe in his attitude at all."

In spite of the losses, slowly the high ground in front of the Gustav Line was being cleared. But the fighting and the conditions had worn out the attackers. Walker wrote in his diary on 22 December of his concerns for his men of 36th Division: "I regret the hardships they must suffer tonight . . . wet, cold, muddy, hungry . . . no sleep, no rest . . . How they endure the hardships I do not understand." Walker himself seems to have been losing heart in the campaign, "taking one mountain mass after another gains no tactical advantage," he complained to his diary. "There is always another mountain mass beyond with Germans on it." But the harder the going, the more pressure was exerted on the generals and frontline troops to produce results. Churchill, who had a proprietary interest in the "southern" theater, complained on 19 December: "The stagnation of the whole campaign on the Italian front is becoming scandalous." In fact, it was to become far worse, and, compared with the fighting at Cassino, the advance through the Winter Line looks almost rapid. Von Senger, who attended mass in the abbey of Monte Cassino on Christmas Day, was astute enough to predict what was going to unfold. "While driving towards the Abbey . . . I noticed how the entire width of the Cassino valley was filled with uninterrupted harassing fire. This continued day and night with very heavy expenditure of ammunition. In contrast to the wide-ranging mobile battles in Russia, the conflict here resembled the static fighting of the First World War."

4

Into the Gustav Line

After the fierce fighting for San Pietro, the 36th Division was relieved by the US 34th "Red Bull" Division. Tom Kindre, now an ordnance officer with the division, describes in his diary how the move was completed in "High winds [and] bitter cold." On the last night of the year "wind started around midnight, blew tents down. Slept under half-knocked-down tent from 3:00 A.M. Sleet, snow, cold." A few days later, Kindre records in his diary: "Several good rumors today." The most outlandish came, supposedly, from Major General Ryder's pastry cook. "Apparently the Germans had been sitting in at the recent Cairo conference and had decided to surrender to the Americans." Most of the other rumors show similar wishful thinking, involving, above all, a departure from Italy: "Starting next month the division will send a thousand men home per month . . . the Division will be out of Italy by the first of the month, relieved by the 88th Division."

The Red Bulls had good cause to be homesick. They had been the first US division to arrive in Europe in early 1942, when they were stationed in Northern Ireland. A National Guard formation commanded by Maj. Gen. Charles W. Ryder, the division had originally been composed of men from North Dakota, Iowa, and Minnesota. Donald Hoagland was one of the few frontline infantrymen who fought with the division from the beginning to the end of the war. The son of a farmer from Brook Park, Minnesota, he was born in 1915 and joined up in 1941, "one of the original in-for-a-year, $25-a-month gang." Growing up in the Depression, "Everybody was broke. There was just no way to make a dollar anywhere . . . A lot of people joined the National Guard because it was a buck or two a month." Even when the war in Europe started it was not talked about a great deal. "It was only about twenty-one or twenty-two years after the First World War," says Hoagland, "and everyone had come home saying no more of that. I think people were reluctant to think about it."

The first contingent of the division had arrived at Belfast in March 1942. Artilleryman Ivar Awes from Minneapolis was one of the few young men arriving in Britain who had been overseas before. The son of Norwegian immigrants, his family had kept in touch with friends and relatives in their homeland. He remembers arriving in Northern Ireland: "We marched in, and we were wearing the old helmets like the British, and everyone asked where the cowboy hats were. I developed a great affection for the six counties [of Northern Ireland]. Over the ten months we were stationed in five of them. We especially liked our first one in County Derry. Coleraine became our place to go on weekend passes. There was a fine dance hall and very nice friendly girls. There were also several fine pubs." Don Hoagland remembers, "We trained physically hard but everybody got a lot of passes." One favorite in Belfast was the Belgravia Hotel, quickly renamed the Belgravia Riding Academy.

Ivar Awes was one of the Americans given training by British troops who had returned from Dunkirk. "We had a very capable cadre of British artillery officers and other ranks that introduced us to straw bolsters, palliasses, ablutions, lorries, their bonnets, shillings, pounds, quids, Guinness, and best of all the British 25-pounder." The men of the division also acquired a taste for the whiskey produced by the Bushmills distillery in Port Rush. There was a brief stay in England as the division prepared to board a ship in Liverpool to take them to North Africa for the Torch landings. Awes managed to "learn to dance the Hokey Cokey and the Lambeth Walk at a dance hall in Chester." He was also invited to spend the night with a local family, who treated him "like a visiting dignitary."

Robert Koloski, a medic with the division's 135th Regiment, remembers that when the Red Bulls were shipped to Africa to take part in Torch, the thinking was: "My, we are the elite, we have been chosen. We didn't know any better." The regiment stayed in Algiers for five weeks before going to the

Tunisian front to face seasoned German troops for the first time. "We found out we were not elite, anything but, and we took a terrible beating," says Koloski. "We were rescued, although some of the guys won't agree with that word, by the Coldstream Guards. Those crazy Limeys were amazing. By that time I realized that this was not some sort of game, but a deadly serious operation, that war was going to be a nasty, drawn-out process." As Donald Hoagland puts it: "After you got whipped and humiliated a couple of times and you have seen your friends killed, then killing becomes a business and you get pretty good at it pretty fast."

After a shaky start, the formation had fought with increasing distinction in Tunisia, and was the first reinforcement division to arrive at Salerno after the initial landings. In the advance from Salerno to Cassino, the Red Bulls saw a lot of hard fighting and long, exhausting periods in the line. Crossing the Volturno at the beginning of November, a battalion of the 168th Regiment suffered grievous casualties from mines. Once across the river, there were two thousand yards of flat ground in front of their objective, dotted here and there with orchards. The leading platoon decided to advance through the trees, but found themselves in a minefield, and only eight of the thirty-odd men emerged unscathed. Exactly the same thing happened to the next two platoons, and by now commanders and staff watching from the other side of the river could follow the progress of the advancing troops by the explosions.

But all the time lessons were being learned and experience gained. After the Volturno River crossing, there would be more properly trained engineers with the assault companies; the division learned also, where possible, to drive flocks of sheep or goats in front of them through mined areas. The division was changing in other ways, too. Originally, it had been a close-knit outfit, with many of the men familiar with one another from home life. This caused its own problems, as Tom Kindre explains: "My company commander had his brother as shop foreman and there were at least three other sets of brothers within our company, lots of prior relationships. Lots of people were now in the command structure higher than the people they had worked for back home. I remember a guy saying one time, 'Well, I can't do anything to him. When I get home he's my boss. I can't discipline him.' There were many problems like that." In Tom Kindre's ordnance company and in other rear-echelon units, the original National Guard composition of the division remained fairly unchanged. But in the small proportion of the division that made up the frontline rifle companies, casualties had meant that few remained from the complement that had sailed to Ireland two years earlier. By the beginning of 1944, of a frontline rifle company of around two hundred men, only about a dozen would be of the original intake. These Iowan veterans found themselves surrounded by men from all over America, and the division at frontline level had become more cosmopolitan. Journalist Ernie Pyle, who traveled with the Red Bulls in late 1943, described the division as "wise and worn, like a much-read book, or a house that wears its aging stone stoutly, ignoring the patchwork of new concrete that holds it together." Tom Kindre also comments on the "constant turnover" in manpower, but finds the original veterans somewhat less "stout": "There were old timers and among the infantry units there were real problems because those who were still there were thinking they couldn't last much longer. Something had to hit them . . . Their morale was very bad."

Artilleryman Ivar Awes's letters home from this period identify the key concerns of the men fighting in Italy, namely food, cleanliness, and home. "I'd certainly like to be home, married, and raising a family rather than being over here decreasing the male population of Germany," he wrote. But, like most of the servicemen's letters, there is little complaining or direct reference to their suffering or the heartbreaking sights all around them. Instead, there is a rugged cheerfulness and an effort to write about anything but the front line, born of a constant wish to reassure family at home whom the men knew would be worried sick, often literally. "It's raining like mad," Awes wrote on 8 November. "It's a relief anyway because it gives us an opportunity to clean up, change clothes, and that means a lot to the men. It keeps up their morale and self-respect. You would be surprised to see the way the men clean up when given the opportunity, even though there is no one to see them except the rest of us. Of course, half an hour afterward they are just as dirty as before but that doesn't seem to bother them."

The men were concerned, also, that the folks back home appreciate their efforts. "The news broadcasts . . . always make it sound so easy," Awes wrote on 13 November. "From listening to them, I suppose you think that these Jerries give up easily. I think I've said before that they are pretty good soldiers." Nevertheless, like many on the Allied side, including the most senior politicians, Awes was optimistic that German resistance would suddenly end: "I hope they break internally and save us the long drawn-out struggle of slowly defeating them," he wrote on 11 November. "Seems to me that

Adolf should see the 'writing on the wall' by now. I'm sure he isn't as jubi-
lant as he was when France surrendered. He must surely be the worst thing
that ever happened to this world."

While British and American divisions were forcing their way through the
Mignano Gap, 34th Division had been fighting further north, nearing the
Gustav Line above Cassino. It had been slow going, and the exhausted division was pulled out of the line for two weeks' rest around Christmas. Now
the priority was to scour the countryside for food and, of course, alcohol, to
mark the festive season. The two main drinks the private soldiers got in Italy
were "vino"—"really rough red wine"—and vermouth. Homer Ankrum,
who served with the 133rd Regiment of the division, describes how Christmas 1944 was celebrated in somewhat greater style by one artillery unit. The
divisional artillery commander, Gen. A. C. Stanford, dispatched a sergeant
and a cook by the name of Rusch to procure some wine. This they achieved,
but the wine tasted very green so Rusch offered to distill it. "In no time at all
[Rusch] was producing a product guaranteed to remove only half the
enamel from your teeth." To this he added a dash of lemon juice and all was
ready. Soon afterward the general himself paid the unit a visit: "Generals are
known to mellow a little at Christmas time," Ankrum begins. "Snarls turn to
toothy smiles and for a few days one would actually believe them to be totally devoid of abnormal temperament. So it was when Gen. A. C. Stanford,
the Division Artillery Commander, drove into the area the next day to pay
his respects to the Red Bull Cannoneers. The General dismounted from his
vehicle, with such a beaming face the men felt like singing 'Joy to the troops,
the General's come!' As Gen. Stanford sauntered over to the headquarters
area, Sgt. James Gregg, Minneapolis, Minn., saluted and offered him a can-
teen cupful of the pulverizing potion. Gen. Stanford, in a holiday spirit and
wanting, for the time being at least, to appear to be one of the boys, accepted
the drink. With his first sip there are those who say his eyeballs rotated, others say his nostrils quivered and still others maintain his ear lobes flapped.
However, the General weathered it all, but noticeably took smaller sips
thereafter."

———————

As the Red Bulls prepared to go back into action straight after Christmas,
criticism of the slow progress of the campaign in Italy was mounting. On 3
January, *Time* magazine asked, "What price success?" and pointed out, per-

haps slightly erroneously, that Tito's partisans in Yugoslavia were tying down more German divisions than the Allies were in Italy. But the "United Nations" were still eight miles short of the Rapido–Garigliano River line. The main effort to clear the remaining villages and high ground in front of the Gustav Line fell to the 34th Division. The town of San Vittore was captured on 6 January after hard fighting, and the division pushed on to Cervaro, the last hamlet before Cassino. This was not cleared until 12 January, by which time, following heavy air and artillery attacks, and serious losses among the Americans, the place was demolished.

The final piece of high ground, which faced the monastery across the Rapido valley, was Monte Trocchio. To the surprise of the assaulting companies of the 34th Division, the Germans had withdrawn. The summit was reached on 15 January by E. W. Ralf's 3rd Battalion, 168th Regiment. "With the heights seized Capt. Earl W. Ralf cut across the hillsides to rejoin his unit," writes Ankrum. "En route he came upon a German position. Several German soldiers could be seen in a firing position. Going closer, Ralf could see they were covered with ice and snow, still gripping their weapons. Whether they had been killed by American fire or had frozen to death, Ralf doesn't know."

From Trocchio the division moved forward again, taking up positions just slightly to the north of Cassino town. Ivar Awes found himself in the lead truck as his battery sought out their new firing position. It was somewhat chaotic, as he explains: "When we moved up I was leading my battery and we got to a fork in the road. There was an MP there and there wasn't anybody ahead of us. I asked him, 'Which way do we go?' and he says, 'Damned if I know, Lieutenant.' 'Oh, God,' I said, 'hasn't anybody gone before?' 'No, you're the first one.' I asked the guy inside who was our instrument sergeant, but he was usually a little bit drunk, he had got a hold of Italian brandy." Eventually Awes took a gamble on one of the turnings and luckily it was not the one that would have led his column into the enemy lines.

Wishing to conserve troops, the Germans had now withdrawn into their meticulously prepared positions on the Gustav Line and there were hardly any enemy soldiers in front of the river lines. For the German high command in Italy the task was simple: to hold the line. The wider strategy for 1944 was focused on defeating the expected Anglo-American forces as they landed in France. Amphibious operations are among the riskiest taken in war, and the Germans saw the chance to drive the landings back into the sea and then counterattack in the East. For the time being, ground would be surrendered to the Soviets—who were still a long way from the German heartlands—in favor of guarding the shorter distance from northern France to Berlin.

For Mark Clark's 5th Army, the breaking of the Gustav Line had acquired a new urgency. Since November 1943, plans had been afoot to land an amphibious force behind the German lines at Anzio, just south of Rome. The logic was impeccable: the Allies had control of the sea and the air, and the German lines of communication were long and vulnerable. As progress slowed in November and December, the plan was dropped, but it was resurrected by Churchill at the end of the year when he persuaded the Americans to allow a small number of landing craft scheduled to return to the UK to stay in the Mediterranean. This was a considerable concession—shortage of landing craft was the bottleneck delaying amphibious operations across the Channel—and caused the invasion of Normandy to be postponed by a month to June 1944. Any further delay would have pushed the operation into 1945. The Anzio attack, Operation Shingle, was planned for 22 January, the last possible date before the landing craft had to be returned to the UK. To link up with this force, Clark would need to break through the defenses of the Liri valley as quickly as he could, preferably within days, and to do this he planned an assault across a wide front. On the left the British X Corps, now bolstered by the arrival of the British 5th Division from the moribund 8th Army front, would cross the Garigliano in three places, establish bridgeheads, and then secure the high ground on the left of the Liri valley. On the right flank, attacks would continue around the north side of Cassino, and in the Liri valley itself would be the main effort, on 20 January, by American soldiers of the 36th Texas Division. The 5th Army planners hoped in the first instance to draw forward German reserves away from Anzio for Operation Shingle, and also to break through to meet up with the landing forces. What they believed would happen is indicated in an "intelligence summary" of 16 January: "It would appear doubtful if the enemy can hold the organized defensive line through Cassino against a coordinated army attack. Since this is to be launched before Shingle it is considered likely that this additional threat will cause him to withdraw from his defensive position once he has appreciated the magnitude of that operation." With the Anzio force threatening lines of communication to the Gustav positions, and faced with a wide attack, the Germans would have no option, so the thinking went, but to withdraw north of Rome.

First off were the attacks north of Cassino, the right hook. This was the responsibility of the French Expeditionary Corps (FEC), commanded by Gen. Alphonse Juin, with the objective of attacking towards Sant' Elia and Atina, and seizing the high ground immediately north and northwest of Cassino.

The French were, to put it mildly, not highly rated by the Allied high command. In 1940, of course, much to their surprise and horror, the French army had been overrun by the German blitzkrieg in a matter of weeks, and the establishment of a collaborationist regime based at Vichy under Marshal Pétain had, in the eyes of the Western Allies, further disgraced France. The Germans had occupied the north part of the country, but allowed the Vichy regime to rule the south as well as France's overseas colonies, most of whose garrisons showed no signs of switching to the Allied side, even when invaded by British or American troops. In Syria in mid-1941 there was even bitter fighting between an Anglo–Free French invasion force and the Vichy garrison, and after the latter's defeat, only 20 percent of the Vichy army agreed to come over to the Allies. When, in Operation Torch, Allied troops had landed at Oran, Algiers, and Casablanca in November 1942, there had been resistance to all three attacks by the French, who for the most part held their oath of loyalty to the Vichy regime to be sacrosanct. In Algiers, American troops had landed and then been cut off when the ships accompanying them were forced back by shore-based fire. Among them was Cpl. Vern Onstad, who relates what happened next: "My instructions were to take my group and take over the power plant. Everything was peaceful until one of the ships sounded the alarm to return. We started going back and that's when the fire really started. The ship pulled out and left us stranded. We had eight men shot, and the forty-eight of us surrendered to the French. I remember a French woman coming up and spitting in the face of one of the injured men . . . we all thought the French were allies, but here we were fighting them." Onstad and his companions were shut in a cavalry stable and kept there for three days. On the third day a French sergeant came in and said, "Boys, I'm afraid you all have to be shot." "Then twelve Frenchmen pulled up in front of the building, a firing squad," Onstad continues. "But after half an hour, the sergeant came back in and said that it had all been a mistake."

Threatened with naval bombardment, the French troops in Algiers had surrendered, but they had hardly increased the Allies' trust in them.

But throughout North Africa, the French now fought alongside the Allies, who set about reequipping and expanding the Armée d'Afrique. A general call-up mustered a total European force of 176,000 men, which were supplemented by French troops from Corsica as well as by 20,000 men who had escaped from France itself. To this were added just over 230,000 native Moroccans, Tunisians, and Algerians, and in September 1943, General Juin was charged with assembling an expeditionary force to fight in Italy.

Born in Algeria in 1888, the son of a gendarme, Juin had had his right hand shot off in the First World War in March 1915. In 1940 he had fought against the Germans and been taken prisoner in Lille. Released in 1941 at Pétain's request, he was then made commander in chief of the French forces in North Africa. After dithering over his oath of loyalty to Vichy, Juin approved the plan for the French African army to fight alongside the Allies to liberate Tunisia, and, it was hoped, eventually France itself. As bickering between the various French factions in North Africa continued, so did British and American exasperation with their newly restored allies. Even the Free French under Gen. Charles de Gaulle were deeply mistrusted, Roosevelt commenting that they were "riddled with spies." For operations in Italy, the Allies envisaged the French very much in a supporting role, as reserve or garrison troops.

The French themselves, however, saw things a little differently. For them the chance to fight in Europe presented the opportunity to make up for the humiliation of 1940, demonstrate their loyalty to the Allied cause, and restore the honor of France. Jean Murat, born in Morocco in 1922, had been in Algiers at the time of the American landings and was about to enter officers' training. In April 1943 he joined the 4th Tunisian Tirailleurs (infantrymen) Regiment (4RTT), part of the 3rd Algerian Infantry Division, as a senior officer cadet commanding a section of the 1st Battalion. Like many of the French, he was highly impressed by the enormous quantities of American equipment becoming available to the French soldiers: "The wealth of ammunition was remarkable," he says, "as was the entire organization . . . in every instance the automobile equipment is efficient and brand-new . . . the food is less exciting." Like most of his fellow *pieds-noirs* (ethnic French who were born in France's North African colonies), he had never been to France, but still felt that he was fighting for the noble cause of a "Free France," which was unquestionably the "homeland." In sharp contrast to the majority of the Allied soldiers at Cassino, patriotic rhetoric had real currency among the French forces. Murat characterizes the *pieds-noirs* as "boastful braggards, noisy perhaps—but dynamic, enterprising, courageous, free-willed and hard-working." Fighting was also, for Murat, "a way to erase the shame of the defeat of 1940 and for the professional soldiers to give the army back its past glory." This, he continues, explains the lack of complaint about the draconian measures of enlistment that had produced so many European soldiers for the French African army, the 176,000 representing some 18 percent of the entire population, a proportion never reached in France even in the worst days of the First World War. A typical FEC unit in Italy would have a European contingent of just under 50 percent. The motivation of the rest, North African Muslims, is harder to specify. Most were professional soldiers, volunteers imbued with warrior traditions who had fought for France in local conflicts with tribesmen. Murat's view is that they fought "less for the love of France than in recognition of the country which, by welcoming them into its army, gave them entrance into a family in which they feel good." It has also been suggested that the North Africans fought for the "chance of proving that they had earned in combat a Frenchman's rights."

In any event, throughout the battles in Italy, the FEC would prove to be one of the Allies' most effective formations. This was partly due to the terrain, which held few surprises to troops recruited from the mountainous regions of North Africa. But the French soldiers were also well led and well suited to the sort of battles that the terrain created, where initiative and exceptional bravery were of such vital importance. This leadership, as shall be seen, depended largely on the European officers putting themselves at the front of the fighting, with inevitable consequences.

The first FEC contingent to arrive in Italy was the 2nd Moroccan Infantry Division, which started disembarking at Naples at the beginning of December 1943. The Americans were concerned that training standards were below those of the US Army, and were also alarmed by the fact that the division's ambulance drivers were women. The Americans suggested that they be kept to the rear as the roads were in poor condition and under fire in some places, but Gen. André Dody, the Moroccan division's commander, "exploded at the suggestion . . . The women of France, like the men, are proud to die for their country," he exclaimed.

Among the division's personnel was twenty-one-year-old ambulance driver Solange Cuvillier, a nurse from Rabat, whose memoirs document the mixture of dread and excitement she felt on leaving Africa. "The column stretches over many kilometers," she writes. "It takes four days to reach the port. Our ambulances are still pristine and we use the bunks and the stretchers as beds. How many wounded and dead would we transport during the conflict? My comrades celebrate my birthday (21st) at a stop we make in the middle of nowhere. We joyfully toast each other throwing back our pitchers of rough red wine . . . Our resolve is unwavering, with only one question: how many charming boys of every race and every faith, who have in common a 'tricolore' in their hearts—how many will make it through this adventure? It's best not to dwell on what will happen."

Dody's force was put into the line northeast of Cassino, where two American divisions—the 34th and 45th—had stalled in the face of terrible terrain and fierce resistance. On 16 December, having relieved the US 34th Division, the Moroccan division launched an attack around a piece of high ground where the Americans had been held up for some two weeks. The success of the operation astounded the Americans, and the Allies' low opinion of the French began to alter. Together with the US 45th Division, the Moroccans advanced some seven miles and made contact with the Germans again on 21 December. At this point the 3rd Algerian Division replaced the US 45th, and Juin's FEC headquarters became operational. Commanded by Gen. Joseph de Monsabert, the 3rd Algerian also contained Jean Murat's Tunisian regiment (as in the American armies, the regiment was the equivalent of a British brigade, made up of three battalions of infantry).

There followed a period of settling in as Juin tried to work out the best way of advancing across the almost trackless, desolate Abruzzi Mountains that constituted his area of operations. More than any of the other Allied generals, he appreciated that the nature of the terrain made the widespread mechanization of the American and British forces ineffective, if not an actual disadvantage. His corps, in contrast, had few tanks, but many more mules than the others. This led him to aim for a breakthrough over the mountains north of Cassino, thus bypassing the most heavily defended sectors of the Gustav Line around the town. But for the moment, he was still facing a German defensive line a few miles in front of the Gustav Line proper, which in this sector was anchored on high ground just beyond the Rapido River.

By 11 January, everything was ready for the right-flank assault ordered by

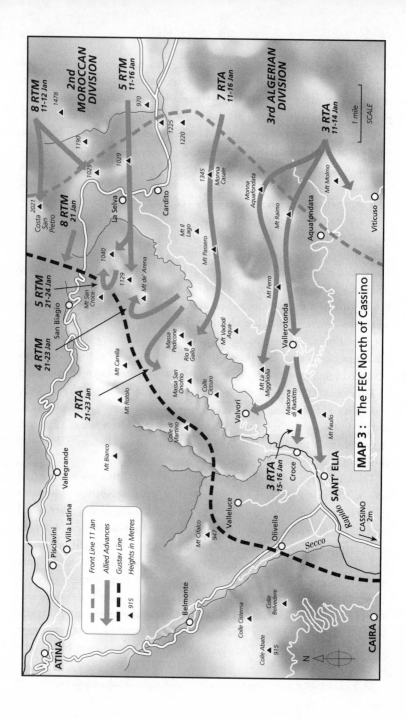

MAP 3 : The FEC North of Cassino

Clark for the next day. Juin planned to attack across a broad front, with two regiments of the Moroccan division to the north and the same number of Algerian regiments on their left. Perhaps the most difficult objective was that of the 7th Algerian Regiment, who were ordered to capture Monna Casale. It was their first taste of combat. "It was a tough assignment," Juin later commented, "whose success would have seemed improbable to those who didn't know the character of [those who made up] the 7th. They were asked to launch, directly ahead of them, an assault on a cliff which seemed impregnable and dominated the plain in such a way that the slightest movement could not escape the enemy's view nor their gunfire." After a short, intensive bombardment of fifteen minutes, the Algerian regiment prepared to advance soon after 5 A.M. But before they even set off, disaster struck when all the officers of the 3rd Battalion, standing on a rock giving out their final orders, were killed by friendly fire.

Other battalions took over the attack, determined that their first action in Italy should not end in disaster. The account of the 3rd Company, 1st Battalion shows the importance of officers leading from the front: "The section under Sous-lieutenant Vétillard is in front; Captain Boutin follows with the rest of the Company. At this point, a shell drops close to the captain, knocking him down." Although wounded, Boutin refused to be evacuated, saying, "This is the first time that my company is engaged in the heat of battle, how could I not participate alongside them?" After the advance was held up by machine gun positions, Boutin led a section to outflank the Germans. "While machine-guns open fire on the summit," the account continues, "[Boutin] leads his last section away crying, 'You see the summit; we need it!' And he is the first to tackle the crest, leading his tirailleurs with his walking stick, shouting words of encouragement. And it's there, as he stands scenting victory, that a bullet hits him straight through the heart." By this time Sous-lieutenant Vétillard was also struck by a bullet that lacerated the skin around his hip. "His wound was extremely painful, but he too refused to give up," the account goes on. "He realized the responsibility that now faced him. It was absolutely necessary, despite the incessant counterattacks, despite the continuous bombardment, to hold on to his positions and hold back the enemy. He goes from group to group, encouraging his men and pushing them ever forward. He uses any weapons he can get hold of, shooting without counting. It's while carrying out this superhuman endeavor, his face contorted with pain, that an exploding mortar knocks him dead."

A postcombat analysis of the 3rd Battalion elaborates on the dilemma that strong leadership was required but also suicidal: "The . . . young officers . . . led their units forward magnificently . . . In our North African units the mettle of the Tirailleur depends entirely on his officers. He follows them blindly. The officers thus have to lead by example, to inspire the men. Each leader is destined for the sacrificial altar." With the objective captured, there were fierce counterattacks, and possession of the summit of Monna Casale changed hands several times. Eventually, after more than a thousand grenades had been used by the French, the top was secure and the advance could continue, as the Germans, in some disarray, retreated to the Gustav Line.

To the north the Moroccans attacked right behind a creeping barrage, and succeeded in taking some of the German defenders on the run. An officer of the 4th Regiment reports that although several blockhouses held up the advance, in many places the troops "pushed on into the night. They were now no longer men, they were there to kill. Grenades exploded in the dugouts and screams came from within; elsewhere the Germans rushed out into the snow, some still in stockinged feet. Half-dressed, they rushed towards their weapons pits through bursts of machine gun fire which forced them to throw themselves flat."

By 15 January the FEC had advanced nearly four miles and were in contact with the main defenses of the Gustav Line. The German commander, von Senger, who was aware that there were no rearward defensive positions between the Gustav Line and the Atina basin, was very concerned that the entire Cassino position might be outflanked. A mountain division, just arrived from Russia, was immediately deployed, but the harsh terrain and climate of the Abruzzi Mountains came as a shock even to hardened troops from the Eastern Front. "Here and also later on," wrote von Senger afterward, "we found that divisions arriving from other theaters of war were not immediately equal to the double burden of icy mountain terrain and massed bombardment." He remarks that in the Abruzzi, "the snowstorms could be so dangerous that the troops had sometimes to descend from a crest toward the enemy in order to survive." He was also concerned that his troops were simply not as skilled as their opponents: "Moroccan and Algerian troops under Gen. Juin. These were native mountain people, led by superbly trained French staff officers, equipped with modern American weapons."

The offensive spirit of the Algerians in particular was noticed by British and American liaison officers, too. Colonel Robert T. Shaw noted of one attack: "I had the occasion to move forward with the advancing troops; there were no stragglers; nor were any weapons or equipment abandoned. I was able to see numerous dead Germans; many showed signs of bayonet wounds; some had their skulls caved in. Morale excellent: very few prisoners have been taken."

Although his troops were also suffering from exhaustion, frostbite, and exposure, Juin ordered an attack on the Gustav Line itself on 21 January. The assault on Monte San Croce was preceded by a heavy bombardment. As always, the Allies had a far greater supply of artillery shells than the Germans. A German *Gefreiter* who had fought in Norway, Greece, and Russia was captured on the first day of the assault. He told his interrogator that he had never had to "endure such violent artillery." His captors were also able to read his diary:

12 Jan. Constantly on alert. Morale is dropping.

17 Jan. Climb into positions on Monte San Croce.

18 Jan. Heavy losses.

20 Jan. Tonight will be decisive—the assault section will not return, wiped out 500 yards from our positions.

21 Jan. Terrific artillery fire. Huddled in my slit trench, unable to leave it. 14.00 Am a prisoner.

22 Jan. Treated well, am at my nerves' end.

The next day the German soldiers in the Gustav Line were informed that the Führer expected every yard of ground to be bitterly defended. In addition, von Senger acted with characteristic speed and decisiveness to bring his artillery to bear on the attackers. To the amazement of the Moroccan division's intelligence units, the Germans they captured simply did not believe in defeat. With the attackers exhausted the drive faltered, and counterattacks restored the outposts of the Gustav Line to German control. Juin, although pleased by the combat performance of his men and the great impression it had made on his allies, later gave vent to his frustration: "With an extra division, perhaps it could have been possible on the evening of 15 January to penetrate more deeply toward Atina, a strategic point on which we could develop a wide flanking movement above Caira and Cassino before descending again into the Liri valley. But behind my two joined-up divisions, who

were somewhat exhausted, there was nothing left. The original plan con-
ceived by the Anglo-Saxon high command failed through the lack of a no-
tion of an army 'maneuver' logically and clearly defined."

It is the great "what if?" of the Cassino story: had reserves been available
and there been willingness to back Juin's plan, much of the bloodbath to
come might well have been avoided.

––––––––––

In closing the gap between the outlying German positions and the Gustav
Line, the French forces had overrun the villages of Sant' Elia and Valvori in
the Rapido valley. It had been just a week since the departure of the Germans from the vicinity of young Gemma Notarianni's house in Valvori. It
had been an eerie time, listening to the artillery fire coming closer: "We
knew which the shells were," Gemma remembers. "There was one noise
from the German ones and another from the Americans. The Germans used
to shoot—boom, boom, boom, boom—and you can rest assured that went
to the right place. Then the Americans start. God knows the ammunition
they used to use! Then someone shouted, 'The soldiers have arrived!' and so
we went to watch. But it wasn't soldiers, it was Goumiers [Moroccan irregular mountain troops]. On the little hill facing us we could hear screaming,
women screaming."

The divisional historian's account only hints at what was happening: "On
the 16th and again on the 17th our patrols had to cross through the olive
groves of the plains to get through to the ruins of Sant' Elia, to push through
to the right up to Valvori, to the left up to the first buttresses of the mountains without finding in front of them any occupants except in some caves
100 or so terrorized Italians." The reason for the terror was not so much the
artillery fire, but the attacking troops themselves, who, Gemma Notarianni
maintains, started raping women at gunpoint. "We thought that once we
were behind Allied lines our troubles would be over. In fact, they were just
beginning. The men would point the gun at the man and rape the woman.
Practically all the women who were violated by them died, through the effect of it. Slowly they all died."

In Valvori itself the family was safe, and Gemma's father, previously a po-
liceman, was installed to keep order in the village. He reported every day to
the French officers stationed there and made sure that the women of the
town were kept inside at all times. Then, a few days later, they were told to

leave the village and head for Sant' Elia. "But the bridge had been blown up," Gemma explains. "So my father said, 'When no one's looking we have to go behind the church and head toward Vallerotonda [across mountain roads].' And we did that and we had a bad encounter with the Moroccans. All the roads were twisting and turning. We were nine altogether with two mules. I had a big basket on my head with a meal for when we arrived there. It was polenta, survival food. My brother had ten liters of oil in a tin. The Bedouins started jumping out from the olives. My brother was learning French and started talking but you know the more you talked the more it was as if they were raining from the sky. We went round the bend, heading for the bridge over the Rapido. They wanted to take the basket. My grandmother had a walking stick and swung it at anyone who came near. She was swearing in Italian. We had to tell them she was barmy, while trying to get the mules going again."

After three or four days in Vallerotonda, the family was told to assemble in the square with only a little bag each. At about midnight they were loaded into a big lorry, which took them to Venafro. "We just wanted them to disappear," Gemma now says of the French North Africans. "It was them that broke through. They broke a lot of things."

Tony Pittaccio's family, too, had found themselves by mid-January in a no-man's-land between the approaching Allies and the Gustav Line farther down the Rapido, where the advance was being carried out by the US 34th and 36th divisions. "We could hear the artillery," Pittaccio remembers, "and see the gun flashes that silhouetted the mountains. And we thought: That's coming here, and we were a bit afraid." They were staying in a farmhouse about three miles outside Cassino, with eight adults and nine children in one room. When everyone was lying down to sleep, the floor was entirely covered. It was a very difficult time: there was no food or medicine, and many were being injured or becoming sick. Pittaccio puts their survival down to the extraordinary efforts of his uncle, but they were also lucky. On three or four occasions they had to move when they were shelled out of their houses. This was German fire, probably range-finding or clearing fields of fire. Once, a family of three sheltering with them was killed. On another occasion they were making a dash for a farm building but it took a direct hit just before they reached it. Tony's uncle unsuccessfully tried to amputate with a pair of scissors the smashed leg of a young girl who had been sheltering inside.

One night soon after, in yet another half demolished farmhouse, Pittaccio woke in the middle of the night to hear his sister talking English. "The window was open and there were Americans below. It didn't last long. The following night we heard again these noises, opened the window, saying, 'Hello, hello' and they were Germans." The Americans were soon back, looking incongruous to Pittaccio as they scuttled and crouched down under cover while the civilians walked around upright. A couple of days later the family found a stack of American rations hidden in a haystack. Thinking they were abandoned, they had their best meal for a long time. But the Americans returned for their rations and were distraught to find them gone. When everything had been explained, the troops were invited into the farmhouse to sit around the fire. Once inside, one of the men took off his helmet and started to cry. "All in the room were silent," Pittaccio remembers, "and the women sobbed with him. Quite likely he had lost a good friend that day."

PART TWO

The First Battle

"I'm afraid."

"That's nothing to be ashamed of," Major Major counseled him
kindly. "We're all afraid."

"I'm not ashamed," Yossarian said. "I'm just afraid."

—JOSEPH HELLER, *CATCH-22*

Those who occupied the lower level were up to their knees in
mud and water; for the extensive rains and the inundation of the
Garigliano had converted the whole country into a mere quagmire . . . Those on the higher ground were scarcely in better
plight. The driving storms of sleet and rain, which had continued
for several weeks without intermission, found their way into
every crevice of the flimsy tents and crazy hovels, thatched only
with the branches of trees, which afforded temporary shelter to
the troops.

—W. H. PRESCOTT, *HISTORY OF THE REIGN OF
FERDINAND AND ISABELLA*, 1858

5

British X Corps on the Garigliano: The Left Hook

The fighting for Monte Camino in early December had hit the British 56th Black Cat Division hard. Worst affected was the 9th Royal Fusiliers Battalion, part of the 167th Brigade, along with her sister battalion, the 8th Royal Fusiliers, and one other battalion. The 9th Fusiliers had lost 25 officers and over 500 men, and few of the original complement who had landed at Salerno back in September were left. Nineteen-year-old fusilier Len Bradshaw, who had been in the army for less than a year, was now a veteran of the battalion. His first taste of combat had been at Salerno, and he remembers that, initially, "I was a bit naïve. I didn't think it was real at first. I was taking too many chances." But, after three months of fighting, he had become increasingly phlegmatic: "It was fate. The more you go on the more you are tempting fate. I really never thought I'd reach twenty-one."

After Camino, contact was made with the Germans again at the Garigliano River on 14 December when the 167th Brigade was brought up to face the enemy across the wide waterlogged plain of the river. "It was an extraordinary existence," wrote one officer of Bradshaw's battalion. "The two sides sat and glared at each other with a wide no-man's-land in between where the Italian peasants quite imperturbably continued to plough and cultivate their land. This was a mixed blessing. It was quite impossible to check who was who. At the same time, by making oneself look as unmilitary as possible one could tag on to an Italian bullock cart or plow team and thus re-connoiter ground quite unapproachable by any other means during daylight."

On 21 December, the 9th Fusiliers were relieved by their sister battalion and withdrew to the village of Cupa to celebrate Christmas. Every turkey that could be found in the local countryside had been purchased at fifteen shillings each, and the promise was that every man in the division would have some fresh meat for Christmas. But when the cooks went to collect the birds, they found that many of them had been subsequently bought by the Americans at five pounds a throw. In the end there was tinned turkey and pork, plus a bottle of beer per man. Like many, Len Bradshaw's unit made their own arrangements. For once they had a dry billet in farm buildings. "We had a fire, and a rum ration in the evening," he remembers. "The signalers had the radio on tuned to an American station. At one point it played 'Silent Night' in German. It was one of the better times." The Italian owners of the farm kept their distance, except when the farmer's wife came to speak to the men. "Don't touch my chickens," she said. "But if you get one from the farm down the road, I'll cook it for you." "So we had fried chicken," says Bradshaw. "It was smashing."

There were many new faces in the division, most of whom had never been in combat before. One battalion had just received men originally from fourteen different regiments, leading its commanding officer to request cap badges, "so that at least the men could have with them the badge of the regiment in which they had to be prepared to die." As some replacements had been arriving in the line poorly equipped and frankly unready for combat, a reinforcement camp had been set up to reorganize new arrivals and men returning from the hospital. It was also designed to "receive men from the units within the Division who, as a result of the stress and strain of what they had gone through, required a period of building up physically or morally or even militarily," as the division's historian reports.

Along with a number of other former Royal Welch Fusiliers, Glyn Edwards now found himself in the 8th Royal Fusiliers, who had relieved Len Bradshaw's battalion. They remained in the line until 1 January, and then headed to the village of Casanova for a belated Christmas celebration. It would be Edwards's last, as he was killed at Anzio seven weeks later. On 3 January, he wrote home to his family:

Dear Mam, Dad & all

These few lines to let you know I am still alive and well . . . I have not been able to write for a couple of weeks now, as you may guess where I've

civilians who had crossed th
questioned and screened fo
man or Allied mines or boc
ardous journey, and there
"The smell inside the priso
no facilities and they had h

Arriving in their position
gan's battery the inevitable
nervousness about the forth
Milligan wrote in his pock
next morning his piles start
had a terrible foreboding o
hang around all day. The w
don't know why, it's already

Swollen by rain, the Gar
bridges across it had been
were on high ground about
river. In front of them, in tl
rigation ditches, were a nu
deterrent, however, was mir
gering number. Most were o
little pressure to activate an
which threw a charge into
called it a Bouncing Betty;
Both types were often hous
ficult.

The night of 17 Januar
once, Len Bradshaw didn't
moved up to the river just l
his system—but he had the
The crossing itself, in boats
fairly smoothly. Then, on tl
separated from one anothe
fire. Among many other c
killed, adding to the confu
Bradshaw. "The night was
Bradshaw was kept busy tr

been, but now we are back for a rest for a few days and, believe me Mam, we need it, as we had such terrible weather while in the line . . . How is Dad these days? Is he still working regular and I suppose is still in the Home Guard and doing his soldiering. I wish I was in that mob.

We are having our Christmas day tomorrow 4 January, as we were in an awkward spot for Dec. 25th, but it doesn't really matter what day we have it out here, as every day is the same now: I hope you had a good Xmas at home, I hope to be with you for next year, as I hope to God that 1944 will see it all over with, and that I am away from *stinking* Italy . . . while we were down in the line it rained continuously . . .

He makes an effort to end on an upbeat note: "I'm feeling quite fit since I've been here, Mam (despite the conditions I have had plenty of oranges and other fruit. I suppose I shall get sick of them soon). I am getting to pick this language up OK now. You should hear me and one of these Italians in conversation, it's a scream to see."

In the center of X Corps' line was 56th Division, alongside the newly arrived 5th Division on its left holding the ground down to the coast, and 46th Division on its right. McCreery's plan was for 5th and 56th Divisions to cross the Garigliano River at separate points and "turn right" driving up the valley of the Ausente River which flows south into the Garigliano almost at its mouth. This valley leads into the Ausonia defile, a narrow mountain gorge that provides a way into the Liri valley behind the main German defenses. In the meantime, the 46th Division was to cross the river opposite Sant' Ambrogio to secure the high ground on the left of the Liri valley to protect the flank of the Texans when they crossed the Rapido in the main thrust of the army attack. The first Garigliano crossings by British X Corps were due to take place during the night of 17/18 January. For 5th Division it was decided to dispense with any preliminary artillery bombardment in order to try to achieve surprise, but for the 56th Division crossing, the artillery would pull out all the stops.

On 4 January, X Corps gunner Spike Milligan was awakened at 4.20 A.M. It was "pitch black cold, and a howling gale." In the back of the battery's wireless truck he traveled to Lauro, a small village on the foothills that ran down to the Garigliano plains. "Across the brown Garigliano were towering mountains," Milligan wrote. "In these Jerry was waiting, among them a Jerry who was going to do for me. Slitheringly, we pressed forward on our muddy narrow road." In Lauro, Milligan had a look in the police station, where

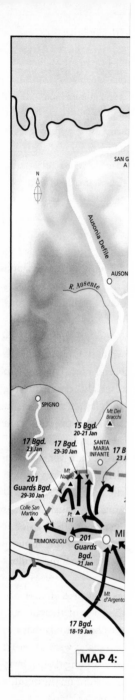

parts of the battalion. Eventually an officer managed to collect together enough soldiers, and the battalion's initial objective, a hill called Colle Salvatito a little under a mile away from the river, was captured just before ten o'clock the next morning. Reinforcements arrived, and the battalion readied itself for the inevitable counterattack.

Crossing to the right of the 9th Battalion, Glyn Edwards's 8th Battalion Royal Fusiliers had less trouble at the river, but found their objective, the bulking height of Monte Damiano, fiercely defended. Just getting up the mountain was a considerable task. Gilbert Allnutt, another fusilier from the 8th Battalion, describes his trek toward the top: "Well before dawn we were at the foot of the mountain . . . Major Allison set off at our head striding towards the summit at a pace that no one could match. Our advance began to look like a sadist's cross-country race for, weighed down by our packs, we grimly tried to keep up with our leader—an impossible task for many. Ahead of us we could see that the mountain was terraced with rocks; many broken and out of place following bombardment. Behind us the sergeant major chased around ordering the stragglers to keep in some form of military formation. I kept my eyes firmly on Major Allison who cut an impressive figure as he strode on, pausing only to shout out encouragement to the men who followed him. Suddenly shells began to fall in front of us and Major Allison was hit. I see him now, in memory, with blood streaming down his face, wounded for the second time, and forced to go back and leave his company."

Without their leader the Fusiliers pushed on, and by evening had reached the summit. The cost had been high, with some companies down to thirty or forty effectives from an original strength of about a hundred. Patrols were pushed forward the next day but came under fire from Allied artillery and were forced to withdraw. After another day enduring sporadic mortar and machine gun fire, the twentieth saw the main German counterattack with heavy mortaring and artillery fire landing on the exposed position, and infiltration by infantry units and individual snipers. After fierce fighting the attack was beaten back by the evening, but the battalion was by now in very poor shape. That evening they were relieved by the 1st London Scottish from the division's 168th Brigade and were moved to the village of Lorenzo, supposedly a quiet sector behind the front line. But when they arrived they found the Germans still in occupation, and there followed two days of house-to-house fighting. Finally, on the twenty-third, the remains of the battalion was moved back over the river to Dodi San Marco for a proper rest.

Glyn Edwards had just enough energy for a short letter on 24 January. It starts in the same way as ever, but shows a young man considerably hardened after the previous week's fighting:

Dear Mam and Dad & all

These few lines to let you know I am still alive and well (thank my God) as I have just got back out of action. It was 8 days of hell up on earth and a hard fight (very hard).

I don't know how long I shall be out of the line. I hope it's for ever as Jerrie is a tough customer: I have lost a few of my pals and it's hard . . . I shall have to end now and shall write again soon. But I have had revenge for some of my mates that got killed so that's one consolation.

All my love, Glyn.

The main enemy counterattack on Len Bradshaw's 9th Battalion Royal Fusiliers was broken up by Allied artillery, but infiltration and sporadic mortar and machine gun fire continued over the next three days. By this stage, says Bradshaw, "We were quite depleted, we'd had a lot of casualties." On the morning of 21 January he was improving his position by piling rocks in front of it when he was hit by a sniper. The bullet smashed into his hip, and the impact knocked him down: "It was like a big kick," he says. "I couldn't get up." A stretcher bearer arrived quickly and put a field dressing on the wound. It was a long and painful journey back to the valley behind him, but, Bradshaw admits, apart from being separated from his friends in his unit, he was glad to be going, and when he reached the dressing station and saw some of the other casualties, he even felt lucky. He was given pain relief and woke up in a hospital. "There were clean sheets," he says. "The bullet was on a cabinet by the side of the bed. A nurse came up and gave me a glass of real lemon juice. I thought I was in heaven."

———

If anything, the 5th Division crossing nearer the coast was even more dangerous. The crossing sites were completely dominated by German positions on the high ground to the north of them. The flat, waterlogged plain had been cleared of obstacles, giving the Germans excellent fields of fire. Both sides of the Garigliano were heavily mined, and German patrols operated at night on the Allied side of the river. The division had only very recently arrived in the area, but its engineers set to work clearing the near side of the river of mines and marking safe paths with white tape. But when the attack started, just before 56th Division went in on their right, the leading troops found themselves in trouble before they even reached the river. The war diary of the 1st King's Own Yorkshire Light Infantry explains what went wrong: "It was difficult and unpleasant, mines were a very real danger and a single-line track had been marked across country with tapes by the Royal Engineers. This may well have been good enough for men in daylight, but for heavily laden men in the dark it was a nightmare, despite the new moon." Many of the assaulting companies had to carry their own boats to the river, across the "mine marsh" with its deep dikes and ditches every hundred yards. The attack by the 6th Seaforths on the extreme left of the front had seemed to be going well, as the Germans were unaware of their progress until they were a few hundred feet from the river. The battalion's historian described the scene: "At last the river itself could be seen, water running smooth and oily, catching bizarre reflections from the sky. The far bank could also be seen, and so far, the enemy did not seem to smell a rat. Apart from the distant sounds of gunfire exchange upstream, all was quiet on our sector. It had to be too good to be true." Then, just moments before the time for the crossing, "Lieutenant John Holcroft . . . stood on a mine. His left foot was ripped straight off with a hideous wrench. Majors Lowe and McKenzie, who were moving up to join him, were both blinded by the sudden night explosion and also generally shredded in the face . . . Already, some of our best officers were incapacitated. Something was going horribly wrong, and the alarm was well and truly raised. As more mines went off, bright green flares suddenly soared into the sky" and defensive fire from machine guns and mortars started hitting the river's edge. Elsewhere, promised guides failed to appear, and many other men found themselves marooned in minefields, taking heavy casualties. As with the Seaforths, when the mines started to go off, incoming fire from the German mortar and artillery began, further breaking up the taped paths.

There had been an ambitious plan to use amphibious craft at the mouth of the river to land troops a short distance to the north of the estuary. But, again, the confused reality of war intervened. Strong currents at the mouth of the river made navigation very difficult. The American crews of the boats were relying on landing lights that failed to materialize or were too late to be of much use. Phosphorescence in the sea stirred up by the boats must have been obvious to the Germans, who brought down defensive fire on the amphibious craft when they were still some two hundred yards from the coast. In the confusion, a party of Royal Fusiliers landed on the wrong bank of the estuary and nearly attacked their own brigade HQ. First to land in the correct place was a detachment of the 141st Field Ambulance along with a small stores party from the Northampton Regiment. True to their training, they started setting up store dumps even though there were no other soldiers ashore to supply.

Several of the amphibious craft were swept out to sea. One company's boat went so far out that it came into contact with a cruiser, busy shelling German positions to the north. They were about to hail her to ask directions when a submarine suddenly surfaced immediately to port. Uncertain of its nationality, the Fusiliers manned their PIAT bazooka and were about to sink it when a head popped out of the conning tower and shouted: "Who the hell are you?"

"Royal Scots Fusiliers" was the prompt and somewhat relieved reply.

"Never heard of you" was the even prompter rejoinder as the hatch closed and the submarine submerged.

As the men of the 17th Brigade were struggling to the river and somehow getting across, a short distance up the Garigliano two battalions of the 13th Brigade—2nd Wiltshires and 2nd Inniskilling Fusiliers—had been approaching the river. Jack Williams, a stretcher bearer with the Fusiliers, describes what happened: "At that point it wasn't too bad, because Jerry hadn't been alerted that we were about to cross the river. It was quiet at the river and we took up positions and waited for the carriers behind us. Waiting. It was the nerves, not knowing what was going to happen. Everybody was in a nervous state. I became very quiet." After this nerve-racking delay, the boats arrived carried by a contingent of the Royal Army Service Corps (RASC). At the crossing site the river was about twenty feet wide. All was still quiet. "When the boats arrived we were ordered across the river," Williams continues. "We thought we were going to get over with no trouble at all, as some of them did." The first company started crossing. Still "nothing happened, no gunfire, no shellfire; and then we went to get over—A Company—and we got in and everything happened—mortars, 88s, machine-gun fire, a really heavy stonk. The effect was pandemonium, really. Everybody was flapping and running about, trying to get in the boats, trying to get over."

Williams managed to cross in one of the eight-man boats, but soon all but one of the battalion's twelve craft were damaged. There were several direct hits on the crowded boats, and many others overturned, throwing their heavily laden occupants into the icy water. Some managed to loosen their pack, wriggle out of it, and swim to the far bank. Others sank like stones to the bottom. Williams's platoon sergeant told him the next day that as he was swimming toward the bank, he could feel hands desperately grabbing at his feet from below.

"We got out of the boats," Williams continues, "and straightaway we had to get up to our objective, which was a farm on the right. We had to get down there immediately; we couldn't hang about on the bank. We could hear the shouts and screams of the people there who were thrashing about in the water, who had been hit. It was a bit of a do at the time, and everyone was panicking."

The farm was cleared by grenade and bayonet, and prisoners were taken, but during the engagement Williams's company commander was killed by mortar fire along with four German prisoners he had captured. The next morning, says Williams, "It was just a question of finding people from your battalion, as everyone was scattered. Everyone was looking for their mates, to see if they had survived. Everybody was in a state of panic, after such a bad experience the night before. We wondered what we were going into."

In fact, the company, with nearly eighty casualties, was unable to take part in further battles until the losses were replaced. The only NCOs left were a sergeant and a lance corporal. Williams, who had been in the army since 1940 and fought throughout the Italian campaign, describes the night of 17 January as his "worst moment. Salerno was pretty hectic, but in my experience nothing before or after compared to that river crossing."

By the end of the following day, 5th Division had secured a shallow and precarious bridgehead, but losses had been so heavy that the reserve brigade, the 15th, had to be committed far ahead of schedule to continue the attack against Minturno, which was cleared by the end of 19 January. As in 56th Division's sector, the next couple of days saw counterattacks by the Germans, but renewed attacks, supported by naval gunfire from off shore, started to force the defenders out of their positions on the high ground overlooking the valley. The British troops were impressed by the strength and comfort of the Germans' dugouts. One was captured with a fully cooked breakfast intact. But just holding on to the gains proved very difficult as the Germans continued to counterattack in ever greater strength, and by 24 January the offensive in 5th Division's sector had ground to a halt. The bridgehead was being sealed off without the intended breakthrough toward the Liri valley anywhere in sight.

As had been the case throughout the Italian campaign, high ground was important most of all because of the powers of observation it gave its possessor. Observation was the key to success in land battles in the Second World War, particularly in the mountainous terrain of central Italy. The gunnery technology and wireless sets of the time could direct the guns of an entire army on to any visible target within minutes. As long as the Germans controlled the high ground running from near the coast to Monte Damiano and Castelforte opposite 56th Division, they could prevent the engineers from bridging the river. Without a bridge, it was impossible to transport the tanks or men in large enough numbers to expand the bridgehead across the river.

After the initial crossing in boats, various ferries, rafts, and floating treadways were employed to get light vehicles and men across, and to ferry back the ambulances with the wounded. But mines and artillery fire hampered the moving up of the heavy bridging equipment and dispersed working parties. Soon damaged vehicles completely blocked the routes to the bridging sites. The engineers called for smoke to shield the river, but the wind was blowing the wrong way and work on the Bailey bridges had to be abandoned. In the meantime, what rafts there were in operation worked day and night. The engineer Matthew Salmon was employed in building and manning a ferry, which consisted of a single span of Bailey bridge fastened to two large rafts. Because of incoming fire there were constant delays and repairs needed to the boats, and the rest of the time was spent trying to clear bridging lorries that were stuck on the way to the site. Now at least the smokescreen was starting to work, although Salmon reports how the Germans sent Italian civilians—presumably under duress—often with pale sacks on their backs, toward the river to try to get them to give away the exact crossing site. The British engineers had no choice but to turn them away as quickly as they could, even if it meant opening fire on them.

On the other side of the line, the German 94th Division, although rested, had been thinly stretched over a long section of the Gustav Line. Enduring the same cold and wet conditions, the German soldiers were particularly affected by the heavy weight of the Allied artillery and, when the weather allowed, the attacks of fighter-bombers. "To one of our shells you send ten or twenty to our side" was a comment made repeatedly by prisoners of war. "Barrages all day," reads the diary of the eighteen-year-old German soldier who had been given a crucifix by an Italian family. "The Tommies are attacking . . . more barrages. A wounded man lies beside me and ahead of me, three dead. I have changed a good deal. I cannot smile now." A letter home from a soldier of 276th Regiment, 94th Division shows the suffering endured by the Germans in the Garigliano sector: "On the way to Company HQ, a distance of less than 200 meters, there are at least twenty German dead—how it happened is all too evident. One tries not to look at them. At night one falls rather than walks over the rocks. The Tommies creep stealthily around. Their snipers shoot only too well. Again and again head wounds. The mortars fire and the whistle and explosion of shells goes on, day and night. Sometimes, for a moment or two only, there is peace, and then I think of home. Sunlight by day, the night spent on cold stones." An NCO of the same regiment managed to keep a diary, which was later found and translated by British intelligence officers. The entry for 22 January reads: "I am done. The artillery fire is driving me crazy. I am frightened as never before . . . cold . . . During the night one cannot leave one's hole. The last days have finished me off altogether. I am in need of someone to hold on to." Three days later he writes, "I start becoming a pessimist. The Tommies write in their leaflets that the choice is ours, Tunis or Stalingrad . . . we are on half rations. No mail. Teddy is a prisoner. I see myself one very soon." Five days later: "The lice are getting the better of us. I do not care any longer. Rations are getting shorter, 15 men, three loaves of bread, no hot meals . . . my laundry bag has been looted."

Kesselring and von Senger had been concerned about the strength of 94th Division on 10th Army's right, but were still surprised by the British success in crossing the river and reaching the foothills beyond. Von Senger visited the 94th Division's area early on 18 January, and, believing the British were capable of breaking through to the Liri valley behind Cassino, outflanking the defensive line anchored on Monte Cassino, he immediately went straight to Kesselring for reinforcements. Kesselring had two veteran divisions—the 29th and 90th Panzer Grenadiers—in reserve near Rome, earmarked to move against any amphibious landing behind the Gustav Line. He had long feared an amphibious landing on one of his long flanks and was loath to part with this crucial reserve force. He had received contrary reports from his intelligence officers about the imminent likelihood of such a landing, but knew from spies in Naples that there were considerable numbers of ships in the harbor. But believing that the fate of the whole of 10th Army "hung by a slender thread," he authorized the move and the fresh divisions started arriving at the Garigliano within two or three days of the Allied attack.

This is what accounted for the increased weight of the German counterattacks on the British 56th and 5th divisions following 21 January. In a typical action, an assault through Castelforte on 21 January by the 29th PG Division caught the British just at the moment when the first impetus of their own attack had waned, the men were tired, and the artillery was in the process of taking up new positions. Numerous prisoners were taken, and the British advance, already well behind schedule, began to look as if it would be reversed.

Private S. C. Brooks of the 6th Cheshires, a machine gunner attached to the same brigade as Len Bradshaw and Glyn Edwards, wrote in his diary on 22 January: "No bridge across the river yet, all troops etc. are rafted, a bad state of affairs. Our platoon come out 12.00 last night and are in action again tonight, have our own views on this. Two lads, Mcnab and Beresford, can't be found, that makes 4 altogether from this Company, I'll say no more. 9 men arrive as reinforcements, the oldest is 20, they are from N. Africa and have done 9 months in the army with a total of two months' service abroad, naturally no action. We take them down the field and show them where our shells are landing and where theirs are dropping, they move on to their platoons. I wish them every luck." Matthew Salmon, on the overworked ferry, could see that morale was now low. "People were getting edgier with each other and asking, 'How much longer are we going to be here? It's about time we were bloody relieved.' People weren't very happy."

On the same day, the successful landings at Anzio, Operation Shingle, were announced. Leaflets were fired into the German lines explaining that they were about to be trapped. The British soldiers on the Garigliano front were expecting the Germans to withdraw, or at least be looking anxiously over their shoulders, but "it appeared to make no difference to them." On 23 January the Germans counterattacked again on the Damiano ridge and regained positions won by the 8th Fusiliers on the first night of the assault. A Company of 1st London Scottish were ordered to attack that night to restore the situation. The company advanced with two platoons forward, but the commander and the only other officer were both wounded in the very early stages of the attack, which was now held up by some enemy machine guns. No. 9 Section of No. 9 Platoon was ordered by the platoon commander, Sergeant Hancock, to carry out a right-flanking movement against the German position. Almost as soon as he had issued the order, he was killed. The section now consisted of a lance corporal and three men, but they were shortly joined by two men from the platoon's two-inch mortar section, Privates Miller and Mitchell, the latter a thirty-one-year-old regular army soldier from Highbury in London. During the advance the Germans opened up with heavy machine gun fire at point-blank range. Mitchell dropped the mortar he was carrying and, seizing a rifle and bayonet, charged alone up the steep and rocky hill through intense Spandau fire. He reached the German machine gun unscathed, jumped into the weapons pit, shot one, and bayoneted the other member of the crew, thus silencing the gun. As a result the advance continued, but shortly afterward the leading section was held up by the fire of approximately two German sections that were strongly entrenched. "Private Mitchell," his citation for bravery reads, "realizing that prompt action was essential, rushed forward into the assault, firing his rifle from his hip, completely oblivious of the bullets which were sweeping the area. The remainder of the section, inspired by his example, followed him and arrived in time to complete the capture of the position, in which six Germans were killed and twelve made prisoner."

Several other positions were cleared in the same way, Mitchell assuming the command of the section and leading by example. More prisoners were taken, but one, having surrendered, picked up a rifle and shot Mitchell through the head. By this time the wounded company commander had decided that the objective would not be taken before daylight and had ordered a withdrawal. But it was only after Mitchell's death that the section received the order. His body had to be left on the hillside. George Mitchell received a posthumous Victoria Cross, Britain's highest battlefield honor.

"God made gentle people as well as strong ones," Spike Milligan wrote. "Alas for the war effort, I was a gentle one." The beginning of the attack on 17 January had attracted counterbattery fire from the Germans, and the next day a direct hit left four dead and six wounded. For Milligan's unit, it was the most grievous blow of the war so far, and everyone was depressed. In the afternoon, guided by men from the battery in a forward observation post right on the front line on Monte Damiano, they shelled a crossroads behind the German lines and were in turn dive-bombed and strafed by the Luftwaffe. The next day one of the forward observers returned to the battery in tears, "finished," and volunteers were requested to cross the river and help man the radios in their tactical headquarters, where their unpopular major had his forward command post. Milligan stepped forward and the next day traveled by jeep up to the river, noticing the stream of ambulances coming the other way. As he neared the front line, the sound of the artillery faded, to be replaced by the noise of small-arms fire and mortars. Milligan was already tired from being up for two nights and was finding his piles increasingly painful. "We approached the ferry bridge over the Garigliano," he wrote. "Jerry was lobbing occasional shells into the smoke that obscured the crossing . . . 'Any more for the Woolwich Ferry?' says a cheerful voice."

Once across the river, Milligan could see Monte Damiano looming ahead. The jeep turned off to the right and arrived at a small, partly destroyed farmhouse that was serving as tactical HQ: "All around are dead Jerries. MG [machine gun] bullets are whistling overhead as we duck and run inside." It was about four o'clock in the afternoon. He was immediately put to work on the radio and kept on the set for the next seventeen hours as harassing fire, aiming for the crossing, continued to land nearby. By dawn he was "numb with fatigue, and my piles had started to bleed." But at nine o'clock in the morning, he was sent with four others to the observation post (OP) with fresh batteries, each weighing fifty pounds, and another radio. The small party started on the road to Castelforte and then turned left into a gully leading up the mountain, passing infantry dug in inside a ravine to their left. At the end of the gully the exhausted men started climbing the mountain, at this point terraced for olive trees. It was here that they must have been spotted by a German observer.

"CRUMP! CRUMP! CRUMP! Mortars! We hit the deck," writes Milligan of the fateful attack. "A rain of them fall around us. I cling to the ground. The mortars rain down on us. I'll have a fag, that's what. I am holding a packet of woodbines, then there is a noise like thunder. It's right on my head, there's a high-pitched whistle in my ears, at first I black out and then I see red, I am strangely dazed. I was on my front, now I'm on my back . . . I know if we stay here we'll all die." Shocked and wounded, Milligan started to scramble down the hill. He heard shouting, but cannot remember the journey back to the HQ. "Next I was at the bottom of the mountain, next I'm speaking to Major Jenkins, I am crying, I don't know why, he's saying 'Why did you come back?' He is shouting at me and threatening me . . . Next I am in an ambulance and shaking, an orderly puts a blanket round my shoulders. I'm crying again, why why why?"

He had a small wound in his leg, and at the forward dressing station he was given hot, very sweet tea and some pills. He was still crying, but did not know why. Drowsy from the tranquilizers and still confused, he was given a label and put into another ambulance with seriously wounded people. "Suddenly we are passing through our artillery lines as the guns fire. I jump at each explosion, then, a gesture I will never forget, a young soldier next to me with his right arm in a bloody sling put his arm around my shoulder and tried to comfort me. 'There, there you'll be alright, mate.' "

The ambulance deposited Milligan at a casualty clearing station, where he discovered he had been labeled "battle fatigue." Still "terribly emotional," he felt isolated and off balance. "It was a wretched time," he writes. "No small kit, no towel, no soap, no friends. It's amazing what small simple things really make up our life-support system." He was given more tranquilizers and taken to see a psychiatrist, a captain, who asked him a lot of questions and then ended, in a loud voice, "You are going to get better. Understand?" Three days later Milligan returned to the battery, still in the same position near Lauro. "How I got back to the battery I don't know," he writes. "This was a time of my life that I was very demoralized. I was not really me anymore."

Back with his unit, feeling like a "zombie" due to the tranquilizers he had been given, Milligan was marched in front of the major and told he was to lose his lance corporal's stripe "owing to my unreliable conduct," he writes. "I suppose in World War I the bastard would have had me shot . . . I didn't represent the type of empty-minded soldier he wanted. I had been a morale-booster to the boys, organizing dances and concerts, and always trying to keep a happy atmosphere, something he couldn't do . . . I am by now completely demoralized. All the laughing had stopped."

Another week of crying, stammering, and distress at the noise of the guns made it clear that Milligan's battlefield days were over and he would have to leave his beloved battery for the last time. It was, he later recorded, "one of the saddest days of my life . . . I got up early. I didn't say good-bye to anyone. I got into the truck . . . as I drove back down that muddy mountain road, with the morning mists filling the valleys, I felt as though I was being taken across the Styx. I've never got over that feeling."

In the Minturno–Castelforte bridgehead there were renewed British attacks from 23 January, the fighting continuing until 9 February as X Corps tried to batter its way onto the top of Monte Damiano and up the Ausente valley toward the Liri River. Commando and marine units were employed on the bleak slopes of Monte Ornito, and gains were made, but McCreery had insufficient reserves to keep the momentum going. The accepted wisdom of the day was that offensive action required an infantry advantage of at least three-to-one; against troops well dug-in in fixed positions more like six-to-one was needed. X Corps, having attacked in the first place with tired and depleted forces, had nothing like this advantage, and the cold and wet conditions on the exposed mountain slopes were taking a toll on the attackers. By the end of January the corps had suffered over four thousand casualties.

Conditions were made worse by the isolated nature of the forward units, who were miles away from any roads. When the road ended, supplies would be loaded onto mules, but in many cases rations, water, and ammunition had to be carried to the advanced positions by porters or the soldiers themselves on slippery, narrow, and treacherous paths. Movement had to be at night and done as quietly as possible to avoid attracting fire. George Pringle, then twenty-six years old, served with the 175th Pioneer Regiment in the Garigliano bridgehead and recalls the exhausting and nerve-racking process of keeping the troops in the mountains fed, watered, and equipped: "Transport brought supplies to the nearest road in the foothills and mules took over, led by Pioneer mule transport companies climbing the narrow and winding trails until the pathways ceased. Here we took over, unarmed so that our hands were free for climbing. With a load of fifty pounds securely fastened, we inched forward in the darkness. We paused breathlessly lest we made our presence known to an enemy patrol. Each time a loose rock was dislodged and fell noisily to the valley below we froze in our tracks as enemy or our own forces fired an inquisitive flare into the sky. No one spoke or sneezed or even breathed too loudly, terrified in case we gave our position away. Finally we would reach our infantry and hand over the supplies, which were always welcomed." This was far from the end of the night's work as, for the descent, the Pioneers would become stretcher bearers. Where the track was wide enough, it would be four men to a stretcher, but often "it was two men slipping and stumbling over the rocks while the wounded man would be groaning and cursing in the dark."

From the beginning of the attack the corps had been desperately short of mules. They were also short of men who knew how to handle them. David Cormack was originally a tank man, but because he was familiar with horses from before the war—his father was a veterinary surgeon—he was put in charge of forty mules and an Italian army cavalry regiment of sixty men acting as muleteers. Communicating in rusty French, Cormack soon had the men of the unit handling their mules well in spite of the soldiers being poorly fed and clothed. On 29 January he made his first trip across the Garigliano, carrying water, rifle ammunition, mortar bombs, and food. Having negotiated the river crossing on a pontoon, he found it difficult to get the mules to keep to the narrow, white-taped path across the ever-present minefields. The journey took six hours up and a little less back.

Trips continued, and on 7 February he took a hundred mules up to Colle Salvatito. He was back again the next morning: "Spent day making two trips up hill, Salvatito, with 3" mortar," his diary reads, "damn tired, as steep and mostly loose rocks . . . rained like hell, cold."

By the next day, offensive action in the Minturno–Castelforte bridgehead had ended. The Germans had successfully sealed off the salient, and the British troops went over to active defense, patrolling and harassing the enemy but not launching any major attacks. McCreery's men were left in the foothills in possession of the original forward positions of the Gustav Line on a frontage of some twelve miles. The depth of the bridgehead was only a few miles instead of the hoped-for seven.

Although the British commanders were disappointed, in the light of the momentous events taking place in the Liri valley to their right from 20 January onward, it was a considerable achievement. The small bridgehead would be of vital importance later, and, crucially, German reserves that could have destroyed the landings at Anzio had been drawn into the Gustav Line from 18 January onward, thus achieving one of the key objectives of the wider army attack before the main thrust into the Liri valley even started.

But there was to have been a third crossing by 46th Division on 19 January on the south side of the Liri valley opposite Sant' Ambrogio. This was to support the left flank of the forthcoming American attack. In Clark's view this was the most important of X Corps' objectives, but inexplicably McCreery attacked here with much less conviction than further south. On the day of the attack the Germans opened the sluices of a dam higher upstream on the Rapido so that the Garigliano was some six feet higher and flowing faster than predicted. Crossing by assault boat became chaotic, made worse by river mist, and only one company of the only brigade involved succeeded in establishing itself on the far bank. The German defenders of Sant' Ambrogio, bolstered by reinforcement divisions from near Rome, counterattacked hard. The arrival of daylight helped the accuracy of German fire, and the success of a second crossing became increasingly unlikely. The men across the river were ordered to return to their side, and, to the subsequent fury of the Americans, no further crossing was attempted.

Clark had few illusions as to what the failure of the 46th Division would mean for the Americans due that night to cross the Rapido a short distance upstream. In his diary he bemoaned the "mental reservations as to the possibilities of success of the operation" of the British divisional commander, and went on: "Although the 46th effort would not entirely have protected [the US 36th Division's] left flank, its failure would leave it entirely uncovered during the crossing of the Rapido River." Maj. Gen. Fred Walker, who was to command the attack by the US 36th Division, noted in his diary that the British 46th Division commander had come to his command post to apologize. "His failure makes it tough for my men who now have none of the advantages that his crossing would have provided. The British are the world's greatest diplomats," Walker continued, "but you can't count on them for anything but words." In his own diary, Clark noted a warning from McCreery that the attack of the 36th Division had "little chance of success on account of the heavy defensive position of the enemy west of the Rapido." Clark concluded: "I maintain that it is essential that I make that attack fully expecting heavy losses in order to hold all the troops on my front and draw more to it, thereby clearing the way for Shingle. The attack is on."

6

Bloody River

Following their mauling in the battles for San Pietro in December, the US 36th Texas Division had needed numerous replacements to bring it up to strength. Now faced with its toughest objective yet, the division contained a large proportion of untried troops. In an article in *Yank* magazine from June 1944, "combat-wise platoon sergeants" explain the typical and often fatal errors that "green" soldiers always made in their first combat: "The first mistake recruits make under fire is that they freeze and bunch up. They drop to the ground and just lie there; won't even fire back. I had one man just lie there while a German came right up and shot him. He still wouldn't fire back," said one sergeant.

"None of the new men dig deep enough or quick enough," another sergeant commented. "I've seen a lot of men die because they didn't dig their holes deep enough," said a third. "Most of them were crushed in tank attacks. Ninety-five per cent of the men in my company are alive today because they dug down the full six feet." There were also complaints that some of the new men did not know how to use their weapons properly, but above all, a high influx of new troops meant that few units knew one another well, and many of the men were not even aware of the name of their squad leader.

Among the junior officers, where casualties were always the highest, there was an even greater proportion of untried troops in the 36th Division fol-

lowing the San Pietro fighting. In one battalion, 75 percent were replacements. One such new arrival was twenty-three-year-old Carl Strom from
Grand Rapids, Michigan. Strom had been in the ROTC (Reserve Officers'
Training Corps) at high school and, as a college-educated boy, had been assigned to the air force ground crew when he volunteered. However, his father, a First World War veteran, pulled some strings and Strom got his wish
to be an infantryman. Having finished Officer Candidate School, he was
shipped to Oran with other replacement second lieutenants and arrived in
Africa at the time of the Salerno landings. There, he was given specialist
training by British Commandos before boarding a ship to Naples. After a
boring wait at a replacement depot, he was assigned to 1st Battalion, 141st
Regiment of the 36th Division on 1 January 1944. When he arrived he was
surprised to find that of the seven officers in his company, four were brand-
new replacements.

After a week's mountain training, he was assigned his own platoon of just
under forty men. Of these, half were, like himself, about to face their first
combat. "There were always jokes about the brand-new second lieutenant,
greenie officers," Strom remembers, "but there was no resentment there. The
older guys recognized that, hey, this is a precarious thing and we don't know
how long this guy is going to be with us. We'll just do the best we can with
him." Strom was acutely aware of his own inexperience. "I got my platoon
sergeant and my squad leaders together, just the four of them and said, 'OK,
now look, guys, I haven't been in combat and you have. You are going to help
show me the ropes. I want you to be perfectly honest with me. If you think
I'm not doing something the right way or in the best way, you let me know.
You guys know more about this than I do even with all my training. I can't
match what you've learned even in three or four days' combat.' "

On 14 January, Strom's platoon—No. 3 in B Company—moved up to a
staging position just behind Monte Trocchio. The next day the company officers climbed to a vantage point on Trocchio to look at the ground over
which they were to attack. Directly ahead of them was the entrance to the
Liri valley, some ten miles wide, flanked on the left by Monte Maio and on
the right by Monte Cassino. This was, then, the route to Rome, the only
space where the Allies could deploy their superiority in tanks and the key
objective of 5th Army's massive attacks across the whole front. "Of course, I
had no experience in that sort of thing," says Strom, "but it was evident to
me right away and to all the officers in the company that this was not going

to be a cake walk. We could see the area where we were going to attack: it was basically flat, sloping towards the river and there was no cover. All the brush was removed and on the other side of the river we could see it was the same thing sloping up. You couldn't see any German fortifications or anything like that, they were too well camouflaged, but you knew they were there."

Strom's divisional commanding officer, Maj. Gen. Fred Walker, was also concerned about the success of the attack and the lack of time for preparation. As well as holding the high ground on both sides of the Liri valley, the Germans had excellent observation from the fortified village of Sant' Angelo on a forty-foot bluff on the far side of the river in the center of the valley. This meant that it would be impossible to move troops forward across the two miles or so of flat ground during daylight without their being decimated by artillery fire. So it would have to be a nighttime attack, which was always more difficult, particularly for inexperienced troops. Heavy rain and deliberate flooding by the Germans had made the valley a sea of mud, and there were no approach roads of sufficient quality to make the bringing up of vehicles easy. The river itself was a formidable obstacle. Although only twenty-five to thirty feet wide, it was up to twelve feet deep and had high, steep banks and icy, fast-flowing water. The very narrowness of the river meant that the Allied artillery would be unable to plaster the far bank as the men started to cross. On the near side were numerous mines, and on the far side the Germans, it was believed, had constructed a layer of dugouts protected by extensive barbed wire, machine gun nests, booby traps, and trip-wired mines. The attacking troops would have to carry their own boats to the river's edge, where engineers would need to construct footbridges to get the majority of the vanguard troops across. But such bridges, Walker had discovered, were in very short supply, along with other engineering materials.

On 7 January, Walker had told his divisional staff engineer, Maj. Oran C. Stovall, to make an estimate of the crossing for planning purposes. Stovall flew over the river and went as far forward on foot as he dared—the near bank was far from being secured. He interviewed civilians and prisoners of war, made maps, and looked for possible crossing sites. His report to Walker did nothing to allay the general's fears: "First," Stovall said, "it would be impossible for us to get to the river. Second, we couldn't cross, and third, if we got across the river there was no place to go." Other engineers agreed that although the Liri valley offered the only way forward not blocked by mountains, it was a "muddy bottleneck" and very well defended.

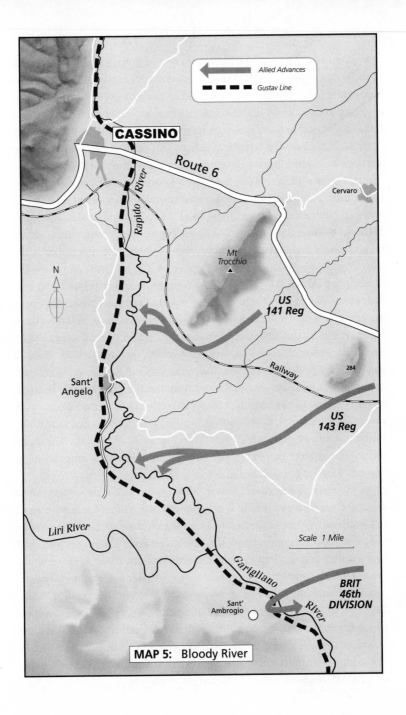

MAP 5: Bloody River

Allied Advances
Gustav Line

CASSINO

Route 6

Rapido River

Cervaro

Mt Trocchio

US 141 Reg

N

Railway

284

Sant' Angelo

US 143 Reg

Liri River

Scale 1 Mile

Garigliano

Sant' Ambrogio

River

BRIT 46th DIVISION

Walker had other, personal reasons for worrying about the river crossing. In the First World War he had been decorated after twelve hundred US soldiers under his command had fought off an enemy force eight times its size as it tried to cross the Marne during the Germans' final offensive. The Americans had slaughtered the attackers. He was well aware that here the defenders would hold a similar advantage to the one he had enjoyed in 1918. There were also unhappy reports from patrols that had ventured to the river's edge. Few had succeeded in crossing the river to reconnoiter the German defenses on the other side, and mine-clearing teams had had insufficient time to dispose of all the devices planted in the flooded Rapido plain on the Allied side. Even when safe paths were marked by the engineers, German patrols would cross the river and move the white marker tapes or plant new mines in the "safe areas."

Although Walker confided his doubts to his diary, he still told Clark on 18 January that he believed his division would achieve its objective of opening up the entrance to the Liri valley. His plan was to start the crossings three hours after sunset, at 8:00 P.M., on 20 January. Upriver of Sant' Angelo, 141st Regiment would cross at two sites, led by Strom's 1st Battalion. About a thousand yards downriver from the village, 143rd Regiment would also cross at two points. The division's third regiment, the 142nd, would be in reserve. This plan would give his six battalions eleven hours of darkness to get across. When the riverbanks were no longer under enemy fire, two Bailey bridges were to be built, which would carry tanks into the battle. The initial troops would ferry themselves across either in pneumatic dinghies or in thirteen-foot-long assault boats.

As the time of the attack neared, Major General Walker's nervousness about the operation increased. During the afternoon of 20 January he wrote in his diary: "We might succeed but I do not see how we can. The mission assigned is poorly timed. The crossing is dominated by heights on both sides of the valley where German artillery observers are ready to bring down heavy artillery concentrations on our men. The river is the principal obstacle of the German main line of resistance . . . So I am prepared for defeat. The mission should never have been assigned to any troops with flanks exposed. Clark sent me his best wishes; said he has worried about our success. I think he is worried over the fact that he made an unwise decision when he gave us the job of crossing the river under such adverse tactical conditions. However, if we get some breaks we may succeed."

As darkness fell, fog developed rapidly in the valley, reducing visibility at the river to a few yards. Back at their jumping-off point, Strom's company platoon leaders drew cards to see who would lead the attack. "I drew the high card so I had the lead platoon," says Strom. The men set off at 6 P.M., each carrying an extra bandolier of ammunition. Bayonets were fixed. Soon their guide, an engineer, took a wrong turn in the pitch darkness and the group ended up near the forward battalion command post. A noisy turnaround started attracting enemy fire, and when the men tried to take cover away from the paths, they immediately started setting off mines. When they at last located the dump where the boats had been left, the men found that some had already been damaged by shellfire. It was now just before 7:30 P.M. The heavy and bulky boats, weighing over four hundred pounds, were then lugged toward the river just as the Allied artillery barrage started, bringing an immediate German retaliation. Some quarter of a mile from the river, disaster struck for Strom: "For my platoon I had two boats and it took six to eight men on each side to carry them. We had to go down this sunken road to the river and the Germans had these places all zeroed in for their artillery so they could fire blind. We were about halfway down the sunken road . . . I was up front with my runner and an engineer guide and I was probably about three hundred feet ahead of the company. As I turned around to look back, two German shells came in and they hit right in my platoon. They killed or wounded every man." Both the company commander and his number two were among the dead. "So now there were only three officers left in charge of the company, none of whom had ever been in combat before. Lieutenant Taylor, who was senior to me by a couple of weeks, assumed command."

Strom attached himself to another platoon. "It took quite a while to clear up the mess in the sunken road," he says. Then, having got lost again, and having been forced to drag the boats as there were no longer enough men to carry them, Strom and the leading men of 1st Battalion finally reached the river at about 11 P.M. "We started to try to launch the boats," Strom continues, "and because it was pitch dark we couldn't see. We put a couple of boats into the water and loaded guys in them and we discovered right away that there were holes in the boats from the shelling and they sank. We lost ten to twelve men who were fully loaded with ammunition, rifles and grenades and so forth, and naturally were heavy. Well, we realized then we weren't going to get the boats in, so we sent word back to try to get some engineers up there to get some kind of a bridge across."

Attempts to launch undamaged boats also met with failure. C. P. "Buddy" Autrey, a sergeant in Strom's company, remembered, "At the river they slid the first boat down the bank, which had a forty- to fifty-degree slope, and put it into the water tip first. It sank immediately. I tried to tell them to put the boats into the water sideways because of the slope and the current." When Autrey got into a boat, it was swept downstream and started taking on water. The men inside, still paddling furiously, were thrown into the river as the boat capsized. Although he was weighed down with equipment, Autrey tried to help a young private, Carl W. Buckley, who was struggling to stay above the water: "Our gear got wet and pulled us under," said Autrey. "I had to let go of the young man and he drowned . . . Eight of twelve of us drowned and four swam to the German side." Wet, cold, and without weapons, the four men tried without success to shout over the river to the Allied side.

C Company of 1st Battalion had similar difficulty in even getting to the river. Bill Everett, a twenty-two-year-old from Baltimore, was in the heavy weapons platoon in charge of a mortar section. Like Strom, it was his first time in combat. "I remember talking to my guys when we were taking off with our boat," he says. "I told them that tonight they were going to have to pay their dues for being an American. They knew they had no chance of getting across because we had been patrolling that river. We couldn't even get recon patrols across."

Because of the small number of crossing sites and narrow approaches, the men made good targets for German fire. As artillery and mortar shells came in, the troops scattered for cover, dropping the boats, and blundered into minefields. The markers showing the cleared routes were soon smashed by shells or buried in the mud, and the approach roads were blocked by abandoned boats and the bodies of men. It was like the Garigliano, only worse. Here the Germans had a far greater weight of artillery and used it very effectively.

"We were very lucky," says Everett. "We couldn't get across. The reason being they blew the hell out of the boats that we had. It was just mass confusion. You couldn't tell what the hell was going on. We were carrying these big 400-pound wooden boats through minefields with our gear in the dark. We had to carry them, I don't know, about two miles maybe. Of course, a couple of guys set off the mines and that blew things all to hell. One of my boys set off one, lost his eyesight. Machine gun fire was all over the field. Lost quite a few men. But when we got down to the river's edge, we tried to launch our boat. We put it in the water and it went right through the bottom. We had to pull back to our original positions. That was that night. It was a real disaster. It was my first operation. I lost a lot of my friends that came with me up there that night, other fellows that had been in the same group coming over with me as replacement officers."

Carl Strom had to wait until 4 A.M. to get across the river on a footbridge. Originally there had been four for the regiment but one was found to be defective, one was destroyed by mines on the way, and the other two were blown up at the river's edge by artillery fire. Eventually the engineers cobbled one together from the remnants. The men of 1st Battalion started to make their way across while the men who had been detailed to go over at the regiment's second crossing site waited behind them to follow over the single footbridge. On the German side the men of Strom's battalion immediately encountered mines, booby traps, and wire as well as machine gun fire from well-fortified positions some 250 yards from the riverbank. They tried to dig in, first probing the ground for mines with their bayonets, but found that in the damp earth their foxholes collapsed or quickly filled with water up to their waists. Most took shelter in ditches or water-filled shell craters. None of their radios worked after the crossing and signal wires were soon destroyed, so they remained out of contact with those on the near bank.

––––––––––––

Initially the crossing downstream by the 143rd Regiment went much better. The first company got across the river without too many problems but then enemy fire destroyed all the boats and inflicted heavy casualties on the next two companies. A footbridge was destroyed almost as soon as it was assembled. Nevertheless, by 5 A.M. most of the 1st Battalion was across. The 3rd Battalion, detailed to cross at another point nearby, failed to even reach the river. Instead they got lost in the darkness and the fog and stumbled into a minefield. All of their flimsy rubber boats were destroyed.

Meanwhile, the men of the regiment's 1st Battalion on the German side of the Rapido were unable to expand their narrow bridgehead and were effectively pinned down in a small pocket with the river at their backs. At 7:15 A.M., the battalion's commanding officer asked for permission to bring back his men. This request was relayed to Major General Walker, who refused, but by that time the commander on the spot had ordered a retreat on his own initiative. By 10 A.M. all the men from the 143rd Regiment were back on the American side of the river.

The German 15th PG Division reported that morning: "Strong enemy assault detachments, which have crossed the river, are annihilated." The 10th Army commander, von Vietinghoff, hadn't even been aware that this was the major attack on the Gustav Line. He considered it merely a reconnaissance in force.

Upstream from Sant' Angelo, Carl Strom and the four-hundred-odd men from 1st Battalion, 141st Regiment who had crossed the river and stayed there were completely exposed as daylight revealed their positions. "I stuck my head up one time to see what was going on ahead of me and got a shot off the side of my helmet," says Strom. A man next to him "stuck his head up" and got a bullet between the eyes. "It went on all day that way with intermittent shelling on us," Strom remembers. "If anyone stuck their head up or revealed themselves they immediately drew fire . . . we were getting no place. At about three or four o'clock in the afternoon a good-sized group from the company—probably twelve to fifteen guys—got up and surrendered. I yelled to them to get down, hold on till night."

Strom waited until dark and then ordered the men with him to move back. "There were not enough of us left to do anything over there, we were running short of ammunition, we had no communications with the rear, and so we picked up as many of our wounded as we could and brought them back across the bridge." When he got back, Strom discovered that from his company there were fourteen men and two officers left out of about 145 men and six officers.

On the morning of 21 January, as the survivors of Strom's 1st Battalion cowered under fire on the German side of the river, the leaders of the 36th Division tried to plan their next move. Colonel William Martin, commanding officer of the 143rd Regiment, held a conference at 9:45, furious that there were many men "who complain and try to return to the rear under pretense of illness." Walker came under intense pressure from Clark to get more men across the river in renewed attacks, even in daylight. Reluctantly, Walker ordered fresh assaults at both crossing points as soon as they could be organized. "I expect this attack to be a fizzle just as was the one last night. The stupidity of the higher command seems to be never-ending," Walker confided to his diary.

Little of the confusion in the killing field of the open Rapido plain had dissipated from the night before. Nobody seemed to be able to locate sufficient boats to make the crossing, and there was still no communication with the 141st Regiment men across the river. Smoke was used to shield the troops moving up to the crossing sites, but as the Germans were firing on preregistered targets, it had little effect apart from confusing the Allied gunners who were trying to fire in support of their men. Nevertheless, most of the 3rd Battalion of the 143rd Regiment succeeded in getting across on footbridges south of Sant' Angelo by about 6:30 P.M.

Bill Hartung, a twenty-one-year-old scout from the battalion, described his experience crossing the river, his first time in combat: "We went down a little horse and wagon road, and on the right side was an embankment about six feet high. We had already picked up our rubber boats, so we scraped against the side as we headed toward the river. A couple of hundred yards from the river, it didn't seem what we were walking on was dirt and rocks. We soon found out that it was dead GIs, stacked sometimes six high. They were from the crossing the night before. They never made it across the river." Hartung reached the Rapido at about 4 P.M., found a footbridge, and crossed together with his company commander and platoon leader. Immediately they became separated, and Hartung did not see either officer again. "The second scout and I continued forward. (We didn't know any better then.) Rifle fire was cracking around my head from all sides," Hartung continues. "Rodgie, the second scout, and I kept going, following the tape laid by the engineers the night before, until it ran out. I didn't know how I made it this far, as German rifle fire was that close to us. Finally it started getting a little lighter, and we saw where someone had started a foxhole the night before, but it was only about ten inches deep. The GI was still lying there, what was left of him. This was my first sight of a guy killed in combat, but wasn't going to be my last, even for that day."

The two scouts took off their equipment and started working to deepen the hole. For the moment they were protected by a smokescreen as well as mist and fog from the river. "We were about three feet deep when the Germans spotted us, then all hell broke loose. Screaming meemies [*Nebelwerfer* mortars], mortars, artillery fire, and machine gun fire about six to eight inches above ground hit us. Our equipment lying outside was blown to hell, the dirt we were piling up was blown back into the hole. We still didn't know how bad off we were because when they stopped firing for a few minutes, we would stand up and try to see what was going on. All we could see were GIs being lined up and taken prisoner. The enemy also had tanks dug in up to the barrel, and fortified as bunkers with steel and concrete about two feet thick. Anyone caught above ground was gone. We finally dug to about six feet deep, and water started coming in so we quit. By this time I was bleeding from the nose and one ear. Nothing was left above ground, and the side of the hole was caving in from almost direct hits."

Most of the 143rd Regiment troops were soon pinned down about five hundred yards from the river. Behind them, engineers struggled to build pontoon and Bailey bridges, but it was almost impossible to get the equipment forward, and the bridging sites were under constant fire. More men, however, were able to cross on footbridges later that night.

Second Lieutenant Robert Spencer of the 2nd Battalion, 143rd Regiment was called to a briefing held by the regimental officers late the same day. "The officers were noticeably nervous and upset," he recalls, "emphatically telling us that we were to launch another attack across the river the next morning and that we would succeed in breaking through the German lines. Failure would not be tolerated!" Spencer remembers the morning of 22 January as "cold, damp, and foggy . . . Our artillery had covered the area with smoke shells, making visibility near zero. Some time before daylight I was ordered to lead Company F across a narrow footbridge and engage the enemy along with the units who preceded us a short time earlier. At this time German mortar and artillery and small arms fire were extremely heavy."

After getting across by footbridge, Spencer and his men passed through a hole in the outer barbed-wire fence and continued to move forward. "Shortly afterward," he continues, "I came upon men from a preceding unit whose casualties were so numerous that many in the foxholes were afraid to move. The terrain over which we were attacking was level with no physical depressions to use for protective cover, and the Germans had their machine guns coordinated for defensive fire about two feet above ground. In addition, their mortars and artillery were zeroed in just in front of their lines, making it impossible to conduct an organized attack. Things were even more complicated because of poor visibility . . . I lost contact with part of my company."

As Spencer moved forward, he could hear Germans in the distance yelling to one another, but he could not tell how near they were. He remembers the cold and the darkness adding to "the terrible feeling of not knowing what could happen next, or where." Suddenly he was knocked out with a wound to the head. "When I came to I was dazed, sick, and scared," he continues. "As I lay in the cold not knowing how badly I was injured or what would happen to me, my head throbbed and I was afraid to move, or touch my wound." Luckily, he was discovered by a sergeant from his platoon, who bandaged him as best he could.

"As time passed I began to think and feel better," says Spencer. He decided to attempt to move to the rear on his own. "Visibility had improved and I could see an irrigation ditch that appeared to head toward the river. I slowly crawled to it and tumbled in, ignoring the foot of water since the protection was well worth my getting wet." Spencer inched his way along the ditch until a barbed-wire fence prevented him from moving farther. "I peered out of the ditch and saw that there was a hole in the fence a few yards over; but there was heavy fire at this time and I had to work up the nerve to chance it. I scrambled on all fours out of the ditch, pushed through the hole, and flung myself into the ditch again." The ditch brought him to the river's edge and he could see the footbridge over which he had earlier crossed. It was still intact, though most of it was underwater since the flotation had been hit by artillery. "I decided to crawl to the bridge, staying as low to the ground as possible," he says. "Again I had to work up nerve enough to attempt crossing to the other side as the only way I could possibly make it across was to crawl, holding on to the bridge to keep from being swept away by the strong current of cold water. Still sick and somewhat confused, I started across on all fours. How long it took I really don't know; I do know it was the longest few minutes of my life."

With his energy almost gone, he reached the other side. There he met an officer he knew waiting to lead his company across the river. "My appearance must have been terrible as I was bloody, wet and muddy. 'My God, Spencer,' he said, 'what happened to you?'"

On the morning of 22 January, Robert Spencer's company from 2nd Battalion, 143rd Regiment had consisted of three officers and one hundred and forty enlisted men. Twenty-four hours later, all the officers had been wounded and only fifteen of the enlisted men, many also wounded, made it back to safety.

Sunrise on the twenty-second had revealed the whereabouts of the attacking troops of 143rd Regiment to the Germans, and heavy fire plastered the small bridgehead. Increasing numbers of men—wounded, "helpers," shock cases, or those "carrying messages"—started trickling back across the river. At noon the regimental commander knew it was hopeless and ordered back the rest of the survivors.

Three hours later Bill Hartung, unaware of any orders, decided that enough was enough: "I told Rodgie we were getting out of there. I left first, not knowing which way was back. I never saw Rodgie again. I finally found parts of the tape and made it back to the Rapido. There were bodies everywhere, mostly parts: arms, legs, some decapitated, bodies with hardly any clothes left on. I thought I was going to get sick, but I guess I didn't have time, and there was always that spine-chilling cry for 'medic.' But there weren't any left. The bridge was about a foot under water most of the way, and stacked with bodies from upstream. A lot of the men drowned with all their equipment still on. I looked at some, that is when I noticed most died with that look of surprise on their face, like 'What happened?' and 'Why me to die this way?' "

Hartung made it back to the American side, and to the road he had come down the night before. "The piles of bodies were gone. I got back to our bivouac area out of artillery range. I laid down completely exhausted, and felt like I had turned into an old man overnight. I know I was never the same person again. When it hit me, I was angry; I cried and shook all over."

He was given a pill by a medic that sent him to sleep and when he awoke it was nearly dark. He spent the night in an outpost near the river, guarding against a possible German counterattack. "The cry for 'medic' was still heard from the other side of the river. Very sad."

At the 141st Regiment crossing site, men had also been able to make it across during the night of 21/22 January and then forced their way a thousand yards from the river. But again no Bailey bridges could be built, and soon all the company commanders had become casualties. When the 143rd withdrew around midday on the twenty-second, the Germans were able to concentrate all their fire on the 141st, with devastating effect. All the bridges and boats were destroyed, the men could neither escape nor be reinforced, and communications irretrievably broke down. Those on the Allied side of the river could only listen to the sounds of fighting ahead of them. By 10 P.M., the last of the American fire had died away.

Three days later the Americans requested a truce so that they could collect their dead and any wounded who might still be alive. The Germans
agreed, and carried the bodies down to the riverbank so that the Americans
would not be able to mark their positions. Several conversations took place
and hands were shaken as the work continued. Corporal Zeb Sunday from
the 143rd Regiment remembers: "This German came to our side and . . . I
gave him a cigarette. I talked to him just a few minutes. He talked pretty
good English. He said he had a brother in Brooklyn named Heinz." The Germans maintained a friendly atmosphere and were anxious to help. But it was
a gruesome business. "At the river Germans and Americans labored side by
side," a veteran reported. "A stack of eighty bodies was piled up along the
bank to be recovered later; these had received direct hits from mortar shells
while standing in their fighting holes and had no heads, shoulders or arms.
They proved difficult to identify."

The attack had been a bloody failure, and the Germans hadn't even
needed to reinforce their positions. They counted 430 American dead, had
captured 770, and there were another 900 dead or wounded on the American side of the river. Precisely nothing had been achieved. German casualties were 64 killed, 179 wounded. US newspaper reports described it as the
worst disaster since Pearl Harbor.

After the war the 36th Division demanded and received a congressional
investigation, hoping that Clark would take the blame for what amounted to
ordering a suicidal attack. A junior officer told his interrogator: "When I saw
my regimental commander standing with tears in his eyes as we moved up
to start the crossing, I knew something was wrong. I started out commanding a company of 184 men. Forty-eight hours later, 17 of us were left." Perhaps inevitably, Clark was exonerated by the investigation, but he remains a
hate figure for the division.

Maybe Clark should have learned some of the lessons of the difficulties
faced by the British in crossing the Garigliano. Maybe he thought his American boys would show the lackluster British how it should be done. In all
events, it was a badly prepared attack. The initial assault strength was only
four battalions, the enemy was alerted, and the infantry had to carry heavy
assault boats for two miles over boggy ground. From the first, the approaches and crossing places came under such intense fire that many of the
infantry threw down their loads and quit. The New Zealand officer Howard
Kippenberger stated bluntly two weeks later: "Nothing was right except the

courage." Even this, though, was not universal, and the US commanders came to have real cause for concern about the fighting spirit of the Texans. There are dark stories, many impossible to corroborate, about men refusing to cross the river or being sent forward at gunpoint. No doubt common sense and the instinct for survival prevailed over hopeless gallantry. With so many inexperienced men, and in conditions that were anyone's worst nightmare, it is hardly surprising that some of the men were, as one historian puts it, "found wanting."

When questioned about this, Bill Everett angrily denies that there were any cases of cowardice, but admits that many of the men simply cracked. "Guys disappeared and then would show up later, you know? Obviously, men maim themselves, blow off toes and stuff like that. They just lost it. A combat soldier has a funny psychology. We used to say, 'Every man has a string so long. You don't know how long yours is. I don't know how long mine is,' and you play it out. There is understanding about that—I'm talking about the people that would blow their fingers off with an M-1. You can imagine what that does. It blows the rest of the hand off. They're under stress. The men at the front understand. As you go back you hear stuff about you're a coward and this and that. That comes later. That's shit for guys like Patton. His closest place to a front line would be a tent somewhere. Those men up there [on the front line] are completely understanding of what happened. The compassion is great there. I mean, I've seen them take care of [one another] like they were little kids, you know, because they understood. They knew tomorrow they may be in the same slot."

7

Anzio and Cassino

As hopes faded for a breakthrough on the Rapido, on 22 January, British and American troops landed amid huge publicity at Anzio and nearby Nettuno, some sixty miles behind the Gustav Line. They met almost no resistance, men and arms poured ashore, and the accompanying press gleefully celebrated a great success. By the end of the day, thirty-six thousand men from the British 1st and US 3rd divisions were ashore, along with Rangers and Commandos, with the loss of only thirteen casualties.

For the Germans it had been a tactical rather than a strategic surprise. They had expected—and feared—a landing on one of the coasts of Italy from the start of the campaign. Although the Germans' aerial reconnaissance was virtually nonexistent, they knew of the buildup of ships in Naples harbor prior to 22 January. But the place and precise date of the amphibious landing were unknown. On the three nights before the landing, Kesselring had ordered a general invasion alert throughout Italy. But on the night of Operation Shingle, warned that the troops were tired by the continuous stand-to, he had countermanded the order. General Siegfried Westphal, Kesselring's chief of staff, adds in his account the story of a visit on 21 January to the Army Group headquarters by the chief of German counterespionage, Admiral Canaris: "His opinion of the enemy's amphibious intentions was urgently sought. Above all, we wanted to know the number and where-

abouts of warships, aircraft carriers and landing vessels. Canaris was unable
to give figures in detail, but firmly believed that there was in any case no
landing to be feared in the near future. It is evident that it was not only our
aerial reconnaissance that was practically paralyzed, but the counterespionage system as well. The enemy landed at Anzio and Nettuno a few hours
after Canaris's departure."

The news of the landings was greeted with alarm by the Germans. There
were only two battalions between Anzio and Rome twenty-two miles away,
and the tactical anti-invasion reserve was, as has been seen, fighting the
British in the Garigliano bridgehead. Precious Luftwaffe aircraft were sent
against the invasion armada, and troops as far away as France and Yugoslavia
were alerted to move to Anzio.

After the landings Churchill had envisaged that the commander of the
bridgehead, the American major general, John Lucas, would strike inland to
cut the supply route from Rome to the Gustav Line. But Lucas had had his
own guidance from his commanding officer, Mark Clark. "Don't stick your
neck out, Johnny," Clark had said to him as the expedition set sail. "I did at
Salerno, and I got into trouble." Lucas, led by Clark, was determined that the
bridgehead be secured against the inevitable counterattack, and in the vital
days after the landing the men dug in and established artillery positions. All
the time, troops and vehicles poured ashore, but the Germans recovered
from the shock remarkably quickly and within days Kesselring had moved
powerful forces to seal off the bridgehead, without, as had been hoped by the
Allies, weakening the garrison of the Gustav Line. The result was hard fighting but stalemate.

Churchill was incensed, commenting that he had hoped "we were hurling
a wild cat on the shore, but all we got was a beached whale." By the end of
January, Lucas had 70,000 troops and 356 tanks ashore. (And 18,000 other
vehicles. Churchill asked in amazement, "How many of our men are driving
or looking after 18,000 vehicles in this narrow space? We must have a great
superiority of chauffeurs.") Yet Lucas was still unable even to attempt a
breakout. His feelings were committed to his diary, which shows that he had
had grave reservations about the landings even before they were undertaken:
"This whole affair had a strong odor of Gallipoli and apparently the same
amateur was still on the coach's bench," he had written on 10 January.

The fighting at Anzio, among the most difficult in the war, is outside the
scope of this book, which is concerned with the larger-scale fighting on the

Gustav Line. Whether more boldness in the first few days would have delivered the desired results has been much debated. In fact, the perennial problem of shortage of shipping meant that not enough troops could be landed quickly enough both to secure and to break out of the bridgehead simultaneously. Even one of Lucas's severest critics, the British major general, W. R. C. Penney, has admitted, "We could have had one night in Rome and 18 months in P.W. camps."

With the bridgehead sealed off, the realization came that the Germans could move reinforcements by land to Anzio quicker than the Allies could by sea. From being the move that would clear the way for the troops at Cassino, Anzio itself now required assistance from those soldiers. The tail had begun to wag the dog. Because of Anzio, it was impossible to do the logical thing and wait for spring and improved conditions for the Allies' armor. A move that was meant to help the attackers of Cassino ended up doing exactly the opposite. When the inevitable German counterattacks started at Anzio, Clark was forced to launch further rushed assaults on Cassino to take the pressure off his precious bridgehead.

It was bad timing. The Anzio force landed just as attacks by the British and French on the flanks of Cassino were running out of steam. Neither British X Corps in the Garigliano bridgehead nor the French Expeditionary Corps in the mountains north of the monastery were about to "nip out" the Cassino position, and the main frontal attack on the Liri valley had, of course, ended in disaster for the US 36th Division. But the pressure on Clark, not just from Anzio but from opinion and politicians at home, made it essential that he kept his men at Cassino on the offensive. "We have a great need to keep continually engaging them," Churchill was urging at this time. "Even a battle of attrition is better than standing by and watching the Russians fight."

The only reasonably fresh force that Clark had available was the US 34th Red Bull Division, which had been earmarked to exploit a breakthrough into the Liri valley. This division was holding the front between the French on their right and the US 36th Division on their left. In front of them was Cassino town and the Cassino Massif, topped by the enormous monastery.

It was here that Clark chose to send in the 34th Division while at the same time urging Juin and McCreery to do all they could to press attacks in their sectors. As has been seen, there was little the British could achieve, having only just held on against the German counterattacks of the previous two

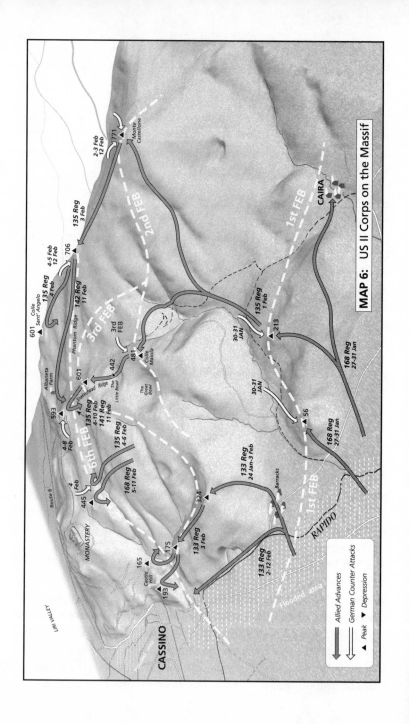

MAP 6: US II Corps on the Massif

LIRI VALLEY

MONASTERY

Castle Hill ▲ 165

193 ▲

175 ▲

CASSINO

Route 6

445 ▲

4 Feb

168 Reg 5-11 Feb

135 Reg 4-6 Feb

141 Reg 11 Feb

135 Reg 4-10 Feb

601 ▲

593 ▲

Albaneta Farm

Snakeshead Ridge

442 ▲

The Little Bowl

481 ▲

Colle Maiola

3rd FEB

Phantom Ridge

142 Reg 11 Feb

706 ▲

135 Reg 7 Feb

4-5 Feb 12 Feb

Colle Sant' Angelo

601 ▲

135 Reg 3 Feb

771 ▲

Monte Castellone

2-3 Feb 12 Feb

2nd FEB

135 Reg 1 Feb

213 ▲

30-31 JAN

168 Reg 27-31 Jan

CAIRA

1st FEB

56 ▲

30-31 JAN

168 Reg 27-31 Jan

The Great Bowl

324 ▲

133 Reg 24 Jan-3 Feb

133 Reg 3 Feb

Barracks

133 Reg 2-12 Feb

1st FEB

RAPIDO

Flooded area

6th FEB

Allied Advances

German Counter Attacks

▲ Peak ▼ Depression

days. The French, too, were exhausted after their failed attempt to take and hold Monte San Croce, but Juin reluctantly agreed to ready his men for a new attack on 25 January.

Clark's plan was for Ryder's 34th Division to attack along the far side of the river into the north of the town and, in a separate thrust, directly across the Cassino Massif to emerge in the Liri valley some three to four miles behind the Rapido and Monte Cassino. The first objective was an old barracks two miles north of Cassino, near the river, and a piece of high ground to its left known as Point 213, which guarded the approach to Caira village. Here the Rapido was less wide and deep than further downstream, but it still presented a formidable antitank barrier. In addition, the ground around the river on both sides was flooded and soggy. On the German side of the river was a belt of antipersonnel mines some three hundred yards deep, after which the attacking troops would have to cross an absolutely flat plain from which all vegetation had been removed to provide a perfect field of fire for the numerous machine guns emplaced in portable steel pillboxes and elaborately prepared bunkers at the base of the hill. The few buildings on this plain had been heavily fortified and housed self-propelled and antitank guns. About one hundred yards from the base of the hill there was a continuous band of high barbed wire approximately fifteen yards in depth as well as more protecting individual foxholes. One battalion leader with the 168th Regiment commented that there was "enough barbed wire to fence in all the farms in Iowa and Illinois." If the attacking troops broke through all this, they were faced with the daunting task of capturing a series of steep mountains behind, all protected by barbed wire, mines, bunkers, and steel-turreted machine gun positions. Simply the terrain up on the massif presented the attackers with serious challenges. "The ridges, when seen from a distance, look like smooth, bare slopes running up and down," says an Allied official account of the fighting. "At Cassino this appearance concealed the horrible nature of the ground. This was unspeakably rough and broken with minor ridges, knolls and hollows jumbled all together. At one point deep clefts might be the obstacle, at another sheer rock faces or steep slabs, or all three might be found in a few acres . . . To attacking troops the ground set vile tactical puzzles one after another. This or that knoll or ridge might seem to be promising objectives but would turn out to be commanded from an unlikely direction by another knoll or ridge or by several. A line of approach might look as if it would 'go' and would turn out to be blocked by some impassable obstacle. The advantages of the ground lay wholly with defending troops."

The initial objective, the barracks, was heavily fortified with pillboxes built under the rubble of the old building. Two battalions of the 133rd Regiment, supported by tanks, attacked across the Rapido at 10 P.M. on 24 January, aiming for the barracks and Point 213. They immediately ran into trouble. Exploding mines on both sides of the river caused casualties and confusion. The tanks tried to break down the high far bank of the river by blasting over a thousand high-explosive 75mm shells into it, but without success, and heavy fire from the barracks drove back the infantry advance. By midnight on 25 January, although the regiment's third battalion had crossed, the Americans had only a shallow bridgehead on the German side of the river.

During the day of 26 January, attempts to reinforce the beleaguered infantry with tanks failed when the first half a dozen became bogged down before reaching the river, blocking the way for those following. That night 1st Battalion, 135th Regiment got a company across the river, but they, too, were unable to move forward. The smoke of battle had made American artillery support difficult during the day. Watching from an observation post on Monte Trocchio, Ivar Awes remembers, "You felt so bad for the infantry." During 26 January he had had a call from his commanding officer: "Ivar, what's going on up there?" the major asked.

"Well, I can hear a lot of noise over by the barracks," Awes replied.

"Can you see it?"

"No, it's completely fogged from the smoke mixing with the mist."

"Oh, God, I wish you could see it," the major exclaimed.

On the morning of 27 January, the 168th Regiment was committed at a crossing site slightly upriver, preceded by a platoon of tanks. Some tanks slipped off the narrow routes that were underwater in many places, but two were across by 8:30 and two more an hour later. None could follow as these leading tanks had so churned up the ground. But the infantry advanced closely behind the four tanks. The commander of one of the battalions reported later: "As I see it, there were three main functions performed by the tanks of the 756th Tank Battalion. The first was to provide a passageway through the antipersonnel minefields by driving through them and exploding the AP [antipersonnel] mines. The infantry could follow the tank tracks without setting off more mines . . . The second main function of the tanks was to get the infantry through the high barbed wire. The third and probably most important was to scare 'hell' out of the German machine gunners to such an extent they fired little for fear of catching a 75mm shell at point-blank range." In turn, the infantry helped the tanks by giving them protection against antitank and self-propelled guns. As the report continues, "Once an SP [self-propelled artillery piece] was definitely located and foot troops moved in on it, it did not stay long in that locality."

All four tanks were out of action by 1 P.M., two hit by antitank fire, one by a mine, the fourth by an artillery shell, but infantry got to the base of Point 213 very early on the twenty-eighth. But then the company commander, deciding that his position would become untenable with daylight, withdrew from this vital position. "As he did so," the official history reports, "the withdrawal turned into an uncontrollable rout. The troops fled across the river."

Believing a general withdrawal was taking place, other men on the far bank of the Rapido panicked and started retreating back across the river. Only here were they stopped, but the two remaining companies on the far side were now too exposed, and they also had to to be pulled back. These men were then sent to another crossing place five hundred yards to the north. Here they went over and advanced about a mile towards the village of Caira, where they dug in. Meanwhile, engineers worked to create "corduroy" roads of tree trunks lashed together in order to try to get more tanks across in support of an attack planned for the next day, the twenty-ninth.

———————

On 23 January, Clark had ordered Juin to turn his French corps sharply to the left to attack Colle Belvedere and the high ground to the right of the 34th Division's effort, thereby, he hoped, protecting the Americans' flank and drawing German troops away from Cassino itself. The French were less than amused, one commander commenting, "Storm Belvedere? Who dreamed up that one? A crazy gamble, *mon général!*"

Juin, too, was loath to give up his attack toward Atina, which he saw as the key to a wide outflanking of the Gustav Line around Cassino: "I was asked to carry out a mission," he wrote after the war, "which under other circumstances I would have deemed impossible, first of all because I didn't like the idea of changing course for the sake of such a negligible distance, that it would extend my front which was already sufficiently stretched and would distract me from my objective, Atina, which I regarded as essential for the development of the army maneuver. I was therefore obliged to suspend all operations on my front except the very eccentric one suggested to me by the Commander of the Fifth Army." It was also, Juin noted, one of the least accessible parts of the Gustav Line, backed by the enormous snow-tipped peak of Monte Cairo, which at 1,669 meters dwarfed even the monastery. The initial advance would involve crossing two rivers, the Secco and the Rapido, and then breaking through the defenses in the valley, before climbing more than eight hundred meters over bare rock, all the time under direct observation by German artillery spotters on Monte Cifalco.

He also had very little time to prepare. Clark wanted the attack two days later, and saw it as essential to the safety of his American Red Bulls. For the French, the supply difficulties were acute. Juin had only one inadequate mountain road serving his sector, and the route was under constant German artillery fire. Nevertheless, preparations started immediately with Juin's Tunisians from the 3rd Algerian Division chosen to lead the attack.

Because of a shortage of mules, the attacking troops were forced to carry all their equipment on an eight-hour hike through the mountains to the French forward positions. To avoid artillery and mortar attack, this had to be performed in the dark, on treacherous mountain slopes, guided only by a small white patch tied onto the pack of the man in front. Among them was René Martin, a sergeant in charge of one of the regiment's 3rd Battalion mortar sections. Just to get into position for the main attack, his unit had to cross the Secco River. "[The engineers] built a small provisional bridge which was destroyed by German fire so a rope was stretched across the river—it seemed enormous. In front of me was a little corporal, he was tiny." Martin himself had water up to his neck as they waded through, holding onto the rope. "This little guy, he held his pack in the air and was walking underwater and hoisting himself up by the rope in order to breathe. That's just to tell you how we reached the [jumping-off] site. We had to begin combat soaked to the skin." Martin had seen plenty of fighting. He had started his military service in southern Tunisia on the frontier, was released, got married, and had a son. The infant was three months old when Martin was recalled as the Americans landed at Algiers. He was then sent to fight for the Germans. When the cease-fire was announced, he went home, only to be recalled once more two days later to fight again, this time against the Germans. But in all his experience, this objective was something else. "When we looked up and saw what we had to do, we said that it was impossible. Everyone thought it was madness."

Early on 25 January, Martin's battalion, led by Commandant Gandoët, began the new offensive. "The battalion is physically and mentally ready," Gandoët wrote in his diary. "Ready to lead a bayonet charge, to be killed on the mountainside, to deal the enemy all sorts of blows." The aim was to capture Hill 470 to secure the entrance to the Secco valley and then push on along the north side of Belvedere to seize high ground on the northern end of the Belvedere/Abate escarpment. A ravine had been chosen—and named the *ravin Gandoët*—as an axis of attack since it seemed to offer cover from artillery fire and the possibility of surprising the defenders on the objective. As ever, the Germans counterattacked every gain the French made, and the early objective of Hill 470, high ground near the front line, was very hard won.

A French account written directly after the war relates how the wounded French officer in charge of the initial attack handed over command to a trusted Tunisian, Lieutenant el Hadi. Twice the summit was captured and twice the attackers were driven off by fierce counterattacks. Finally, at about 10 P.M., el Hadi rallied his troops and pressed forward. "His forearm has been shot off by a shell," the account reads. "For half an hour he leads the company, dragging it behind him. A veritable flag to his men, he shrieks and carries on like a madman. The small groups advance step by step. They arrive at the summit. At that moment Lieutenant el Hadi is blasted by a machine gun bullet that pierces his body. He shouts to the Tirailleur Barelli who is just next to him, 'You, send up a flare.' Then he collapsed and crying up to the heavens, 'Vive la France,' he died on the conquered peak."

The rest of 3rd Battalion made their way across the valley and into the mountains beyond, supported for part of the way by American tanks. The story of their attack has been documented by René Chambe, an eyewitness, albeit one keen to stress the heroic nature of the French forces' effort. He describes how the leading company, commanded by Lieutenant Jordy, reached the *ravin Gandoët* and were shocked by the task that lay ahead of them. From afar it had looked manageable, but up close "the slope of the gorge was so steep that it sent a shiver down one's spine . . . To make things worse it was blocked with slabs of rock, some of them enormous . . . Getting across them would involve a combination of mountaineering and acrobatics. Climb up there? All of 2,500 feet, every man with an enormous load, using

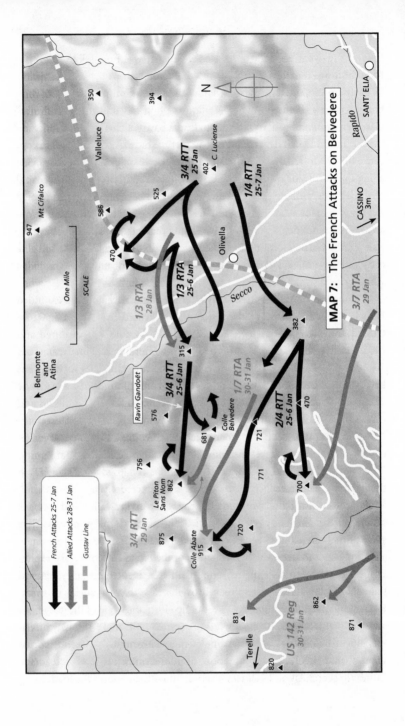

MAP 7: The French Attacks on Belvedere

French Attacks 25-7 Jan
Allied Attacks 28-31 Jan
Gustav Line

SCALE
One Mile

N

Belmonte
and Atina

Mt Cifalco
947 ▲

350 ▲
Valleluce ○

394 ▲

SANT' ELIA ○

586 ▲

525 ▲

470 ▲

C. Luciense
402 ▲

Olivella ○

3/4 RTT
25 Jan

1/4 RTT
25-7 Jan

CASSINO
3m

Rapido

1/3 RTA
28 Jan

1/3 RTA
25-6 Jan

Secco

315 ▲

382 ▲

3/7 RTA
29 Jan

3/4 RTT
25-6 Jan

Ravin Gandoët

576 ▲

1/7 RTA
30-31 Jan

Colle
Belvedere

721 ▲

470

2/4 RTT
25-6 Jan

756 ▲

681 ▲

771 ▲

700 ▲

3/4 RTT
29 Jan

Le Piton
Sans Nom
862 ▲

875 ▲

720 ▲

Colle Abate
915 ▲

831 ▲

862 ▲

US 142 Reg
30-31 Jan

871 ▲

Terelle

820 ▲

only his feet, his hands, his knees and his teeth. Almost three times the height of the Eiffel Tower, to be clambered up foot by foot with no steps, no handrail, no one to help."

Nevertheless, they began the epic climb and soon found that at various points the ravine came under German machine gun fire. This necessitated volunteers emerging from cover to launch grenade attacks against pillboxes. At 4 P.M. German shells started falling, but still the men climbed, tired, parched with thirst, and drenched in sweat in spite of the cold. "The climb became a nightmare," Chambe continues. "The physical and moral effort demanded of them stretched the men to the limits of human resistance, eventually taking them beyond. Tirailleurs who had so far passed through unscathed felt a black veil fall over their eyes, the result of overstrained hearts and complete muscular exhaustion. They had to stop, to fight against blacking out, to hang desperately on to the edge of the void."

Eight hours after beginning their climb, the men reached their objective, Point 681. They found it lightly manned and proceeded to clear out the Germans they encountered. As darkness fell, they dug in, elated at their victory, but out of contact with their superiors and having almost completely exhausted their food and water.

All along the front, gains had been made, but at a great cost. To the south of Colle Belvedere, the 2nd Battalion of the Tunisians had attacked toward Point 700, which dominated the Sant' Elia–Terelle road. Driven off by a counterattack, they remained in control of the southern slopes of Belvedere. The French commanders did all they could to push more men forward and plug the gaps in the line. The next day more of Gandoët's men made the terrible climb up to Jordy's company, arriving at 2 P.M., and were immediately ordered to continue the attack toward Point 862. At the same time, 2nd Battalion would clear Belvedere and also push on to Colle Abate, Point 915. By 8 P.M. Belvedere was secured, but Captain Léoni, who had taken over command of the 2nd Battalion, urged a rest before pushing on for Colle Abate. This was refused, and the remnants of the battalion pressed forward at 9 P.M. With hardly any men left, they reached the summit at 2:30 A.M. the following day. Gandoët's men, attacking from the north of Belvedere, also secured their objective, Point 862, known to the French as *le Piton sans Nom*. They were greatly aided by having reestablished contact with the rear, which enabled them to bring down a huge weight of artillery fire on the peak.

Von Senger had good cause for alarm at this deep thrust into his line, and moved quickly to reinforce the sector. The next day he launched counterattacks that drove the French off their forward positions and back towards the Secco River. René Martin had only just succeeded in setting up a position for his mortars when "a warrant officer suddenly shouted 'Get out, get out, get out' because the Germans were advancing with an entire regiment and we were so few. We had to retreat towards Gandoët's Command Post. He told us to stay there." The counterattacks continued the next day, and Belvedere itself looked like being surrounded. "Belvedere was covered with little bunkers," says Martin. "We entered them and the Germans began shooting from all sides. We were trapped. There were only six or seven tirailleurs left out of a company of thirty-eight."

Luckily, Martin found a well-built former German position. "The Germans had dug a hole in the rock like a round well sheltered by a boulder above creating a sort of hat. I found myself stuck there with Sergeant Blanchard and, as it was completely round, like a well, we slept me with my head between his legs, him with his head between my legs, curled up like two dogs. At this point, the Germans were shooting sixty shells per minute. For five nights without water, they continued to shell; without food, nothing. Scientifically after five days, you go mad. My lips were painfully dry. I had a little tin of peas that I would crush against my lips to ease the chapping. I gave some to Blanchard too and like this we eased the pain."

But the situation was restored, with the help of the Allied artillery, now familiar with the various peaks and ravines on the Belvedere Massif. The Germans were also beginning to weaken, and on the 29th Gandoët succeeded in recapturing *le Piton sans Nom*. Two days later Colle Abate was also recaptured, and at last the remnants of the Tunisian regiment were relieved by Algerian troops.

"The Arabs did things the Europeans would never have done," says René Martin. "It's the Arabs that say this, 'The Moroccans are warriors, the Algerians are men and the Tunisians are women.' But for women they managed the impossible. It's for that reason that so many of them were killed."

As the survivors of the Tunisian regiment trudged back to Sant' Elia, they were greeted by Juin. "Our hearts overflowing with pity and pride," he wrote. "We saw them coming back, haggard, unshaven, their uniforms in rags and soaked with mud, the glorious survivors of the regiment." Glorious but few. Of the assaulting companies only 30 percent had returned unscathed.

For Juin, the action of the previous five days was more fuel for his dissatisfaction with the Anglo-American leadership. With the Gustav Line pierced at last, why was the French effort not properly reinforced? Were the French still not trusted? If the two attacks were supposed to occur simultaneously, why were the Americans still down in the Rapido valley rather than on the heights to the south of Belvedere as scheduled? On 29 January, with the 168th Regiment of the US 34th Division dug in only a mile from the river, Juin wrote to Clark, "The 3rd Algerian Division has carried out, at an unbelievable cost and with severe losses, the mission you entrusted to them . . . I have absolutely no further reserves to supply an offensive effort. Also, on its left, the 34th US Division hasn't yet set foot on the heights southwest of Caira and the current situation for the 3rd Algerian Division is extremely hazardous." He went on to threaten that unless the US troops started getting on to their objectives, he would be forced to withdraw his men from their exposed and isolated positions on the Belvedere Massif for which they had fought so hard. According to Juin, the letter "arrived like a bombshell in General Clark's headquarters."

In fact, on the same day that Juin was writing this letter, the 168th Regiment launched a full-scale attack across the Rapido against the high ground blocking the way to Caira village, Points 213 and 56, and the ridge running between them. At first no tanks could get across, and the infantry found itself pinned down again by minefields and barbed wire, but in the afternoon the tanks started arriving. More than fifty had been sent forward, of which about a dozen succeeded in reaching the infantry across the river. This was largely due to the more favorable northern crossing point and the efforts of the division's engineers to improve the approach routes. The others were knocked out or simply bogged down in the mud. But the few vehicles that made it were enough to explode the antipersonnel mines and clear the wire, and by dusk all three battalions of the regiment had secured their objectives.

Elaborate defenses were found within the knolls—concrete bunkers big enough to house up to thirty men, with bunks, plentiful food and ammunition, and efficient heating arrangements. The following day German counterattacks were beaten back and Caira village captured. A state of confusion still existed with German and American positions so close that the soldiers could hear the enemy talking. One US officer, returning from the hospital with thirty replacements, led his men straight into the German lines, where they were captured.

Further back, ever-wishful rumors made up for the lack of information from the front line. On 30 January, Tom Kindre, the ordnance officer with 34th Division, wrote in his diary, "Every day Cassino is reported taken, every night the rumor is disproved." Ryder, at least, was aware of the hard fighting still needed before Cassino could be captured. From intercepted radio messages he knew that von Senger had been busy reinforcing the Cassino sector. A fresh German regiment was put into the town, and on the thirtieth two battalions of the 90th Panzer Grenadier Division were alerted to move from the Garigliano sector to the Cassino Massif. With them came the headquarters of the division, commanded by Maj. Gen. Ernst Günther Baade. A close friend of von Senger, Baade was an eccentric officer and popular with his men. He liked to wear a kilt over his uniform and instead of a pistol he sported a huge bone-handled dagger. Although like von Senger an Anglophile, he was determined to resist capture and kept a monk's cowl in his bunker to disguise himself if need be. Baade assumed control of the whole sector and brought with him a battalion of the 1st Parachute Division.

On 1 February, Ryder ordered the 133rd Regiment to attack the barracks again in the hope of opening the narrow road into the northern end of Cassino town. Now supported by tanks, the Americans were at last able to clear the wrecked building and, the next day, advance down the small shelf, some 300 to 400 yards wide, between the sheer walls of the massif and the Rapido River. At the same time, one of their companies pushed along the ridge above the road, heading for Point 175 over the north end of the town. Once they had battered their way into the northern outskirts of Cassino, there ensued vicious street fighting. Each building had been converted into a strong point and progress was measured in yards. The Germans had excellent observation from the high ground behind the town, resulting in heavy American casualties. The tanks found they had little field of fire, and when one was knocked out by an antitank shell it often blocked the progress of those behind. "Gun emplacements were also camouflaged in piles of rubble presumably created by our own artillery and tank fire," Maj. Warren C. Chapman of the 133rd Regiment reported after the fighting. "Their fires were well planned and coordinated so that each gun was covered by another." The bazooka, by which infantry could fire antitank projectiles from a shoulder-borne tube, was of utmost importance, not just for taking out German tanks, but for blasting holes in the sides of buildings to gain entry. "In many cases 'No Man's Land' consisted of about a 10-yard space between two houses," Chapman continues. "This was ideal for playing catch with grenades." The fighting continued for over a week, but the attackers made little headway.

A key objective was Castle Hill, which rose almost vertically from the northern end of the town to a height of 193 meters, topped by the ruined fort in which Tony Pittaccio and his friends had played at soldiers. Men from the 100th Nisei Regiment, made up of Japanese-Americans from Hawaii, attacked across the deep ravine that separated the castle from Point 175 but were unable to hold the position.

Up on the massif, however, luck had been with the Americans.

8

The Cassino Massif

While the 133rd Regiment of the US 34th Division was still clearing the barracks, Ryder launched his 135th Regiment on to the Cassino Massif to take the high ground on the left of the French and push on to seize the monastery and the mountains beyond it. Their first objectives were Colle Maiola and Monte Castellone. "Initially we were in reserve," remembers Don Hoagland of the 3rd Battalion, 135th Regiment. "Then we moved to the little town of Caira. We moved up from there and our mission was to get up on the hill behind the Germans. It was so foggy that morning—we were lucky." Moving in single file up the mountain, the men were completely hidden from the German defensive positions dug in to the forward slopes of the range. As they passed invisibly, the men could hear Germans talking nearby. "We were way up above them and got past in the fog. We could never have done it otherwise," says Hoagland. Both objectives—Colle Maiola and Monte Castellone—were captured by 10 A.M., 1 February. Hoagland, now preparing defensive positions on Maiola, had not even had to fire his rifle.

The next day, while the men on Castellone fought off a counterattack from the alarmed Germans, others from Hoagland's battalion pushed forward from Maiola along a ridge that led, eventually, to the monastery. Because of its shape, it was named Snakeshead Ridge. By the end of the day they were some 850 yards from Monte Calvary, better known at the time as

Point 593, a hillock with steep sides about two thousand yards from the rear entrance to the monastery. This position, on top of which lay the ruins of a small fort, blocked progress to the monastery itself and provided its occupiers with good observation and field of fire in all directions.

At the end of 2 February, Clark was much encouraged by these successes, informing Alexander that "Present indications are that the Cassino heights will be captured very soon." On the next day, the 135th Regiment was reinforced by a battalion from the 168th and continued the drive southward toward the Liri valley. From Castellone, a battalion advanced along Phantom Ridge, which ran, parallel to Snakeshead, along to Colle Sant' Angelo, and seized the high ground in the middle known as Point 706. On the left, however, fierce resistance on Snakeshead Ridge and from the high ground to its right meant that there was little progress. On the same day, the Germans counterattacked Colle Maiola, where Don Hoagland's section was in a defensive position.

Underneath about a foot of soil there was solid rock, so it was impossible to dig in. For protection the men had to scrape small hollows and then pile stones around them to create "sangars."* The attack was repulsed, and the rest of the battalion advanced the next day to within two hundred yards of Point 593, while on their left another battalion of the 135th Regiment pushed forward close to Point 445, even nearer the monastery. Over on the right-hand Phantom Ridge, progress toward positions on Colle Sant' Angelo was briefly made before the attackers were driven off back to Point 706.

The Germans were now clinging to the last slopes in front of the Liri valley. Immediately behind them lay the sought-after route to Rome. If the Americans could just clear these last positions, the monastery and the entire Gustav Line would be outflanked. But the attackers themselves were suffering. "There was never a time that we were free of intermittent or heavy mortar fire," says Hoagland. "We took lots of counterattacks up there. You have your men placed expecting that you are going to be hit. It was almost always at night, and they came in quietly to get as close as they could. All of a sudden there's bodies moving out there in front of you. Every night there would be another attack and although we were able to beat them all off, eventually

---

*"Sangar," a corruption of the Hindustani word *sunga,* was a rock parapet that was created in front of a position by moving loose stones into a defensive wall. The British had become very familiar with these during warfare along the Northwest Frontier.

it's fatigue that hits you as much as anything. I remember hearing Leroy Rogers, who was one of my platoon leaders, hollering at them one night, saying, 'Come on, you sons of bitches Krauts, come and get us.' "

Once the Germans had recovered from the deep incursions of 1 February, they quickly reorganized and made the attackers aware of how carefully the avenues of approach to the monastery had been covered by mortar and machine gun fire. "The Germans knew how to set defensive positions," says Hoagland. "They had all this low land covered and of course they had had the time to tell where were the likely spots that you could attack or set up your own mortars."

As much as enemy fire, it was the conditions up on the massif that wore out the attackers. "It was brutal country to fight in," says Hoagland, "with cliffs that you could walk into in the dark without realizing they're there." On 4 February the weather worsened, and there was a heavy snowstorm, further increasing the misery of men already soaked by freezing rain. Intermittent mortar fire kept the men from sleeping, as well as causing casualties. "You'd lay down at night in your shallow hole," remembers Hoagland, "and if you had a couple blankets you would put one down in the wet hole, lie down, and pull a wet blanket over you. That's the way you slept."

Although, of course, the weather was the same for the defenders, at least the Germans had had plenty of time to blast deep dugouts in the rocks, and they had also stockpiled food, water, and ammunition on the massif. For the Americans, the closer they advanced to the monastery, the more difficult it was to supply the forward troops. Everything had to be carried by mule or porter up the narrow, steep paths from Caira down below.

The division was now suffering appalling casualties. Journalist Gordon Gammack reported after the battle, "In deep snow banks, up and down rocky, slippery, treacherous slopes there was established here during the first two weeks of February probably the longest litter train for the evacuation of the wounded in the history of the American army."

Medic Robert Koloski, in charge of the battalion aid station for Hoagland's unit, had set up his post in Caira in "a farm outbuilding, with only a partial roof, but it did have walls. By that time," he says, "they were suffering a large number of casualties. There were some pretty extensive wounds, and more numerous than we had handled prior to that, including the African campaign and the early campaign in Italy. We had never experienced the volume of casualties we had then. We knew that our guys were taking a rather considerable beating." When a man arrived at Koloski's station, his wound would be doused in an antibiotic powder (which Koloski kept in a large salt shaker) and then bandaged up. "We also tried to minimize the effects of shock and we used a great deal of blood plasma," he remembers. "We also used morphine very liberally. To start out we were told not to use more than one syringe on a badly wounded man, but we ended up knocking in about two or three of them, which we slammed right through the clothing."

In a division of some 15,000 men, 1,000 were medics. There were three enlisted medical aid men with every company, with their own station, from where the wounded would be evacuated by litter bearers to the company or battalion aid station. "Early on we learned that if you could get them out of there just as quickly as you can, patch them up, they could make it back. At that point in time, you were probably accomplishing all that you could accomplish," says Koloski. There might have to be emergency surgery, particularly with stomach wounds, but speed was of the essence to get them out and back up the chain, not just for their own well-being, but also to keep the decks clear in case of a sudden catastrophic run of battle casualties.

From Koloski's aid post the men were taken back to a collecting station some quarter of a mile behind the lines, then to a clearing station, really a small hospital, then finally to proper hospitals outside the control of the division. "So you were no longer the glamorous doctor, you were a first-aid man," says Koloski, "but it was a good feeling too: the opportunity to do something with these people. You felt you were doing something."

The largest percentage of wounds were from mortars rather than artillery shells or bullets. "Considering that every soldier had a rifle and there were machine guns and pistols, a startlingly small number were bullet wounds," says Koloski. "All rifle fire really did was keep your head down." Mortars were the most feared of the enemy's weapons as far as infantry were concerned. They "are more severe [than artillery]," another American doctor has written. "Mortars are more accurate. Falling close to men, they cause extensive mutilation. It is not unusual for one man to have compound fractures of several extremities at one time as well as numerous penetrating wounds of the abdomen and face."

Ernie Pyle, on one of the few occasions he talks graphically about the reality of battlefield wounds, expresses his amazement at some of the lucky escapes: "Sometimes a bullet can go clear through a man and not hurt him much. Bullets and fragments do crazy things. Our surgeons picked out more than two hundred pieces of shrapnel from one man. There was hardly a square inch of him from head to toe that wasn't touched. Yet none made a vital hit, and the man lived."

But the inverse was also true. A single tiny, white-hot piece of shrapnel could do enormous damage. "If there was blood pumping out of an artery, that we could do very little with," says Koloski. "We had no equipment and for the most part none of us had the skills, except the surgeons, and by the time you got that man down to the surgeons he would have bled out. Usually if they lived past a clearing station they were going to make it."

However, the greatest drain on the manpower of the 34th Division up on the massif was not battle wounds but "trench foot." If a man's feet remained wet and cold for a long period of time, he would soon be unable to walk. "We didn't really understand a lot of it," says Koloski. "The feet swelled to the point that men's toes literally looked like sausages and if it was untreated long enough the man lost his feet. It encompassed having frostbite and chilblains; cold and damp were the two factors involved. You tried to keep your feet dry as much as possible. To do that, of course, you needed extra socks, which weren't usually available. Once their feet swelled up, if they tried walking they were in great pain. As they swelled they turned blue. If it wasn't treated for long enough it turned into gangrene." Trench foot was treated with gentian violet, a cure-all also used for crab lice. "It's a very old-fashioned remedy," says Koloski. "It's not a true antibiotic, more like hydrogen peroxide. It was largely ineffective." The result was that the men were lost to the division. "We early on realized that there was no point in keeping these people around; there was nothing they could do. For all practical purposes they were useless as soldiers so they were evacuated. A lot were assigned to various base-unit operations. I don't think we got more than about 10 percent back to the line. It was equipment failure. We never really had the right equipment at the right time. Someone apparently decided that Italy was going to be dry, but it was anything but dry."

Battle wounds, trench foot, and pneumonia were steady drains on the 34th Division troops trying to break through the mountains beyond Cassino. Clark already had one regiment from the US 36th Division—Clare Cunningham's 142nd, which had escaped the Rapido bloodbath—fighting up on the massif, and he now ordered that the shattered remnants of the other two regiments should be sent up. The 142nd had been fighting on the left flank of the French, and were now ordered to reinforce 34th Division positions on Monte Castellone. On 5 February, Cunningham's unit made the climb up the mountain among the dead of the 34th Division, and Cunningham took over a two-man foxhole built by the Germans. This was about six feet wide and seven feet long. He shared it with his buddy, Stanley Katula. It was a frightening spot. "It seemed like we were under observation all the time," says Cunningham. "They were just looking down on us all day long. They knew every move we were making." Huddled together for warmth, the two men nevertheless suffered from the 'bitter, terrible cold . . . frozen feet.' There was also a sense of powerlessness—Cunningham had no idea what was happening fifty feet away, and movement in daylight was impossible. "Some would just go berserk," Cunningham remembers. "A forward artillery observer who had been with us just two or three days panicked and took off, no rifle, no nothing, running right through to the German lines. We yelled at him—he was so new we didn't know his name—we just kept hollering, 'You're going the wrong way, you're going the wrong way.' We never heard from him again."

While their rear was being guarded, the troops on the Snakeshead and Phantom Ridges, and directly in front of the monastery, continued to press their attacks, small groups of men inching their way forward across ridges or up slopes. The focus was now firmly on Monte Calvario, Point 593, identified as the key tactical position on the massif. In confused fighting the vital hill changed hands several times over the next few days, as attacks on the monastery itself were pressed on the left by the 168th Regiment. John Johnstone, a Chicago-born private, was just coming up to his twentieth birthday when his unit was ordered to attack on 8 February. He had been with the 168th Regiment for only three months. "The first sergeant came round," explains Johnstone, "and said, 'OK men, here's what's going to happen. At three o'clock there is going to be a rolling barrage for fifteen minutes, then I'll blow the whistle and we're going to move forward.'" Before the sergeant left, he asked Johnstone his name. When Johnstone replied the sergeant said, "OK, you're an acting sergeant for now."

"At three o'clock the rolling barrage came," says Johnstone, "and at three-fifteen we heard the whistle, although we didn't know where the sergeant was." Johnstone turned to his buddy and said, "Come on, Harry, let's go."

"I'm not going, you go," he replied.

"We're a team, we've got to go."

"I am not going," came the final reply.

So Johnstone emerged alone from his sangar and, together with a lieutenant, his runner, the BAR (Browning automatic rifle) man, four other men, and a sergeant, started the attack. Having advanced about a hundred yards, "we fell under small-arms fire. We all hit the dirt and I laid on my back," says Johnstone. "I couldn't see a thing, except the BAR man firing. Then he rolled over to take out his clip and put a fresh clip in, and as he was doing that a hand grenade came over. He rolled back over, not seeing it, and it went off. He had a big hole in his stomach. He came running back saying, 'Am I going to die? Am I going to die?' When he got to me I said, 'No, lie down, relax, don't run around, relax, relax, relax, you will be all right.' Then the sergeant got up on one knee with his gun and he started firing. Then he fell over. He had a bullet in his thigh."

Johnstone remained lying on his back, but was soon after injured himself by a German grenade. "The lieutenant then came running back saying he was going back for help and that we should hold out a little longer, and then he took off." Three times the Germans called out for the Americans to surrender as they were surrounded, and on the third occasion Johnstone and his companions slowly stood and raised their hands. "Four that were all right helped the wounded and the Germans took us to a cave behind the monastery," says Johnstone. There they were searched and had their personal items removed. The wounded, including Johnstone, were patched up, and to his surprise his watch was returned to him.

The regiment tried attacking again, but once more was caught by flanking fire and forced to withdraw. Often when just about to launch an attack, a German counterattack would come in and the men would be hard pressed to hold on to their existing positions. It was clear that the defenders were determined and well organized. From 7 February, von Senger had started moving more reinforcements to the Cassino Massif, and by 10 February, Baade had several more parachute units under his command. The latter was well aware of the importance of Point 593, and ordered continual attacks until, on 10 February, it was firmly back in German hands.

By now the men of 34th Division were worn out by stress and a lack of hot food and sleep. Attacks were repeatedly arranged and then postponed because the infantry were physically incapable of movement or so demoralized that they refused to leave their foxholes and sangars. Don Hoagland remembers that "after about a week there were several times when an attack was planned but before it could take place, somebody would recognize that there just wasn't enough push in the outfit to do anything. So it then became a case of just hanging on." The 135th Regiment was now very short of men, with few of its rifle companies able to muster more than about thirty troops, less than a third of full strength. The 168th Regiment was in a similar state, and the 133rd, down in the outskirts of the town, was faring no better. But still the American high command continued to order attacks, seemingly unaware of the realities of fighting and surviving on the massif. On 9 February a New Zealander officer, newly arrived at Cassino, went up to the forward lines to see the conditions for himself. He reported back that "the American infantry was worn out and quite unfit for battle without a thorough rest . . . it was very plain that none of [the senior American officers] had been forward or was at all in touch with his men." Soon afterward Alexander sent his chief of staff, the American general Lyman L. Lemnitzer, to assess the mood of the troops himself. He "found morale progressively worse . . . [the troops] disheartened, almost mutinous."

A series of letters found around this time on a captured soldier from Baade's 90th Panzer Grenadier Division seems to indicate that the situation was similar on the other side of the line. "For two weeks we have been in action," wrote the man to his father, who was fighting on the Eastern Front. "The few days were enough to make me sick and tired of it. In all that time we've had nothing to sleep in but foxholes, and the artillery fire kept us with our noses in the dirt all day long. During the first few days I felt very odd and . . . didn't eat anything at all. I lost my appetite when I saw all that . . . not a single man from my original squad is left, all of them missing. And it seems to be the same in the entire company." Also found on his person were letters from his father in Russia and his mother in Germany. The father's reads, "We are on the retreat, and have retreated quite a bit . . . Everybody is sick and tired of the war, but it does not look as if the nonsense will come to an end. I feel that it will go on until everything is completely destroyed." The mother, while bemoaning the constant air raids, implores her son in Italy, "I'm waiting and waiting always worried about my sons at the front. To have you in this great danger is hard for a mother. Be careful, do it for me."

Clark was determined that his men could still break through the last defensive positions before the Liri valley, aware from intelligence that the Germans had also been taking heavy losses. On 11 February the 141st Regiment from the US 36th Division moved up to Snakeshead Ridge and was ordered to clear the gorge between Snakeshead and Phantom, and then break out into the northern side of the crucial valley below. In charge of the Regiment's 3rd Battalion was Capt. C. N. "Red" Morgan. On arriving as an advance party during the morning of 10 February he reported to the battalion command post of one of the 34th Division's units, "located about 1,000 yards from the abbey of Monte Cassino and 300 yards east of Snakeshead ridge . . . The Bn CO gave us all the information he had," Morgan's account reads. "As he pointed out his positions on the map, we began to suspect that everything was not in accordance with what we were previously led to believe. Our reconnaissance of the area confirmed this." Contrary to what the men of the 141st had been told, Point 593 was not in the hands of the Americans. Their closest positions were about one hundred yards short of the summit on the near slopes. It would clearly be impossible to attack to the right of the position if it was still controlled by the enemy. "There was talk of another attack by the 34th Division troops against hill 593," Morgan wrote. "This attack was to be launched during the night of 10–11 February. After they had reached their objective, we were to attack through them. This attack failed to materialize. The few survivors of the 34th Division on Snake's Head, after more than two weeks of bitter fighting, were utterly exhausted. The attack was called off. The 1st and 3rd Battalions of the 141st would relieve the troops of the 34th Division on Snake's Head. The two battalions arrived after their long struggle over the slick mountain trails. Relief of the 34th Division troops on Snake's Head was accomplished and by the morning of 11 February, the 1st and 3rd Battalions were in position. An attack was scheduled for 11:00 that day."

"We started up the trail in a blinding rain and it turned into snow and we got up there late at night," remembers 141st Regiment's Bill Everett. "We moved into position in the driving snowstorm. The next morning all hell broke loose." They attacked at eleven o'clock in freezing rain and gusts of wind of up to fifty miles an hour. Soon after, the Germans counterattacked fiercely, and the Americans were hard pressed to hold on to their starting positions. "We lost the company commander and a couple of the guys early that first morning," remembers Everett. "I just told the guys, 'Hang on. Somebody wants this hill pretty bad. Let's hang on and hold it.' We soon lost the rest of the officers and most of the enlisted men. The officer situation was so bad in our outfit they were going into the hospitals and getting guys that had been wounded at the Rapido River and bringing them back up. The attrition rate on company-grade officers, second lieutenants and first lieutenants in rifle companies, was tremendous." Lieutenant Carl Strom, also from the 141st, whose company, with about forty men, had been made up to roughly platoon strength after the disaster on the Rapido, says that they simply didn't have enough troops to be able to attack successfully. Instead they were assaulted by the Germans, who "attacked several times. They came up the hill from down in the gorge. We used up box after box of hand grenades on them because, of course, you could take a hand grenade and just throw it down there and catch any number of them but they kept attacking and attacking."

"Confusion reigned that day," said Red Morgan. "The only thing that kept the Germans from overrunning our positions was the tenacity and guts of the officers and men of the line companies. When the attacks and counterattacks were over, the two battalions wound up relatively on the same line that they had taken over from the 34th Division. The Germans were in command of the situation on Hill 593. Their meat grinder was ready to grind up any troops that we were willing to throw in."

On the same day, Major General Ryder, in command of 34th Division, had ordered yet another attack by 168th Regiment on the monastery. By this time the three battalions were at about a third of their full complement, and most of these few men were replacements hurriedly raised from intelligence, antitank, and reconnaissance platoons. Even drivers, cooks, administration, and service personnel were ordered forward to bolster the line. But with Point 593 still under German control, the regiment had no protection on its right, and in spite of a spirited dash forward in a thick snowstorm, they were soon driven back to their start line.

On Snakeshead, the men of 141st and 142nd regiments were counting their losses. "At about 1700 Feb. 11," wrote Red Morgan, "the combined strength of the 1st and 3rd Bns was about 20 officers and 150 enlisted men. The normal complement of the combined strength of these two battalions would have been approximately 70 officers and 1,600 enlisted men." In such circumstances, Morgan continued, "the walking wounded were carefully screened. We could not spare a man that could still throw a grenade or fire a rifle." The next day brought little respite: "During daylight hours, practically any movement of any member of the battalions could be observed. This brought in small-arms fire as well as the heavier ordnance."

But finally the generals relented and, over the next two days, the Americans were relieved by fresh British troops. The 36th Division men were to be moved to another position on the ridge some five hundred yards back, but for 34th Division, or what remained of it, it was the end of their ordeal at last. As they climbed out of their foxholes in darkness, many collapsed through cramp and exhaustion. Others found they were unable to walk due to trench foot. "My ass was dragging just like everybody else," says Don Hoagland. "But as I was a first sergeant I took a responsibility, so I was going to be the last one off. I watched them come down and I can't imagine men being in any worse shape than that bunch. They were like zombies shuffling along. They were just absolutely exhausted, and it was not our company alone; it was all of them. It was just continual lack of sleep, continual pounding, continual action. It was a nasty, nasty battle in a nasty, nasty war."

One of the trucks carrying the Red Bulls away from the front became bogged down in a small stream. Nearby was the photographer Margaret Bourke-White. "This gave me the opportunity to study the faces of the human cargo the truck carried," she wrote in a book published before the end of the war. "I knew from the division emblem they wore on their sleeves that these men had been up in the mountains around Cassino . . . I thought I had never seen such tired faces. It was more than the stubble of beard that told the story; it was the blank, staring eyes. The men were so tired it was like a living death. They had come from such a depth of weariness that I wondered if they would ever be able quite to make the return to the lives and thoughts they had known."

Clare Cunningham from the US 36th Division's 143rd Regiment had been on Monte Castellone for a week when the big German counterattack began. It was Baade who had realized the vital importance of Point 593 and who had insisted on its recapture, whatever the cost. Now Baade decided to launch a counterattack on Monte Castellone, which anchored the Allies' positions on Snakeshead Ridge. Code-named Operation Michael, the attack was launched at 4 A.M. on 12 February, preceded by the heaviest German bombardment of all the Cassino fighting. Cunningham was an early casualty: "Katula and I got hit before daylight. A shell went in right at the end of our foxhole, blew us out and filled in the foxhole with dirt." The two buddies had been blasted out of the hole in opposite directions. "I was unconscious for a few moments, then I tried to get back in the hole, but there was no real hole there." One of his legs was completely smashed and the other broken. "I crawled back to the remains of the hole, while Katula lay unconscious in the open. Most of the day I dozed off. I could hear the firing going on."

Right behind the bombardment came two battalions of Baade's best troops moving forward across the bare slopes of the mountain. It was bitterly cold. The Americans on the summit found that some of their weapons were frozen; one man was lighting matches to try to thaw out his machine gun, others were instructed to urinate on their rifles: "It didn't smell so good after firing a couple of hours, but it saved our lives," one platoon sergeant reported.

At first the Germans were successful, capturing the near slopes of the mountain, but just after sunrise the worn-out German artillery started landing shells on the attackers. At the same time the Americans on the summit rallied and the assault was beaten back. At noon Baade called off the operation. The Germans had left at least 150 dead on the slopes, most killed by their own artillery. The Germans were now learning the same lessons that the terrain had been teaching the Allies: up there the defender had an immense advantage, and artillery is as likely to hit your own men as the enemy.

Clare Cunningham was evacuated at about five o'clock that afternoon, but didn't even get to an ambulance for another ten hours. Once eventually at the casualty clearing station, his leg had to be amputated below the knee.

The next day, 13 February, the German regimental commander sent an English-speaking officer to ask the Americans for a truce in which the Germans could pick up their dead. The break in the fighting was arranged for between 8 and 10 A.M. on the next day, St. Valentine's Day, and the American chosen to administer it was Lt. Col. Hal Reese. Having made the grim journey up the mountain, past dead soldiers of both sides, he arrived minutes before the truce was due to take place. At that moment a white flag appeared on the German lines, and Reese and the battalion commander started off down into the valley, carrying a small Stars and Stripes. At a plateau they found two Germans who had a Red Cross flag. A third German was watching from behind a bush. It was a strange and tense battlefield encounter, and Reese found himself interpreting in spite of his rusty German. A group of Germans assembled, and one said he was from Koblenz and remembered American soldiers being stationed there at the end of the First

World War. Reese said he had been one of those Americans, and, faced with German skepticism, he pulled out an old ID card with a picture of himself taken in the town in January 1919. Soon they were all pulling out wallets and showing photographs of parents, wives, and children. A camera came out and new photographs were taken.

All the while, German stretcher bearers were busily moving their dead back to their lines. Reese spotted two men carrying interesting-looking heavy packs going into a clump of bushes about two hundred yards away in the direction of Monte Cassino. Smiling, one of the Germans engaged Reese in conversation again, moving closer to impede his view. The truce was then extended by half an hour as the Germans struggled to collect all their dead, and Reese and the other officer sat down in no-man's-land in full visibility, in order to assure the Germans that the truce was still on. When Reese got out his binoculars and started to scan the hills behind the German lines, he heard the ping of a bullet, and then another, nearer. "Colonel," said Reese's companion, "I don't think they like us using those glasses on them." They then checked their watches: five minutes to go. It was time to get behind their own lines again.

Troops from the 36th Division were to remain in the salient around Castellone for another week. "It was snowing part of the time and raining part of the time and always cold," remembers Carl Strom. "I lost about half of my outfit from trench foot." Bill Everett was also "in real bad shape when we pulled back. I had developed pneumonia from being wet in the driving rain and snow in the mountains." When they finally reached safety on the Allied side of the Rapido, the survivors were rewarded with a lavish steak dinner. After weeks of dried rations, all the men were made sick by it.

In spite of the bravery of the French and the sacrifices of the Americans, the first battle had been a failure for the Allies, a defensive victory for the Germans. Clark's original plan had indicated his aversion to attacking the Cassino fortress head-on, and when he was forced to change his mind, only one tired and understrength division was committed. Troops sent in piece-meal had been repulsed by determined defenses and the effective moving of reserves from quiet to threatened sectors. The cost had been high for the Allies—five divisions (US 36th and 34th, British 56th and 5th, Algerian 3rd) had been rendered unfit for further battle. Domestic opinion was dismayed. Armchair generals in government and the media had been promised Rome by the end of January and couldn't understand how things had gone so wrong. British high command in particular was deeply concerned—above all that the Americans might lose interest in the Italian campaign and further downgrade the southern theater. Moreover, there was deep worry about the survival of the increasingly embattled bridgehead at Anzio. The landings had become a liability. Something had to be done at Cassino.

PART THREE

The Second Battle

Cold are the stones
That built the walls of Troy,
Cold are the bones
Of the dead Greek boy
Who for some vague thought
Of honor fell,
Nor why he fought
Could clearly tell.

—PATRIC DICKINSON, C. 1946

In these old hackneyed melodies
Hollow in the piano's cage
I see the whole trash of the age—
Art, gadgets, bombs and lies.

—ROY FULLER, C. 1949

9

The Destruction of
the Monastery

Although Anzio and the Monte Cassino battle had been at the front of people's minds back home in London, Berlin, and Washington, the destruction of the ancient monastery on 15 February 1944 would make Monte Cassino front-page news all around the world, and it has remained one of the iconic moments of the war. It was no secret that it was going to happen, and the world's press had assembled. John Lardner in *Newsweek* called it "The most widely advertised bombing in history." A group of doctors and nurses came by jeep all the way from Naples so as not to miss the spectacle. On the hills opposite the monastery, the generals watched; nearer by, soldiers from both sides gazed, awestruck. Only to these frontline troops did it come as a surprise.

To make the fresh attacks demanded by the perilous situation at Anzio, Alexander had assembled a multinational force of elite troops consisting of the 4th Indian Division, the 2nd New Zealand Division, and the British 78th Battleaxe Division. In his account of the Cassino battles, Maj. Rudolf Böhmler, who fought with the German 1st Parachute Division, called the trio "the finest weapons in the whole of Alexander's armory." Replacing the shattered remnants of US II Corps on the Cassino Massif was the 4th Indian Division, brought over from the Adriatic front. Originally earmarked to exploit through the mountains beyond the monastery after its capture by the US

34th Division, the 4th Indian now had the task of taking Monte Cassino it-self. Confidence in the division was high; from its fighting against the Ital-ians in Eritrea in 1941, it had experience of mountain combat, and there had been notable victories in the Western Desert and in the long pursuit to Tunisia.

Commanders, senior staff officers, and most of the regimental officers of the 4th Indian were British, as was the artillery and one battalion in each of the three infantry brigades—1st Royal Sussex, 1/4 Essex, and 2nd Cameron Highlanders. Each brigade also contained one battalion of Gurkhas and one of Indian soldiers. The Indian component was drawn from the traditional "martial races"—Punjabis, Pathans, Sikhs, Rajputs, Dogras, Jats, and Mah-rattas—and all were volunteers and men of high social standing. Most were from families boasting generations of soldiers, and they had a collective identity as members of an honorable profession. Commanding them were only the very best British officers, who received higher pay than their equiv-alents in the British army.

The Nepalese soldiers of the division's three Gurkha battalions had also traveled a long way from home to fight for the Western democracies. Not that democracy would have meant anything to them. Nepal at this time was almost entirely closed off from the outside world, a caste-bound, poverty-stricken feudal autocracy where education was forbidden and there was al-most total illiteracy in the general population. Becoming a soldier was the only way out of a life that has been described as consisting of "poverty, pri-vations, drudgery and weariness." In theory all Gurkhas were volunteers, al-though in some cases village headmen simply received orders for all the men of military age to be sent away for enlistment. Men of all ages were recruited: some of those fighting in Italy were probably as young as fifteen (although hardly any of the Nepalese knew the year of their birth) while others were in their fifties. The 1/2nd Battalion of 7th Brigade even had a father-and-son mortar team. As in the Indian battalions, the most junior British officer, however young, would outrank the most experienced Nepalese.

As late as 1942, few people in Nepal were aware that there was a war go-ing on. "I joined the army for money and honor and so I was pleased when I was enlisted, on 31 October 1939," one Gurkha veteran told interviewers in Nepal. "No one told me that a war had started." Astonishingly, nearly a year passed before his British commanding officer let him know that a war was happening, and that he was on his way to fight in it.

Balbahadur Katuwal joined up November 1942. As soon as he was accepted, his head was shaved, as was the case for all Gurkha soldiers until the end of the war. "I went to Dehra Dun for ten months' recruit training," he remembers. "It was so hard that some of the men ran away." Jumparsad Gurung, who also fought at Cassino, describes the severe regime at the training camp: "Our NCOs punished our mistakes by twisting our ears or striking us. They used harsh language. We had to mud-smear the floors every morning and that meant us getting up in the dark to get everything ready for parade that started at 0700 hours. We paraded till 0900 hours. British officers rode past us on horses during this first parade but they never spoke to us. Our morning meals were from 0900 to 1000 hours and there was never enough food." After a breakfast, usually of rice, the recruits had school until noon, where they were taught to count and write in the Roman alphabet as well as learning Urdu. Physical training and rifle practice took up the afternoon, and then there would be an evening meal consisting of chapattis or, twice a week, meat, and then, Gurung continues, "we would wash our clothes or have a singsong. We had to open our mouths and have a spoonful of fish oil poured in every evening by an NCO. I never knew why this was. I often thought of my village."

In late 1943, Balbahadur Katuwal's training was complete: "Then it was time to go overseas. The families saw us off with much waving and many tears. No one told us where we were going. Even when we were in Italy we had to be told where we were." But Katuwal, whose work as a dispatch rider allowed him to see a bit of the country, soon developed a liking for it. "I went around Italy a lot and one of the girls, a general's daughter I think she was, was very kind to me," he remembers. "I met her when she was washing her clothes and she said she would wash mine for me. She would feed me with bread and butter. She wanted to marry me because I spoke some Italian. Italy's great place and they're great people. They said that the 'hairless ones' (because we Gurkhas shaved our heads) were the best people and the Germans were the worst people. No one misbehaved. I have no idea why the Germans were in Italy," he adds. "It might have been better had we been told."

Kharkabahadur Thapa of the 1/2nd Gurkha Rifles was one of the few literate recruits and was earmarked as a signaler: "I was enlisted on 19 November 1940 as a boy soldier," he says. "My grandfather had been a soldier and had taught me how to read and write. I went to Dehra Dun where I was

taught the rudiments of signaling after a week in a rest camp where we were
taught basic discipline and school. That was how to behave, how to recognize the colonel and how to answer the NCOs. We were issued clothes and
taught how to put them on. We had milk daily to help us develop. We had
lectures every night. The boy's training lasted a year but after six months I
was taken from boy training and made a recruit. The pay was five rupees a
month but after cuttings for laundry and barber we were left with two rupees. It was enough.

"I was still on the small side and also underweight. The CO ordered that
I should continue with the milk. After six months' recruit training I passed
out as a trained soldier at the proper time and took my regimental oath on
the Nishani Mai [the regimental truncheon Queen Victoria gave to the regiment instead of a third color after the siege of Delhi in 1857]. We were
played away from Dehra Dun by the brass band as we left for Karachi."

By 1944, Thapa had fought for the British in the Middle East and North
Africa. "In Italy," he says, "we passed fields of wheat and many grapes. We
drank wine."

The Gurkhas, generally extremely polite, were comparatively well liked by
the Italians: "We didn't speak to the girls until they spoke to us," one
Nepalese veteran recalls. But they were much feared by the Germans, particularly for their skill at nighttime ambushes. Lurid stories were soon circulating in Italy, one of which is retold in his diary by a British major from
78th Division: "I came across some Gurkha soldiers who were laughing up-
roariously. When I asked what the joke was, one who spoke some English explained that they had been out on patrol when they came across three
Germans asleep in a slit trench. They cut off the heads of the two outside
men but left the chap in the middle as he would have a terrific shock when
he awoke!"

Beneath the pleasant, smiling exterior, the Gurkha rifleman had an iron
nerve and a great ability to survive in hostile environments. The Allied leaders considered them excellent mountain troops and had great faith that they
would be able to take the monastery.

In his memoirs, B. Smith, a signaler with the 4/16th Punjab Battalion, describes his division's journey from the Adriatic: "In transit, the various battalions and companies made an odd-looking convoy. The trucks carrying
the men sprouted all kinds of excrescences such as crates of live chickens,
fire buckets, water bags, bits of furniture and clothes drying in the wind.

From some of the trucks came the bleatings of sheep and goats for both Moslem and Hindu carried their meat alive and killed it ritually as required. The whole convoy was like a traveling circus, albeit bristling with weapons, and the spectacle was watched with wonder by the war-weary Italian populace."

While the divisional headquarters was being established at Cervaro, the scene of bitter fighting by the US 34th Division a month earlier, Smith billeted himself and a couple of companions on an impoverished old Italian couple. It was an anxious time. "The war was thirty miles up the road," he writes, "and had been banished to no more than a dull rumble at night and occasional flickering like summer lightning; but it was waiting for us and we knew it and we were no heroes." The next day he ventured up the road and took in the battlefield—the mountains and the Liri valley entrance. "At the center of this scene," he writes, "was the monastery itself perched dramatically a thousand feet above the town, gleaming white in the sun, immense, ancient, beautiful, brooding, an enigma."

Replacing the US 36th Division in its soggy foxholes opposite the Liri valley was the 2nd New Zealand Division, utterly different from the 4th Indian Division except that it too was considered one of the best fighting units on either side. New Zealand had declared war on Germany at 9:30 P.M. on 3 September 1939. The prime minister, Michael Joseph Savage, had announced, "Both with gratitude for the past, and with confidence in the future, we range ourselves without fear beside Britain. Where she goes, we go, where she stands, we stand." Beneath the rhetoric was a grim understanding that this would be a war of survival for New Zealand as well. However geographically distant from the fighting in Europe, New Zealand was dependent on Europe and America politically, economically, and culturally. Despite grave reservations in the country, Savage decided to raise a large expeditionary force, but promised that there would be no conscription.

But Savage was already terminally ill with cancer, and when he died on 27 March 1940, his successor Peter Fraser immediately introduced conscription for men over eighteen. For those who resisted there were draconian punishments, and high-profile conscientious objectors were immediately taken off the streets. This was ironic, as Fraser himself had briefly been imprisoned during the First World War for his conscientious objection. But in truth, he had little option other than to introduce conscription, as in the previous world war many had volunteered and been shipped to Europe only to be laboriously shipped back again when it was discovered that they performed vital jobs at home. It was a question of manpower management: New Zealand had to mobilize itself industrially as well as militarily when the supply of manufactured goods from Europe ceased.

Initially, however, there were plenty of volunteers. On the first day that recruitment offices opened and the posters declared "The Spirit of ANZAC Calls You," there were 5,000 volunteers, and by August 1940 there had been over 60,000. Even when conscription was introduced, the men sent overseas were in theory volunteers, although one veteran explains that, for those over twenty-one, the minimum age for going overseas, there was a certain amount of arm-twisting involved: "It was just after I'd turned twenty-one that our unit was earmarked for joining overseas reinforcement and we were asked to volunteer . . . Those who didn't, the officers went along asking their reasons. In many cases married men were expected to remain but those younger and single were severely questioned."

Clem Hollies was twenty years old when the war started, employed by the National Bank of New Zealand at their Onehunga, Auckland, branch. "A few hardy souls rushed to enlist," he writes in his account of his war. Christmas came and went, and he was still "in no hurry to enlist," but with the New Year more and more of his friends began to join up. "Why did this young man volunteer to fight in a war which at that time was thousands of miles away?" Hollies asks. "Patriotism and jingoism certainly did not influence him nor was there any thought of 'doing his bit.' He had no real reason to leave these shores. His life was predictable and safe. Perhaps therein lies the answer. He and thousands of others maybe saw an opportunity to change their lives of quiet desperation by going overseas, for in that slow-moving world very few had that chance. Little did he realize that his overseas trip was going to last for four years."

To get overseas Hollies lied about his age and, after a period of training, found himself in April 1941 with a corporal's stripe and on a troopship leaving Wellington. Everywhere there had been cheering crowds. "Here we were," he writes, "safely on our transport, eagerly awaiting departure and the beginning of our BIG ADVENTURE, not knowing and probably not caring what the future might bring."

In North Africa, Hollies joined the 21st Battalion of the New Zealand Expeditionary Force, which had already seen combat in Crete and Greece. After time in Syria and Palestine, Hollies fought at El Alamein and was promoted to second lieutenant. "With officer status," he writes, "a new life opened up—access to better restaurants and nightclubs was available, which made my new life very enjoyable."

The New Zealand soldiers tended to be hardy and used to the outdoors and to assessing ground and terrain, that most important skill of an infantryman. They were also well educated, practical, and skilled at improvisation. The German general Erwin Rommel rated them as the best troops he had fought against, and by the end of the African campaign the New Zealand Division had become a hard-hitting mobile force adept at outflanking maneuvers and fast movement.

In command of the division was Lt. Gen. Sir Bernard Freyberg. Already in his fifties, Freyberg had fought in the Mexican civil war and distinguished himself on the Western Front in the First World War, winning a VC and being wounded nine times. He was an imposing figure, a national hero, and vastly more experienced than his commanding officer at Cassino, Mark Clark. Considering how many times he was wounded, it is a miracle that Freyberg survived the First World War. Too many of his New Zealand compatriots did not. Eighteen thousand were killed and many more maimed out of a population of just one million, a higher proportion of casualties than any of the major belligerents. This had had a profound effect on Freyberg. The British Chief of the Combined Staff, Alan Brooke, referred to him disparagingly as "casualty conscious," and he has been accused, among other things, of failing to push through attacks. But Freyberg was more than just a divisional or corps commander. He was New Zealand's representative in the Mediterranean theater and was answerable only to his own government. He was well aware that he was responsible for the lives of a high proportion of his country's men of military age.

Jack Cocker, the sixth of seven sons from the extreme south of South Island, had all his brothers except the youngest in the service. He trained as a machine gunner and, in 1943, age eighteen, joined the New Zealand Expeditionary Force. He was "duly . . . jabbed and stabbed with sundry injections [until] it only took someone to glance at my swollen arm to have me flinch." He left Wellington and, having spent time in a "gigantic tented camp alongside the pyramids," sailed for Taranto as a reinforcement for the 27th Machine Gun Battalion. "It took us a while to acclimatize after Egypt," he remembers, "but we soon were old hands and enjoying the vino and the *sig-norinas*."

The New Zealand Division had originally arrived in Italy in October 1943. Shipped with it in different lifts were forty-six hundred vehicles, an indication of its mobility in the desert. The original agreement with Prime Minister Fraser had been that the troops would return home after the end of the North African campaign. The Australians, fearing Japanese attacks at home, had already left. There were theatrical appeals from Churchill for the New Zealanders to stay, but it had been Roosevelt, pointing out the logistical problems of shipping the troops home and then replacing them in Europe with Americans already in the Pacific, who persuaded Fraser to relent and allow the division to continue fighting in the Mediterranean.

At the end of 1943 the New Zealanders had been involved in fierce fighting on the Adriatic front, on the Sangro, and at Ortona. When it became clear that further gains were impossible, the division received orders to remove all its badges and markings, and prepare for a secret move over to the 5th Army front on 20 January, just as the US 36th Division was attacking across the Rapido. The silver ferns on the vehicles—mockingly called "white feathers" by the "Poms"—were duly painted over, but, Clem Hollies remembers, "This 'secret' move was ridiculous as we were greeted everywhere by the locals as 'Kiwis.' "

The historian of the New Zealand medical units attached to the division describes the journey across Italy: "During the day's travel, Italian civilians, including an incredible number of unwashed children, begged vociferously for biscuits, chocolate, and cigarettes. Most of the villages passed through were small and filthy, each having its distinctive odor and all united in poverty."

On 3 February, Alexander established a new corps within Clark's 5th Army, to be called the New Zealand Corps, consisting of the 2nd New Zealand Division and the 4th Indian Division. Another high-quality British division, the 78th, was also to join the corps from the Adriatic front, but had been held up by snow on the mountain passes and did not arrive at Cassino until 17 February. The new corps also contained British artillery and American armor, but was desperately short of experienced staff for planning and logistics. Freyberg was to command the corps and Brig. Gen. Howard Kippenberger took command of the 2nd New Zealand Division.

It was a rushed arrangement and, not for the first nor the last time, the international flavor of the Allied armies caused resentment, confusion, and indecision. Clark was well aware of the special status of Freyberg, a prewar dinner guest of Churchill, and of his men, and wrote in his diary on 4 February: "These are dominion troops who are very jealous of their prerogatives. The British have found them difficult to handle. They have always been given special considerations which we would not give to our own troops." Clark found the imposing figure of Freyberg difficult to deal with and resented not being consulted about the role of the new corps in his 5th Army. Noting that he now had five corps under his command, only two of which were American (II Corps and VI Corps, which were at Anzio), he confided to his diary: "And thus I was about to agree with Napoleon's conclusion that it is better to fight allies than be one of them."

For the moment, though, the troops were exhausted by the hard fighting and miserable conditions on the Sangro front. Second Lieutenant Alf Voss, an intelligence officer with the 21st Battalion, had lost good friends in the fighting. "At the end of the Sangro campaign we were completely done in," he says. "My hair had begun to turn gray . . . I had also started to smoke. Calling down the artillery was particularly stressful. At one stage I went seventy-six hours without sleep, then I fell asleep while smoking a cigarette and woke with my map board on fire . . . We were always getting wet then constantly trying to dry ourselves out, and spent quite a lot of time digging our trucks and guns out of the mud." Jack Cocker joined his 27th Machine Gun Battalion on the Sangro as a "red arse," the term used for someone who had not yet been under fire. "We arrived at the platoon headquarters," he remembers. "No one even looked up as we entered the house. It was the normal welcome to red arses." He soon learned the fate of the men they were replacing. A complete machine gun section of about twelve men had been taken prisoner after crossing the Sangro. Having waded, waist deep, through the river carrying their guns and ammunition, they had had to dig in on the opposite bank. By the time they had done this they were so exhausted that, even though they were the front line, they promptly fell asleep and were captured by a German patrol.

Now the men had a short break at Piedemonte D'Alife in the Volturno valley. It was much warmer than in the mountains where they had been stationed, and they were in pleasant country that was relatively unscarred by the fighting. Several homesick New Zealanders could even fantasize that they were back home. John Blythe, a twenty-eight-year-old artilleryman, wrote of this time: "Although still winter, it seemed almost autumnal in the Volturno valley after the snows of Ortona. We bivouacked in a pleasant spot with lots of trees near Alife, and from an upstairs window of a better class of farm house it was easy to imagine one was looking out on a pastoral scene back home in Otago." There was dry frost at night but sunshine during the days, and visits to Pompeii, hill-climbing, plenty of "vino," meals with local Italian families, and games of rugby rejuvenated the men. Twenty-year-old North Islander Brick Lorimer, a tank driver in the 19th Armoured Regiment, remembers how the Italians had treated them with caution initially: "We were depicted by the propaganda as savages with painted faces, wearing grass skirts and eating people," he says, but there are many stories of the locals showing the New Zealanders the same kindness with which they treated other troops. The New Zealanders also got to use the luxurious American showers nearby, entertainments were laid on, and there were even trips to the recently reopened opera house at Caserta.

"Daily I could see their faces losing the strained look," their commander Kippenberger wrote in his account of that time. "What matter that all the summer campaign lay ahead; for a little while we were very content with life." As well as entertainments there were route marches and training on river crossings on the Volturno, remembered by one veteran as "a great laugh." It was explained to the troops what they were up against at Cassino, but it failed to shake the confidence of the division. Jack Cocker remembers, "They told us all about the terrain and what it was like but we thought it was going to be a doddle."

The New Zealanders also came across American soldiers for the first time, with their "unfamiliar green combat jackets and differently shaped helmets . . . They probably thought we were 'Limeys' and took little notice," writes John Blythe, "but they were closely scrutinized by us." Most amazing were the lavish amenities laid on for the GIs and the prodigious use of valuable materials. Vehicles broken down were simply abandoned and, Blythe goes on, "the roads were festooned with telephone wires on a scale never previously experienced . . . the Yanks must be great talkers." They also noted a different style in the 5th Army: everything was shiny and brusque. It was, Blythe writes, "a whole new milieu and mood completely alien to our old informal Eighth Army routine." The New Zealanders in particular prided themselves on their informality and had little time for spit-and-polish or niceties of rank. When out of the line there was seldom a distinction between officers and men; British troops were amazed when New Zealand officers dropped in and had a meal in the men's mess. One veteran explains it thus: "New Zealanders are a law unto themselves. We were a civilian force, not a strictly military one, you see. We lived as near to a civilian life as possible, apart from doing the job we had to do."

There is a famous though probably apocryphal story that captures the reputation of the New Zealanders. During the African campaign, a senior British general visited the New Zealand Division. At lunch he said to Freyberg, "Your chaps don't salute, do they?"

"You should try waving at them," Freyberg replied. "They always wave back."

Certain factors beyond national characteristics and the special status of the New Zealand force contributed to this unique character. As the whole New Zealand Army in Europe was one self-contained division, many officers who would, in bigger armies, have been promoted out of the division, remained. A large number knew one another from home, or as one veteran puts it: "New Zealand is such a small place that if you came across a bloke there was somebody who knew somebody, who knew somebody, who knew your family." By the time of the Italian campaign the division was a well-oiled machine. Before an operation they would require only one sheet of orders rather than the thirty or so common in the British army. It was this relaxed professionalism more than anything else that accounted for the division's informality.

After an "idyllic two weeks," during which the troops had been lulled into thinking that the west coast was milder, drier, and sunnier than the Adriatic, on 4 February heavy rain began to fall. On the same day, Clem Hollies's 21st Battalion was ordered to relieve the 143rd Regiment of the US 36th Division on the Rapido River opposite Sant' Angelo. "The whole area around Cassino had an ominous air," Hollies reported. "Flat expanses of flooded countryside interspersed with drier ground churned up by shellfire; derelict vehicles, including bullet-ridden assault boats; neglected rows of grapevines and forlorn, shattered trees; stone houses less roofs and with gaping holes in their walls (some of the houses were still occupied by Italian families). And, glaring down at us from 1,700 feet, was the omnipresent bulk of the Monte Cassino monastery."

On the same day, artilleryman John Blythe moved up to his position near Monte Trocchio. "The regiment started advancing to the front," he writes.

"The hills closing in on us were dark and the mountains ahead looked bleak and depressing. It was clear the country had been fought over; there were shell holes, bomb craters—some quite big—tree stumps and blackened trees raising scratchy outlines. We had plenty of time to look around because congestion on the only road to the front caused many stops and starts. There was time to sit and think; to become aware of the old, cold, gut feeling."

Clark was confident that the New Zealand Corps would capture the monastery and maintained that, had his US II Corps possessed just a few more reserves, they would have done it themselves. He was even resentful that the honor of capturing the monastery would fall to the "British" after all the hard fighting of his American troops.

Freyberg was not so sure. After touring the forward areas, he reported back to the New Zealand government that, "We are undoubtedly facing one of the most difficult operations of all our battles." But the soldiers themselves arrived at Cassino full of confidence in their ability to get the job done. Here was the 8th Army coming to the rescue again, as they had done in Africa. Here were the invincible divisions, feared by the enemy, who had known nothing but success.

The original plan was for the New Zealand Corps to perform a wide-flanking attack through the mountains north of Monte Castellone. This was certainly the French commander Juin's preferred option, and he had lobbied Clark to reinforce the French attacks north of the monastery and make it the major thrust. But there were doubts about the possibility of supplying and supporting forward troops across the towering, snow-clad mountains, and to move troops into position to attack in that sector would require significant time that was not available. Instead, it was decided that "one more push" by fresh, high-quality troops would achieve what had only just eluded the exhausted Americans. The 4th Indian Division, spearheaded by the 7th Brigade (containing 1st Royal Sussex, 4/16th Punjab, and 1/2nd Gurkha Rifles), would storm the monastery, clear the surrounding high ground, and then enter the Liri valley several miles north of the Rapido River. Immediately behind would be 5th Brigade (containing 1/4th Essex, 1/6th Rajputana Rifles, and 1/9th Gurkhas), standing by to occupy the monastery and Monastery Hill after its capture. The 2nd New Zealand Division was to cross the Rapido just north of Sant' Angelo, take Cassino town, and open up the

Liri valley for the US 1st Armored Division to charge through and meet up with the hard-pressed Anzio force.

The experienced commander of the 4th Indian Division, Maj. Gen. Francis "Gertie" Tuker, was horrified at the plan. Like Juin, he favored "turning" Monte Cassino by a wide outflanking movement. But if it was to be a frontal attack, then, Tuker insisted, it must be accompanied by an overwhelming concentration of firepower. By this, he meant aircraft as well as artillery. But Tuker was ailing. Afflicted by a mystery illness, he was undergoing exhausting treatment and showing no signs of improvement. One of the doctors attending him was thirty-two-year-old John David. The son of the bishop of Liverpool, David had arrived in Italy having served in India and North Africa. On 6 February he wrote a letter home: "General Tuker apparently has a flare-up of chronic sinusitis and is to have a course of penicillin . . . no efforts are to be spared to achieve perfect sterility and comfort." A large dose was administered every three hours. "The course of penicillin is arduous in the extreme," David wrote. The next day Tuker discussed with his doctor the possibility that the monastery would have to be bombed. In his diary entry for 7 February, David reports he told Tuker that such an act would be sacrilegious. Tuker asked him if he had a better idea. He didn't.

The Allies were well aware of the national and international importance of Monte Cassino. An Italian from Cassino has since described it as the equivalent of Italians bombing Westminster Abbey. As early as October 1943, Italian museum authorities had drawn 5th Army's attention to its unique status, and Clark's headquarters had stressed the need to preserve the building from bombardment. At the end of December, Eisenhower, then still the Allied supreme commander in the Mediterranean, had reiterated that all efforts should be taken to avoid damage to Italy's many historic and religious buildings. "Today we are fighting in a country which has contributed a great deal to our cultural inheritance," his message to "all commanders" read, "a country rich in monuments which by their creation helped and now in their old age illustrate the growth of the civilization which is ours. We are bound to respect those monuments so far as war allows." But he had continued with a cautionary note: "If we have to choose between destroying a famous building and sacrificing our own men, then our men's lives count infinitely more and the buildings must go . . . Nothing can stand against the argument of military necessity."

At the beginning of January, after receiving complaints from the Vatican that Allied shells had hit the monastery, Alexander repeated the order that the building should not be targeted, but ended with, "Consideration for the safety of such areas will not be allowed to interfere with military necessity." The Germans had assured the Vatican that their troops would not occupy the abbey, but few on the Allied side believed the promise. In Britain and America, the press argued about whether the abbey should survive. In early February a debate in the House of Lords saw the archbishop of Canterbury urge the protection of the treasures of Italy, which "belong to the world . . . not to any particular time." Lord Latham had replied, "I do not wish to see Europe stocked with cultural monuments to be venerated by mankind in chains and on its knees . . . The people of this country will not submit to their boys being sacrificed—even one of them sacrificed—unnecessarily to save whatever building it may be."

In early January the Germans had established an exclusion zone around the monastery, and the gate was guarded by military police. A diary kept by the abbot's secretary, Don Martino Matronola, testifies that the Germans kept to the letter of their promise not to station troops in the building. But this did not change the fact that the monastery was sitting at the center of the Gustav Line. All around, fortifications had been constructed, and a deep cave under the walls was being used as an ammunition dump. The outbuildings of the monastery had been razed to the ground to clear fields of fire, and observation posts and crew-served weapons were situated in the shadow of the walls. At this time the Germans also sought to clear the monastery completely. All the refugees were evacuated, with the exception of three families too sick to be moved, and the abbot was asked to leave. He refused and stayed put with his half dozen companions from the order, including Don Martino. Stray hits from artillery from both sides continued in January in spite of the protestations of the Vatican, and on 5 February, as the US troops continued their attacks along Snakeshead Ridge, a civilian was killed by shrapnel landing inside the building. That night there was a heavy thunderstorm as well as a violent artillery bombardment on nearby German positions. Driven from the caves where they had been sheltering, some 150 civilians pounded on the door of the monastery. When they threatened to set fire to it, the door was opened and the refugees, cold, starving, and crazed with fright, rushed in. The next day the remaining monks did what they could to calm and accommodate the refugees, but food and water were running out, and soon sanitary conditions were appalling. Inevitably illness, later thought to be parathyphoid fever, broke out. No one thought the situation could become any worse.

———————

On account of his illness, Major General Tuker had been forced to hand over command of the 4th Indian Division to Brig. Harry K. Dimoline on 6 February. Tuker's doctor, John David, called this "an ominous change . . . [It] means they go into this next highly critical battle without the old man!" But Tuker continued to badger Freyberg to reconsider his plan for the frontal attack on the monastery and at the same time tried to find out what he could about the building itself. Receiving no help from the 5th Army's intelligence, he sent an adjutant to Naples, who eventually found a book, dated 1879, which gave details about the construction of the monastery. On 12 February, Tuker communicated his findings to Freyberg: "The main gate has massive timber branches in a low archway consisting of large stone blocks 9 to 10 meters long. This gate is the only means of entrance to the Monastery. The walls are about 150 feet high, are of solid masonry and at least 10 feet thick at the base . . . Monte Cassino is therefore a modern fortress and must be dealt with by modern means . . . It can only be directly dealt with by applying blockbuster bombs from the air."

Freyberg had already warned Clark that the monastery might have to be "blown down," and on 12 February he officially requested that it be attacked from the air. Clark was at Anzio, so Freyberg spoke to the American's chief of staff, General Gruenther. "I want it bombed," he demanded. "The other targets are unimportant, but this one is vital. The division commander who is making the attack feels that it is an essential target and I thoroughly agree with him." Gruenther contacted Clark and other senior US ground commanders, none of whom thought that bombing was warranted. Major General Geoffrey Keyes, commander of US II Corps, even warned that bombing would "probably enhance its value as a military obstacle, because the Germans would then feel free to use it as a barricade." The Allied commanders were also aware of the presence of refugees within the building.

In his memoirs, Clark maintains that if Freyberg had been one of his American corps commanders, he would simply have refused the request. But "in view of General Freyberg's position in the British Empire forces" the matter was referred to Alexander, who instinctively backed the New Zealander. "When soldiers are fighting for a just cause," Alexander wrote, explaining his decision, "and are prepared to suffer death and mutilation in the process, bricks and mortar, no matter how venerable, cannot be allowed to weigh against human lives." But the decision rested with Clark as army commander, and he continued to argue that bombing the monastery would not only hand the Germans a ready-made propaganda coup, but would hit civilians as well as be of doubtful military value. However, when Freyberg pointed out that a higher officer who refused to authorize the bombing would have to take the blame if the attack failed, and then uttered Eisenhower's magic formula—"military necessity"—Clark conceded and agreed to give the order as long as it was approved at the highest level.

In the meantime, the evidence was weighed up as to whether the monastery was occupied by the Germans. There were reports from men on the ground: a man had been sniped, there had been a flash of field glasses at one of the windows, small-arms fire had been seen and heard coming from the vicinity of the abbey. On 13 February, Gen. Ira Eaker, supreme air force commander in the Mediterranean, flew over the monastery at two hundred feet and thought he saw a military radio aerial as well as army personnel moving in and out of the building. The same day, Gen. Maitland Wilson, who had replaced Eisenhower as supreme Allied commander in the Mediterranean, claimed "irrefutable evidence" that the monastery was part of the German main line of defense. This was deemed enough, and at the Foggia airfields as well as at those in Britain and North Africa, preparations started for a massive attack.

In fact, "evidence" of German occupation—endlessly argued over since and largely proved to be partial and faulty—was something of a red herring as far as the British commanders on the ground were concerned. To them, the building and the hill were a single military objective and could not be separated. Furthermore, in his memo to Freyberg, Tuker had pointed out that: "Whether the monastery is now occupied by the German garrison or not, it is certain that it will be held as a keep by the last remnants of the garrison of the position. It is therefore essential that the building should be so demolished as to prevent its effective occupation." The argument was not about whether the Germans were inside at that moment, but more about whether the troops could be expected to attack toward an undamaged building that had massive walls and only one door. The New Zealander Kippenberger, writing after the war, backs up Tuker's point: "Opinion at NZ Corps HQ as to whether the Abbey was occupied was divided. Personally, I thought the point immaterial. If not occupied today it might be tomorrow and it did not appear that it would be difficult for the enemy to bring reserves into it during the progress of an attack, or for troops to take shelter there if driven from positions outside. It was impossible to ask troops to storm a hill surmounted by an intact building such as this, capable of sheltering several hundred infantry in perfect security from shellfire and ready at the critical moment to emerge and counterattack."

In his memoirs Alexander revealingly admits that the destruction of the monastery was "necessary more for the effect it would have on the morale of the attackers than for purely material reasons." In this, he shows that the British commanders were more in touch than the Americans with the feelings of the frontline troops. For the men in soggy slit trenches down in the Rapido valley or struggling up the mountain paths to the salient north of the building, the massive abbey, with its small, cell-like windows, towering over them, had become a malign presence. It dominated their lives. No movement during the day was possible without first checking whether you could be seen from the monastery, or "the all-seeing eye," as one veteran called it. Fred Majdalany, who served in the Lancashire Fusiliers, 78th Division, described how it felt to approach the ridge on which the abbey stood: "As the road became less crowded, you began to have the feeling the monastery was watching you. When you have been fighting a long time, you develop an instinct for enemy observation posts . . . it is like being suddenly stripped of your clothes. We were being watched by eyes in the monastery every inch of the way up the rough little road through the olive groves." David Cormack, who had moved from the Garigliano with his team of Italian muleteers, remembered the "Bloody monastery gazing down at you. You couldn't scratch without being seen. And it was a psychological thing. It grew the longer you were there." Most would have approved of the bravado of Gen. John Channon, commander of the 15th Army Group Air Force, who said to Alexander, "If you let me use the whole of our bomber force against Cassino we will whip it out like a dead tooth."

On 13 February there were severe snowstorms in the Cassino area, but the next day the meteorologists forecast clear weather for the next twenty-four hours. Without delay, the bombing was scheduled for the morning of the fifteenth. On the fourteenth, artillery shells filled with leaflets were exploded over the monastery. The leaflets in Italian and English read: "Italian friends, beware: we have until now been especially careful to avoid shelling Monte

Cassino Monastery. The Germans know how to benefit from this. But now the fighting has swept closer and closer to its sacred precincts. The time has come when we must train our guns on the monastery itself. We give you warning that you may save yourselves. We warn you urgently: leave the monastery. Leave it at once. Respect this warning. It is for your benefit.— Fifth Army."

None of the leaflets fell within the monastery walls, but a refugee picked one up just outside and showed it to the eighty-year-old abbot. As word of the warning spread among the refugees, some fled to nearby caves, some made for deeper shelters, others put their faith in God that He would not allow the tomb of St. Benedict to be destroyed. It was suggested that everyone should leave the building under a white flag, but this was considered too risky. Instead, the abbot decided to contact the Germans for help in evacuating the monastery. Don Martino Matronola recorded in his diary that a German officer, a Lieutenant Daiber, and another soldier arrived the next morning, a little before five o'clock, for an interview with the abbot. Shown the leaflet, the officer replied that he thought they were "to intimidate and for propaganda purposes." Pointing out that immediate evacuation was impossible because of the fierce fighting around the monastery, he said that if the population taking refuge in the monastery "chanced to flee, about a third of them, judging from previous experience, would perish on the road." The monks shared the German's skepticism; surely the Allies would never carry out such a threat. In any event, there was an agreement that everyone would leave the monastery at five o'clock the following morning.

After the interview, the officer asked Don Martino if he might view the church. "It was not possible to see anything for the darkness," the monk wrote, "so with great care I lit a lamp briefly and immediately afterward we left." Lieutenant Daiber was the last foreigner to see Monte Cassino's great shrine. Four hours later the Flying Fortresses of the 13th Strategic Air Force arrived overhead.

While the Allied leaders were debating whether to bomb the monastery, Anzio had been at the forefront of everyone's mind. Reliable intercepts from Ultra indicated that a massive German counterattack on the fragile beachhead could be expected on 16 February. There were widespread fears that there would be "another Dunkirk," save for the successful evacuation. Once the bombing was approved, there was added urgency to carry out the Cassino operation as quickly as possible so that the aircraft would be available for Anzio for the sixteenth.

But transferring troops up the mountain to relieve the Americans and getting into position for an attack on the monastery had proved extremely arduous. The isolated salient above the monastery was effectively a separate battlefield some distance ahead of the main Allied front line. For the troops of the 4th Indian Division moving up from the rear, the roads immediately behind the Allied lines were in a very poor condition and congested. Once these had been negotiated, the journey to the forward salient involved crossing the flooded Rapido valley, exposed to German observers on Monastery Hill, then clambering up a succession of narrow, slippery goat tracks, all effectively a no-man's-land behind the forward front line.

The division's attack was to be spearheaded by 7th Brigade, commanded by Brig. O. de T. Lovett, with the 1st Royal Sussex Battalion due to take the forward positions. The battalion started moving up on the night of 10 February to a new concentration area near Caira. There were insufficient vehicles that could cope with the muddy conditions, and as the rain lashed down and the wind howled, the men had to cross the sodden Rapido valley on foot while lorries carried the supplies. Two of the trucks skidded off the road and fell down a steep embankment. The two vehicles were carrying the entire reserve mortar ammunition and grenades for the Royal Sussex.

Twenty-year-old Douglas Hawtin was a lance corporal in the Royal Signals attached to the Sussex Battalion. From a family of Northampton builders, Hawtin had been in the army for two years. The next two months, he has said, "were the grimmest of my army career, and I suppose in my whole life." As he was in charge of heavy radios and radio batteries, he was one of the lucky ones who was driven across the exposed Rapido valley. "We loaded a lot of equipment on to an American jeep which took us forward over an extremely rough and almost impassable cart track . . . right into the valley of the Rapido River completely in view of the enemy in the mountains above. Shelling was constant . . . this area was known as the 'Mad Mile.' Casualties and vehicles were everywhere, troops marching across."

Hawtin arrived at the forward camp near Caira on the evening of 12 February. There was steady shellfire, some of it from the Allied guns. This was not to be the last "friendly fire" that the division would suffer as the Allied gunners struggled to master the intricacies of the mountain salient. From this base they had a seven-mile journey to the positions in front of the monastery, and much of the track was impassable even to jeeps. Also, only about a third of the required mules were available, and there was not enough time to concentrate the meager resources of the division. Hawtin, however, was issued with three mules and their Arab handler. "At nightfall, having loaded up, we set off with mules and hundreds of troops marching up into the mountains." The track soon narrowed to only eighteen inches wide, with a sheer drop of a thousand feet on one side and steep cliffs on the other. "It was tortuous, pitch-black darkness, we were tired, having had little sleep for days, still wet through," Hawtin remembers. The mules started losing their foothold, and one of Hawtin's, top-heavy with the weight of spare radio batteries, slipped and plunged over the edge. It was a very long and exhausting climb, and when Hawtin finally reached the battalion headquarters in an old German bunker, he immediately had to get to work. In his diary for Monday, 14 February, he wrote: "Traveled all through the night nearly unto death . . . set up the station and built ourselves a hideout. Still trying to dry ourselves out today so quite miserable all day."

On each journey, nearly a third of all the mules were lost as Hawtin's had been, making the supply situation for the Sussex Battalion critical. "We had no reserve rations and barely one blanket per man," the commanding officer of the battalion, Lt. Col. J. Glennie, wrote in his diary. "Admin situation bad."

Other battalions were having similar difficulties. The 4/16th Punjab was to take up positions to the left of Snakeshead Ridge, but, along with the brigade's other battalion, the 1/2nd Gurkha, they had been delayed on 12 February when they had gone to the aid of the Americans being counterattacked on Monte Castellone. Having had an exhausting journey across the Rapido valley, Signaler B. Smith was with his battalion, the 4/16th Punjab, negotiating the trek from the forward camp to the top of the massif. One part of the journey was known as Death Valley as it was under German observation and frequently shelled. Smith, leading mules carrying his signal equipment, got through, but part of the battalion was still making its way across the valley floor when "a string of flares lit the whole valley with an eerie blue light." The inevitable shellfire followed, causing severe casualties. At daybreak Smith found shelter in a tiny farmhouse, where Indian and British soldiers squashed in with an American grave party. The following night there were no spare mules. Instead, for the next stage of their ascent they had to carry all their radio equipment with the help of two porters. Weighed down with a thirty-five-pound lead-acid battery along with his personal gear, side pack, and sleeping bag, Smith found that his regulation shoes, studded with flat metal protectors, gave little grip on the slippery track. At one point on the way up to Snakeshead Ridge in the darkness, they got lost: "It was now a brilliant moonlit night," Smith recalls, "there was no sign of our HQ; indeed, there was no sign of anybody . . . Our track dwindled into a diverging maze of minor trails and we were confronted with a choice of routes. The two porters patiently followed without question and presumably believed we knew where we were going. We held to the same line, uphill and westward, moving carefully, talking little and listening hard. The little trail we were following led us across the heads of two steep gullies and proceeded toward the moonlit silhouette of a long spur. Coming around a sharp corner we stopped, petrified. The ground fell away steeply in front of us into a dark void, and high above us on the opposite side rose the monastery, its whole southern face brilliantly lit by the moon. It was beautiful, a breathtaking moment before we hastily retreated back round the corner. I can't understand why we didn't receive a hail of bullets: we must have been clearly visible to the Germans dug in around the base of the walls perhaps four hundred yards away."

Eventually, a full three days after having originally set off, they found their battalion headquarters, "a battered white farmhouse on a terraced hill," and looked for somewhere to sleep: "Just below the farm on a small terrace we could dimly discern a line of sleeping figures with room to spare at the end. So we joined them, unrolled our waterproof bags, used a side valise for a pillow, and dog tired we promptly fell asleep. It was broad daylight when we were awakened by shouting and laughter. Grinning down at us from the terrace wall were three gunners, friends of ours, members of the elite fraternity of artillery observers. 'Morning sigs,' they shouted. 'You sleep in strange company.' We looked to our left at the recumbent forms. They were all on stretchers with blankets over their faces and with their boots sticking out uncovered. We had slept with the dead, poor fellows, American dead. We grimaced and then joined the laughter. So does war debase man and so does man hide his finer feelings in sheer self-protection."

Close behind the forward troops, the division's doctors moved up to Caira to establish an advanced dressing station (ADS). John David was among them, and wrote in his diary about the American soldiers he came across. They were complaining about their generals twenty miles behind the lines, saying, "Let the boys have another crack at it." One "shell-shocked" young soldier he spoke to had "seen six of his buddies killed . . . The Americans have done no mean job, the way they have plugged along. Everyone's opinion has risen a great deal. The only trouble seems to be in their generals."

But the exhausted state of the Americans combined with the paucity of tracks up and down the mountain was delaying the relief further. Douglas Hawtin sums up the situation: "[There were] live, or just about alive, Yankee soldiers departing . . . they had had enormous casualties and were delighting at being relieved. The whole operation was due to be completed during the previous night, but with limited access, atrocious weather and enemy activity the whole operation took much longer and all day Americans could be seen appearing as if from nowhere and making for this goat track to go down the mountain. There was no passing bay, so no chance of them descending until all of our division was up."

The bottlenecks and constricted tracks meant that two extra battalions—the 1/9th Gurkhas and 4/6th Rajputana Rifles—put under the command of 7th Brigade, found it impossible to get onto the massif in time for the forthcoming attack. The ever-dwindling number of mules also meant that not only men from the division's reserve brigade, the 11th, but from the attacking brigade as well had to be used as porters. When finally in position on Snakeshead Ridge, it soon became apparent what a simply awful place it was, overlooked from three sides by enemy positions. Twenty-year-old John Buckeridge was a platoon commander in C Company of the Royal Sussex Battalion, and took up a position on the ridge a mere fifty yards away from the Germans. "You had to build sangars from the boulders and rocks strewn all around," Buckeridge recalls. "The Americans had built these little oblong shelters which were not more than eighteen inches high, and in which not more than two people could go. As dawn came, it was quite clear that these walls were not high enough to prevent the Germans from observing us. During the course of that morning I was sitting with my batman in my sangar and he was shot dead by a sniper from across the valley from a place called Phantom Ridge. He wasn't the first to be sniped and killed. That was my initiation into this ghastly place called Snakeshead Ridge."

There was worse to come. Having ascended Snakeshead on the night of 13 February, the Sussex Battalion found reconnaissance extremely difficult,

as movement during daylight attracted instant fire, and at night it was difficult to work out the complicated terrain. One thing became clear, though:
Point 593, Calvary Mount, from where the battalion was supposed to launch
its attack on the monastery, was still in German hands. It was decided that a
separate attack on this crucial strong point would have to precede the assault
on the abbey. It also became apparent that the fifty or so American soldiers
holding on in the most forward positions were so exhausted they would
have to be carried out on stretchers. With each stretcher needing four bearers to carry it over the rough ground, nothing could be done on the night of
the fourteenth, so the attack on Point 593 was ordered for the night of the
fifteenth.

The gravity of the task facing the 4th Indian Division soon became obvious. Bodies in various states of decay and mutilation were scattered everywhere. "It was like a cemetery up there," says Royal Sussex veteran Jack
Turner, "devoid of all greenery . . . and the desolation and the misery. Dead
all round you rotting." Signaler B. Smith was equally shocked: "There were a
number of dead GIs lying around," he writes. "Thank God their mothers
couldn't see the sadness and indignity of it all."

The bombing began at 9:45 A.M. on Tuesday, 15 February. It was a huge display of strength. The army commanders had requested dive bombers to
break the monastery walls, but somewhere along the line the scale had
mushroomed. Perhaps the air commanders, aware that this was the first
time that heavy bombers of strategic air forces were to be deployed as tactical support for infantry, were determined to put on a show to demonstrate
the power of the weapons at their disposal.

That day BBC war correspondent Christopher Buckley broadcast from
Cassino. He described how the attacking aircraft "flew in perfect formation
with that arrogant dignity which distinguishes bomber aircraft . . . As they
passed over the crest of Monastery Hill small jets of flame and spatters of
black earth leaped into the air from the summit. Just before two o'clock . . .
a formation of Mitchells passed over. A moment later a bright flame, such as
a giant might have produced by striking titanic matches on the mountainside, spurted swiftly upwards . . . For nearly five minutes it hung around the
building, thinning gradually upwards into strange, evil-looking ara-
besque . . . Then the column paled and melted. The Abbey became visible

again. Its whole outline had changed. The west wall had totally collapsed, and the whole side of the building along a length of about a hundred yards had simply caved in. It lay open to the attacker."

In the first wave, 142 B-17 Flying Fortress bombers from the 13th Strategic Air Force stationed at Foggia dropped a total of 253 tons of high-explosive and incendiary bombs. New Zealander John Blythe was watching from the gun lines by Trocchio: "As wave after wave came in the smoke began to rise, the vapor trails grew and merged, and the sun was blotted out and the whole sky turned gray." The monks were at prayer in a small room below the northwest wing of the monastery. When they heard the first bombs hit the abbey, they gathered on their knees around the abbot, who gave them each absolution. One of the monks, Don Agostino, has explained, "We heard the planes coming then huge explosions. Everything shook, smoke was everywhere." "The whole mountain was alight," says a German veteran who had been stationed nearby. "The olive trees burned for days. It was a torch, a real inferno." The second wave, of 47 twin-engined Mitchells and 40 twin-engined Marauders from the Mediterranean Air Force, unloaded a further one hundred tons of bombs from about 1 P.M. Staff Sgt. Kenneth E. Chard, on board the lead medium bomber, reported, "Target cabbaged real good." Only film footage can really do justice to the fury and viciousness of the bombing, as high explosive is seen to rip apart the monastery.

The bombing was followed by an artillery bombardment, and the effect on the building was spectacular. The *New York Times* called it the "worst aerial and artillery onslaught ever directed against a single building." Lieutenant Daiber, the German officer who had met with the abbot early that morning, said it was "as if the mountain had disintegrated, shaken by a giant hand." The monks in their refuge deep in the abbey were unhurt but had to dig their way out. The scene that greeted them when they emerged was one of utter destruction. There was a huge crater in the middle of the priory courtyard, the cloisters had collapsed, and the beautiful central courtyard was completely destroyed. The basilica, with its frescoes, magnificent choir, and wonderful organ, was now a heap of rubble. The sacristy, too, with its beautiful murals and carvings, had been leveled to the ground. All around were injured or killed refugees. It is thought that over one hundred perished. Not one German soldier was killed by the bombing.

A British artilleryman, flying with an American pilot in one of the ever-present spotter planes over the battlefield, commented, "The sight that confronted us will never be forgotten by all who witnessed it. The monastery was unrecognizable." Those watching had mixed reactions. There was much cheering, particularly among those who had already been fighting in the malign shadow of the monastery. One American wrote approvingly the next day, "It was a tremendous spectacle to see all the Flying Fortresses come over and drop their bombs." The veteran war correspondent Martha Gellhorn was a spectator of the bombing and wrote, some thirty years later, "I remember the actual bombing of Monte Cassino. I watched it, sitting on a stone wall or the stone side of a bridge, and saw the planes come in and drop their loads and saw the monastery turning into a muddle of dust and heard the big bangs and was absolutely delighted and cheered like all the other fools." Others who had just arrived at Cassino had rather more mixed reactions. New Zealander Brick Lorimer said that it was "soul destroying to watch . . . the realization settled on us finally what we were here for, that it was essentially a sad time." A young Gurkha officer, Eric "Birdie" Smith, newly arrived at Cassino, wrote in his diary on that day: "The Allied air forces bomb the monastery. Awe-inspiring to watch. It is now shrouded in dust. There was no opposition from the Germans, no antiaircraft fire. I suppose you could call the monastery another tragic casualty of war."

For young Tony Pittaccio, however, there was no ambiguity, only a deep sadness and despair: "As for Monte Cassino, whereas the military may have felt spying enemy eyes looking down on them, we felt that benevolent eyes were looking down on us. The monastery was to us the assurance that goodness would triumph over evil and the promise that it would never be destroyed meant that life would continue. We said our daily prayers with our eyes turned toward the monastery. It was a source of great comfort. When it was bombed we just could not believe what we were seeing. A part of all of us, and especially me and my family because of what it had meant to us, died with it. Nothing was sacred anymore and the world had truly become a darkened place."

At 8 P.M., Lieutenant Daiber returned to the remains of the monastery. He found the monks gathered at the Cappella della Pietà and immediately asked the abbot to confirm in writing that there were no German troops in the abbey when it was bombed. The exhausted eighty-year-old signed the declaration on the altar of the chapel. At dawn the next day many of the surviving civilians fled the abbey. Don Martino's account of the day is concerned with the discovery of three small children, their mother dead, abandoned by their father. His diary entry concludes with the reflection that man is beyond hope.

Early the next morning the remaining survivors, led by the abbot carrying a large wooden crucifix, set off in the direction of Piedimonte, behind the German lines. During the journey Don Martino was wounded in the arm when a shell landed nearby. A woman who had lost both her feet had to be left to die on the way. They reached the shelter of a small house, from where a German ambulance picked them up late in the afternoon and took them to von Senger's headquarters. Von Senger sent them the next day to the Benedictine monastery at Sant' Anselmo on the Aventine, but outside Rome they were intercepted by the SS. In his memoirs, von Senger writes, "the weary old man was dragged off to a big transmitting station, where he was not even given a meal. Here he had to give an account [broadcast on the radio] of the difference in the behavior of the Germans and the Allies . . . Tired, hungry and dejected, the abbot was dragged to the German Embassy in the Vatican, where he was asked to sign a memorandum that bristled with propaganda against the Allies . . . The abbot refused to put his name to such a document."

The diarist Iris Origo, an Englishwoman married to an Italian marquis, recorded the effect of Abbot Diamare's radio broadcast: "Without a single adjective, quietly, in a tired and saddened tone, he told the story as if it had happened a hundred years ago. It was terribly moving and I can hardly imagine what the Benedictines from the monastery now scattered all over the world must have felt in hearing that quiet, heartfelt account of the end of that source of civilization—now, after fourteen centuries of religious life, buried forever."

The treatment of the abbot enraged the Vatican, but the Germans had their propaganda coup and were going to make the most of it. A film was made of the ruins of the abbey and flown to Berlin. "In the senseless lust of destruction is mirrored the whole fury of the British–US command," Propaganda Minister Goebbels told the nation. "It is one of the grotesque manifestations of history that British–US youth risks its life to carry out the Jewish desire to destroy." It was the Germans, he declared, who were the true defenders of European civilization.

The Allies in turn insisted that the fault was with the Germans for occupying the monastery. "It was necessary," the Pathé news service announced. "[It] was turned into a fortress by the German Army." A spectacular film of the bombing taken from the Allied lines was shown, followed by the announcement, "so ended an extremely unpleasant task."

Kesselring was infuriated that his men were being blamed for the destruction, saying that allegations of German occupation of the building were "a baseless invention." It was the fault instead, he said, of "United States soldiery, devoid of all culture" and "Anglo-Saxon and Bolshevik warfare [which] has only one aim: to destroy the venerable proofs of European culture."

Arguments about the justification for the bombing have continued ever since. In fact, the destruction shocked both sides. One perhaps unanticipated consequence was that it may have convinced Kesselring to spare Rome, Venice, and other places of outstanding historical and artistic importance. Indeed, the impact was felt by all who watched the film of the bombing or saw photographs of the ruined abbey. That a treasure of civilization such as Monte Cassino should have to be destroyed reverberated around the world as the culmination of the pity, stupidity, and barbarism of war.

10

Snakeshead Ridge

Almost everything of value in the monastery had been destroyed. But how did this help the Allies? The massive walls were still intact at their base, so there was no easy way in for attacking troops. And there was not even a force ready to storm the building when the bombing and artillery stopped. The 4th Indian Division's commanding officer, Dimoline, had repeatedly asked Freyberg to delay the air attack until his assault troops were in position, but the pressures of Anzio and the weather, and a failure of coordination between the air forces and the ground troops, meant that the bombing occurred twenty-four hours earlier than Dimoline expected. The commander of 7th Brigade was told that the attack was going ahead only fifteen minutes before it started. So, to the forward troops of the 4th Indian Division opposite the building, who were supposed to rush in before the Germans could recover, the bombardment came as a complete surprise. Glennie, the commanding officer of the Sussex Battalion, later wrote, "Everyone, including the monks and the enemy, seemed to know about the timing of the bombing except us."

The 4/16th Punjab Battalion was positioned to the left of the Sussex men on Snakeshead. Their war diary describes the bombing from their point of view: "We went to the door of the Command post, a derelict farmhouse, and gazed up into the pale blue sky. There we saw the white trails of many high level bombers. Our first thought was that they were the enemy then some-one said 'Flying Fortresses,' then followed the whistle, swish and blast as the first flights struck against the Monastery. Almost before the ground ceased to shake the telephones were ringing. One of our Companies was within 300 yards from the target and another 800 yards. All had received a plastering and were asking questions with some asperity."

The Sussex men, too, were uncomfortably close to the monastery. John Buckeridge of C Company explains: "I could see hordes of Flying Fortresses in groups, and as I was watching I suddenly saw, as they got over Cassino, the bomb doors open and watched the bombs come down. Some of them hit the monastery, a lot of them didn't. As the terrain was granite, exploding bombs caused granite splinters and the casualties we endured during that particular bombing came from granite splinters, and not from any direct hit." Twenty-four of the battalion were wounded.

As the artillery bombardment continued during the afternoon of 15 February, Freyberg, who seems still to have been unaware that the crucial Point 593 was in enemy hands, urged action on the part of the 4th Indian Division to take advantage of the bombing. But the commanders on the spot refused to attack the monastery until 593 was captured, arguing that any move across the open ground toward the abbey would be cut down by flanking fire from this position, and stipulated that this preliminary attack must take place after nightfall. Thus—after all the sound and fury, the thousands of tons of bombs flown from as far away as Africa, the terrible destruction—nothing happened.

Even organizing the preliminary attack was causing appalling difficulties. It had been very difficult to establish the true lie of the land, or the enemy's strength on Point 593. Because of the steep slopes either side of the ridge, there was only a very narrow strip along which men could attack. It was therefore impossible to deploy large numbers of men, who would have just presented a larger target to the Germans. In any event, only one company, of three officers and sixty-three men, was detailed to attack that night. One of the three officers was John Buckeridge: "We were to attack and take Point 593 with a view to the battalion passing through and trying to take the monastery; the monastery now being reduced to rubble and the Germans being in defensive positions. C Company got up from their sangars to attempt to wheedle the Germans off 593." The men moved forward as quietly as possible and the company thought they'd succeeded in surprising the

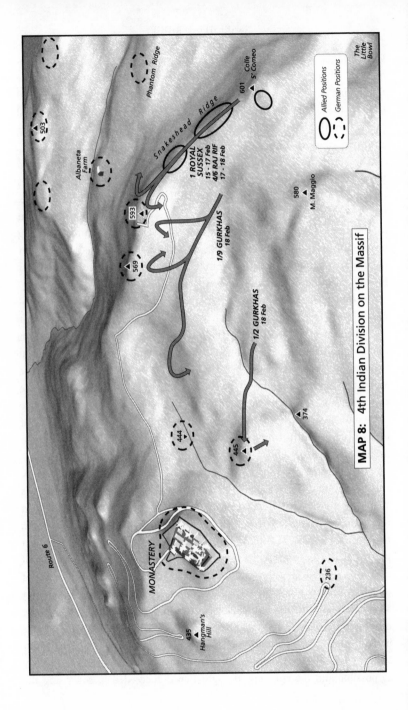

MAP 8: 4th Indian Division on the Massif

Allied Positions
German Positions

The Little Bowl

Phantom Ridge

503

Albaneta Farm

Snakeshead Ridge

601 Colle S' Comeo

1 ROYAL SUSSEX
15 - 17 Feb
4/6 RAJ RIF
17 - 18 Feb

593

569

1/9 GURKHAS
18 Feb

580
M. Maggio

1/2 GURKHAS
18 Feb

374

444

445

236

MONASTERY

435
Hangman's Hill

Route 6

Germans. But at the last moment, at a distance of about ten yards, the defenders opened fire with machine guns and hurled a volley of grenades. "You had it coming at you from about three or four different directions and it was very, very uncomfortable," recalls Buckeridge. For the attack, Signaler Douglas Hawtin had moved up with the battalion's commanding officer on to the ridge: "It was fierce close-quarter fighting. There was I, completely exposed on this bare rock face, operating the wireless with bullets and confusion going on all night, no cover whatsoever, not even a pebble." The attackers tried to infiltrate around the side of the position but soon ran out of grenades, essential for this sort of fighting. Before first light, Glennie ordered them to withdraw. Buckeridge's two fellow officers were both casualties, as were thirty-two of the men.

In the meantime the Germans occupied the monastery ruins and repaired their strong points around Monastery Hill. One of the reinforcements moved up on the night of 15 February was eighteen-year-old Werner Eggert. It was just as dangerous and difficult for the Germans to move men and supplies up to their forward positions as it was for the Allies, and as his unit made the climb up to the monastery, Eggert came under shellfire. "Suddenly a whistling came at us, mercilessly hitting the high retaining wall in front and behind us," he recalls. "Groaning and calling, I got back up on my legs. The wall, coming down with masses of earth, buried some of our people. I shook the dirt off and checked myself out. I had not got a scratch . . . In the fire of more impacts, we feverishly excavated the buried and helped the ones wounded by shrapnel and stone fragments. Two medics ran from one injured to another, but that was not enough. A few syringes already filled were put into my hands. 'Give it to him in the arm, to that one in the butt, quickly, through the trousers!' one of them said to me. He pointed with the torch. I heard a groaning . . . Suddenly, somebody stood beside me. He held his right hand to the place where his chin had been. I called for the medic, but the man had already fallen over. The medic tore up package upon package and tried to stop the pulsing blood rushing out. I gave him my last syringe. I don't know whether the man survived. Here our company suffered the first Cassino losses, two dead ones and four severely wounded people; six men were assigned to carry the stretchers. Maybe not even five minutes had passed since the whole thing started. The largest portion of the remaining people had already hurried past us in express step. I just about managed not to fall behind as I followed them, gasping for breath, moving up a slope."

In the darkness, some of the men began to doubt whether they were on the right track, and Eggert was sent ahead to find the way. "I headed up to the saddle . . . It was not yet dawn. I had waited for the end of one of the sporadic artillery assaults and started by running, as fast as the trampling path permitted, in the direction of the monastery. Suddenly, when the vapor had somewhat disappeared, the southwest portion of the abbey which had withstood the bombs stood before me—an enormous column—defiantly, threateningly and like a monument. The thing grew like a gray-white nose of a ship, diagonally from the black soil above me."

For Eggert, as for soldiers on both sides, the waiting to go in and the feeling of helplessness when under shellfire was worse than actual combat: "Every human has fear," he says. "It is a natural component of the self-preservation instinct. However, I observed in myself certain moments when rage and anger anesthetized the fear. I am sure others also experienced this—when normal reactions are out of order. When exposed to the shells, against which one has no chance, rage over one's own powerlessness surfaces. When humans approach you to kill you it is already different. They are your equals. You see the human for one instant as human. In the next moment you see him as a killing machine. The picture jumps back and forth until it stays as the human killing machine. And that's where the rage comes from. That's when you shoot. Without fear. Without scruples. As soon as the finger has curved, you become completely calm."

The next day, 16 February, there were more Allied fighter-bomber and artillery attacks on the monastery, but the crucial Point 593 itself could not be targeted as it was too close to the Sussex men's positions. After several delays, while the men waited for mules to arrive with more grenades, the battalion launched another attack in the evening, still trying to clear and hold Point 593. Glennie was unhappy that he had not had more time for recce and for amassing more ammunition, but, he said, "We got on with it because a: it was repeatedly emphasized that we must do something to take the pressure off the Anzio beachhead which was in imminent danger of collapse; b: we had so far always been successful. We had the superiority complex common to the rest of 4th Indian Division." As the attack started, Allied shells hit the men as they formed up on the start line. The attackers had advanced only fifty yards when they came under withering fire and a shower of grenades landed in their midst. However, some men from D Company managed to get around a flank, and fierce hand-to-hand fighting ensued on the peak. A sharp German counterattack added to the confusion, and the Sussex men found that, again, grenades were running out. Glennie sent in his reserve company, which had been earmarked to consolidate on 593 after its capture, but at that point the Germans fired three green Very lights (flares), which just happened to be the Sussex's signal to withdraw. Some of the attackers, even those who had reached 593, started pulling back to their own lines. By this time, though, daylight was approaching, which would have left the Sussex men fatally exposed, and Glennie was forced to halt the attack. During the two nights, of the men used, the Sussex had suffered over 50 percent casualties.

Now Freyberg's patience wore out. Having twice allowed the 4th Division to attack in small parties on Point 593, he demanded a larger-scale attack the next day, 17 February, on a wider front directly on the monastery, in effect returning to the approach taken by the US 34th Division two weeks before. The commanders on the spot protested that there was simply not enough room between the huge crevices and steep slopes to deploy three battalions in the attack, and that they were having to use a high proportion of the division's assault troops as porters. But, under pressure from Clark as the situation at Anzio deteriorated, Freyberg insisted, and instructed that at the same time an attack would be made by the 2nd New Zealand Division down in the Rapido valley.

Kippenberger, in his first divisional command, had been experiencing similar problems to those of the 4th Indian Division. Although his supply situation was better, the flooding of the Rapido valley by the Germans had effectively built a moat in front of Cassino town and the Liri valley entrance. The heavy rain from 4 February onward had worsened the situation, with much of the valley underwater and quite impassable to tanks and other vehicles. The only axis of attack was along the raised railway embankment into the station. But this had been substantially demolished and mined, and would require numerous repairs and two Bailey bridges before it could be used. As up on Snakeshead, this narrow space could accommodate only a limited number of assaulting troops, so Kippenberger decided that he would attempt to seize the station with just a single battalion, then engineers would repair the causeway and he could push through the armor and the rest of the division. It was above all essential, Kippenberger realized, that tanks reached the attacking battalion before daylight made them sitting ducks. The force he chose as the spearhead was the 28th, the Maori Battalion.

This had been formed at the behest of a senior Maori politician to prove the bravery of New Zealand's indigenous people and demonstrate their willingness to make sacrifices for the nation. Recruitment remained voluntary for the Maori and, according to a historian of the battalion, "had little to do with patriotic duty, rather it was the age-old tradition of maintaining the *mana* or status of the family, the *hapu* (subtribe) and the *iwi* (people)." Companies within the battalion were formed on a tribal basis, which made for tight-knit groups, and many sets of brothers served in the same unit. George Pomana, from C Company, remembers that most of his platoon went to school together, and forty-eight men from his small township were in the battalion: "When you know people from way back," he says, "you never think of letting anybody down." Pomana's father had died just before he was born, from the aftereffects of a gas attack during the First World War, and he remembers lots of hard, physical work growing up on the family dairy farm: "None of us had much in the way of education," he says. "We were taught to use our muscles more than our heads."

The Maoris, of course, came from a tradition of endemic warfare and were unquestionably aggressive and effective soldiers. But they were also warm and humorous. Brick Lorimer remembers them as "full of tricks. Inimitable jokers ... [with a] distorted sense of humor." Lorimer himself was part of the armored force lined up to exploit into the Liri valley. "The story was that the Maoris would make the breakthrough, the bridge would go in, and then here come the cavalry, Rome next stop."

At 8:45 P.M. on 17 February, the leading companies set off for the attack. It was a dark and cold night, and the men first had to cross six hundred yards of sodden ground to reach their start line. From there, at 9:30, they moved forward. Almost immediately they encountered minefields and freshly laid barbed wire, as well as mortar fire. But after an hour they reached the station yards. In command of B Company was Capt. Monty Wikiriwhi. Already wounded and decorated in the desert, he was one of three brothers in the battalion. "My 12 Platoon on the right wavered in the face of a particularly violent burst of MG fire from two Jerry posts," he recalled. "I immediately ordered a charge—the men leapt forward and, as in training, two men leapt on to the wire—the others jumped over (there was sufficient light from flares and gun flashes) and, with bayonets and grenades, cleaned the posts out. Others were busy with cutters on the ordinary wire and the platoons were soon through on to the first objective." This was the Round House, a large building immediately south of the station. From there, with artillery support, the Maoris moved toward the station. For an hour a confused battle raged for control of the buildings. "That night it was all hand to hand with bayonet and Bren guns," said Wikiriwhi. "How my men ever sorted out who was who and what was what I will never know. It was a pitch dark night. Anyway by morning they had cleaned everyone out of this place." A Company's objective was a small mound close to the station known as the Hummock. Here, though, it was discovered that the position was protected by a deep ditch that was impossible to cross. Nevertheless, work was proceeding rapidly behind the forward troops. By 2 A.M. the engineers were working on three demolitions simultaneously, with only one still untouched.

Two thousand feet above them in the mountains behind the monastery, 4th Indian Division's attack started at midnight. The first assault, as before, was on Point 593, with two subsequent attacks planned for Gurkha battalions across the broken terrain to the left of Snakeshead directly onto the high ground immediately in front of the monastery. An eyewitness, Peter Cochrane, a captain in one of the battalions portering for the attackers, describes how, after an intense barrage, Indian soldiers of the 4/6th Rajputana Rifles moved off along Snakeshead Ridge. "The Germans put up flares, unusually short-lived, so that one saw the battlefield in a series of brilliant flashes." Through the smoke and dust from shell fragments, he could make out that things were not going well: "The sepoys went in like tiger cats, but the hillside, the barbed wire and fierce defensive fire were too much for them. There were many casualties." Most were pinned down some one hundred yards from the objective, but a handful of men reached the summit of 593. However, they were unable to clear all the German positions on the near slope and could not, as planned, advance along the saddle of rock toward the monastery. Nor could they prevent fire coming from positions around 593 disrupting the subsequent attack, about three hundred yards to their left, by the 1/9th Gurkhas. Having endured a four-hour approach march, the Gurkhas attacked at 2:15 A.M., heading downhill toward Point 444. They were subjected to withering fire from around 593 as well as in front of them, and the leading company was driven off course. An attack on the left side of 593 by the second company made little headway. To their left, the 1/2nd Gurkhas had an even worse time. Kharkabahadur Thapa remembers his part in the fighting: "We also opened fire from time to time. One GOR [Gurkha other rank] was hit, a bullet in the stomach, from LMG [light machine gun] fire from below. I threw a grenade in the direction from where the fire had come, fired my rifle and killed a German machine gunner. We put dressings on the wounded man and pulled him to where the adjutant was. We moved our position a little and shells landed where we had been. The man died. The adjutant asked about relatives and I said I was a close relation and his neighbor in the village . . . I was not afraid when the bullets started flying. British soldiers said, 'Die, go to heaven. Very good, Johnny, very good, Johnny,' laughing with us."

Attacking directly toward the monastery, the leading company had to proceed through a patch of chest-high gorse scrub that had looked innocuous in aerial photographs. But the Germans had liberally sown the thickets with mines and tripwires linked to booby traps and established fire pits nearby. Nearly every man in the leading platoon was blown up by mines, and as the rest of the company tried to push on through, they were hit by grenades and machine gun fire. The next two companies worked their way around the left of the scrub and fought to the top of Point 445, only eight hundred yards from the monastery itself. There, fire raked them from three sides as they frantically tried to scratch together some cover on the rocky summit.

Up on Snakeshead Ridge, communication had broken down between the companies of the Rajputana Rifles and the battalion headquarters, so at 4 A.M. the battalion's commanding officer went forward himself to assess the situation. Half an hour later he called for Maj. John ffrench, the officer in charge of the last remaining uncommitted company. "He said that we had had heavy casualties, but that he had been up on Pt 593 which was clear of the enemy and that I was to take A Company forward to secure it," recalled ffrench. "I sent my runner to bring the company up. There was some delay, owing to a porter party having just arrived with a supply of grenades, which Subedar Mohammed Yusef had then ordered to be primed and distributed among the men. I was with the forward platoon as we reached the low wall which had been the start line and the sangars still occupied by the Royal Sussex, when we were met by a burst of firing from the crest of Pt 593 only 70 yards ahead. We were too late. The Germans had already reoccupied it. Two Royal Sussex stretcher bearers got up to bring in one of their wounded lying only a few yards forward and were immediately shot dead. The Germans evidently had snipers with telescopic sights lined up on any movement forward. It was just getting light, so I signaled to the other two platoons to take cover. The forward platoon had already gone to ground."

With the coming of daylight, it was decided that the entire attack would have to be abandoned. The men were ordered back to their starting positions, only the 1/2nd Gurkhas holding out until they could evacuate their wounded.

Together with the losses sustained by the Royal Sussex Battalion, it was a grievous blow to what had been an elite division. The 1/9th Gurkhas had lost nearly 100 men killed, wounded, or taken prisoner; the 1/2nd Gurkhas 149, including nearly all its officers; and, worst of all, the Rajputana Rifles had lost just short of 200. "The battalion, which had contained many veterans, was never the same again," wrote a 4th Indian Division officer in his account of the battle, "and it was a sad and costly defeat after a string of victories in past battles." For eyewitness Peter Cochrane, the failure was due to the mistimed bombing of the monastery and Freyberg's scratch corps headquarters: "It was typical of this hopelessly disorganized battle that through no fault of the army, the divisional attack could not be synchronized with the bombing of the monastery; it would have given the unfortunate infantry a sporting chance . . . Cassino was our first experience of an 'allied' battle and we did not like it. We could and did respect our fellow soldiers of all nationalities, but the command structure and staff work seemed to us below par." Certainly, as before when the Americans were attacking over the same ground, the Allied high command seemed to have little knowledge of the realities of the fighting up on the massif. What looked like a tiny distance on a map might contain deep gorges, vertical cliffs, or impassable rocks. Added to this, they had underestimated the problems of supplying the frontline soldiers as well as the tenacity and determination of the German defenders.

The next day, Dr. John David wrote a long entry in his diary that vividly captures the confusion and shock in the division: "Very eventful day for me today. Fearful noise all night, then fairly quiet this morning. No news again, monastery believed to have been taken by our boys but they need reinforcements to hold." After lunch an urgent message came for twenty-four stretcher bearers and an officer to get up to the front line as quickly as possible. David reached the forward camp near Caira but could find "no coherent news about what was going on . . . Patients are being brought down in a steady stream. About 240 had come down in two days." He trekked up to the farmhouse where 7th Brigade had its headquarters. On the way, among the dead mules, he saw a total of thirteen stretcher parties digging in to positions every 300 to 400 yards. Finally he reached the advanced dressing station just short of the front line. "Here I found a lot of white-faced officers from whom I could get no sense whatever."

Down in the valley, the New Zealanders' plan began to unravel at about 3 A.M. when the moon came out, revealing to the Germans the positions of the engineers working on the causeway to the station. Accurate mortar and machine gun fire started to hit them, and just before dawn they were withdrawn. When it was clear that there were no tanks on the way that morning, the Maoris in the station, under fire from three sides, asked permission to withdraw. To do so would have meant that all the sacrifices made would be for nothing. But to stay risked the attacking soldiers being wiped out or taken prisoner. Kippenberger decided that "It was just possible that the enemy would not counterattack with tanks," and he ordered a smokescreen and as much supporting fire from the Allied side of the Rapido as possible. Machine gunner Jack Cocker remembers firing all night and all the next day in support of the Maoris in the station.

At around ten in the morning Kippenberger tried to send reinforcements from George Pomana's C Company, but moving along the narrow causeway, observed from the monastery and elsewhere, was "like walking a tightrope in a shooting gallery," and heavy fire drove the company back. The Maoris in the station held on grimly that morning, but at about 2 P.M. the rumble of tanks could be heard through the smoke. The Germans were obviously massing for a counterattack.

Just before 3:15 P.M., using the cover of the smoke to creep close to the Maoris, German infantry attacked from two sides, supported by captured Sherman tanks. Soon the ammunition for the Maoris' handheld antitank PIAT bazookas was expended, and the situation looked desperate. Tank shells fired at a range of just fifty yards blew some Maoris clean out of their positions. The force of the blasts tore the clothes off others. "During the afternoon he came at us with his infantry and tanks and that's what tossed us out," says Monty Wikiriwhi. "I was telling my colonel over the radio, 'We've had it,' and he said, 'Stay there. Hold it! Hold it at all costs!' I told him virtually to go and get stuffed, saying, 'No, to hell with that,' and ordered all my men out."

As men started to fight their way back, Wikiriwhi, already carrying a mine wound from earlier, was hit in the leg by an explosive bullet. Seeing the blood pumping out of his commander, a junior officer applied a makeshift tourniquet and dragged him to the embankment, in spite of Wikiriwhi's protestations that he should be left behind. Moments later the junior officer was himself killed. Wikiriwhi lay on the ground as the Germans advanced past them. "I and a lot of my men too were just lying here," he says. "One German came round and kicked us in the guts and shouted 'Raus, Raus' as if to wake us up. I just lay there with my men. He went away, then I started my crawl back." Although the bones in his right leg were smashed, he applied his pistol lanyard as a tourniquet and fashioned a wooden splint. "I started at about ten o'clock that night," he continues, "just pushing myself along on my backside." In spite of the loss of blood and the pain from his wrecked leg, Wikiriwhi kept going all night. By sunrise he was about four hundred yards from the station, and although now clearly visible to the Germans and under fire, he made it back to the New Zealand forward lines by five o'clock that afternoon.

It had been a massacre. Of the 200 troops who set off the previous night, some 130 were casualties. Freyberg had no option but to admit the attack was over.

Six weeks later, in the hope of recovering their dead, a reconnaissance party of Maori returned to the site, led by the battalion commander, Peter Awatere, as well as the regimental sergeant-major, Martin McCrae, the padre, and another officer, Norman Perry. The first body they discovered was that of Lt. George Asher, who had had both legs blown off during the fighting on 18 February. The corpse was so badly decomposed that they were able to identify it only by the distinctive way he had swished back his hair. They could see, however, that before he died he had tried to apply a tourniquet made of wire to stem the loss of blood. Next they found the remains of a platoon, all lying in the same direction: facing Cassino. It seems they had all been hit by a single burst of machine gun fire. Then Norman Perry heard what he described as "an awful keening sound." He turned round to see that McCrae had identified one of his relatives.

The party returned the next day to take away the dead, but were interrupted when a jeep of military police arrived. None of the officers was wearing his insignia, so the police instinctively addressed Perry, the only European in the group. Told that they should not have been there and that burying the dead was a job for the graves registration unit, Perry replied that they would bury their own. The senior officer, Awatere, remained silent, but at that moment a truck carrying the burial party arrived. Awatere called out to them in Maori, "Come forward, but come slowly." He then turned to the military policemen and said, in English, "The men you see approaching are from 28th Battalion. They have come to bury their friends and relations; one of them has come to bury his brother. I will not be responsible for what happens here if they are not able to do so." The red caps wisely withdrew.

The Germans were delighted to have recaptured the station and to have "given the New Zealanders a bloody nose." For them it was another defensive victory. Furthermore, almost simultaneously, the hastily assembled but powerful German 14th Army had smashed through the perimeter of the Anzio bridgehead and was heading directly for the coast. It looked like the Allies would be driven back into the sea. At Cassino some of the Allies' finest troops had been slaughtered for no gain whatsoever. It was the low point of the entire campaign.

11

Lull at Cassino, Counterattack at Anzio

After an intense artillery barrage, the German counterattack on Anzio was launched at 5:30 A.M. on 16 February, the morning after the bombing of the Cassino monastery. It was the heaviest German offensive of the campaign, with three divisions, 452 guns, and 270 tanks, including 75 heavy Tiger tanks. By early the next day they had penetrated over two miles into the Allied defenses, but sodden ground meant that the tanks had to keep to the metaled roads. Here, they were easy prey for Allied aircraft and artillery, which had responded to the German assault with a huge weight of shells. The German infantry was left without its support, and the attack faltered the next day, having been within an ace of success.

Alexander had already ordered a fresh offensive on the Gustav Line to help relieve his beleaguered forces at Anzio. His first instinct had been to wait for better weather in order fully to employ his superiority in armor and aircraft, but pressure from London and Washington, Anzio, and the New Zealand Corps commander Freyberg persuaded him otherwise. Freyberg wanted to try again on the monastery and Route 6 but on a different axis of attack from the north into Cassino town and against Castle Hill, which stood between the monastery and the town. After the failure of previous attacks towards Sant' Angelo and the station and with the Rapido valley still largely underwater, this was the only approach to Route 6 open to the Allied armor. The town was heavily fortified, so Freyberg planned an enormous aerial and artillery bombardment that would entirely flatten Cassino; thereafter the New Zealanders were to clear the town and open the way to the Liri valley for the massed Allied tanks. From Castle Hill, units of the 4th Indian Division, spearheaded by 5th Brigade, were to fight their way up the hairpin road to the monastery and capture Point 435. This was known to the Allied soldiers as Hangman's Hill, as on the peak stood a wrecked pylon that from below looked disturbingly like a gallows. Hangman's Hill was only three hundred yards from the outer wall of the monastery. From there an assault would at last be launched against the remains of the abbey itself, clearing the vital observation point.

Alexander agreed, as long as the attack was preceded by three clear days to allow the ground to firm up enough for the four hundred waiting tanks to be able to exploit in the Liri valley. On 22 February, New Zealand units relieved the last men of the US 34th Division holding the northeastern corner of the town of Cassino, and the British 78th Division took over the New Zealanders' positions opposite Sant' Angelo. Everything was due to be ready by 24 February, when the code words "Bradman bats today" would signal the order to attack.

But on the twenty-third the weather worsened, and there was continual rain for nearly three weeks. The new offensive had to be postponed. Down in the Rapido valley, continuous duty under observation from the monastery was beginning to affect engineer Matthew Salmon. Soon after the bombing of the monastery he was put in charge of a water pump near the Rapido River. The pump, driven by a small two-stroke motor, filled two 200-gallon tanks, to which Salmon added purification chemicals. Day and night, working alone, he had to fill containers to be taken to the frontline troops. "I couldn't understand it," he says. "The Germans must have known I was pumping water there." After about a fortnight he was exhausted from lack of sleep. Being under observation made him increasingly shaky, as did the lack of contact with his friends in his unit. Then the inevitable "stonk" happened. "As the shells came in I threw myself to the ground. There were seventeen in as many seconds," he says. The water tanks were wrecked, but Salmon was miraculously uninjured. He was not going to stay there, though, and headed back to his headquarters. "I walked up the track and was spotted by our RSM, who said, 'What are you doing here? Who is supplying water up at the front?' I went to reply to him, but discovered I couldn't talk properly and I kept stammering." The regimental sergeant-major told him to get a jeep, load it up with supplies, and start again. "I replied that I needed some rest and a break before I returned," says Salmon, "but he insisted that this was not necessary and told me to go back straightaway. When he knew I was serious about some rest, he consulted the CO who was upstairs."

The commanding officer, the fearsome Major Smith, asked to see him.

"What's all this about then?" he asked me. I explained to him in the best way I could about the attack at the river, but he seemed to be unimpressed by the difficulty I was having with my speech.

"Do you expect someone else do your shift for you?" the major asked.

"No," I replied, "all I ask is that I am allowed some rest."

The CO went berserk and called me a coward.

"OK, call me a coward if you like," I replied. "How long do you have to be in the army fighting to become a coward? Whatever you say, I'm not going back there until I get some sleep. I don't care if you take me outside and shoot me because I am at my wits' end and I've had enough."

At last the major conceded and sent Salmon to the field dressing station. There, the doctor asked him to give the wounded men some tea and cigarettes. "There were some wounded German prisoners," Salmon remembers, "but they were frightened about drinking our tea or smoking our cigarettes because they had been told we would try to poison them. Some of them even messed themselves with fright . . . Not long after that I started shaking and realized that I had been badly affected."

Evacuated to a field hospital, he was sedated and asked a series of questions by a doctor. "He told me to think back as far as I could in my life so he could establish the reason for my troubles," Salmon continues. "He asked if there had been any insanity in the family. For three days he interrogated me about my life. I began to wonder who needed remedial treatment—him or me? Surely he could see that the trauma I had been through during the war was the cause of my nervous state."

Moved back again, this time to the No. 2 General Hospital in Caserta, he found himself in the same ward as Spike Milligan. "Most of the men were what we used to call 'bomb-happy,'" Salmon explains. "Some were walking about as if they were drunk, but I had difficulty walking because I was shaking so badly. I was still having difficulty with my speech and couldn't get words out." At the end of the ward there "was another place, with the doors locked. In there were the blokes vastly more battle-fatigued than us. They were really out of their minds, had really gone off their heads. It was very sad really, that people should be put in a situation where they lose their minds. Bloody war. They were human beings, soldiers, a lot of them were Guardsmen. They said they could see the fairies and this sort of thing. It was very sad."

The chief psychiatrist at the hospital was Maj. Harold Palmer, a tough, no-nonsense northerner, "A rugged-looking man with a broken nose." He had written papers before the war about the value of "narcosis" for the treatment of psychiatric symptoms and was well respected in psychiatric circles for his energy and optimism that he could treat anything. He was disliked by some, however, for his direct methods and the way he talked about "cowardice." "Men who broke down in war," he wrote, "failed in their job as soldiers . . . A community at war has as much right to demand that a soldier gives his 'nerves' for his country, as in principle it exercises the right to demand that a soldier gives his eyes, limbs or even his life for his country."

Both Milligan and Salmon were treated by Palmer. Milligan had spent several days reading in bed in the ward, where, he writes, "About two-thirds were under drugs, and slept most of the day. The remainder were very silent and morose. No one spoke to anyone." When he finally saw Palmer, he told him that he needed a job to occupy himself. "I appreciate that," Palmer replied. "A lot of the bastards like to malinger here as long as they can." Milligan was posted to a rehabilitation camp north of Naples and given a job as a clerk.

Salmon had a rougher ride. Palmer, he says, shouted at him, "questioning me over and over again and accusing me of lying. I just couldn't make him understand that I was telling the truth, and the difficulty I was having with my speech made things even more distressing." Then Salmon was given an injection of sodium amytal, a barbiturate sometimes called a "truth serum," that had been used with some success on patients who had broken down during the nightmare evacuation of Dunkirk. Its use was controversial as it caused some patients to relive the horrors of what had led to their breakdown in the first place. But for others it was a shortcut away from the symptoms associated with "battle fatigue"; and for Harold Palmer, at least, it was a way of checking the men for "malingerers." Once the drug had taken effect, Salmon found he could speak again, and Palmer questioned him, more gently this time. He told his story once more, and finally Palmer said to him: "Right, you will not be going back up the front anymore. You will be put in a ward, and given some treatment." "I thought, Thank God for that," Salmon remembers. "I didn't want to go back up there; nobody does if they've got any sense." Once in bed, he was given a drink. "I don't remember anything more until the next morning, when I said to the doctor, 'Oh, that was a smashing sleep, I must have slept the clock round.' " In fact, he had been "asleep" for two weeks, a treatment known as "deep-sleep" narcosis, brought on by a heavier dose of barbiturates. Many other people in the ward, Salmon now noticed, were lying in bed or walking around "like zombies," undergoing the same treatment. For Salmon it seemed to have worked in that his symptoms—the shaking and stuttering—had disappeared. He doesn't resent the initial aggressive approach of Major Palmer. "You've got to take into consideration that there were some very clever people in the army who said, 'I'm going to get out of this lot,' and made out they were up the wall when they were not. You've got to have a person make sure they're genuine. That's why he was so abrupt."

Salmon was classed B1 Permanent—unfit for frontline duty—and was given a job in the hospital as a carpenter. "I was glad to be out of it, after what I'd been through," he says. "I have to be honest about that. I'd have given everything I owned not to have to go up the front line anymore. No, no, I didn't want no more of that."

Back at Cassino, the attack was still due to start as soon as the weather cleared, so the men detailed for the offensive were kept in their forward positions just behind the front line. Losses were steady and demoralizing. John David was now working as supply officer for 5th Brigade's advanced dressing station. His diary tells of a stream of shellfire casualties from the Essex Battalion. "Essex people very fed up," he wrote on 18 February as more severely injured men were brought in. "They complain they cannot retaliate."

The 1/4th Essex Battalion had arrived at Taranto on 22 November the previous year, having spent five months training in Syria and Egypt. Many were still the local men who had made up the territorial regiment before the war, although some were replacements brought in to make up for losses sustained in the desert fighting. One such was Ken Bond. He remembers joining the battalion after the fighting in North Africa, and being so impressed by the brown knees of the veterans that he promptly got himself very badly sunburned, an offense that rated as a self-inflicted wound. Happily, a kind medical orderly, Cpl. Ted "Nutty" Hazle, came to his rescue with some calamine and promised not to report him. Born and brought up in an industrial part of Bristol, Bond's father had been a furnace worker at a chemical factory, and Ken had left school at fourteen and done a succession of jobs, ending up, aged seventeen, as a milkman. He was the youngest of eleven children, three of whom did not survive into adulthood. "My mother was forty-five or forty-six," Bond says. "So I was the last of some who weren't wanted!" At eighteen he was conscripted and, after a period of training and the usual ferocious array of injections, he was shipped to the desert. Arriving as a young replacement meant that Bond had to do all the guard duties and other jobs. Many of the men were up to ten years older, and it was difficult to make friends. "I never felt that us West Country people were ever accepted," he says. "The Londoners didn't like the people from the West Country, and they were a close-knit band, from the fighting in the desert . . . I didn't know where we'd ended up, till someone said, 'You're in Italy.' " It was bitterly cold arriving in Taranto from Alexandria, and Bond remembers feeling particularly sorry for the Indians in their brigade. There was a short period spent in the line on the Adriatic front before the transfer of the division over to the 5th Army.

The battalion had arrived in the Cassino area on 4 February and eight days later moved forward to a gully near the village of Valvori. Under enemy observation and sporadic shellfire, the battalion watched the bombing of the monastery on 15 February. Three days later they were moved forward in darkness into Wadi Villa, a valley about a mile up the Caruso Road from Cassino. From here, it was planned, they would be able to exploit the success of 7th Brigade's efforts up on Snakeshead Ridge. But after the bloody failure of those efforts, the Essex were earmarked as the assault force for the next attack and kept in position. Wadi Villa was overlooked by German observation posts on Monte Cairo, so no movement was possible during the day, and the men had to stay in their bivouacs situated on the forward slopes of the valley or down on the dry riverbed below.

Within days, they had suffered their first casualty from shellfire, a Private Cole, and another man deserted. When the weather changed on 24 February, conditions for the men in the Wadi deteriorated further. "It rained as only it can in southern Italy, and down the mountains it came," the officer in charge of B Company, Capt. J. Beazley, has commented. "It filled the riverbed and swept through our lines, taking with it blankets, equipment, and even a medium machine gun."

Corporal Ted "Nutty" Hazle was one of the unlucky ones who had camped down at the bottom of the valley: "We were laid up in what was a dry ditch. We put a bivvy in it, made it comfortable." Then when the waters arrived, he was reduced to sitting on his tin hat for most of the night, which just about kept him out of the water: "The only one better off than me was the sergeant-major, who was sitting on an ammunition box!" Hazle was now a stretcher bearer in D Company, and as a veteran of North Africa—he was decorated with a Distinguished Conduct Medal (DCM), having been severely wounded at El Alamein while rescuing injured men—was still unfazed by the task ahead: "We were well hardened," he says. "We weren't worried about the attack."

For Maj. Denis Beckett, C Company's commander, it was "a strangely unreal situation. There certainly seems to have been a lack of planning in keeping the men in such an unpleasant and dangerous position for so long before the attack. It was an extreme case of that eternal order to army troops: 'Hurry up and wait.' "

Charlie Fraser, a signaler attached to the brigade, wrote in his diary on 27 February: "Again it rained nearly all day. I think everyone is fed up with these positions in Wadi Villa. Five more Indian ranks killed by shellfire. Roll on the attack, let's get it over with. Still raining, gullies and track flooded. More shelling and mortar fire in 5 Brigade HQ area. Rained all night."

Ken Bond celebrated his twenty-first birthday on 5 March "in a hole in the ground waiting to go in . . ." By then he was cold, tired, and frightened. "I was soaking wet. My bedding, blankets and the like being the same." The sleeping was very limited and the mortar and shellfire seemed nonstop. He was terrified most of all by the *Nebelwerfers,* six-barreled mortars that the Germans had originally designed to fire smoke canisters but had converted to firing high explosive. For infantrymen, this weapon, known variously as "screaming meemies," "moaning minnies," or "screaming sisters," seems to have been the most frightening in the Germans' arsenal. "I never drew pictures about 'screaming meemies,' " wrote American cartoonist Bill Mauldin, "because they just aren't funny." Just as terrifying as their effect was the noise they made as they came in. Ernie Pyle wrote, "The gun didn't go off with a roar, but the shells swished forward with a sound of unparalleled viciousness and power, as though gigantic gears were grinding." A British officer described the noise as "like someone sitting violently on the base notes of a piano, accompanied by the grating squeak of a diamond on glass." "That frightened the hell out of me," says Ken Bond, "the scream of six mortars coming over all at once."

Originally, the orders for the battalion for the forthcoming attack were to defend Castle Hill and its environs, but on 3 March at another conference at corps headquarters, the battalion commander, Lieutenant Colonel Noble, learned that the Essex were now to capture the monastery as well. John David wrote in his diary ten days later: "The Essex are said to be getting the honor of taking the monastery and have an Essex flag ready to put on it." Captain J. Beazley adopts a rather different tone: "Just when our morale was sadly needing a fillip, we had news that the attack on Cassino was to start."

During this period, from 19 February to 14 March, the newspapers back at home reported that all was quiet on the Italian front. "A report both misleading and untrue!" exclaims a British captain in his memoir of his time at Cassino. "It is never quiet to the soldiers nearest the enemy!" Up on the massif above the Essex men, hemmed in on three sides by enemy positions, the other two brigades of the 4th Indian Division cowered in their shallow sangars, desperately trying to get shelter from the freezing rain and snow as well as mortaring and sniping, with only their leather jerkins, gas-capes, and greatcoats for warmth.

Signaler B. Smith, of the 4/16th Punjabis, described life opposite the monastery at this time: "On many nights we heard the odd crack of a rifle and we groaned. The pattern was invariable. The initial crack would be answered by a couple of shots which prompted a burst of Bren gun fire which bred a rapid stutter from the German LMGs which started the mortars off, then the 25s and the 88s and finally the mediums and heavies and the whole area would be dancing, booming and crashing like Dante's *Inferno.* All this used to happen in minutes because of one itchy finger and one nervous eye. After a while both sides would realize that no one was attacking and the guns would grumble into silence." His battalion had not fought in the second battle, but between 15 February and 23 March they suffered 250 battle casualties as well as many more from sickness and exposure. In all, 7th Brigade was losing sixty men a day.

The Sussex Battalion signaler Douglas Hawtin was becoming increasingly exhausted: "I did not undress at all for two months; in full battledress and overcoat all the time. I got hold of some empty sandbags and wrapped these round the legs from knees to ankles and tied with string, and then let the mud cake on for extra warmth." He was wounded in the leg by shrapnel but could not for the time being be evacuated as there was no one left who could operate the wireless link back from battalion to brigade headquarters. The wound was dressed twice a day, but it still went septic. "Naturally we were alive with lice," he says. "We used to light a cigarette and pop them, usually helping each other out with this task." Hawtin was also suffering from a violent attack of dysentery, and soon he was almost too weak to stand. At this point the medical officer ordered him back while he could still walk.

John David was transferred to a Gurkha battalion's advanced dressing station on the massif to replace another doctor who had been killed. "Our troubles now begin in earnest," he wrote in his diary on 25 February. "It rains continuously . . . mud now rises in a sea outside the door, and our boots are never dry. All night we hear the unfortunate supply people sloshing past. Anyone who arrives wounded in the evening is always soaked through. We have no means of drying their clothes. It is impossible to send them down the track these dark nights, so we have to put them in the room above. Our blankets are all damp. My feeling of helplessness, being unable to mitigate their lot, increases with the hours."

The next day he was called out to help bring in a signalman, a Private Jennings, attached to the 1/2nd Gurkhas. With four stretcher bearers, he ventured out into the night: "We slithered along the path, fell twice flat in the mud. At last against the skyline we saw an agitated party of bearers coming down with the unfortunate patient groaning at every jolt." A shell had landed in the signaler's foxhole and not exploded, but had smashed both his feet, which were "only hanging on by skin. Now he was coming, cold with shock, soaked with rain and [we had] no means except morphia, which he had already had, of relieving his troubles." David saw that immediate amputation was needed on one foot. "We transfused him and warmed him up, and he seemed quieter but by midnight he was showing that peculiar jerky restlessness which they have before death, and by morning he was dead." David had to prepare Jennings for burial, "which only consists of putting a blanket over him. It also necessitated a lengthy search for the amputated foot, which had been thrown on to the rubbish dump. I did not want someone later on suddenly to find it there, so after some time I was able to return it to the body."

As the rain continued, the supply situation on the massif, already difficult, worsened, and many of the "rubbish dumps" were scoured by the British soldiers for discarded American rations. Coffee, biscuits, and sugary sweets were found and greedily consumed. David Cormack was now attempting to supply the Gurkhas on the massif with his company of Italian muleteers. It made the supplying he did in the Garigliano bridgehead seem easy. "Went out with fifty mules," he wrote in his diary on 28 February, "long way, guides not at all efficient, & began to rain just as starting to climb the mountain . . . Hell's own trip to top, heavy rain, mud, pitch black, lost a few mules. Stopped trying to go back at 12:30, as lost." On the way back he was usually assigned to carrying down American corpses in body bags. Some had been dead for nearly a month. "They weren't fresh," he says.

––––––––––––

In and around the monastery, the Germans continued to improve their defensive positions, but they also were losing men, both on the supply journey up a path behind the monastery and from the heavy weight of continued Allied artillery. Born in Berlin in 1917, Kurt Langelüddecke was an artillery observation officer stationed in the monastery at this time. "I had to tell what I had seen and if it was worth it to shoot somewhere," he says. "I reported this back to the general. The general needed to be able to observe. That's why Monte Cassino was so important. Whoever had that mountain was the master!" However, the targets had to be considered carefully. "We weren't allowed always just to shoot. We had to divvy up our ammunition," says Langelüddecke. "We didn't have enough shells. We had many cannons that wouldn't shoot or couldn't shoot because they didn't have ammunition." Langelüddecke had already fought in Poland, Holland, Belgium, France, and the Soviet Union, but he describes the fighting at Cassino as the hardest of the war. He had been positioned three hundred yards from the monastery when it was bombed and, together with the paratroopers, had moved into the shell of the building soon after: "The ruins were dusty and dirty. In the booth of the holy Benedictine monks I found a spoon that I ate my soup with. I needed it; we didn't have much." As with the Allies, movement in daylight was suicidal, and only at night would the ruins come alive with men bringing up supplies, the wounded being evacuated, or commanders visiting their outposts. "I was up there for twelve weeks and never went outside in the sunshine," says Langelüddecke. "I began to look totally different."

For some, this period was their first experience of the Cassino battles. Birdie Smith, subaltern in the 2/7th Gurkha Rifles, had been left behind at a replacement camp, much to his frustration. On 4 March, he wrote in his diary: "Day passed slowly. Few odd jobs. Still bored. All I want is to join my battalion. After all, the war is into its fifth year and I have yet to see a German soldier." Three days later he got his wish and started the climb up to the battalion's positions on the massif. In no time, his "romantic notions" had been "destroyed." On the way up he came across a trickle of men coming in the opposite direction: "tired, disheveled, many of them wounded . . . prematurely old bedraggled men . . . few of them showed any interest in us." When he reached his battalion HQ, he reported to his colonel. "He was a different man," Smith writes, "a pale, strained face, deep dark circles around his eyes; I was shocked at the change in our CO." A week later, having survived a near miss that left him shaking uncontrollably, he wrote in his diary: "Have we been condemned to live forever in this cold, damp hell on earth?" Only when alone in his foxhole did he feel he could release his fear out of sight of his comrades.

On 10 March, John David left the forward advanced dressing station for the rear. By now even his steadfast spirit had had enough. "I left the farmhouse where I was in the last letter," he wrote home that night, "where everything was very difficult, so difficult I cannot tell you till later. It will rank in my life and in a good many other people's as a period when our optimism and endurance and 'British fortitude' were tested to the limit . . . [T]he weather was such that I hope I shall never experience again . . . I am now picturing a nice hospital job in Naples and when we finish, will try to apply for one."

All across the front, the men dreamed of Naples and cursed the appalling weather. Frenchman Jean Murat, of the 4th Tunisian Regiment, had still been at officers' school in Algeria when his regiment was decimated during the attack on Belvedere. At the end of February he was among those relieving the last of the American contingent on Monte Castellone and spent much of March on the mountainside. The first relief, on the night of 28–29 February, was particularly grueling. "Rain has been falling for several hours," he writes, "so the night is so black that, for fear of getting lost, we all attach ourselves to the belt of the man ahead." Such had been the losses in the company, that "All its officers, the great majority of its *sous-officiers* and the best part of its men are new." Concerned most of all that he might not be up to the job, Murat quickly becomes acquainted with the familiar frontline feeling of confusion and helplessness: "I have no information about what awaits us. I have no map. What use would it be in the driving rain and in this darkness, where I can't even make out the man ahead of me whose belt I'm hanging on to?"

The climb was steep and slippery, and Murat, at the back of the company, felt the weight of his greatcoat and pack, now completely soaked with rain. When the guide ahead turned off the mule trail, "the column now climbs straight up, on to the steepest slope. The men, completely out of breath, are exhausted." They paused frequently, but when one rest had gone on too long, Murat struggled forward to find that fifty or so men, himself included, had lost the remainder of the party. He instructed the men just to keep climbing, and when the gradient lessened, he writes, "I advance cautiously. From time to time I call out tentatively, 'Yoo-hoo, Lieutenant, yoo-hoo.' This would be highly amusing if I wasn't so terribly anxious. I called out again [and] an irritated voice, much more confident than mine, answered, 'Shut it, you idiot!' " Murat was led by the hand by a section leader, but "It is so dark that I can't even see him. He puts me in what had been his command post . . . It is in fact a hole where, soaked to the bone, I wait for daybreak. And when the sun rises, I discover in the pale light that throughout the night I had had my back to the enemy, with my gun pointed toward our side!"

For the moment, Murat remained dug in on the reverse slopes of Castellone. On his first day up there he discovered a boot containing a decomposed foot. At the summit, "the situation is much more difficult . . . Every day hundreds of shells pepper our position. The German artillery have their preferred hours, from eleven o'clock until noon and from 1 to 2 P.M. No one knows the reasons for this programming."

In this sector, too, the Germans were busy improving their defensive positions, and the occasional sound of dynamite could be heard as they blasted themselves deeper into the rocks. For some, though, the psychological effects of being under sporadic shellfire were beginning to take their toll. "I've been in the line for several days now," an unnamed machine gunner from the 115th Panzer Grenadier Regiment wrote in his diary on 13 February. "We have taken up new positions close to Tommy. I'm sure I can maintain that the Somme battlefield did not look worse. It is fearful and horror overcomes you as you wonder when this misery will stop. The air vibrates with shells and devils and death."

In the Garigliano beachhead conditions were no better. "The weather did not improve," recalled a Pioneer officer, F. G. Sutton, from the 2nd Beds and Herts Battalion, the first from the newly arrived British 4th Division to go into the line. "Cold, rain and sleet made life miserable. Movement during the day was restricted; there were no sanitary arrangements and, as the area had been occupied by troops for over six weeks already, the smells were not too savory." As on the Cassino Massif, just getting to the front line was an exhausting and dangerous business. Charlie Framp, from the 6th Battalion Black Watch, another British 4th Division unit, who went into the line near Monte Ornito for the first two weeks of March, recalls how the men were issued with five-foot staffs to help them climb to their new position. "The only paths were goat tracks which twisted and writhed agonizingly up and across the mountain slopes. It seemed we marched miles just to make a few hundred yards' upward progress. Higher and higher we climbed, despite the intense cold, very soon we were bathed in sweat, my legs ached cruelly from the effort involved."

Once in position, it was, according to one of the regiment's historians, "a curiously hole-and-corner life. The companies could see into the German positions, and the Germans could see into theirs, in an almost indecent fashion." "My sangar replaced one situated a couple of yards away which had received a direct hit by an enemy shell," Charlie Framp continues. "It had contained two men, at the time, now it was just a mound of stones with an up-ended rifle stuck over it bearing a tin hat upon its stock. A blue-black hand poked out from the rocks and hung slackly down on the outside. Even though we were several thousand feet up and the wind blew fresh and cold, the sweet, sickly smell of death hung heavily about the area."

Once in their lofty positions on the mountain, "It was bitterly cold, blizzards were frequent, icy winds blew the snow through unprotected openings in the sangars . . . The Germans, over on the other side of the crest, some two hundred yards away, were rumored to be suffering from the cold even more than we. One of our patrols reported finding a German position with a dead man in it, he wasn't even wearing an overcoat, there were no wound marks on him, it was readily believed he'd died of exposure."

The men were not allowed to return fire as it would have given away the position, but there was regular patrolling and infiltration at night by both sides, a particularly stressful activity in which the slightest noise, the tiniest stone disturbed, could attract fatal fire. A Coldstream Guardsman recalled how the German snipers would always target the very rear of a patrol, so they "scrambled like scalded rats not to be the last man."

Patrols were easily ambushed in the mountainous terrain. A corporal in the Durham Light Infantry tells of one such occurrence: "We were spotted. Jerry brought his mortars down on us, so we had to get back to our positions. I've never been under shellfire like it before or after. He tossed everything at us that afternoon. We had a string of blokes went shell shocked—just lost their nerve—they were crying, laughing, crying one minute, laughing the other . . . Babyish."

Both sides attempted to infiltrate between the other's sangars to set booby traps and lay mines in supposedly safe areas. Forward observation positions would also be occupied during the night. Framp tells the story of one patrol that went out from his battalion to see if a cottage in "no-man's-land" was being used in this way by the Germans. The officer in charge split the platoon in two in order to approach the objective from both sides. The cottage was empty, but the two sections opened fire on each other and there were several casualties.

Corporal Walter Robson was a stretcher bearer in the 1st Battalion, Royal West Kent Regiment, another British 4th Division unit arriving at Cassino in March. The eldest of eight children from a working-class family, his formal schooling had ended at fourteen. He had married his wife, Margaret, only two months before being sent overseas. He would survive the fighting, but in the summer of 1945, when the division was in Greece for the civil war, worn out from fatigue and battle strain, he was hospitalized for "heat stroke" and died almost at once of pulmonary tuberculosis. His moving and eloquent letters to his wife were published after the war. As his wife, Margaret, wrote in the introduction to the slim volume, "Almost our whole marriage was contained in our letters."

"In Cairo I saw a newsreel showing our boys in Italy," he wrote to Margaret in the middle of March. "You've seen similar films I expect. I saw mule teams toiling up the snowy heights and I shuddered." Soon after arriving at Cassino, the battalion took over part of the line in the Garigliano sector near Tufo. One night Robson heard a noise outside the sangar he shared with his friend Steve. They crawled out to find a "chap, tin hat, overcoat, leather jerkin, balaclava, all muffled up, but shivering and sobbing that he couldn't stand it." The two stretcher bearers took him to the advanced dressing station and gave him a cigarette and hot tea. He "sat shivering with two tears crawling down his nose. A doctor felt his pulse and we left him." On the way back it was so dark that he and Steve had to hold hands as the only way of keeping contact. "We talked loudly for the benefit of the sentries who, blind as we were, might fire at anything sounding too quiet and creepy. We got tangled up with phone wires, climbed over boulders . . . and finished the journey on our hands and knees. All the time it was raining. Eventually we got back to our blankets and shivered all night . . . the next morning everything was white. A thick fall of snow. Oh, darling, and back in the village, in our kit-bags, we still had our tropical shorts. 'What a birthday,' I said, for it was March 16th." For Robson, his role of stretcher bearer was the only consolation. "I would I think, be haunted all my life if I knew I had killed someone," he writes.

Eleven days later they were to be relieved: "Jerry hadn't started his nightly bout of shelling. We wanted to be out of it before he did. A fortnight of this was enough for anyone. In our sangar, the paper stuffed into the chinks not really effective against the draughts, we knelt in a peculiar position. Our heads on the ground and our feet drumming rapidly for warmth, something like ostriches. Miserably, miserably cold."

For those on the Rapido valley floor the "lull in operations" meant shivering in slit trenches, being continually soaked, and bailing out their holes in the ground. "There was a lot of sickness," remembers New Zealander Brick Lorimer. "The conditions were terrible. Mud and rain and snow and no cover at all." Artillery bombardment went on sporadically, and German snipers were on the lookout for anyone who left his shelter. Even a short distance behind the lines there were casualties. Favorite targets included men assembling for mealtimes. Machine gunner Jack Cocker was nearby when Americans in their rest area were "lined up for chow when Jerry sent in a few rounds of artillery. The result was something like a slaughterhouse."

The mood of the New Zealand Division was not helped when, on 2 March, their respected commander, Howard Kippenberger, had his feet blown off by a mine that had been left behind on Monte Trocchio. In the New Zealand artillery lines, John Blythe could sense the failing morale: "People appeared subdued," he writes, "and there was a somberness about the whole rotten deal. Perhaps it was the dark hills, the brooding mountains, the mists on the plain, or the regiment on the left which forever fired smoke shells to blind Jerry. Or was it the smell of death? The whipcrack explosions of the 88s by day and the dull boom of the 170 at night? The slashed trees, the rubble, sour stomach in the mornings and the cold? Would it never end?" The "sour stomach" was not helped by the poor-quality food and the large amounts of low-grade wine the soldiers consumed each night in an effort to sleep through the shellfire. As the days dragged by, the men became less confident that they would survive this particular battle. "I was too young and too bloody ignorant to die yet," Blythe writes.

In early March, however, he was given a few days' leave. He went to Naples.

Although many of the Allied soldiers at Cassino, particularly the frontline infantrymen, went without a period of leave during their entire time in the battles, for a large number the port of Naples was their first sight of Italy. Many others visited Naples at some point, and the city looms large in their memories of the Italian campaign. One US artilleryman sums up the town: "There was a lot of booze . . . and a lot of women." The comedian Tommy Trinder, who toured the rear areas entertaining British troops, always got a knowing laugh when he told a story about first arriving at Naples harbor. His instructions, he said, were to report immediately to the harbormaster, who would have a car ready to take him to his first troop concert. As Trinder left the boat he was accosted by one of the many pimps who frequented the port. "I will take you to pretty girl," the tout offered. Tommy walked on. Still pursuing him, the tout repeated his offer. The comedian stopped and said, "I don't want a pretty girl. I want the harbormaster." The Italian looked to heaven, his expression indicating his amazement at the peculiar tastes of the *Inglese*. "The harbormaster," he repeated. "It is very difficult—but I try."

Norman Lewis vividly describes life in the city in his book *Naples '44*. Installed in a grand palace overlooking the bay soon after the capture of the city at the beginning of October 1943, his ill-defined job included screening Italians whom the Allied armies wanted to employ in various roles. Later he would interview young women who wanted to marry British soldiers. There was great suspicion about spies and saboteurs: Lewis tells of "a plague of telephone-wire cutting" at the beginning of January. The army was convinced that this was deliberate sabotage, "whereas we know full well," wrote

Lewis, "that lengths of cable are cut out purely for the commercial value of the copper, and that like any article of Allied ownership, the copper is offered openly for sale in the Via Forcella."

Alan Moorehead visited Naples, intrigued to see something of "The first great city of German Europe to fall into the hands of the Allies." He was shocked by the poverty, prostitution, and blatant criminality: "Army cigarettes and chocolates were stolen by the hundred-weight and resold at fantastic prices. Vehicles were stolen at the rate of something like sixty or seventy a night (not always by the Italians). The looting of especially precious things like tires became an established business. In the whole list of sordid human vices none I think were overlooked in Naples during those first few months."

Jean Murat spent an afternoon in the city, concluding that it was "a vision of a den of iniquity where everything was for sale." Norman Lewis exclaimed in his diary in early February: "Nothing had been too large or too small— from telegraph poles to phials of penicillin—to escape the Neapolitan kleptomania . . . Even the manhole covers have been found to have a marketable value, so that suddenly these too have all gone, and everywhere there are holes in the road."

There is no denying that the inhabitants of Naples were in extremis. Even when the German shelling of the city ended, there were sporadic air raids. The Germans had left behind time bombs not just on infrastructure such as bridges, but in post offices, telephone exchanges, and other places where only civilians were likely to be injured or killed. The Germans had carried off what meager stocks of food the city had possessed and there was widespread starvation. With the water supply smashed, some were reduced to trying to distill drinking water from seawater, and in the unsanitary conditions, disease broke out. In November a typhus epidemic started; in December there were forty cases a day, and the following month this rose to sixty. Only by dusting 1.3 million people with the new "wonder" insecticide DDT was the outbreak brought under control. The Allied soldiers there, heavily immunized before they left home, were safe, but hundreds of Italians perished.

As Allied supplies of food, medicine, clothes, and luxuries like cigarettes and chocolate poured into Naples harbor in eye-boggling quantities, it soon became obvious that up to a third of it was going missing. One Allied report in the spring estimated that 65 percent of Neapolitans' per capita income de-

rived from dealing in stolen Allied supplies. The authorities hit back, arrest-
ing and dealing out harsh prison sentences, but, as Lewis pointed out, "The
victims who fall are always those who have no one to speak for them, and
cannot bribe their way out of their predicament." He considered the "war on
the black market" a bit of a joke: "It is impossible to stop and search a single
Neapolitan on the street without finding he was wearing an overcoat or
jacket made from army blankets, or army underclothing, army socks, or at
the least had American cigarettes in his pocket."

Soldiers sometimes took matters into their own hands. A juvenile gang
started jumping into the backs of lorries when they were halted by traffic
and seizing whatever they could. The soldiers countered this by having a
man hidden in the back with a bayonet, which he would bring down on the
hands of the boy as he grabbed hold of the tailboard, resulting in numerous
severed fingers. Not that the soldiers themselves were always above reproach.
The army bureaucracy in Naples had its fair share of corruption and theft,
and Jack Cocker cheerfully admits that he and his mates were not averse to
a bit of wheeler-dealing: "Whenever you went on leave, especially to a place
like Naples, you'd go with a sackful of gear—all sorts of gear that you could
hock off."

Like many of the Allied "invaders," Norman Lewis grew to love Italy and
the Italians. At the end of his year there, he wrote that if he had had a choice
of where he was born, it would have been Italy. Soon his attitude to the extensive thieving was one of almost amused amazement. "The impudence of
the black market takes one's breath away," he wrote in early May. "Stolen
equipment . . . is now on blatant display, tastefully arranged with colored
ribbon, a vase of flowers, neatly-written showcards . . . YOU CAN MARCH
TO KINGDOM COME ON THESE BEAUTIFUL IMPORTED BOOTS . . .
IF YOU DON'T SEE THE OVERSEAS ARTICLE YOU'RE LOOKING FOR,
JUST ASK US AND WE'LL GET IT."

For the victors, or those with money, Naples still had plenty to offer.
There was fine food at the black-market restaurants on the quay below the
Excelsior Hotel, where musicians strolled among the diners. The San Carlo
Opera House had been miraculously unaffected by the bombing and re-
opened in December with a good Italian company performing *The Barber of
Seville, Lucia di Lammermoor,* and *Il Trovatore.* If you were an officer—other
ranks were banned—or a journalist like Alan Moorehead, you could take a
boat out to the beautiful island of Capri, where "the same international so-

Carl Strom, who crossed the Rapido with the US 36th Division on 21 January

Engineer Matthew Salmon, who ended up in the same psychiatric ward as Spike Milligan

John Johnstone of US 34th Division. He was taken prisoner during an attack on the monastery

Paratrooper Robert Frettlöhr, on the right, with three friends. Frettlöhr was the only one of the group to survive the war

Tony Pittaccio with his mother and sisters

US artilleryman Ivar Awes, in a photograph taken while his division was stationed in Northern Ireland

An American soldier shares his food rations with hungry Italian villagers in the Cassino area, 1944

Gemma Notarianni with her family. She was seventeen when the fighting reached her home in Valvori, near Cassino

British and US soldiers assist civilians injured following the explosion of a time-bomb in the Naples Post Office on 20 October 1943

With the fertile valleys a sea of mud, motor transport was paralysed. Instead the Allies had to rely on men and mules

IWM; NA 8787

IWM; NA 11342

January 1944. Men from Basutoland carry supplies for troops of British 56th Division

IWM; NA 13282

17th Indian Mule Company supplying 4th Indian Division in March 1944

A Moroccan medical battalion bring wounded down from the mountains, April 1944

IWM; NA 13884

Italians with mules on their w
towards the Castelforte front, Janua
1944, following a mine-cleared pa
marked with white tap

Gurkha despatch rider

IWM; NA 11154

A ferry, constructed from a single span of Bailey bridge fastened to rafts, carries ambulances back across the Garigliano River, January 1944

The mountains and valleys of "Sunny Italy" WANT TO SEE YOU....

Shellfire lands near Castle Hill, with the monastery behind, January 1944

Eighty-year-old Abbot Gregorio Diamare leaves the headquarters of von Senger (second left) on the morning of 16 February. He was soon afterwards intercepted by the SS

The Germans moved quickly to occupy the ruins of the monastery

'This ghastly place called Snakeshead Ridge.' Troops of the Royal Sussex Battalion in sangars on the ridge overlooking the monastery

IWM: MH 11246

IWM: NA 12252

Men of the 1/4 Essex in Wadi Villa, 27 February 1944. Already they had been taking steady losses from shellfire

Men of New Zealand 22nd Motorised Battalion playing rugby while on rest in the Volturno valley, early March 1944

While the Americans were often provided with lavish hot showers, other Allied troops had to make do with a tub

IWM: NA 12670

IWM: NA 12208

Above: In some of the most vicious fighting of the battles, New Zealand troops attempt to push through the smashed town

Below and right: Elite German paratroopers emerge from the wreckage of the town to fight off the New Zealand attacks

Indian stretcher bearers bring down a wounded man from the Cassino massif

IWM: NA 12032

IWM: NA 13746

...eared by both sides, the irregular Goumiers ...vere instrumental in the breakout through ...ie mountains to the south of the Liri valley

Solange Cuvillier, the French nurse attached to 2nd Moroccan Division

Werner Eggert, one of the few German paratroopers to escape from Cassino

Ken Bond, one of the 1/4 Essex men to struggle up to Hangman's Hill

A damned hard nut,
just the right job for our **New Zealand pals**

Indeed, an amusing war
— FOR THE AMERICANS

German propaganda leaflets aimed at New Zealand and British troops

Polish troops haul supplies up the mountain prior to the final offensive

Polish soldiers of the Kresowa Division launch a grenade attack on German positions on Phantom Ridge

IWM; MH 1984

A painting by Terence Cuneo of Amazon bridge being pushed over the Rapido

British troops advancing towards Amazon bridge through a smokescreen

IWM; NA 14809

Dead in Cassino

Graves of members of the 16th Battalion, New Zealand Expeditionary Force, near Cassino

A wrecked Sherman tank near the Rapido

An engineer feels under a doll with a bayonet, finding a wire attached to a large mine

Wherever the troops might want to go, ther were mines. This is from February 1944, ne the Garigliano

Clockwise from above:

The remains of Cassino

The town, with the castle in the background, before and after the fighting

The smashed monastery as seen from Snakeshead Ridge, May 1944

IWM: NA 15808

4 June 1944: US troops move into the
suburbs of Rome as Mark Clark looks o
He was later to have the 'Roma' sign take
down and shipped back to the USA

American GIs march past the Coliseu

IWM: NA 15913

Cheering crowds in
Rome, 5 June 1944

Dead at Pignataro
in the Liri valley

ciety, a little diminished, had continued somehow through the trouble, although with the slightly beaten air of a worn-out roué." Even some British residents remained there, still carrying on their languid lives in their luxury villas. According to journalist Christopher Buckley, who visited the island in October 1943 with an introductory letter from Gracie Fields to her tenant, it was "rather bad form" to refer to the war raging all around. Buckley went back to Naples in mid-December, having been reporting from the front line: "To return to Naples from Monte Camino was like stepping from the atmosphere of a street accident directly into a crude and noisy cabaret," he wrote. "Naples was beginning to be an excessively gay place . . . There was all the spurious brightness which you find whenever there is a rapid turnover of money. There was a general atmosphere of jolliness . . . Quite suddenly I realized that I couldn't stand it a day longer."

Meanwhile, the starving people of Naples continued to do whatever it took to survive. For most, the only way to do this was to steal from or sell something to the Allies. When the Germans had been in occupation, they had wanted to buy food and clothes to send home. The Americans and British wanted stockings and jewelry or cheap souvenirs. Treasures were dug up and put on sale or cheap fakes hastily assembled. Like any army, the new occupiers of the city also wanted alcohol in vast quantities, and when the supplies were exhausted, the Neapolitans were happy to make often dangerous bootleg liquor to meet the demand. Then there were other inevitable appetites. Moorehead writes about "Six-year-old boys . . . pressed into the business of selling obscene postcards; of selling their sisters, themselves, anything." A report by the Allies in April estimated that, out of a nubile female population of 150,000, 42,000 were engaged in prostitution. For most, the only other option was to starve to death. As Norman Lewis writes, "Nine out of ten girls have lost their menfolk, who have either disappeared in battles, into prisoner-of-war camps, or been cut off in the North. The whole population is out of work. Nobody produces anything. How are they to live?"

There was a range of reactions among the soldiers to this situation. For some, trips to a brothel became the be-all and end-all of their lives. The American ordnance officer Tom Kindre tells of one man in his command who "just couldn't stay away from the prostitutes," however many times he got the clap and was punished for it. Others guiltily confided to their diaries that they had visited a prostitute the night before, but now regretted it. "Not all of the men participated as much as some of them," recalls an American artilleryman who spent time in the city. "I suppose about fifty percent did." For many, it "just was not for them," although few seemed to condemn those who did succumb. Months of close male company created something of a "stag night" license in many groups, where behavior such as very heavy drinking and trips to sex shows was accepted without comment. There was also the fact that the men were very far from home. As Tom Kindre comments: "It was totally liberating. Most of the people that I was with were from small towns and fairly restricted upbringing. Everybody knew everybody else and you couldn't get into too much trouble. So here they were in a foreign country with license, they felt, to do just about anything they wanted to and I think the sexual mores were very open." Bill Mauldin's tactful gloss is: "They all feel a certain freedom from the conventions they would observe in their own countries."

Many liked the idea of exercising this license, but then found that the reality of the situation was far from erotic. When first entering the city, Norman Lewis came across several American supply trucks parked outside a municipal building, surrounded by soldiers "helping themselves to whatever they could lay their hands on." Thereafter they streamed into the building, and Lewis followed them. There was, he writes, "much pushing forward and ribald encouragement on the part of those in the rear, but a calmer and more thoughtful atmosphere by the time one reached the front of the crowd." Inside the building, "a row of ladies sat at intervals of about a yard with their backs to the wall." Lewis was struck by how ordinary they looked, with the "well-washed respectable shopping and gossiping faces of working class housewives." There was "no enticement, not even the most accidental display of flesh." By the side of each woman stood a small pile of tins. It was clear that if one added another tin to the pile, "it was possible to make love to any one of them in this very public place." Those of the soldiers who had pushed themselves to the front, tins in hand, "faced with these matter-of-fact family-providers driven here by empty larders, seemed to flag . . . the air went limp. There was some sheepish laughter, jokes that fell flat, and a visible tendency to slip away."

The official position, Tom Kindre explains, "was do whatever you want to . . . there was no moral judgment." The only caveat was "Don't get sick because we need you to do your job in the army." The American authorities had set up "prophylactic stations" throughout the city and offered an effective, if nasty-sounding, "day-after" treatment, but few were inclined to use them, and by Christmas an epidemic of gonorrhea had struck the city, with several hundred new cases every week. The Germans when in occupation had been very careful to maintain the strictest medical supervision over the city's brothels, and there were reports that the German-occupied north was, in contrast to Naples, virtually free of streptococci and gonococci, which, Norman Lewis writes, "to all intents and purposes were reintroduced to Italy with the arrival of the American troops." There were even crazy schemes to send infected prostitutes through the lines to infect the German infantry and close the "VD gap."

The Allied authorities reacted by sealing off areas of the city—restrictions easily evaded by the determined—and posting notices everywhere warning of the disease. Lurid films were shown to the troops showing its hideous effects, and prophylactics were made even more widely available. Other efforts were more ham-fisted. In mid-March a leaflet was printed in Italian and given out to the soldiers to pass to anyone offering the services of prostitutes: "It begins," Lewis reports, " 'I am not interested in your syphilitic sister.' Whoever dreamed this one up clearly had no idea of some of the implications or the possible consequences. Remarks about sisters are strictly taboo to Southern Italians, and the final insult *tua sorella* (thy sister) is calculated instantly to produce a duel or vendetta. Many soldiers have already handed out these dangerous notices to people who accosted them for reasons other than prostitution, and there are bound to be casualties."

There were some backlashes from the Neapolitans. In early March some women were attacked by youths when out walking on the arms of Allied soldiers. Even the chronically poorly paid British soldier was better off than a skilled Italian worker, and the American private soldier earned more than any native of Naples. For the young women of the city, Lewis writes, "the temptation is very great, and few seem able to resist. Thus the long, delicate, intricate business of Neapolitan courtship—as complex as the mating ritual of exotic birds—is replaced by a brutal, wordless approach, and a crude act of purchase. One wonders how long it will take the young of Naples, after we have gone, to recover from the bitterness of this experience."

New Zealand artilleryman John Blythe's rest period involved three days and two nights out of the line. First, he moved to the rear, where he could have a shave and a decent night's sleep, then he left for Naples the next morning.

"I departed with the others in a somewhat funny mood," he writes. "To date in this war there had been no involvement with women, but there had been too many near-misses lately, and if an opportunity arose to sleep with a woman it would be taken. The matter was mental rather than physical; a state of mind, a rejection of firmly held principles. Who the hell cared anyway? The Army equipped everybody with various types of prophylactics against disease, so why mess about? In the morning before we left for Naples I dosed myself."

He and his half dozen companions found Naples hot, dirty, and smelly. "Children played in the narrow streets amid rotting garbage under lines of washing strung between buildings," he writes. "They were undernourished, some wizened like little old men, but indomitable and hard as nails. They would have had your bootlaces if you'd let them, and when they knew you were on to them, caution was returned with flashing smiles." Blythe wanted to see the famous Bay of Naples, but found masses of barbed wire and huge mounds of military stores impeding the route to the sea. Instead the party went to an outside café, where they drank Marsala. This left Blythe lethargic, "and as the sun grew hotter [it] produced a dull headache." They repaired to a restaurant, where there was a choice of polenta or spaghetti. As they continued drinking one of the men announced that he wanted a woman. "For the first time I had ever known we were all of the same mind," Blythe writes. "Perhaps we had reached a milestone in our lives? In the past we had turned down scores of opportunities. There had been the odd individual like Ernie who wanted sex, but never the whole group. Perhaps the others felt the bell tolling for them too?"

One by one the men were led away. When eventually it was Blythe's turn, he was taken to a house around the corner. There, "an attractive young woman" led him upstairs. "My eyes were on her slim figure as we climbed the stairs and entering a bedroom she promptly kicked off her shoes and stretched herself out on the counterpane of a double bed. She was wearing a thin summer frock and nothing else." He started to take off his boots, and the girl told him it wasn't necessary. He insisted, feeling increasingly awkward. "This whole exercise was crazy," he remembers. "I wished I had never got myself into this situation. I felt ridiculous trying to be nonchalant, as if I had gone through this performance many times before." The girl clearly wanted it over with as quickly as possible: "With a head thick with wine and rising anger at the whole cold-blooded business, I entered her. At one stage she plucked the dress from one shoulder to bare a breast, perhaps to hurry me on, but the sight of the brown flaccid nipple nearly stopped me in my tracks. It was nothing special and soon over. Without warmth and emotion."

Blythe returned to the restaurant to find his companions had all left, but he remained there "brooding and drinking in the foulest of moods as the afternoon wore on." When he started to attract looks from the other diners, he left, revisited the prostitute, and then just caught the transport out of Naples. The next day he was back at Cassino.

PART FOUR

The Third Battle

I only know what we see from our worm's eye view, and our segment consists only of tired and dirty soldiers who are alive and don't want to die; of long darkened convoys in the middle of the night; of shocked, silent men wandering back down the hill from battle; of mess queues and atabrine tablets and the smell of cordite and foxholes and burning tanks and Italian women washing and the rustle of high-flown shells; of jeeps and ammunition dumps and hard rations and olive trees and blown bridges and dead mules and hospital tents and shirt collars greasy black from weeks of wearing; and of laughter too and anger and wine and lovely flowers and constant cussing. All these it is composed of: and of graves and graves and graves.

— ERNIE PYLE, CASSINO, MARCH 1944

What I saw took me back across twenty-eight years, when I experienced the same loneliness crossing the battlefield of the Somme.

— FRIDOLIN VON SENGER UND ETTERLIN

12

The Battle for
Cassino Town

On 14 March the weather at last cleared long enough to launch the attack the following day, and the code "Bradman bats today" was finally passed down the ranks. Early in the morning the forward troops of the New Zealand 25th Battalion holding the northern outskirts of the town withdrew up the Caruso Road and at 8:30, in bright sunshine, the first wave of heavy bombers appeared overhead.

Never before on the Italian front had a town been obliterated by carpet bombing. For three and a half hours, 575 medium and heavy bombers and 200 fighter-bombers, the largest air forces ever assembled in the Mediterranean theater, dropped nearly a thousand tons of high explosive on roughly one square mile of land. In terms of weight of bombs, it more than doubled the amount dropped on the monastery a month before.

A New Zealand signaler from the 25th Battalion, watching from the old barracks about a thousand yards up the Caruso Road out of Cassino, remembers that "after the first bombs fell there were a few seconds before the shock wave, which blew me over backwards about ten yards." "The impressive spectacle was an exhilarating sight to the waiting troops below," the 25th Battalion's historian wrote. "A huge and dense pall of smoke and dust rose over Cassino as the heavy bombs burst with a shattering roar." Alexander, Clark, and Freyberg watched from a VIP enclosure on high ground near

Cervaro, in almost a picnic atmosphere. Freyberg commented that "None who saw it will forget the terrible one-sidedness of the spectacle."

A machine gunner from Jack Cocker's platoon, in position on the near side of the Rapido to give covering fire to the attack, saw "Mitchells in a long column of groups of three . . . [they] weren't much above 3,000 feet and in the clear air we could see the four bombs detach themselves from each plane and go plummeting down in a shower. It was easy to follow the 1,000-pounders right to the ground, where an enormous geyser of black and orange mud and debris leapt into the air, and fell back again while a pillar of smoke unfolded."

The first wave of bombers scored with impressive accuracy, but soon the "pillar of smoke" obscured the target. So, while half of all the bombs fell within a mile of the center of town, the other half went seriously astray. Four Fortresses and thirty-nine Liberator medium bombers missed the target and dropped their bombs on Allied areas. Jack Cocker's 27th Battalion lost an officer and a gunner and six men were wounded; a Moroccan casualty clearing station was hit, causing sixty casualties; another fifty were killed or wounded in British 4th Division's rear echelon. David Cormack was with his mules and his Italian muleteers when the bombs started landing on them. The next day he wrote in his diary, "Just back to camp, when Americans very kindly put a dozen or so bombs slap thru', blast their gum-chewing land . . . killed Razzi [an Italian officer], wounded 1/2 dozen, had to shoot 15 mules in two hours . . . Hell of a mess . . . general opinion of USA air force v. low."

Worst of all, one group of aircraft mistook for Cassino the town of Venafro, eighteen miles away. Gemma Notarianni and her family had been evacuated there. One bomb killed twenty-two of their friends from Valvori. In all, 140 civilians died or were wounded. In the final reckoning, more civilians and Allied soldiers were killed than Germans.

Up on the massif above the town, there were near misses but no one was hurt. The scale of the bombing, though, affected all. Gurkha officer Birdie Smith was near the Allied front line in the mountain salient: "When four or five bombs had landed a few yards from A Company's position, no one poked his head out of his foxhole. After a few minutes I felt like shouting, that's enough! But it went on and on until our eardrums were bursting and our senses were befuddled . . . I found myself shouting curses at the planes. Later I was to write: 'What an inferno is Cassino now. Dear God—take pity on those men, if there are any survivors within the town, which I doubt.' "

Stationed in the fortress-town were about three hundred Germans of the 3rd Regiment of the 1st Parachute Division. This elite formation had been brought into the line by von Senger at the end of February, and the division now held Monastery Hill as well as the town. In command of the 7th Company of the regiment in the town was Lieutenant Schuster: "Tensely we waited in our holes for the bombs to drop," he reported. "Then they came. The whining scream of their approach, the roar of their explosions and the noise of the aircraft themselves mingled with echoes flung back from the hills to produce an indescribable and infernal bedlam of noise. The whole earth quaked and shuddered under the impact." Also underneath this inferno was Sgt. Georg Schmitz, a Pioneer attached to the regiment: "The first wave dropped most of its load near the station, but before we could think straight there was a second wave coming and this time we were in the midst of it. The air vibrated, and it was as if a huge giant was shaking the town." Sheltering deep in a cellar underneath one of the thickly built stone houses of the town, his group survived. "Well, we had been lucky," he says. "Dirt and dust got into the cellar, into our eyes, ears and mouths, tasting of bones." But the initial waves of bombers were coming at intervals of only ten minutes. As the next one arrived, the men clung to one another "as if we were one lump of flesh." The entrance to their cellar was now blocked. "This was terrible," Schmitz says. "We were buried alive. Frantically we started to claw in a mad, haphazard way at dirt and stones. And then there was another wave just overhead."

After the first half hour, the bombers came in at intervals of fifteen minutes for the next three hours. "More and more sticks of bombs fell," another German soldier in the town reported. "We now realized that they wanted to wipe us out, but we could not grasp that this terrible episode would go on for so long . . . The sun lost its brightness. An uncanny twilight descended. It was like the end of the world . . . Comrades were wounded, buried alive, dug out again, eventually buried for the second time. Whole platoons and squads were obliterated by direct hits . . . Scattered survivors, half crazy from the explosions, reeled about in a daze, avoiding all cover, until they were hit by an explosion and disappeared."

It was not just the force of the bombing, but its relentlessness. For Lieutenant Schuster, "The crash of bursting bombs increased in intensity. We clung to each other, instinctively keeping our mouths open. It went on and on. Time no longer existed, everything was unreal . . . rubble and dust came pouring down into our hole. Breathing became a desperate and urgent business. At all costs we had to avoid being suffocated, buried alive. Crouching in silence, we waited for the pitiless hail to end."

When the last aircraft turned for home at midday, the massed Allied artillery opened up on the remains of Cassino and on to the German positions on Monastery Hill. By the end of the bombardment over a thousand tons of shells, the equivalent of 275 truckloads, had been fired. A senior Allied officer commented, "We have fumigated Cassino." No one believed anybody could have survived, and, if they had, surely their nerves would be shattered.

Germans watching from nearby positions certainly thought so. The unnamed machine gunner from the 115th Panzer Grenadier Regiment wrote in his diary on 15 March: "Today hell is let loose at Cassino. Cassino is a few kilometers away to our left. We have a good view of everything. Almost 1,000 aircraft bomb our positions at Cassino and in the hills. We can see nothing but dust and smoke. The boys who are lying up there must be going mad."

Following behind the barrage were two companies of the New Zealand 25th Battalion together with tanks from the 19th Armoured Regiment. They were detailed to take Castle Hill and clear the town up to the east–west section of Route 6, before it veered sharply to the left and ran along the base of Monastery Hill. This was to be achieved by 2 P.M., when the 24th and 26th battalions would continue the fight up to the "Baron's Palace," thereby opening up the Liri valley for waiting New Zealand and US tanks and the British 78th Division. The effects of the bombing were immediately apparent to the advancing infantry. Their approach road into Cassino was a mess, and in the town itself not a single building stood intact. Even those few that had not received a direct hit had lost their roofs and been shaken to their foundations. "Entering Cassino was a vision of the end of the world," remembers a corporal from the battalion. "It was like some ghastly warning. Would this then be the fate of Rome, or for that matter Paris, or London, or Berlin, or even Auckland?" Cassino, he says, "looked as if it had been raked over by some monster comb and then pounded all over the place by a giant hammer."

As they moved forward, there was some sporadic fire from positions around Castle Hill, but the New Zealanders gained their old positions without too much difficulty. But when they advanced into the wreckage of the town, they realized, to their amazement and fury, that this was not to be merely a walk through a shattered town as they had been led to believe. Instead, there was fierce resistance from German paratroopers.

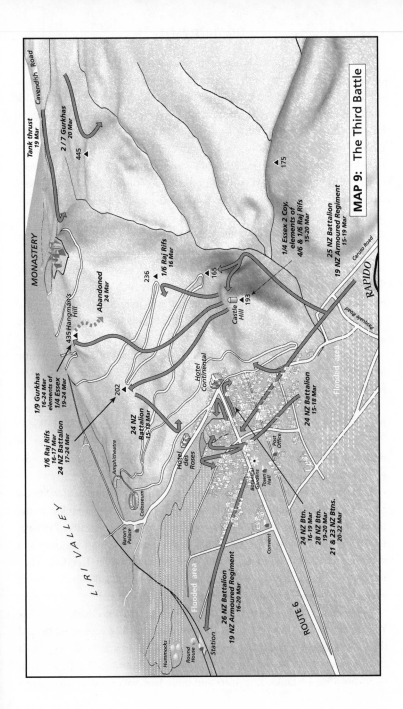

MAP 9: The Third Battle

LIRI VALLEY

MONASTERY

Tank thrust
19 Mar

Cavendish Road

2/7 Gurkhas
20 Mar

445 ▲

175 ▲

1/9 Gurkhas
16–24 Mar
elements of
1/4 Essex
19–24 Mar

1/6 Raj Rifs
16–17 Mar
24 NZ Battalion
17–24 Mar

435 ▲ Hangman's
Hill

Abandoned
24 Mar

236 ▲

1/6 Raj Rifs
16 Mar

165 ▲

1/4 Essex 2 Coy.
elements of
4/6 & 1/6 Raj Rifs
15–20 Mar

25 NZ Battalion
19 NZ Armoured Regiment
15–19 Mar

Castle Hill

193 ▲

Caruso Road

RAPIDO

202 ▲

24 NZ
Battalion
15–18 Mar

Hotel
Continental

24 NZ Battalion
15–18 Mar

Amphitheatre

Colosseum

Baron's Palace

Hotel
des Roses

Botanic
Gardens

Town
Hall

Post
Office

Embankment Road

flooded area

26 NZ Battalion
19 NZ Armoured Regiment
16–20 Mar

Flooded area

Convent

24 NZ Btn.
16–19 Mar
28 NZ Btn.
19–20 Mar
21 & 23 NZ Btns.
20–22 Mar

ROUTE 6

Station

Round
House

Hummocks

The bombing of the town had been on an unprecedented scale, but some of the garrison had survived. Even dropping five tons of explosive for every soldier in Cassino had not completely "fumigated" the town. Through quick thinking, one company commander had moved his men into a cave at the base of Monastery Hill. Others, like Sgt. Georg Schmitz, had successfully dashed there between the waves of bombers. Lieutenant Schuster and his men had almost been buried alive, but emerged unscathed from their deep cellar. Virtually all the Germans' equipment and ammunition had been destroyed or buried along with over half of the three-hundred-strong force, but enough men had survived to clamber out, take up defensive positions, and bring sniper and machine gun fire on the New Zealanders.

The advancing troops were faced with another unexpected problem: such was the mangled state of the town that it was often impossible to find a way forward. Huge craters and enormous mounds of rubble blocked every avenue of advance. Where there was a narrow gap, men could move forward only in groups of two or three. These were then easily forced back by snipers and machine gunners.

The success of Freyberg's plan depended on the first attacks being swiftly and strongly carried out while the defenders were still reeling from the bombardment. But the tanks of the 19th Armoured Regiment were having difficulty even reaching the town from their start line a mile up the Caruso Road. The road itself had an enormous crater in its center, and, with flooding and minefields on one side and steep cliffs on the other, there was no other way forward. It took the leading squadron an hour to reach the northern outskirts of the town.

Once in among the wrecked buildings, the going was even harder. Streets had simply disappeared. Brick Lorimer remembers driving a tank into the town: "There was no way the tanks could get through the heaps of rubble, which were over twenty feet high. There was twisted steel and masonry and of course massive bomb craters, some sixty feet wide and ten feet deep. They were all joined to each other. Thousand-pound bombs had blown horrible holes everywhere. The whole town was in absolute ruins."

In some of the most vicious fighting during the Cassino battles, the New Zealanders pressed forward under the cover of a smokescreen while behind them, engineers worked frantically to repair the damage to the approach road, improve access from the other side of the Rapido, and clear paths in the rubble for the tanks. Engineers and bulldozer drivers made easy targets for snipers and it was hard going. Ahead, the infantry were moving forward much more slowly than had been hoped—each hundred yards took an hour rather than the planned ten minutes. B Company of 25th Battalion had been detailed to clear the houses at the base of Castle Hill and then capture the Continental Hotel, a large building situated on slightly higher ground where Route 6 turned left through the town, but they succeeded in neither objective, being pinned down by heavy fire.

In the middle of the afternoon the Germans started a heavy bombardment on the northern end of the town. Because everything—reinforcements, tanks, and supplies—had to be funneled through the narrow channel of the Caruso Road, there were plenty of targets, and the New Zealanders' difficulties multiplied. As A Company fought its way to the remains of the town's post office just short of Route 6, and at last some tanks worked their way forward, Freyberg was finding it difficult to push reserves into the town. As on Snakeshead Ridge and on the railway embankment, the Allies were forced to attack through a very constricted corridor in insufficient strength to overwhelm the determined defenders.

At 5 P.M. a company of the 24th Battalion was sent in to help to clear the bottom of Castle Hill. Among them was Pvt. Roger Smith, who much later published his memoirs of that time. As they moved along the approach road, they lost five men to machine gun fire, but Smith was nevertheless "thankful that at last we were engaged. That oppressive dread that seemed to sap my whole moral fiber, and always presaged action, had disappeared with the call for constructive action. Fear remained, but it was normal fear, the wariness of a soldier rather than soul-destroying apprehension." Pinned down just inside the town, he became aware of a German voice calling out from beneath the rubble "crying and crying, mad and frantic." The platoon could not move forward, and the calls continued until Smith was driven to scraping at the debris with his bare hands to try to reach the trapped men. But it was impossible, "so we had to abandon them to madness and death, crouched in a black vault." The next day the voice could still be heard, but by the evening there was only silence. Eventually the platoon moved forward, but it took Smith's company five hours to reach 25th Battalion's forward positions in the town around the post office.

Half an hour after 24th Battalion, the 26th moved forward, ordered to take the station. At this moment, contrary to the forecasters' predictions of three clear days, torrential rain started, making the going slippery and soaking the radio batteries, rendering them useless. As darkness fell and the men stumbled forward in single file, each man clinging to the battle dress of the man in front, several fell into the deep craters, which were beginning to fill with water. Soon the rubble of the pulverized buildings had changed to the "consistency of dough," and the heavy bomb dust had mixed with the rain to coat everything "in a thick gray slime."

It had been a disappointing start to the attack in the town, and reinforcement difficulties continued through the dark, moonless night. But half of Cassino was now in Allied hands, and above the town there had been a notable success. D Company of the 25th Battalion had been given the task of taking Castle Hill in the initial attack and, finding that the approach from the town was blocked, its commanding officer had sent a platoon up the deep ravine that ran below the castle toward the monastery. From here they had climbed a near-vertical cliff directly below Point 165, capturing two lookouts who had been sheltering deep in their dugout.

A Bren gun team consisting of Pvt. T. McNiece and Lance Cpl. Bill Stockwell was sent out to protect the platoon's right flank. "As Bill and I came to the edge of the rock," says McNiece, "I noticed a concrete pillbox on the top of the hill—it was about twelve feet square with a small window two feet square and four feet from the ground . . . I raised the Bren to my hip and made a dash for the side of the pillbox." Covering fire from his companion kept the German machine gunner inside occupied while McNiece threw in a grenade. "There was a lovely explosion, dust and splinters of stone and wood came flying out of the window; a few seconds later there was a clatter at my feet and there lay a Jerry stick grenade smoking and spitting out sparks. Without stopping to think, I grabbed it and flung it over the cliff . . . I immediately slipped another grenade through the window and it went off with a bang." Then another stick grenade came out through the window and landed just out of McNiece's reach. "I fell flat on my face and hoped for the best; the seconds seemed like ages; then there was a terrific explosion." But apart from ruptured eardrums, McNiece was unhurt. "When the dust cleared I was standing by the window with the Bren held out at arm's length [firing] through the window." He threw in a third grenade, then called up his companion. Together they took prisoner the occupants of the bunker, which turned out to be a company headquarters. Over twenty men were captured. "At the far end of the pillbox," says McNiece, "there was a ladder down into a huge dugout about twelve feet square and fifteen feet deep. Jerries were filing up the ladder with their hands in the air."

Now the platoon found itself being fired on by Germans in the castle. But on the other side of the castle two other D Company platoons were fighting their way up a steep ridge that ran from the bottom of the ravine. The Germans retreated to the inner keep and were flushed out with grenades. By 5 P.M. the New Zealanders were in command of the castle. With their prisoners, they dug in to await the 4th Indian Division in the shape of the 1/4th Essex Battalion, who were to push up Monastery Hill to Hangman's Hill and then storm the monastery.

It was crucial that there should be no delays that would allow the Germans to recover from the initial attacks. But through a failure of communication, it was two hours before word reached the Essex Battalion waiting down in Wadi Villa. The first to set off was A Company, under the command of Maj. Frank Ketteley. It was immediately clear that this would not be an easy relief. "Darkness brought the rain the Germans needed," an Essex signaler wrote in his diary the next day. "Caruso Road was a shambles: darkness, teeming rain and heavy shellfire had made it a nightmare for the rain-soaked infantry floundering in the night toward Castle Hill." Some of the men of A Company became involved in the close-quarters fighting that continued at the foot of the hill, while others began the climb. Twenty-four-year-old Bill Hawkins, who had already lost his platoon commander in the fighting, remembers, "It was raining and we started to climb, following the white tapes the New Zealanders had laid. We hadn't realized that the hill would be so steep. The only time you saw light was when the gun flashes went off, and there was continual sniping. Shells were going off, which blasted apart the white tapes, and the loose ends were flapping about, so we went by sense of direction more than anything."

C Company followed behind, under the command of twenty-six-year-old Maj. Denis Beckett. "The damage caused by the bombing and the close-quarters fighting going on at the foot of Castle Hill made control very difficult," he says. "We were trying to move up in single file along a tape and then, when it ended, up a path to the Castle . . . From time to time we met parties of Germans and close-quarter fighting developed." The men became strung out and Beckett virtually lost control of his company.

It took Bill Hawkins three or four hours to climb up to the castle: "It seemed to be neverending," he says. "You'd put your foot forward and find a rock in the way, so you'd move it to one side but then you didn't really know whether you'd changed direction or were still heading the same way. You were just hoping you were still heading to the top, but there were so many thickets and rocks to get round and get over to keep going and it was raining and slippery and very difficult."

It was midnight before elements of the two Essex companies reached the castle and relieved the New Zealanders. Hawkins took over a dugout on the outskirts of the building facing the town: "The prearranged plan, that B Company would come up and relieve us and we would go out of the castle and up to the monastery, was knocked on the head more or less from the start," he says. The delay in the relief of the New Zealanders wrecked the carefully worked out timetable and worsened the bottleneck in the narrow corridor at the north end of Cassino. Following behind the leading Essex companies were the 1/6th Rajputana Rifles, whose two rear companies were caught by an artillery bombardment at around midnight as they inched along the congested road and were effectively out of action. Meanwhile, C Company of the Essex retook Point 165, which had been evacuated by the New Zealanders when they moved into the castle and had been reoccupied by Germans late in the evening. The two companies of the Rajputana Rifles that made it to the castle passed through them to attack the next hairpin bend on the road above Point 165, known as Point 236. This was not only a crucial stepping-stone on the way to Hangman's Hill and the monastery, but was also the Germans' last strong point that gave observation on to the roads to the north, along which the attacking troops had to advance. The strongly held position dominated the slopes of Monastery Hill in both directions and could bring flanking fire to bear on any forces that tried to pass below.

At 4:30 A.M., 16 March, the Indian soldiers climbed as quietly as they could toward Point 236. They got to within 150 yards of their objective when they were spotted. Immediately heavy machine gun and artillery fire rained down on them, and they were forced to retreat to the castle. This left the third battalion of the brigade—the 1/9th Gurkhas, which had been detailed to pass through Point 236 once it had been captured and advance to Hangman's Hill—with a dilemma. Eventually the battalion's commanding officer decided to push two companies, C and D, up the mountain and hope for the best. With the main track up to the castle now under heavy enemy fire, another route was found that seemed to head in the right direction. At one point the track split and the two companies separated. D Company then ran into an ambush in which fifteen men were killed, while C Company simply disappeared into the night.

At 8:30 A.M. the Rajputana Rifles were once more sent against Point 236 under the cover of a smokescreen in the continuing effort to widen the bottleneck around Castle Hill. But again the attack was repulsed, and while it was in progress a German mortar scored a direct hit on the battalion headquarters. But at 2 P.M. the brigade had a great boost when news came in that C Company of the 1/9th Gurkhas, which had gone missing in the night, was on Hangman's Hill, less than three hundred yards from the monastery wall. Climbing diagonally across the hillside in the darkness, the company had managed to avoid German positions along the way and had surprised and overcome a small garrison on the hill. The Gurkhas had soon come under retaliatory mortar fire, and the CO, twenty-year-old Capt. M. R. Drinkhall, had been wounded. They had also found that their radio was not working, and several runners sent to the castle were intercepted. At last, after much tinkering, the radio was repaired and communication with the rest of the battalion was restored.

Plans were immediately made for the rest of the Gurkhas to join their comrades after nightfall. Soon after dark the luckless 1/6th Rajputanas made a third attack on Point 236, and this time they managed to hold the hairpin bend for some seven hours before being driven off again. They did succeed, however, in securing Point 202, a hairpin directly above the town. These two attacks were sufficient to keep the Germans busy while the rest of the 1/9th Gurkhas infiltrated themselves, platoon by platoon, up to Hangman's Hill. The whole process took seven hours, and the reinforcements arrived just in time to drive off a fierce counterattack by paratroopers from the monastery. By now the Germans knew that there was a substantial force of Gurkhas just outside the monastery walls.

The price for this success had been paid, in the main, by the 1/6th Rajputana Rifles. With two companies decimated by shellfire before even reaching the castle and the rest depleted and exhausted by the three attacks on Point 236, it was, as the signaler Charlie Fraser wrote in his diary on 17 March, "no longer an effective battalion." The final straw had been the direct hit on the battalion HQ. John David was in the advanced dressing station when the casualties started arriving. "At lunchtime the Raj. Rif. Officers began to come in," he wrote in his diary on the same day. "First Major Samuels: 'I have lost my nerve.' Nothing else. No wounds. I didn't like that. Nobody to ask what to do. What do you do with an officer who just states that he has lost his nerve? Fortunately at that moment his own colonel arrived white and shaking, having been dug out of the building which collapsed and he said that Major Samuels ought to go off sick. Poor Col. West . . . got us all upset by jumping at every sound."

Nevertheless, with troops established on Hangman's Hill, the attack on the monastery was still on. The first priority was to resupply the Gurkhas and attempt to secure the lower reaches of the hillside below them. On the evening of 17 March, two companies of the 4/6th Rajputana Rifles from 11th Brigade set off with mules and porters to take ammunition up to the hill. In command of D Company was Tom Simpson. As before, just reaching the foot of Castle Hill was far from easy. "Just as we prepared to move off we were heavily shelled, suffering heavy casualties to men and mules alike," remembers Simpson. "When the firing stopped I attempted to reorganize the column and get it moving." Another salvo came in, killing two mules and splattering Simpson with blood and skin, leaving him "winded but unscathed." Thereafter, he rushed the remnants of the column down the track into Cassino. "Here the going became very difficult with the rubble from shattered buildings and bomb craters to contend with. As I skirted one stricken NZ tank, its gun at a drunken angle, I stepped off the edge of a huge crater, pitching forward to end wedged in the twisted metal of a bedstead. Struggling to free myself, as my men ringed the rim of the crater looking for me, I clawed my way up and we pressed on until I was able to locate the tape marking a route up to the castle."

Simpson reached the castle to find that the battalion's other company had already passed through. Outside the walls the Germans were keeping up the pressure on Essex men on Point 165. "As I organized my party before following," says Simpson, "the Germans opened up with heavy machine gun fire pouring multicolored tracer down into the courtyard, the red, green and orange bullets bouncing off walls and ground alike. This proved too much for the unarmed porters who refused to go farther despite my best efforts to convince them that my men were the finest soldiers in the Indian Army and would see them safely through. There was nothing for it but to offload everything and, draping ourselves with as many bandoliers as we could carry, together with other supplies, we set off. As we neared Hangman's Hill the Gurkhas guided us through their positions with little hisses of welcome."

Back in the castle, A and C companies of the Essex Battalion had suffered numerous casualties from snipers, and several men and a large quantity of equipment had been buried when a portion of the wall collapsed. But it was decided that the whole battalion should be relieved by the 4/6th Rajputanas and head up to Hangman's Hill to join the Gurkhas. So now it was the turn of B and D companies to make the nightmare climb up to the castle. Stretcher bearer Ted Hazle remembers the pouring rain, and losing his haversack over the edge of the cliff when he stopped for a rest: "I was left with no food, nothing." Ken Bond recalls the darkness, the extraordinary difficulty of the climb, and men falling "down the side. You never saw them again." On the way up, the track came under shellfire: "Men were trying to scramble into the solid rock that was there. You had to do something, when there were shells crashing around you. I was fortunate none were close enough to do any damage."

Very early on the morning of 19 March, the two companies reached the castle. They set off almost immediately for Hangman's Hill. In the castle the relief of A and C companies by the 4/6th Rajputana Rifles was almost complete. Then the rest of the Essex Battalion would proceed to the Gurkhas' position. From there, in a couple of hours, the monastery would be stormed.

————

Almost directly below Castle Hill, the New Zealanders had been fighting their way through the wreckage of the town. On the morning of the 16th, a few tanks reached 25th and 26th Battalions' positions just short of Route 6. "Getting through was difficult," says Brick Lorimer. "The drivers were really put to the test to guide the tanks through the swamp, the mud and water. The massive bomb craters were now half filled with water . . . [there were] sections of masonry and pieces of timber sticking up out of a sea of water and mud." But prodigious work by New Zealander and American engineers had forged a path through some of the wreckage, and the infantry were now able to push forward, albeit slowly. Communication with the tanks was sometimes difficult, as Lorimer explains: "When the infantry located [a strong point] they would tell—a lot of it was pointing—the tank crews and give us some targets to fire at. We would fire all sorts—armor piercing or high explosive or even machine guns—and that way we would winkle them out."

By the end of the day there were New Zealander troops across Route 6 and in the ruins of the convent, and about two-thirds of the town was in Allied hands. The next day the 25th Battalion cleared the botanical gardens, now a "morass of liquid mud," and the 26th Battalion, supported by tanks, recaptured the station.

It was now clear that German resistance in the town was based at two hotels: the Continental and, some five hundred yards to the south, the Hotel des Roses. As long as these could be held, Route 6 would be blocked and the Indians' access to the massif threatened. Repeated attacks by the 25th Battalion had made little headway, and on 18 March a company of the 24th Battalion took over Point 202 from the Rajputana Rifles and tried attacking the Hotel des Roses from the rear. This, too, was repulsed, and it was obvious that the Germans were succeeding in infiltrating reinforcements into the town from Monastery Hill and via underground passageways. House-to-house fighting continued, with attacker and defender often virtually cheek by jowl. One platoon of the 25th Battalion "shared a house with the enemy for three days, and for 36 hours lived on iron rations and cigarettes . . . While the Germans could be heard moving around on the roof, nothing could be done as all exits were covered by a German strong point across the street in front and grenade-dropping snipers on the roof." On 18 March a message from a company of the 24th Battalion to their headquarters reported: "Town literally full of enemy snipers. They inhabit rubble and ruined houses. We are being as aggressive as possible . . . Until Monastery Hill is in our hands sniping problem will continue." Late on that day, as plans were being made for the Gurkhas and Essex men to storm the monastery the next morning, Freyberg called on his Maori Battalion to enter the town to finish off the job.

He had another trump card to play, too. During the three-week "lull" after the second battle, Indian and New Zealander engineers had been busy constructing a road from Caira village right up to the massif. Where under observation, the work and the completed road surface were shielded by netting. Some thirty-seven tanks and self-propelled guns had been assembled, and by daylight on 19 March they were in a deep bowl known as Madras Circus behind Snakeshead Ridge. From that position they were to sweep around to the rear of the monastery. It was hoped that the appearance of tanks from this direction would cause, as one historian of the battles has written, "the consternation that greeted Hannibal's elephants after their Alpine crossing."

The Germans were unaware of this, but there was plenty else to cause them concern. Much of Cassino town was in Allied hands, and the strong points in the hotels—the last-ditch defenses of Route 6—were virtually surrounded. The monastery had Allied soldiers close to it on two sides. They knew that unless they took immediate and drastic action, the Gustav Line would be broken.

13

Castle Hill

About an hour after Ken Bond, Ted Hazle, and the rest of B and D Companies of the Essex Battalion had left the castle to join the attack from Hangman's Hill, half a dozen men from B Company reappeared in the castle gateway. From a position higher up the slope they had seen a large number of Germans approaching the castle from the direction of the monastery. At this point the relief was almost complete, and A and C Companies were preparing to head up to Hangman's Hill. "We were in a pretty fair state of chaos," says Denis Beckett, in charge of C Company. "We were trying to issue rations and ammo, and sort out weapons which had been buried among the debris the previous day." Major Frank Ketteley, the senior officer in the castle, gave the order to stand-to, and the Essex men ran to their posts. At that moment heavy machine gun fire from the summit of Monastery Hill, Point 236, and the town below swept the area. "I had never known anything like it," says Beckett. "It came from every angle. This lasted for about ten minutes and then they were on us."

The Germans had realized the crucial importance of Castle Hill. Not only did it tower over the northern part of the town, it was key to the Allied efforts higher up the mountain. If the castle could be recaptured, the New Zealanders in the town would have Germans observing and bringing down fire on their every move, and the attack force on Hangman's Hill would be isolated. The day before, a series of German infiltrations had begun to establish a cordon around the castle. From broken houses on the upper fringe of the town, these groups blazed away at any men who tried to leave the castle or cross the hillside. The castle gate had been under fire. What now followed early in the morning of 19 March has been described as "nothing less than the last phase of a medieval siege, the only difference being that machine guns were substituted for crossbows and grenades for boiling pitch."

The moment the machine gun fire stopped, some two hundred men of the 1st Battalion, 4th Parachute Regiment swept down from Point 236, overrunning the defenders of Point 165 and surging on toward the castle. "We could not use artillery defensive fire," says Denis Beckett, "because we did not know how the Raj. Rif. [Rajputana Rifles] or our own people were faring out in front. Our mortars had not then been registered. It had to be fought out with infantry weapons man to man." While Frank Ketteley contacted battalion headquarters to let them know what was happening, Beckett tried to organize the defenses. "The first wave very nearly succeeded," he says. "One or two tried to penetrate the courtyard and many were stopped only a few yards from the walls. We broke them up with Mills grenades, Tommy guns and Brens." Beckett himself was wounded in the neck and the arm by a machine gunner just outside the walls. Ketteley then crawled forward in an attempt to pick him off, but was shot in the head. "We talked a bit and then he died," Beckett remembers. Soon afterward the defenders saw a white Very light go up, and the small-arms fire was replaced by artillery and mortars, so Beckett, now the commanding officer in the castle, assumed that the attack had been driven back. "I took stock of the situation," he says. "It was not pretty . . . we had lost a few good chaps in the first machine-gunning . . . and a number were wounded trying to take up fire positions."

The respite was brief. At 7 A.M. the paratroopers came again under cover of a smokescreen. This time a multitude of stick grenades was hurled into the castle and the Germans tried to climb the walls. But now the Essex men were better prepared, and Beckett had arranged for his battalion's machine guns, situated on the other side of the ravine, to bring enfilading fire on the western end of the castle. The three-inch mortars had also now established fire lines and were used to telling effect. The problem was finding an observation point. "Eventually I climbed on top of a wall, exposing head and shoulders. I was a complete bloody fool to do this," says Beckett, "but I could see no alternative. Anyway, a little runt of a Boche chucked a grenade at me and I was lucky not to get it on the head. By sheer luck we got the correction through before this happened."

The fiercest fighting took place in the courtyard. Three times the Germans penetrated, only to be driven back by Bren gun fire and grenades. In the castle's tower, Bren gunners manning the arrow slits were hit repeatedly by snipers. Once the attack was repulsed, there were only 60 men and three officers left from an original complement of over 150. Eight thousand rounds had been fired by machine gunners, and 1,500 mortar bombs had been fired. "One barrel bent under the strain and another became red hot," reports Beckett.

An hour later another attack was launched. Again, heavy artillery and machine gun fire broke up the advancing paratroopers, but several reached the Essex positions just outside the walls. "Fighting at times was at very close quarters," says Bill Hawkins. "German stick grenades were thrown at us; we replied using our Mills grenades, which from my position we were able just to roll down the mountainside. One of my platoon Bren-gunmen, Private George De Court, who'd accounted for a number of the enemy, had three stick grenades fall in his position. Two were promptly returned, but he was just too late to dispose of the last one; sadly he was a fatal casualty."

But the attack was beaten back again, and soon afterward a stretcher bearer approached the castle under a white flag to ask for a cease-fire in order to pick up wounded. "I had never done a truce," says Beckett, "and I got on to battalion and asked if that was all right." The day before, Beckett and another man had ventured out of the castle to pick up a wounded man, and he had been very impressed that no Germans had fired on them. When he had returned to the castle, he had stood in the gateway, totally exposed, and saluted up the hill. This time, the request for a truce was passed up the command and agreed by the divisional CO. For half an hour Germans, British, and Indians worked side by side bearing away the injured. When the Germans ran out of stretchers, they were lent some blankets by the British to help carry away their wounded.

After about twenty minutes, sniping from German infantry further up the mountain brought the truce to an end, and the two sides retired to lick their wounds. Each lacked the strength to swing the battle either way. For the 4th Indian Division, though, the attack from Hangman's Hill, postponed to 4 P.M., was still on, in spite of the vulnerability of their lines of supply and the perilous situation in the castle, and more troops were ordered up to Castle Hill and to continue on further up the hillside. Among them was Birdie

Smith, second-in-command of A Company, 2/7th Gurkhas: "It's the jackpot for us," the company CO, Denis Dougall, told him with a long face. "We're going for the monastery." It took two and a half hours to get the men down from their positions to the left of Snakeshead Ridge; then, writes Smith, "We moved into the town. There was no town. It was an indescribable mess of rubble . . . Everywhere there was a pervading smell of death." To their left they could hear gunfire as New Zealander and German patrols clashed. At the foot of the hill there was a patch of open ground now covered by German snipers, and the Gurkhas had to dash across platoon by platoon. The main track up to the castle was also now under constant fire, so Dougall left his men and went up alone in the hope that one man was more likely to get through.

Some time after, a message came back for Smith to climb up to be briefed. He, too, set off alone, and with great difficulty negotiated a track right on the edge of the steep ravine. "The scene inside the Castle was one of maximum activity, chaos, confusion . . . of men huddled behind piles of rubble, some wounded, many worn out and several who had given up completely." He was greeted by Maj. Denis Beckett: "The commander of the beleaguered Castle was a young major," Smith writes, "with his arm in a sling, unshaven, exhausted but radiating a calmness and courage that was inspiring those men who were still willing to fight and defend the position. Behind his quiet manner was a fierce determination."

Beckett refused to let the company go forward and spoke to his CO on the radio. "I was convinced," he says, "that the castle was the most important place at that time in the whole battle." Instead of going up the mountain only to return, like other units, in tatters, Beckett argued that the company should be held nearby to help defend the castle. While Dougall waited in the castle for agreement from the brigadier for this change of plan, Smith was sent back down the hill to convey the news to the men below. Hoping to avoid the ravine, he took a path to the right, and after a few yards met a group of frightened and tired Indian soldiers hiding behind some rocks. He asked them the best way back to his company. One of the men informed him he could choose between two tracks down the hill: the shorter one was covered by snipers; the other was safer but horribly steep.

"One way you get shot, Sahib, the other you slip to your death. But," he grinned without humor, "if you do go that way (pointing to the shortcut) you are on your own, we will not move to help you, even if you are hit."

"Why?" I asked.

"Why? Why? The Sahib asks why? Because we've already lost men doing crazy things for British Sahibs. Now do them yourself."

The others nodded in agreement.

Smith, still reeling from nearly falling into the ravine on the way up, chose the shorter track. He waited and waited, watching the fifty yards or more of the path obviously exposed to snipers in the western part of the town. "I said a prayer, the only prayer I could think of, the Lord's Prayer. Then getting quickly to my feet, charged down the track. It seemed as if I was going to be lucky when something flicked off my black side-cap as I dived to the ground. I lifted my head and saw the bullet mark. As I dropped so had the bullet missed, but only just, my head. Something had prompted me into diving for cover. In a second I was covered in sweat. Cold sweat. Everything seemed to stop; the noise of battle, the guns." A minute passed that seemed like an age. Above him, Smith could hear the Indians on the other side of the hill. "They were laughing about the young 'boy Sahib' who had refused to take their advice," says Smith. "I longed to call out to them but knew their answer in advance. I crawled forward and willed myself to make another dash. I prayed with great sincerity, prayed for speed, that the sniper would think I had already been hit. Into the open zigzagging down the track at the fastest speed I had ever attempted. Once again the crack, crack, a blow on my haversack, and then the safety of another rock. Breathless, in tears and humbled to find that fear had caused my bowels to open, I lay as dead until a glance at my watch spurred me on." Smith then charged down the lower part of the track and made his company position, to the relief of his men, who had seen him come over the top and fall. "I began giving out orders," says Smith, "trying to ignore shaking hands and the tell-tale wet patch down my trouser leg."

Up at the castle the determined German paratroopers were attacking again. This time, a small group of Pioneers with an officer inched forward and placed an explosive charge under the buttress of the northern battlements. A large part collapsed, burying twenty of the defenders, and the Germans swarmed through the gap. But they were met by concentrated machine gun fire and cut down. A prisoner taken at this time reported that, of the original two hundred German attackers of the morning, only forty were now still fit for combat. They had done enough, however, to force a further delay to the attack on the monastery from Hangman's Hill.

While Beckett's men had been fighting off the first counterattacks on the castle, two companies of Freyberg's Maori Battalion had gone into the attack on the stubborn defenders of the ruins of the Continental Hotel from their positions two hundred yards away. Their bravery and determination won them a few houses on the outskirts of the hotel, and nearly a hundred prisoners were taken, but, as with previous attacks, they found the hotel itself impregnable. Not only did the building and the surrounding rubble bristle with snipers and machine gun nests, but the Maoris found it impossible to form up to attack in sufficient strength. There was little room among the "lunatic maze" of the shattered buildings, and when a force did manage to assemble, a rain of mortar bombs, directed from the high ground still controlled by the Germans, fell on the men. Soon the sections became separated and, in many cases, unsure of where they were. C Company succeeded in reaching the foot of Monastery Hill, but then became cut off. The tanks supporting the attack struggled to approach the objective, and those that did were knocked out by a powerful German tank dug in to its turret in the lobby of the hotel. As before, the Germans relentlessly infiltrated through the scattered New Zealanders, and the latter kept finding that houses they had cleared had been reoccupied, and snipers and bomb squads were hitting the attackers in their flanks or rear.

There was no effective "front line," and in many cases it was not clear whether a building was occupied by friend or foe. Sergeant Mataira, from the same village as George Pomana, ducked into one house to read a map only to find that it was full of Germans. They shut the door behind him and took away his weapons. Pomana continues the story as he heard it from Mataira: "[The Germans] were abusing him, making a game, and then a couple of them had their machine guns on him and then one or two would come along and give him a kick and get a laugh out of it, and he was starting to swear at them, they were getting quite amused because they were really upsetting him, but what they didn't realize, while he was looking at them and they were thinking he was still swearing at them, he was talking to his mates over the wall in Maori, telling them to throw a grenade in. They didn't want to because they were worried about him getting killed as well, but he threatened them, saying, 'If I get out of here, I'll fix the whole lot of you.' It's guts as well as brains. They threw in a couple of grenades and it was enough to distract them, so he was able to grab a machine gun off them and got them out. He had to shoot some of them. He didn't realize there were so many of them: they were all in the rooms out back. They all came out and surrendered. Thirty-two of them."

Private R. Smith's description of one effort by Maori soldiers to clear a building captures the terrifying risks involved in house-to-house fighting. Two Maoris kicked the door in confidently enough but then, "as the door crashed open they were framed for an instant against the shadow of the passage beyond—framed for one second before they collapsed as if their legs had been snatched from under them, to the searing rattle of Schmeisser fire. The squirt of bullets pursued the limp forms as they folded their way down the steps, the bodies pouring themselves to the ground with a ghastly fluidity that is impossible in life." In such conditions, the defender, as the Germans had discovered at Stalingrad, had a huge advantage. By midafternoon it was obvious that the attack had failed.

Freyberg had one more card to play on 19 March. The tank force behind the monastery was intended to attack after the Hangman's Hill force had started their assault. When that attack was postponed, nobody in the scratch corps staff thought to tell the tankmen, who set off as planned. Progress was good initially, with the force passing to the west of Colle Maiola and circling and shooting up strong points on Point 593. From there, with the Liri valley open to their right, they pushed down a narrow defile that led to the rear of the monastery.

Young German paratrooper Werner Eggert was with the 4th Parachute Regiment behind the monastery: "Suddenly we heard tank noises coming up the mountain. This produced quite a bit of nervousness on our side. I was sent around to mobilize everything that had legs. I remember someone running close to me with bazookas under his arm. Behind me I heard even more scrambling. Carefully, looking for cover like a rat, I reached and then bent down with our third group. Everybody was already in his position and nervously expecting the attack." Then came an amazed cry from the German defenders: "No infantry in sight!" "Just when I wanted to go back to the command post, the firing went off," says Eggert. "I found cover in the walls of our watering place. The tanks approached in 'forward line' and without accompanying infantry. The first came through and almost reached my water hideout. Suddenly it was standing there alone and we fired at it with a

Panzerschreck [like an American bazooka] while it was trying to turn back. It came to a halt. The people stepped out and were taken as prisoners. The next tank was disabled further above by a buried mine. MG fire sizzled on its metal. It remained there without moving and blocked the narrow way for all following tanks. Nobody came out of this one. From the next tank, two men managed to step out and escaped in the fire cover of the following tanks, which soon turned around."

When a dozen were disabled, the remaining tanks were ordered to retreat. Had the attack been coordinated with another from Hangman's Hill, or if the tank force had had infantry and engineer support, it might well have broken the Cassino defenses. In the event, as the 4th Indian Division's historian has written, "Once again one fist struck while the other arm hung idle."

———————

By midafternoon on 19 March, Ken Bond and Ted Hazle from the composite B and D Company of the Essex had finally completed the journey from the castle to Hangman's Hill. The hillside was littered, Bond remembers, with "shredded trees, all splintered and rocks and rocks and rocks." It was "just a question of following the man in front. Someone must have known the way." The climb up the terraces on the hillside, or what was left of them, took half a day.

Many did not make it: only seventy, of whom thirty were wounded, succeeded in meeting up with the Gurkhas. Some got lost and ended up with the New Zealanders on Point 202. Many others were killed when caught on the exposed hillside by shell and mortar fire. "We lost chappies," says Ken Bond, "I knew various of them—who either got killed or died of their wounds on the way up, but we had to move on. We scrambled up and up and got into this culvert, a pipe under the road about four or five feet across. No one knew what we were intending to do from then on. Some of the chaps were further up, on another bend in the road, sheltering in another culvert. Fortunately, the culverts were dry. A dozen or twenty of us took shelter there. It was really chaotic, no one knew what was what."

Ted Hazle's section came under machine gun fire on the way up. "Jerry was shooting at us with a Spandau," he says, "so it was a case of make a run for it and hope to get around. I got a nick across the throat with a bit of gravel but got around." When he reached the hill, Hazle found that he was the only medic on the spot. "I made an RAP [regimental aid post] at the edge of this rise. I bedded down just on the side of the hill. The majority of them were around the corner and under the bluff of the hill, but we weren't. It was all right for the colonel of the Gurkhas, he was under a little bluff, but we just laid up at the side and put up sangars. We were being shelled by our own guns and they were dropping smoke shells to cover what we were doing. Trouble is, they weren't high enough. We got smothered in smoke and I still feel it. It made you cough. There were signalers up there, and I said, 'Can't you signal back to get them to raise the guns?' 'I've got no batteries,' he replied. So we just had to grin and take it. There wasn't much grinning."

Late in the afternoon the attack on the monastery was postponed again. It was clear that the attacking force was now isolated up on Hangman's Hill, and reinforcements could not be sent up until the approach to the castle and beyond had been cleared. The surviving men of A and C companies of the Essex in the castle were relieved that night by a battalion from the British 78th Division, and they made their way back to Wadi Villa to await the return of the Essex men on Hangman's Hill. The journey down was, according to Bill Hawkins, "just as difficult as coming up. You were slipping and sliding and you had to sort of lean on the hillside." Once in the Wadi, still under mortar fire, they took stock of their losses. Only twenty-one men had returned from A Company and just thirteen from C Company. As a cohesive force, the battalion had ceased to exist.

––––––––––

This had been the decisive day of the third battle. None of the three Allied attacks planned for the nineteenth—on the Continental, the diversionary tank thrust, and the storming of the monastery from Hangman's Hill—had succeeded. It was now essential to widen the bottleneck around the castle, and to clear the German positions in the town that threatened the left flank of those on the hillside. The next night the 78th Division men attacked Point 165 from the castle, but ran into a newly sown minefield and were beaten back. In the town, fresh New Zealander troops were sent in to try to batter their way into the German strong points at the foot of Monastery Hill.

New Zealander Clem Hollies was with the 21st Battalion when they moved up the line late on 19 March: "We were taken forward by a truck along Highway 6," he says, "and debussed about a mile short of the town and then moved forward by foot along the road, suffering an uncanny feeling of utter nakedness, with no protection, nerves taut for the burst of expected fire or incoming shell. We were lucky, and safely reached our assembly point in a building that turned out to be the convent . . . Tracer and mortar bursts lit up the night sky and gave us occasional glimpses of the devastated build- ings around us." From the convent, the battalion moved through the botan- ical gardens, where they were attacked by a squad of paratroopers. This was broken up by concentrated Bren gun fire. "When the enemy had retired," Hollies continues, "we saw German stretcher parties were busy carrying their wounded and two New Zealanders were in danger of being picked up. There were no Red Cross armbands available, but 'Pom' Pomeroy and I re- moved our steel helmets, and, indicating that we were unarmed, took the risk of being shot at from the Continental Hotel about 150 yards away, and assisted them both to regain our lines. This incident of a few minutes seemed like an eternity and I had a horrible feeling of hundreds of baleful eyes watching us. On regaining our house, we collapsed and didn't stop shaking for hours afterward. When daylight came, the shelling increased in intensity and it was impossible to move in the open without the protection of smoke shells. Our wireless set was destroyed and our house was being blown down around us. It was a great relief when a runner brought a mes- sage from Battalion Headquarters ordering us back to the comparative safety of the convent."

Intelligence officer 2nd Lt. Alf Voss was with the same battalion. He found Cassino "an unearthly place. There was always the smell of cordite in the air and every now and then you could hear the boom of mortars or the swoosh of *Nebelwerfers* opening up." Taking over from a Maori unit, he asked an of- ficer to show him a good place for the battalion headquarters. He was di- rected to a nearby building, but found that it had been reoccupied by the Germans and had to be retaken. Once established inside, "Our existence soon became subterranean," he says. "There were about 18 men in our head- quarters, in two rooms about 20 by 17 feet . . . I was trying to find out where our different units were, but no one was quite sure . . . the situation was very tense." Just before dawn, Voss heard a tank's motor recharging in the build- ing next door: "A German Panzer had sneaked in behind a garage door and just shut it. I borrowed three Kiwi Shermans, which let loose a few shells, knocking the building down on top of the German tank. No doubt the Ger- mans in the tank were in contact with their mates, as there was now a hail of enemy mortar and artillery fire heading at us. We then saw three or four members of the crew running off, heading towards the Hotel des Roses. Some of our blokes fired at them but they disappeared."

Other units did not even see any Germans but were still pinned down. The historian of the 23rd Battalion complains that the men "could see no rifle or other flash to indicate the whereabouts of the enemy who had perfect cover combined with perfect observation, and therefore complete mastery of the situation. Under these circumstances, daylight attacks over ground so cratered and covered with debris did nothing more than give the enemy good targets."

Intercepted German messages indicating pessimism that they could hold out encouraged Freyberg to keep ordering attacks on the Hotel Continental and the small strip along the base of Monastery Hill still in German hands, but none achieved the breakthrough. For Clem Hollies, "Our local war had reached a stalemate as far as our attack was concerned."

An officer in Jack Cocker's battalion summed up the mood of the men in Cassino at this time: "The air in the town [was] heavy with smoke and dampness and the stench of death, seeming to close in around you, almost suffocating you; a dismal place shrouded in thick, clammy mist, giving a feeling of despondency." Cocker himself describes the sensation of being continually under observed artillery fire: "You'd be down in your gun pit and all of a sudden they start shelling. They'd be getting closer and closer and you'd think to yourself, What the hell am I doing here? I don't have to be here—I shouldn't be here, and you'd be getting really upset. Once the shelling finished you were all right, you get used to it. Sometimes when it got a bit close you got a wee bit touchy and you'd think, Well, the next one is going to come and bury me. You were always scared, you couldn't help it."

Clem Hollies's unit was withdrawn back to the convent on 21 March, but was forced to stay there until the 25th. "Our four days and nights were absolute hell," he writes. "Mortar bombs continued to rain down; we had *Nebelwerfer* rockets through our roof; and the never-ending smoke shells meant we lived in a world where there was no day. Our nerves were stretched to breaking point, hands shaking so much cigarettes were hard to light. Hot meals were impossible, as was washing and shaving."

Freyberg was aware that his corps was now exhausted and demoralized. The war diary of the 23rd Battalion reported: "There seems little doubt that the conditions under which the troops are at present fighting are the worst ever yet experienced . . . the town is in ruins . . . every heap of rubble [is] a likely spot for enemy snipers who infiltrate sometimes behind the forward troops. All day long German shells pound the ruins . . . movement by day is made impossible. Fighting at times so close that only a wall may separate friend from foe."

On the morning of the twenty-third, Freyberg admitted that the New Zealand Division had "come to the end of its tether." The men in the 4th Indian Division's sector had their hands full merely holding the castle against continuing German counterattacks, and Freyberg had no option but to bring the third battle to a conclusion. Some on his staff pointed out the terrible losses the Germans must have suffered and urged one more push. To this, Freyberg reportedly replied with one word: "Passchendaele."

Indeed, it is impossible to look at photos of the Cassino battlefield at this time, with its desolate moonscape of craters filled with brackish water and dead mules and men, without being reminded of the infamous scenes of the First World War. For the correspondent Christopher Buckley, usually a forthright propagandist for the Allies' anti-Nazi war aims, the third battle was the "ultimate quintessence of war . . . men were hurling at one another lumps of jagged metal, everything that could tear and rend the living flesh, crush and shatter the bone . . . A wave of total and overwhelming despair swept over me. It was all going to happen again, so many times more. One had to cling hard to the purpose and meaning of it all."

In the town, among the filth and stench of unburied bodies, there were increasing cases of "battle fatigue." The official New Zealand medical history politely reports that toward the end of March, "infantry from Cassino showed signs of prolonged strain and lack of sleep, and cases of true physical exhaustion made their appearance."

It was decided to withdraw the troops isolated on Hangman's Hill and Point 202, disband the ad hoc New Zealand Corps, and establish a new defensive perimeter around the station and Castle Hill. The New Zealanders in the town had been able to see the men up on Hangman's Hill. In spite of their own predicament, it was impossible not to feel sorry for them on their isolated hillock. "If we weren't altogether happy about our own position," one New Zealand noncommissioned officer wrote, "we at least realized that it was infinitely preferable . . . to the undefined area among the barren rocks of the hill where our Indian friends grimly held on under a hail of mortar and shell. Our own twenty-five pounders appeared to rake most of the hillside. One wondered how men could live in such a place."

Since reaching the culvert under the road on the afternoon of 19 March, Ken Bond and the twenty or so men with him had not moved. "There was no one to give us instruction or advice as to what we had to do, whether we were going to go forward or being brought back," says Bond. "We didn't know anything, it was so chaotic." The failure to hold on to the various key positions on the hillside had meant that the troops on Hangman's Hill, who had set off with only twenty-four hours' emergency rations, had had to be supplied by airdrop. A British news film of the time portrays this cumbersome operation in jocular tones: "Chappatis by parachute for Indian troops in Italy" reads the headline. "An hour ago these men were almost at the end of their resources. Now with food and supplies they can hold out and they do . . . For our troops it's literally manna from heaven." However, "You had to scramble out and note not to be shelled and mortared trying to retrieve it," says Bond. "And half the time it drifted elsewhere, away from us, so [food] was very, very minimal." Water was also in very short supply. The Essex Battalion historian tells the story of a sergeant, who every night would take as many water bottles as he could carry and fill them from a shellhole. On the fourth night he returned from his trip later than usual and without any water. He had been about to refill the bottles when a Very light had shown that the hole contained a dead mule, which the sergeant estimated had been there for about three weeks.

Perhaps worst of all were the casualties from "friendly fire." In order to try to shield both the Hangman's Hill force and the New Zealanders in the town from the "all-seeing eye" of the monastery, there was an almost constant laying down of smoke shells around the base of the abbey and on the hillside. The artillery smoke shell had a small explosive charge that ejected the base plug of the shell during flight, permitting smoke-producing canisters to fall to the ground where needed. But the empty shell, still a deadly piece of metal, then proceeded on its way. Three sergeants in a sangar just up from Ken Bond were killed when a shell landed among them. In Ted Hazle's aid post, he says, "It was our own smoke that was doing as much harm as anything." Even the base plug could be fatal. The Gurkhas' commanding officer, Lieutenant Colonel Nangle, reported: "Canisters, shell cases and base plugs continued to fall among us and to cause casualties. One Essex man hit by a base plug ran about forty yards downhill before falling dead."

While Ted Hazle—equipped with only some bandages, a bit of morphia, and a pair of scissors—continued to treat the wounded, the isolated men, tired, hungry, and cold on the exposed hillside, waited helplessly for an order to attack or retreat. "Tiredness was the worst," says Hazle. "You get fed up and not as strong as you should be." Jack Miles, an officer in the 1/9th Gurkhas, recalled: "What growth that was left was just blasted tree stumps. There wasn't a blade of grass, not a leaf, not a tree, just shattered rock. I find it incredible to think that men went up and down these slopes and lived on these slopes, in such conditions, sleeping in the open in cold March weather, soaked with rain, terribly hungry and, twenty-four hours a day, the cacophony of war."

The proximity of the position to the enemy demanded constant alertness, and any movement in daylight brought mortar or rifle fire from the monastery. By 23 March, the original 1/9th Gurkha attack force, which had been on the hill for eight days, had been decimated. One rifleman from the 1/9th Gurkhas, who had been wounded in his arm, thigh, and stomach, told interviewers: "The fire was so heavy we could not lift our heads up. We crawled forward and used the stacks of corpses as cover. We also looked for food in the dead men's kit. We lost a lot of men."

Gurkha rifleman Balbahadur Katuwal, from the same battalion, was also on the hill for eight days. "For a week we were not resupplied," he says, "and then there were two airdrops but we could not go and pick up the packs as the enemy fire was too heavy. Eventually, at the third attempt two packs were dropped on our position containing ready-cooked food and we had a fine meal of rice and pulse. It was a difficult time and we reported the badly aimed fire. My greatest fears were mines, aerial bombs and medium artillery." Another Gurkha says, "We had virtually no food or drink all that time and we wet our mouths with mud. We relieved nature where we were. I had no hope of living, only of being killed and killing the enemy." To keep up their spirits, some of the Nepalese sang a song: "My battalion is One Nine GR/My house is in Dhaireni/After being surrounded for ten days, my mind wept tears."

When it was decided to withdraw the men on Hangman's Hill after dark on 24 March, three volunteer officers climbed up to contact the isolated force. "One young officer came up and said, 'I'm leading you out,' " remembers Ted Hazle. "He took us down the front of the castle, which was supposed to be impossible. I think I slipped from the top to the bottom of that hill on my bottom." While the men made the three-hour journey down, an extravagant artillery shoot as well as diversionary attacks kept the Germans busy and the retreat was completed without upset. "When we got to the bottom the Gurkhas collected us and took us to their place that night," says Hazle, who was to receive a bar to his DCM for his extraordinary medical work on the hill. "They gave us places to sleep, and, after a bit of a meal, we slept." The Germans later counted 165 dead Gurkhas on and around the hill as well as 20 machine guns, 103 rifles, 36 Tommy guns, and 4 wireless sets. Triumphantly, they raised a large swastika flag on the hilltop.

Point 202, the hairpin bend behind the town, was also abandoned on the same night. The wounded were left behind, with a Red Cross flag fashioned from parachute silk flying on the outside of the cave, which straightaway ended German mortar fire on the position. The walking wounded left the next morning, carrying another Red Cross flag, having promised to send stretcher bearers for the others. Left behind were four New Zealanders and a corporal from the Essex Battalion, A. J. Smith, whose platoon had stumbled into the New Zealanders' position five days before while trying to find the Gurkhas on Hangman's Hill. Smith, wounded on 19 March by a mortar explosion, had, he said, "fourteen different holes in me."

The next afternoon a group of stretcher bearers was sent out on Monastery Hill to pick up the men left behind. In charge was a New Zealander, Capt. A. W. H. Borrie. "As we were making our way across, we noticed some figures near old C Company HQ waving a flag," he says. "When we reached them we found they were the four Kiwis and one man of Essex Regiment who had been left behind. They had given up hope of being collected, so an hour previously the fittest of the party had handed round a large bottle of rum, dropped by parachute the day before. Fortified in spirit, these five lying cases had dragged themselves down to the road, a rough journey of twenty yards, and had managed to move a few yards along the road, each one helping the other." Borrie arranged for the men to be carried or stretchered, but as they were setting out a German soldier emerged from the ruins on Point 165, waving a Red Cross flag and advancing along the road toward them. Communicating in schoolboy French, he told Borrie that he was not allowed to pass. "Well, we just sat down in the open, and the officers started appealing to the orderly while we sat very dejected at this turn of events when our long ordeal seemed over," says A. J. Smith. Borrie continued to argue with the German, "and then Thompson and Worth were taken into the ruins on Point 165 to see the Commandant. The Commandant asked for a cigarette—Worth immediately gave him a full packet. The German explained that, as the English had shot at a stretcher bearer at Cassino, the Cassino Commandant had ordered that there was to be no further evacuation of British from Monastery Hill. He gave his approval, however, for our evacuations, coming down with Thompson and Worth to inspect us. We heard them coming but dared not look around until they were beside us. A nod of the head from Sgt. Thompson was the sign for action, so we picked up our wounded and set off for the Castle, making double-quick time before the Germans changed their minds."

"I was so delighted," says Smith, "that I completely forgot the holes in my leg, and started to walk very fast toward the castle, but it only opened my wounds again, causing me to be carried once more."

The hospitals behind the Allied lines were now overrun. In February, following the Maori attack on the station, the number of New Zealand admissions to the general hospital tier of the medical service had been the highest since June 1941 and the fighting in Crete. This record did not last long. In March the fighting in the town had produced nearly twice the number.

Without the satisfaction of victory, the hard fighting at Cassino brought the elite New Zealand Division to the brink of falling apart for the only time in the war. The crucial bond between men and their leaders broke down. By the end of the third battle, the men simply no longer believed that they could do what was being asked of them. The crisis in the division is underlined by the soaring cases of sickness and disciplinary action just after Cassino. Clem Hollies comments on this change in the New Zealanders: "I noticed that there was a different approach to battle in the battalion. The 'old hands' were becoming weary (and wary) and the reinforcements were not up to scratch."

There were still frontline duties to be carried out by the New Zealanders in the town at the beginning of April, but toward the end of the month the division was moved to a "quiet" sector in the mountains to the north where the French had been fighting. Also living in that area was Tony Pittaccio. He soon befriended a Bren gun carrier crew from the 23rd Battalion and was eventually accepted into their ranks, given a uniform and the job of making the small wooden crosses that were used to mark temporary graves. The Maori Battalion was nearby as well, and Pittaccio remembers them as "Great guys, kind-hearted [but] a long way from home, and starting to wonder what they were doing there." All the men he came across were "heartbroken by the destruction and suffering. They didn't talk about their own losses. The approach was 'He was a good old sod, he was an old bastard, let's drink to him.' There was no sentimentality." The Maoris, though, called the attack on the station "bloody futile" and the general mentality had become that everything they were doing was equally pointless. "They complained about the whole strategy of Cassino," says Pittaccio, "blaming the high-ranking officers."

––––––––––––

The 4th Indian Division was also being relieved at last. There were few left. One company of the 4/16th Punjabis had entered the line with 180 men and left six weeks later with 37. This was typical of the attrition within the division. On 26 March, Birdie Smith received the order to leave his position up on the massif and lead his men on a five-mile march down the Pasquale Road to Wadi Portella. "For most of the time in the front line the men had hardly walked at all for six weeks," he writes. "Men were cramped, unfit, mentally exhausted, without any willpower . . . Never will I forget that nightmare of a march. Officers, British and Gurkha, shouted at, scolded, cajoled and assisted men as they collapsed. At times we had no alternative but to strike soldiers who just gave up; all interest lost in everything, including any desire to live."

The shattered remnants of the once proud division were to be moved to the quieter Adriatic theater. "4th Division lost more than a battle," commented Major General Tuker. "They had lost some of its very substance in the shape of the men who had molded it." On 27 March, after a long wait in the Wadi Villa, the remains of the Essex Battalion were reunited with the D and B company men who had been on Hangman's Hill and moved out to Venafro, where they had their first proper meal of "steak, chips and tomatoes, with a steaming mug of tea." Five days later, reports the battalion's historian, "the 1/4th Essex left the 5th Army and the area of Cassino with few regrets." At Cassino the battalion had suffered twice the losses they had received at El Alamein. Replacements could make up the numbers, but the battalion would never be the same again. "After Cassino we had lost quite a lot of our offensive spirit," says Denis Beckett. "The sparkle had gone." Bill Hawkins concurs: "Before Cassino you had the blokes who had been together in civvy life, and from the start. We knew each other's families and that sort of thing. But when those chaps were gone you have a different class of person come in . . . there just wasn't the same feel about things." Most of all, the days in the cramped keep of the castle had been a shattering personal experience. Essex Battalion man Reg Fittock remembered: "There was terrible fear in that castle for those five days. That was definitely the worst five days of my life. I have never been so relieved in my life as when we were withdrawn from the area."

When the doctor John David left Cassino with the division, his sense of relief was overwhelmed by sadness. "I experienced a wave of acute sorrow," he wrote. "So many friends lost or broken, so many with their nerve gone."

14

The Green Devils
of Cassino

In the town, the troops on both sides continued their deadly games of cat and mouse. By now the Germans of the 1st Parachute Division knew they had pulled off a remarkable coup. They had distinguished themselves before, in Norway, the Low Countries, and Crete. During the fighting in Sicily, they had famously dropped into battle at lunchtime and therefore avoided the RAF. But this was in another league. None of their most senior commanders had dared believe that Cassino town could be held, but it seemed the few survivors of the bombing had achieved the impossible. Their superiors, though, appreciated the superhuman effort made by the elite troops. Any parachutist who fought for two weeks in the town automatically received an Iron Cross.

Berliner Joseph Klein registered for the paratroopers in 1941. Previously he had been a pilot with an ocean rescue unit stationed in Belgium, responsible for fishing downed British pilots out of the sea. "I had to go to Brussels to see the chief psychiatrist of the German Air Force—to examine why a pilot would want to become a paratrooper," he remembers. The psychiatrist asked him, "Why do you want to have anything to do with this troop of gangsters?"

"This is no gangster troop," Klein replied. "This is the bravest troop that Germany has."

Klein was told he would be an instructor, but that was not what he had in mind. "Listen to me!" he said to his supervisor. "I did not come to the paratroopers to become an instructor! I want to be in the war. A war unit."

"My dear young man, how old are you?" asked the supervisor.

"Eighteen years."

"Then listen. Be careful not to pee in your pants in the war with your eighteen years."

All the German paratroopers remember their training as particularly hard. Robert Frettlöhr, who had volunteered after seeing a heroic film about the paratroopers, describes the daily regime: "You start at six o'clock in the morning and continue until five o'clock at night. You do not want to go on because you are absolutely shattered after days of training like that."

"There were people who got so worn out and tired that they couldn't crawl to their beds," says Klein. "They were so exhausted that they slept on the floor. We had three-story beds and they couldn't make it up to the top." There were many injuries, and failures were ruthlessly weeded out.

Severe casualties in Crete persuaded Hitler that the paratroopers' days of jumping were over, and the force was broken up into small units and pitched into Russia to fill holes in the line. In spring 1942 there had been a plan to use the paratroopers to capture Malta, but the operation failed to materialize. In the autumn they returned to Smolensk, where Maj. Gen. Richard Heidrich took over command of the division under its new title: 1st Parachute Division. "The 1st Division was the mother division," says Klein, "the elite of the elite!" After a period in France, the division had seen action in Sicily, its last attack from the air. From Salerno onward they had been in the front line and were worn out, with many suffering from malaria.

On first arriving at Cassino, Klein had been responsible for blasting down some of the unsafe ruins of the bombed abbey, and had been with his 3rd Regiment in Cassino town at the time of the New Zealanders' attack. "During the bombing, we were in the cellar of the Hotel des Roses," he says. "The bombs ripped apart the house. But these walls fell on the vault and protected us even more. The rubble and ruins—lying on top of this vault—that was the ideal protection! We were in a fortress."

Klein describes the fighting in the town and the importance of their positions on slightly higher ground along Route 6: "We were in a fortunate position. We were above. That is always how it was. They might come into a destroyed house, and we would be above it and could drop a grenade on their heads."

Klein had fought on the Eastern Front but considers the combat in the ruins of Cassino town as particularly vicious: "Every method was allowed . . . There was basically the rule 'You or me.' A few soldiers mined the bomb craters. The Allies came in and jumped from hole to hole. And when they ran they were fired on with machine guns so that they jumped in the holes, into the bomb craters. When they were in the craters, the mines and explosives which had been prepared were lit. Naturally they were blown into the air. That was very terrible."

The German defenders had sustained massive casualties in the initial bombing, in most units over 60 percent, and more had been killed during the subsequent fighting, but they had saved the town and the road to Rome. Even Allied commentators at home, transfixed by the events at Monte Cassino, spoke in admiration of the paratroopers' fighting abilities and determination. General Alexander was forced to concede that his troops were no match for the elite Germans: "Unfortunately we are fighting the best soldiers in the world. What men! . . . I do not think any other troops could have stood up to it perhaps except these para boys."

New Zealander Alf Voss shared this amazement at the fortitude of the enemy: "Even after those casualties they were still fighting hard," he says. "I wondered how many Kiwis would have continued fighting against such odds. Few, I suspect, and wondered also what on earth had been driving those Germans." *The Times* of London followed Alexander's line that they were simply very good troops, calling the paratroopers "bold and determined," but other Allied commentators put it down to their ideological motivation. Naples radio reported on 21 March: "The German paratrooper today has but one object—to die for Adolf Hitler. He is a fanatic, seldom more than twenty years of age. At Cassino he is sacrificing his life for the Führer and his cause." Certainly many of the paratroopers were, like Klein, "true Nazis." The division was part of the Luftwaffe, the youngest and thus the most "Nazified" of the three services. But there is more to it than this. As Klein explains, it was a self-consciously elite troop, efficient and close-knit. "We are there for each other," he says. "That was built up in Russia and Crete. It's like a chain. Each man is a link in the chain. And if one is missing, the chain pulls apart. In other words, if I would have given up, the whole thing would have fallen apart. In our fighting troop, we were always together. And one always knows where the others stand—I can depend on them. They don't give up."

Paratrooper Werner Eggert says he saw many "so-called heroic acts, the careless ones and the ones that suddenly surpassed themselves." Few, he maintains were motivated by "sacrifice for people and native country." Instead some would come about from "acting consciously on your obligations to a bonded troop, dependent on each other for better or worse," while others would arise from "situations where you were driven by pure despair or where all you could do was fight on in order to save your own life . . . How often such an attitude meant success in the process of our operations. How often this led to survival."

Buttressing all of these various motivations, however, was the threat of severe disciplinary punishment for those who failed to live up to the paratroopers' high standards. Klein tells a story from his time on the Adriatic front when a man was accused of stealing. After he had been whipped "black and blue," Klein had him stripped naked and locked in an unheated room where the temperature dropped to minus twenty degrees Celsius. Care had been taken to remove anything that would have enabled him to take his own life. "When he began to scream I said, 'This goes too far,' " Klein remembers.

Along with esprit de corps, the paratroopers had also been trained to act on their initiative. While to some extent this was true of all German soldiers, it was particularly evident in the paratroopers and encouraged by their commanding officer, Heidrich.

At home in Germany, the paratroopers' resilience in Cassino had a massive impact. A secret report by the SS stated that: "The progress of the fighting in Italy is the only thing at the moment that gives us reason to hope that 'We can still manage it.' It has demonstrated that we are equal to far superior adversaries." The monastery of Monte Cassino had now become an international symbol of German resolve and defensive skill.

————————

The judgment of historians on the third battle at Cassino, and on Freyberg's planning and execution of the attack, has not been kind. Airpower had been overestimated again, and, as with the destruction of the monastery, it had merely created ruins in which the defender had the advantage. Tanks had been unable to support the infantry, who themselves had insufficient space among the wreckage to employ the tactics of fire and movement to clear the town. A senior Allied air commander conceded that the failure of the battle was due to the impossibility of "blotting out all enemy resistance in well-prepared positions," but added, "The other simple explanation [for the failures] . . . was that the killed . . . on the 15th, the day of the attack, amounted to four officers and thirteen other ranks. I hope we shall have learned by the time we attack again that five hundred casualties today often save five thousand in the next week."

Certainly it has been argued that Freyberg should have attacked in greater strength immediately after the bombing of the town, and that even while the battle was in progress he was too cautious about committing his reserves. There may be some truth in this, although, as has been seen, the narrow axis of advance limited the number of troops who could be sent forward, and the breakdown of communications with the forward elements meant that Freyberg could not know where to deploy his reserves. He was also hindered by events outside his control, especially the heavy rain on the second day of the attack and the fierce counterattacks by the Germans on Castle Hill, which ended all realistic ambitions to capture the monastery from Hangman's Hill.

The final irony is that perhaps the main purpose of the attack—to relieve the pressure on Anzio—was no longer valid by the time the delayed assault was launched. The situation on the bridgehead had been stabilized by the beginning of March. Heavy German casualties had stopped their second counterattack on 29 February, and the next day the skies cleared and the Allies were able to use their airpower and naval guns to great effect. In light of this, it is hard to understand why the third battle was launched at all. Certainly the Germans were baffled. Von Senger later called the attack "one of the most perplexing operations of the war."

From the end of March, stalemate set in at Cassino. The front line now stretched from the Garigliano bridgehead in the south, along the Rapido River, and through the wrecked town. Above the town the castle remained in Allied hands, and above that was the awkward salient stretching from Snakeshead Ridge to Monte Castellone and Colle Abate into the Apennines. At many points along this line only yards separated the two sides.

Immediately behind the lines, the local Italians continued to suffer. Artilleryman Ivar Awes, whose US 34th Division was preparing to leave the area to reinforce the Anzio bridgehead, wrote home on 24 March: "These Italians are funny people. Some of them absolutely refuse to leave the battle areas. Especially the farmers—they just won't leave their farms and livestock.

They just go about their business as if things were normal. They even pay social calls on their neighbors and compare the damage that's been done to their houses etc. I've seen young girls riding a bicycle through an area that a soldier wouldn't dare stick his head out of his foxhole in. Many of them have been killed too, and they all wear a black ribbon of mourning but they have such a deep faith in the mother of Christ that nothing shakes them. They just take what comes and carry on. They hate Mussolini, the Germans, and I believe they hate us because we brought the war to their shores. I don't think they go for this 'liberation' idea too well. All they want is peace just like the rest of us and I hope they, and all the rest of the world, get it soon."

Many still tried to cross the lines. Both sides were careful about firing in such a situation, but there were inevitable casualties. "I saw one woman with a little girl and a bunch of laundry going along on a mule," Awes remembers. "A little later I heard an explosion and turned around and there was laundry all in the trees. The poor woman and the mule and kid were killed . . . It was terrible. Oh God, I just cried and cried."

Tony Pittaccio remembers that the biggest killer was malaria: "The Germans flooded part of the valley which, with dead bodies, animal and human, became infected with mosquitoes. Soldiers were protected, they had medicine and proper clothing, but we civilians were not and most of us caught malaria and many died. The danger lasted for many months after the fighting ended."

Once behind the American lines, Pittaccio's family had reestablished contact with their father in Southampton, and while Tony befriended the New Zealand Bren gun carrier crew, his mother and sisters, like many others, eked out a living by doing washing for the Allied troops. The locals soon learned to "grade" the different nationalities in the Allied force. "The most liked," says Pittaccio, "were the Americans, because they were exceptionally generous. Second were the New Zealanders, third the Indians. The British were admired because of their discipline and military correctness but gave little away materially, maybe because they had little to give. Gemma Notarianni is less forgiving of the British: "They would not give us food: they sometimes threw it, but never gave it. All the others would give us leftovers."

"The ones we could have done without were the North Africans," said Pittaccio. "Italian men who had a young female family to protect were in a dangerous situation because they could be dispensed with by a bullet or a knife if they did not permit what was actually rape. I am not saying that it happened on a wide scale, but it did happen. Women sacrificed themselves by offering themselves in place of their daughters."

There are many allegations that the French North African troops, particularly the Goumiers, irregular Moroccan mountain troops now joining Juin's FEC in increasing numbers, indulged in rape and looting on a large scale. Norman Lewis in Naples reported in May 1944 that "the French colonial troops are on the rampage again. Whenever they take a town or a village, wholesale rape of the population takes place . . . children and even old men are violated . . . What is it that turns an ordinary decent Moroccan peasant boy into the most terrible of sexual psychopaths as soon as he becomes a soldier?" Complaints were made to Juin about the behavior of his men. Even the pope was called upon to intervene. Later he would take the extraordinary step of banning Allied "colored" troops from entering Rome.

Like all rumors, particularly in wartime, the allegations took on a momentum of their own and should be treated with great caution. A British journalist commented, "The Goums have become a legend, a joke . . . No account of their rapes or their other acts is too eccentric to be passed off as true." Every large army contains its fair share of sociopaths and criminals, and the degrading conditions of warfare have always facilitated this sort of behavior, so it might be unfair to heap all the blame for atrocities committed against civilians at the door of the "Moroccans." It was noticeable when researching this book that almost every Italian civilian mentions the French North Africans in this context, but it is much harder, although not impossible, to find eyewitness reports that can be reliably checked. "I myself witnessed a most dangerous incident," says Tony Pittaccio. "We only had an uncle to protect his wife and my two sisters. A Moroccan or an Algerian soldier, I am not sure which, came into the room where we were sheltering and demanded that his wife and my sisters follow him. For the first time I learned that my uncle could speak fluent French. He made a strenuous effort to try to keep calm while the soldier was becoming more agitated, but my uncle said something to the soldier with a calm but stern voice which resembled a military command. This stunned the soldier but I am sure that he would have soon snapped out of his perplexity and would have proceeded with his evil intentions had it not been for two other men who were passing by, saw what was happening and came over to help. So, whereas when the Germans were there men had to hide, when the North Africans were there women and young girls had to hide."

Looting, like rape, is also as old as warfare itself, and Allied veterans from all nationalities cheerfully admit to stealing food, wine, and valuables from the houses of Italian civilians. So automatic was this practice that the Germans took to booby-trapping attractive-looking propositions to catch out unwary Allied troops. The New Zealander Jack Cocker reports that in one town "we lost several fellas looking for loot." Prisoners of war were also considered fair game, and few would make it to the prison camp still in possession of their watches. A young officer from the Durham Light Infantry told the story of taking some prisoners on Monte Camino: "We shouted at them to come out with their hands up. They came out, something like 16 or 18 of them. I'm afraid that when we lined those prisoners up, if any of them had any cameras or anything like that, which we didn't want to fall into the hands of the people guarding the prisoner of war camps behind, we helped ourselves—we felt that we were more entitled to them than they were. Perhaps slightly reprehensible in some ways. Among them was a camera and I took some snaps there and then."

German pistols, insignia, belt buckles, and field binoculars were particularly prized, and men would risk their lives to get hold of them. "Souvenir" became a verb, as in "we souvenired his plane's compass." Rear-echelon and air force personnel would pay huge sums for a German pistol.

Other stories are darker and related only with great regret by veterans. Several have told of their revulsion when a comrade stole from a dead body, in some instances cutting off the finger of a dead German to steal his gold wedding ring. Perhaps more than anything else, this illuminates the debilitating effects that war has on the behavior and morality of those forced to fight it.

The weather until the end of March remained cold and wet, and on the mountains there were heavy falls of snow. The unnamed German machine gunner from the 115th Panzer Grenadier Regiment wrote in his diary toward the end of the month: "We are back in the hills behind Cassino. What we are going through here is beyond description. I never experienced anything like this in Russia, not even a second's peace only the dreadful thunder of guns and mortars and there are the planes over and above. Everything is in the hands of fates, and many of the boys have met theirs already. Our 'strongpoint' is built round with stones. If one is dropped among them, then we'll all have had it." A couple of days later he writes, "There has been a heavy fall of snow. It is whirling into our post. You would think you were in Russia. Just when you think you are going to have a few hours' rest to get a sleep, the fleas and bugs torment you. Rats and mice are our roommates too." Most of all, he longs for a return to his family. On 27 March, in his last entry, he writes, "In spite of it all we are still holding out . . . Here I have to suffer the worst privations and want so badly to get home to my wife and son. I want to be able to enjoy something of the beauty of life again. Here we have nothing but terror and horror, death and damnation. When will the day come again when I shall be able to devote myself to my wife and baby, and take pleasure in the birds and flowers? It is enough to drive you out of your mind."

Such sentiments were shared by all the soldiers at Cassino, particularly those with wives and young children. The importance of letters, described by one American veteran as "a lifeline to sanity," cannot be overestimated. The army authorities certainly appreciated this, and great efforts were made to get mail to the troops whatever the circumstances. The written word was the soldiers' only contact with back home, and it was desolation not to receive letters. All veterans pleaded for more replies. On 16 April, Walter Robson, the corporal in the 1st West Kents who had married his wife, Margaret, only two months before leaving Britain, complains: "I've had no letters—well one—one in a fortnight. Which is not good enough. What's the big idea!" But before he finishes writing, his wish is granted and he is instantly overjoyed. "It's arrived," he writes at the end of the letter. "I knew it! The loveliest letter you've ever written, and it's over a fortnight old. I'll write a special letter tomorrow. Me and the nightingale who loves you too, who's telling the world so at this moment outside."

A vast number of letters were written by the troops in Italy. One American veteran sent five hundred in two years just to his parents. While receiving letters gave the troops a window back to their old lives, so the act of writing was seen both as a sane task and an accepted and welcome retreat into privacy, a way of dealing with the long stretches of boredom and forever being in a crowd.

Letters from Cassino also usually contain an appeal for reading matter to be sent out. Books were among the necessities of existence for servicemen, again to counter the boredom and to provide an accepted private space and link with their past lives. "A few magazines and books," one serviceman has commented, "provided the 'civilization' with which to counter the pain, the general racket and the awful, though now much admired, bonhomie, through which we floundered." There was huge demand among the British for Penguin and Pelican paperbacks, and US publishers were quick to launch their own paperback lists during the war. Reading anything was better than nothing, as Bill Mauldin points out: "Soldiers at the front read K-ration labels when the contents are listed on the package, just to be reading something." Most in demand were local, rather than national, newspapers, where the men could read about their hometowns and people and places they knew. Nineteen-year-old Colin O'Shaughnessy, a private from Derby in the 5th Northants Battalion, requested the *"Evening Telegraph* or the *Derbyshire Times* . . . perhaps you could include a *Farmer and Stockbreeder* or *The Poultry World.*" Colin had been hoping to emigrate to New Zealand after the war to work as a farmer. He was killed on 18 May by artillery fire.

Of course, letters could not dispel all the homesickness, loneliness, and yearning for loved ones. "I don't want to write, I want to come home and talk," Walter Robson wrote to his wife at the end of March. In addition, letters were censored, and sometimes soldiers would struggle to find something other than the war to write about. "It's hard to compose a letter that will pass the censors when you are tired and scared and disgusted with everything that's happening," Bill Mauldin commented. But there was also a great amount of self-censorship. Soldiers were concerned about their families, how the worry of their absence was affecting them, and letters often attempted to sustain the morale of those at home. When Colin O'Shaughnessy tells his mother about a friend who has been killed, he instantly follows it up with a reassurance: "It's a rotten shame as he was only nineteen. But don't worry I'm coming back. You're not getting rid of me as easy as that." When Robson does talk about the horrors experienced, he is apologetic: "I should write gay *triviata* but I can't. I think sometimes I ought not to write at all rather than like this. Sorry . . ." Robson's letters show a fascinating conflict between the urge to "tell it how it is" and his desire to protect Margaret from the reality of what was happening at Cassino, itself almost indescribable: "One day I am going to send you a letter packed beginning to end with all the swear words I know, and others far worse which I shall invent," he writes. "You will know then that I am letting myself go about this bloody war."

Robson's letters also illustrate his personal battle against fear: "the feeling that you can't keep on going up these mountains and coming down again . . . You trample these thoughts down, but you might as well trample down gas, they rise again." The greatest concern for Robson, as for many of the men with loved ones and dependents at home, was the effect that their death would have on those left behind. Coming down the mountain after his unit's stint in the Garigliano bridgehead in late March, Robson passed a small, recent grave by the side of the track. The reaction of the men was "Poor devil, he's well out of it . . . But it's not him you think of, it's his people," Robson continues. "Jerry ranged on more than an Italian slope when he got him. He ranged on an English home as well. He launched a shell and a letter. The shell brought peace to one, the letter misery to many, a wife, a child, a mother? Yesterday it was a Jerry's grave. You thought the same thoughts. A home in Wilhelmshaven. You didn't gloat. Didn't even say that's one less. You don't hate Jerry. You just say why can't we all come to our senses and call the whole thing off?"

———————

At the end of the third battle, the 4th Indian Division was replaced on the Cassino Massif by men from the British 78th Battleaxe Division. Fred Majdalany, an officer with the 2nd Lancashire Fusiliers, describes the tension of imagined dread that preceded going "up the line": "You always had that just-before-the-race feeling when the first move order arrived. You took the usual steps not to show it. You made the usual wan little jokes. The others did the same. You knew that the others were thinking and feeling exactly the same as you. You knew they were all thinking 'Oh Christ!' " As he approaches the battle zone the landscape changes, the traffic thins out, and on the side of the road are burned-out vehicles "rusty and hideous . . . Sheaves of telephone cables crisscrossing the ditches and hedgerows like a giant's crazy knitting." They pass the inevitable wounded coming out, and "You thought of a clean hospital bed. And it seemed the most wonderful and desirable thing in the world to be wounded."

The commanding officer of the battalion, John MacKenzie, was shocked by what he found up on the massif: "We eventually reached the Gurkha battalion HQ located in a small, shelled farmhouse whose upper structure had collapsed over two ground-floor rooms. These were barely habitable and crawling with vermin . . . the next night Gurkha guides led the companies to their positions. The three forward ones were right under the noses of Germans fifty yards away . . . In our HQ hovel the Gurkha commanding officer shook hands and wished us luck." His Gurkha regimental sergeant-major was drunk or, as MacKenzie puts it, "unsteady from an overdose of rum." "He shook hands with me and babbled a short speech," MacKenzie continues. "The CO translated, 'He has wished you all a safe return to your families or a warm welcome by your ancestors.' They hurriedly departed down the mountainside and we, the new owners, had to come to terms with a shell-torn, mine-ridden and corpse-filled estate."

"As we approached Snakeshead," writes Majdalany, "we came upon the aftermath of a considerable battle. American equipment was scattered everywhere—tin hats, ammunition pouches, bits of rifles, bits of machine guns, bits of boots and bits of clothing. One of the tin hats had half a head in it. One of the boots contained most of a leg . . ." Aside from the grisly remains, the Lancashire Fusiliers were shocked by the isolated and exposed nature of the positions they were to occupy. "The forward defensive layout was tactically unsound, almost untenable," says MacKenzie. "The Germans held the high points on a rocky ridge overlooking our soldiers in their stone shelters who were vulnerable to bombs from light mortars and even thrown grenades. Furthermore, we were all overlooked by enemy observers around the towering Monastery and by those on Monte Cairo. It was dangerous to move during daylight; toilets had to be performed within the sangars. My request for adjusting the defensive layout was refused; the reason given was that positions won at such great cost during the previous battle must not be relinquished. It seemed illogical to have to defend such vulnerable positions." Nevertheless, the Fusiliers manned the forward outposts, rotating their platoons every forty-eight hours. In their tiny sangars the men slept back to back to conserve warmth and did what they could to improve their dwellings by piling more and more stones and earth around them. As punctual as clockwork, the Germans would carry out their early morning and evening "hates," when the British positions would be plastered by artillery. At dusk, the men would crawl from their shelters, and, writes Majdalany, "you would see small groups of bare hindquarters showing white in the semi-darkness, like grotesque friezes: their owners fervently praying that they might complete the proceedings before a shell struck the area. For shelling—frightening at any time—is worst of all when it catches you with your trousers down."

Soon the men were filthy. One British soldier remembers, "The lines in your hand ingrained with dirt, your hands smelled, everything smelled."

With an improvement in the weather in mid-April came a worsening of the problem of getting water up to the men on the mountain, and there was scarcely enough to drink, let alone wash. One mountain pool just below the monastery was ringed by the dead bodies of soldiers from both sides whose thirst got the better of their common sense. Under cover, snipers from both sides waited for the next man to risk a drink.

Worst was the smell of death everywhere, with mules and men "in an advanced state of decomposition, and black with feasting flies." Rats could be heard at night, tearing at the bodies all around. Many of the men contracted dysentery, making their toilet arrangements even more difficult and unpleasant. "A state of utter timelessness set in," writes Majdalany. "The only war that existed for us was that between ourselves and the Monastery Germans."

If anything, the supply situation of the Germans was worse than that of the Allies, who had plenty of artillery ammunition to rain down on the narrow track known as Death Ravine that led from the German rear to the monastery. During the day an Allied observation plane would circle the supply route almost continually, bringing down fire on anyone who risked the journey in the light. "Our potable water supply was delicate," remembers paratrooper Werner Eggert, who took his turn bringing up the provisions and ammunition at night. Even then, he says, "Incalculable fire assaults thundered into the valley. Many of our men died during the one-hour ascent and half-hour descent. Some mules would continue despite being filled with shrapnel fragments. Besides normal artillery ammunition also a few phosphorus-spraying fire shells hit."

Soon the path had a "white-yellow marking" from the discarded peel of oranges that the carriers would eat to assuage their thirst. The oranges were dragged up in big bags, along with "Thermoses with only lukewarm meals, bread, tea bags, sugar, candles, white alcohol tablets used to heat food, and bandages. Sometimes a few small bottles of rum and chocolate. Primarily, however, crates with hand grenades and ammunition. And deadly plate mines, which hung sometimes loosely from the mule or were carried in the backpack. The artillery assaults were multiplied by their effect: "the plate mines were terrible direct hits," says Eggert. "As a small wheel in this large war machine, I was finally hit at night on the valley way with a few splashes of burning phosphorus on the trousers. I threw myself immediately into the next water-filled crater and waited until somebody passed again. Behind, two mules and a foot soldier loaded with a backpack quickly walked uphill. He stopped for a moment and gave me one of his first-aid packets." By the time Eggert reached the first-aid post at the foot of the path, the phosphorus was burning "like hell" on his skin. "Someone cut the trousers open, washed, rubbed and rinsed. I began to sweat and started to become nauseous." But within ten days, with new underwear, trousers, and boots, Eggert was back with his unit in the monastery.

German parachutist Robert Frettlöhr had taken part in one of the bloody assaults on the castle, and at the beginning of April was sent back to Castle Hill as part of the German defensive ring around the position. "They were shelling us all the time as we were going up," he says. "As a young man of twenty it was impossible to know what you felt. They kept telling you you had to fight for your country. Forget it. You had to fight for self-survival." During the day Frettlöhr would sleep in a rough stone shelter before crawling out at nightfall to man one of the forward machine gun positions. "It wasn't a pleasant time up there, because you were dirty, filthy. You used to get a pint of water but believe me that pint of water didn't go anywhere. But there was a lot of alcohol and we all used to drink, because we always used to say if you get wounded you don't feel it as much."

In the mountains to the north of Cassino, the French troops were also relieved by British soldiers from the 4th Division, and then subsequently by New Zealanders, rested after their efforts in the town. Pioneer officer F. G. Sutton, from the 2nd Beds and Herts Battalion, remembers, "It was obvious the French were very good soldiers. Their positions were well sited and things seemed to run efficiently." The Moroccan Goums had been patrolling in front of the position, and Sutton heard that they had a habit of cutting the ears off Germans they had killed to collect a reward for each one. Three days after Sutton's arrival, three South Africans who had been captured at Tobruk passed through the lines. On the run for six months, they had been clothed and fed by local Italians throughout that time. The next day, indicating that the Germans had not noticed the relief, the Beds and Herts men were showered with propaganda leaflets in Arabic. One was sent back to the intelligence section and translated:

Did you know that the British troops never stay in the front line more than four to seven days and after return to their rest zone? . . . Did you know that thousands of your Tunisian and Algerian brothers have been murdered under the orders of General Eisenhower because they refuse to fight for their oppressors? Arab brothers, did you know as well that only a German victory can put an end to that oppression? This is why we advise you to cross over to our side so that after the war, you will be able to return to a free Arab country, a country where your wives and your families are at this moment waiting for you. Come across the German line, either alone or in numbers.

Both sides had identified the other's "foreign" troops as weaknesses that could be exploited. As well as the French colonial troops, the New Zealanders fighting for the Allies were targeted with leaflets that praised them for being the "pluckiest soldiers of the British Empire," but went on to imply that the Allies were saving all the hard battles for the "Boys of the NZEF." "TO INDIAN TROOPS," read another leaflet. "Without aim or reason [you] are helping a foreign nation, which for the last 200 years has enslaved you."

For the Allies, there were high hopes that the increasing number of *Volksdeutsche* facing them on the other side of the line might be persuaded to desert. The German army, as well as containing Austrian and other largely willing recruits from the *Grossdeutschlander*, had more or less forcibly conscripted French, Poles, Czechs, and Italian Fascists of dubious loyalty. These were targeted with "safe conduct leaflets" that guaranteed fair treatment if the bearer crossed the lines. The fact that few from this group deserted surprised the Germans and Allies alike.

The German approach to their American and British enemies was designed to play on the fears and concerns that plagued all frontline troops far from home. One leaflet designed for British consumption had a picture of a woman pulling up her stockings while a smiling American fastened his tie in the background. The text read: "While you are away . . . the Yanks are 'lend-leasing' your women . . . Their pockets are full of cash and no work to do, the boys from overseas are having the time of their lives in Merry Old England." Certainly the faithfulness of wives and girlfriends at home was a major concern for the troops in Italy, some of whom had already been away for over three years. Nothing would darken the mood of a unit more than if one of them received a "Dear John" letter. Other possible resentments, such as the much higher pay of the American troops, were also exploited.

For the Americans, there were digs at Roosevelt's promise of October 1940 that "No American boys will be sacrificed on foreign battlefields" and numerous references to loved ones left behind. "American Soldiers!" one leaflet read. "She wanted to spend her life in peace and happiness by the side of her husband . . . NOW HE WILL NEVER COME BACK! Far away from his country and his people he was sacrificed for foreign interests on the battlefield . . . What about the girl you love? Will she also be WAITING IN VAIN?"

German leaflets also sought to fuel political concerns, mainly to do with Soviet Russia. "Where will Russia stop?" asked one. Another had a series of cartoons, with Churchill and Stalin portrayed as tiger cubs. As the story progresses, Joe grows and bullies Winston. "In spite of all that, Winston had a great affection for his big brother and, whenever the opportunity offered itself, licked his skin most affectionately." In the final picture, Joe has a tail hanging out of his behind. "One day," the accompanying text reads, "Winston had disappeared. All that could be seen of him was his little tail. It is not known whether he had done so much arse-hole creeping that he eventually finished up in Joe's belly or whether the latter had swallowed him up."

The majority of these leaflets were delivered by artillery fire. The canister from a smoke-producing shell would be removed and the shell stuffed with about 750 leaflets and reassembled. After firing, the ejection charge forced the leaflets out over the enemy's positions. The men of the 5th Army's Combat Propaganda Team could turn out a leaflet on very short notice, which was essential as some conveyed morale-sapping news rather than simple propaganda. Once the content was approved by the chief of staff, it was translated and the leaflet was printed on a Crowell press, which was carted around 5th Army territory on a giant captured German tank carrier. The mobile press could turn out four-by-six-inch leaflets at a rate of eight thousand an hour. One such leaflet appeared in the days after the Anzio landings: Initial Allied successes were listed and delivered to the Germans around Cassino. The Germans had a similarly well-organized routine.

There were even leaflets about leaflets. The German side produced the following: "Those of you who are lucky enough to get out of this inferno of Cassino will always remember the German parachutists, the most ferocious of them all. Yet just imagine, some greasy, slick-haired guy sitting safely way back of you tries to soften us with leaflets, asking us to wave a white handkerchief. Let this guy come to the front and find out that the paper with his trash on it is just good enough to wipe the arse with. On second thought, let him continue sending his leaflets—toilet paper is becoming rare at Cassino, and, tough as they are, even German parachutists don't like using grass." Undoubtedly this was the fate of most leaflets that were picked up. But the thirst for reading matter, and the "saucy" or amusing content of some of them, meant that most would be read first.

In time the propagandists on both sides became more ingenious, sending over material that might hang around longer because of its usefulness. Matchbooks showered down on the 56th Division's positions in late January. On opening, a long strip of paper emerged. It detailed ways to simulate a variety of illnesses, including skin infections, stomach problems, dysentery, conjunctivitis, sore throat, neuritis, heat attacks, hepatitis, and tuberculosis. This approach was taken with simple leaflets, too: "Take a laxative," one advised, "then tell your doctor you suffer from gnawing pains in your abdomen . . . When the doctor examines you, show painful response to pressure on the right side immediately below the ribs . . . Stick to your story at [the] hospital . . . if you're clever, you can keep up the game for weeks and months. The disease is *amoebic dysentery*; but for Pete's sake, don't tell the doctor that, let him find out for himself. Remember: The most important thing about a war is to come back home alive!"

Knowing the demand for reading matter, the Allies produced a special weekly newspaper for the German frontline troops called *Frontpost*, which was fired into German lines. An interrogator of prisoners of war was amazed when one of his charges requested a copy "as if this was a regular service to which he had subscribed."

Morale was an obsession of both sides during the war. For the Germans it was hoped that the "will" of their troops would make up for the increasing shortfall in men and material. For the Allies it was considered essential to keep their "citizen soldiers" fighting at all. Between the wars there had been great advances in advertising and mass communication, most notably radio, and these developments were harnessed in the cause of raising morale or lowering that of the enemy. The Germans set up a special radio station near Cassino that for half an hour each evening broadcast Indian music, and told "the truth from all around the world." Both sides broadcast propaganda continually, but the frontline troops who were able to listen to it were more than capable of perceiving it for what it was. "We always used to listen to the German propaganda," remembered a New Zealander who fought at Cassino.

"You'd get the BBC News and you'd get the Jerry news and between the two of them you'd find out just what was happening."

As the wider war situation worsened for the Germans in spring 1944, with the Russians advancing toward the borders of Poland and the Allied bombing offensive intensifying, the guardians of German morale became more concerned about avoiding the spread of defeatism at home. An information leaflet was produced for those about to go on furlough from Italy: "When you now return home, you will be asked many questions. Remember that you undertake a grave responsibility in what you have to say. Many of you have seen unpleasant and astonishing things in the last few weeks . . . the major course of events is what counts, not what may have happened in individual instances. So be discreet . . . see to it that through your accounts you do not bring unrest to the people or even upset the policies of the Reich government."

Allied intelligence officers made regular appraisals of German morale. One report focused on the impressions of an escapee from a prisoner-of-war camp. It gives an insight into the thinking of the German rear-echelon troops, who would be expected to be of a lower caliber and morale than those on the front line. The prison guards were all under twenty or over forty. "About two-thirds said: 'Deutschland is kaput' and practically all realized that Germany had lost the war," the escaped prisoner reported. "They hoped for a negotiated peace without the military occupation of Germany . . . The first question the guards asked the PW [prisoner of war] was 'Are you in the RAF?' They said that the hatred for England started with the bombings of German towns and asked 'Why do you bomb our women and children?' . . . They seemed to think that German and English people were pawns which were moved about by a machine without realizing why things happened or thinking that they had any control over them."

Certainly many of the reports show this sort of wishful thinking, reflecting the widely held Allied belief that Germans, faced with overwhelming odds, would bring the war to an early conclusion. But most intelligence officers, having looked hard for any encouragement to support this view, were forced to concede that "despite the immense casualties, there are still many Germans soldiers with five to eight years' service; some even longer. Routine, discipline and a merited tradition of efficiency override personal grievances, lack of air support and distrust of Hitler." There were none of the mass desertions of *Volksdeutsche* that the Allies expected, and German resistance at Cassino remained firm.

In late April, Pioneer officer F. G. Sutton's unit was relieved by the New Zealanders. Among the incoming troops was machine gunner Jack Cocker. He remembers this mountain sector as "a very dangerous place. When a mortar bomb or shell landed, the shrapnel and bits of rock were particularly nasty." But after the horrors of the fighting in the town, this was a relatively quiet posting. "It was sort of unwritten law that if we kept quiet, then so did the Jerry—which suited us fine," says Cocker. Nevertheless, there were casualties on the journey back and forward to the jeep head to collect supplies. It was difficult to move at night without "sending up a hell of clatter among the empty tins that covered the ground." Cocker remembers that on the route "there was a poorly buried French soldier whose hand and arm were outside the rocks piled on his body. Each time we passed we shook his hand for luck. When I think of it now it doesn't make me feel very good but in war one's principles and what is right and wrong go by the board to a large extent."

In front of their positions lay the bodies of a number of Moroccan Goumiers who had been cut down by German fire from the high ground they still commanded. Rumors had it that the Goumiers carried large quantities of cash on their persons, as they had no way of getting their pay and loot back to their families in North Africa. "If you wanted to take your life in your hands and go out there, there was plenty of cash to be had," says Cocker. Few would risk it, though, and it was not possible to retrieve the bodies for burial, either. "The stench was bad and so were the rats. One invaded my hoochy and as he was right down by my feet I threw a bit of biscuit. After that he used to appear every morning for his bit of biscuit—until one night he ran over my face. So next morning he was killed in action: I shot him with my service pistol."

Much of the misery of the Allied troops holding the front line in March and April was due to the Germans still controlling the high ground in front of their positions. This was particularly the case in the shattered town, held by units of the British 4th Division and the Brigade of Guards from the newly arrived British 6th Armoured Division. Supplies had to be brought in at night, and any noise would bring fire from German machine guns on fixed lines targeted at the known entry points to Cassino. The troops would wear rubber shoes or ties sacking to their boots for the journey in. Cyril Harte, a stretcher bearer with the 3rd Battalion Grenadier Guards, remembers entering the town on a pitch-black night before creeping into the basement of a bombed building. When daylight came, he looked out through a small hole in the shelter. "I was overawed by what I saw. The town was flattened, not a building stood. Trees were decapitated and everything was quiet. Not a living thing . . . could be seen or heard above ground. Looking upward I could see this huge mountain, surmounted by the Abbey, and I realized why Hitler's Gustav Line had been so impenetrable, for it commanded the valley for miles around. The nights were eerie. Incessant croaking of frogs in the shellholes filled with water, myraid fireflies sparkling in the darkness and the putrid smell of dead bodies lying around unburied contrived to make an unearthly atmosphere."

Walter Robson's 1st Battalion Royal West Kents moved in on 23 April, to hold the more open southern outskirts of the town adjoining the railway station, the scene of bitter fighting by the 26th Battalion of the 2nd New Zealand Division a month earlier. He was stationed in the cellar of a house only 150 yards from the nearest German positions. During the night, some were on guard while others slept, although they would be woken if they made too much noise snoring. The cellar was ten feet square and fourteen feet high, with one entrance through the floor of the house above. As elsewhere in the town, the conditions were filthy. "Can't wash, the water's rationed and there's swill from meals dumped in the rubble upstairs," Robson wrote to his wife, Margaret. "Hellava lot of rubble, hellava lot of swill. The latrine is an oil drum and has to be emptied into a hole in another wreck of a room. Flies. The first mosquitoes. Fleas. And under the fallen rubble of the ruined staircase lies the body of a New Zealander . . . We cook by the grave and there's tea leaves on it and empty tins . . . But none of it is very sanitary and as the days wear on so the smells grow worse."

The battalion headquarters was in the crypt of the old convent. "There was a big German outside," a guardsman remembers. "He must have been there for yonks. His torso had swollen so much it had broken his belt. And the stench, that's what hit me, the stench." Charlie Framp from the Black Watch was there in April and recalls, "During the hours of daylight we looked out upon a dead world. Nothing stirred in the ruins. Even so, hidden eyes watched everything." Nerves were shredded by the close proximity of the enemy. One night Walter Robson saw a German standing in the entrance to his cellar. "The sentry, in the blackness of the interior, just watched him and let him go! The Jerry waved on five others and disappeared. Another sentry saw this, and why they held their fire I can only put down to sheer petrifaction from fright." On one occasion Framp, the company runner, put his eye to a hole in a wall only to see one looking at him from the other side. "And above the entrance to our cellar," says Framp, "poised like a giant boot over a beetle, loomed Monte Cassino."

Naturally, conditions were just as bad for the German defenders of the town, still ensconced in the Hotel des Roses, the Continental, and caves along the western side of Cassino. "I remember being sent to collect dead bodies for burial," says a private in a German Pioneer unit. "They had been piled in a big crater by both sides over the weeks. It was probably the most terrible sight I have ever seen. Green faces, swollen; and all those eyes—staring, loathing. And the rats. The stench was colossal. Even gas-masks were no use. We had to put first-aid packs soaked in cologne over our mouths and nostrils."

The pause in operations gave the Allies time to assess the mistakes and failures of the last four months. One problem was clearly that their huge numerical superiority in planes, guns, and tanks was not matched in infantry. This was particularly the case with the New Zealand Division, which had been designed for an exploiting role. It was not cut out for the type of attritional fighting it had had to perform. But there had been tactical failures, too. Major General Tuker, whose 4th Indian Division had been so mauled at Cassino, was later to criticize the "extraordinary obsession in British commanders' minds that they must challenge the enemy strength rather than play on his weakness . . . the waste of hammering at the enemy's strongest point is seen at its most extreme form at the battle of Cassino . . . where men were hurled time and again against a mountain position which had for centuries defied attack from the south and which in 1944 was not only the strongest position in Italy, but was held by the pick of the German troops in that theater of war." His verdict on the first three battles, albeit with the benefit of hindsight, was damning: "These battles in fact were military sins no less."

If the successful defense of Cassino raised German hopes and morale, events on the Eastern Front were not going their way. By the beginning of May the Russians had advanced to the borders of Hungary and accepted the surrender of the isolated German 17th Army in the Crimea. Paratrooper Joseph Klein relates how his commanding officer, Heidrich, called together some of his men to tell them about his recent visit to Hitler's headquarters in Rastenburg, East Prussia: "We sat under the olive trees and he told us that when he was received, Hitler looked like a ruined man. 'The man, he does me sorrow. He doesn't trust anyone anymore. He knows the paratroopers are courageous. But the man has no more hope,' said Heidrich. 'But we won't let the hope sink until the end.' That was May 1944," says Klein. "And suddenly the Allies attacked."

As the "United Nations" troops suffered all along the line, the weather had improved and the Allies had discovered that they could at last move tanks around on the floor of the Rapido valley. Their gains, however meager, from the third battle had been consolidated, and fresh troops moved in. The skies, too, cleared, and were soon full of Allied fighter-bombers, queuing up in cab rank style to be called down on German targets. And in Alexander's headquarters, the Allied leadership seemed to have at last learned the painful lessons of the previous four months.

PART FIVE

The Fourth Battle

He knew that the essence of war is violence, and that moderation in war is imbecility.

> —Thomas Babington Macaulay, "Essay on Lord
> Nugent's Memorials of Hampden," 1831

I was at Stalingrad, and I had never thought to endure worse.

> —German soldier captured during the fourth
> battle of Monte Cassino

15

Deception

For six weeks after the end of the third battle of Cassino, Alexander steadily enlarged and reinforced his forces opposite the monastery. This time, he refused to be pushed into another rushed attack, instead demanding that he have sufficient resources to break the Gustav Line. In fact, the planning for the fourth battle of Cassino, code-named Operation Diadem, envisaged not only the capture, at last, of the monastery, but also a rapid advance to the north of Rome. From the Anzio bridgehead, secure from major German attacks since the beginning of March, a force of six divisions would be coordinated to break out soon after the main attack and cut the Cassino–Rome road, isolating the retreating troops from German 10th Army. What Alexander was aiming for was no less than the complete annihilation of the German forces in southern and central Italy. This was the priority, rather than the largely symbolic capture of Rome.

He successfully argued that to achieve this he needed: time to retrain and rest divisions exhausted from the winter fighting; good weather, so that the Allies' huge superiority in tanks and aircraft could be exploited; and plenty of extra troops, in order to have at least a three-to-one numerical advantage. Instead of isolated attacks, the Allies would now engage the enemy en masse on a front of twenty miles from Cassino to the sea. For this, seven and a half extra divisions would be needed. Alexander's first move was to switch the dividing line between the 5th and 8th Armies to the Liri River. Thus Mark Clark's 5th Army now had responsibility for Anzio and the Cassino front from the Liri to the sea while the British 8th Army, under Montgomery's replacement, Lt. Gen. Sir Oliver Leese, took over the Liri valley itself and the Cassino Massif, and moved most of its force from the Adriatic front.

Extensive efforts were made to keep this substantial buildup from the enemy, and an elaborate plan was put in motion to deceive the Germans as to the time and place of the forthcoming attack and to induce them to hold their reserves north of Rome, as far from the southern front as possible. On the German side of the lines, the impression was given that the Allies had given up trying to break the Gustav Line. A campaign of misinformation was put in train to convince Kesselring that the next attack would consist instead of a landing at Civitavecchia, north of Rome. There were extensive reconnaissance flights over the area, and Canadian and American troops ostentatiously practiced amphibious landings near Naples. Dummy divisions were invented and movements of real troops disguised as much as possible.

The deception succeeded. When the attack came on 11 May, Kesselring would have two strong divisions north of Rome, too far away to affect the crucial first days of the battle. The timing was also a complete surprise. On the morning of 11 May, von Vietinghoff, commander of the 10th Army, told Kesselring, "There is nothing special going on." General von Senger, whose defensive skills had been so vital to the Germans in the earlier battles, was away on leave in Germany. Furthermore, when the offensive started, the Germans found they were facing seven more divisions than they had bargained for.

As the drier weather drained the Rapido valley, the Germans anxiously watched their "moat" in front of the Gustav Line disappearing. Increased Allied air activity added to their worries. For the Germans, according to Kesselring's account, "Four unknown factors kept the command in Italy on tenterhooks: When would the Allies start operations from the beachhead? Would the offensive be supported by an airborne landing in the Liri valley? Would there be a fresh invasion in the region of Rome or further north?" And, most worryingly, "Where and in what strength would the FEC [Juin's French force] attack?" The poor state of the Luftwaffe meant that Kesselring had little useful aerial reconnaissance, and he largely fell for the deception that there would not be another attack at Cassino and that the Allies would use their superiority at sea to launch another amphibious landing. His difficulties were compounded by the exhaustion of his troops and by an Allied bombing offensive against his long lines of supply.

Since December the Germans, with huge numbers of conscripted Italian laborers, had been constructing a fallback position about seven miles behind the Gustav Line. This was initially called the Adolf Hitler Line before being changed to the Senger Line, and it ran west of the Rapido, crossing the Liri valley from Pontecorvo to Aquino, then climbing the Cassino Massif through the village of Piedimonte before merging with the Gustav Line on Monte Cairo. In effect, the two lines were one defensive system as the intervening countryside was dotted with strong points. Compared with the Gustav Line, though, the Hitler/Senger Line was decidedly makeshift.

Alexander's force was now more multinational than ever, and dealing with the various leaders must have strained even his great powers of diplomacy. But a certain amount of reorganization had simplified the army group's logistics. The Adriatic and Apennine sectors were now lightly held by a British corps consisting of two Indian divisions, with the New Zealan-

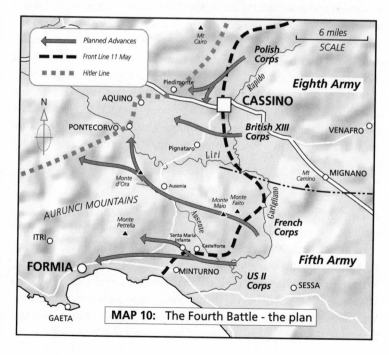

MAP 10: The Fourth Battle - the plan

ders and a small Italian force holding the mountainous country on their left up to the Cassino Massif. Around the monastery, in the salient so hard won by the US 34th Division back in January and February, was Polish II Corps, consisting of two divisions with an armored brigade. Along a front of seven miles facing the town of Cassino and the Liri valley was British XIII Corps. In the line were the British 4th Division, which had been holding parts of the town since the end of March, and the Indian 8th Division, newly arrived from the Adriatic sector. With them, to exploit any breakthrough, were the British 78th Battleaxe Division, the British 6th Armored Division, and a Canadian corps consisting of one infantry and one armored division.

On their left, the FEC, reinforced with two more divisions as well as Goumier irregular mountain fighters, were packed into the Garigliano bridgehead won by the British X Corps back in January. Next to them, holding the front to the sea, were two American infantry divisions, the 88th and the 85th, which had arrived in the Cassino sector in March.

This represented a very substantial advantage over the defending Germans, who had 57 battalions to face the 108 Allied. But the German battalions were only about half the size of Allied ones, so in infantry the Allies had at the very least the three-to-one advantage demanded by Alexander. In addition they had an overwhelming superiority in guns, tanks, and aircraft. Kesselring estimated that he had only a tenth of the aircraft available to the Allies.

So, by 11 May, a total of 1,600 guns, 2,000 tanks, and 3,000 aircraft were assembled along the twenty-mile front, equal to 45 guns, 57 tanks, and 85 aircraft for every thousand yards, not counting infantry with their weapons. As Alexander himself noted, quoting Nelson, "Only numbers can annihilate."

———

It was decided that at exactly 11 P.M. on 11 May, timed to the last pip from the BBC, the massed artillery, lined up hub to hub in the Allied rear, would open fire. Careful plans were laid for each of the forces along the start line. On the left, the two American divisions were to push westward, with the 351st Regiment of the 88th Division detailed to capture the village of Santa Maria Infante. The 88th was the first all-conscript formation to go into combat, and had more than its share of accompanying journalists to see how they fared. The draftees came from all over the United States, but the majority were from the New England and Mid-Atlantic states. They had arrived at Casablanca in November 1943 after a rough passage from the United States, many seasick soldiers crossing the Atlantic "by rail," that is, the ship's rail. Klaus Huebner, an officer medic with the division, remembered feeling "truly sorry for GI Joe. The dark, poorly ventilated holds reek of sweat and vomitus. Men have lost their identity, and seem to be only numbers. No wonder that some soon become bitter." Huebner was born in Germany, but his family emigrated to the United States in 1926, when he was eleven years old. The division trained in North Africa, an experience Huebner found occasionally farcical. "I don't quite understand exactly what is going on," he wrote. "I don't suppose I have to . . . I must learn never to think for myself, for this is the Army."

The untried division started arriving in Naples on 12 February. While most remained for the time being in the Volturno valley, part of one regiment, the 351st, had their first taste of the front line when they did a week's stint on Monte Castellone from 25 February. Like all troops going into battle for the first time, their major concern was that they would fail to do their jobs. One 351st veteran remembers, "As we entered combat I had a strange feeling. All my life I felt secure, knowing the United States would protect me, but now it was reversed. The country was now depending on me to protect them, it was an awesome feeling because I was not sure I could bear so much weight."

The main part of the division went into the line on 4 March, relieving elements of the British 5th Division near Minturno. "This first night no one knows exactly how to behave," wrote Huebner. "The sounds of war are still new." A familiar complaint was the lack of coverage of Italy in the American newspapers. This was keenly felt by all the soldiers in Italy, none more so than "publicity hound" Gen. Mark Clark. He had always been envious of the fine public relations enjoyed by the US Marine Corps, which had made PR a part of their table of organization right at the outset of the war, securing professional advice by hiring a New York advertising and publicity agency. Clark now insisted that all parts of his 5th Army have public relations units.

When the 88th Division arrived in Italy, an officer from 5th Army headquarters visited to check personal records. He found a sergeant, Jack Delaney, who had been a newspaperman in civilian life, and he was appointed to head the new PR section. He needed a team, and the 5th Army officer continued to look through the records. Milton Dolinger was an artilleryman who had joined the division in Africa, but before being called up he had graduated from Penn State University with a degree in journalism. "One day while helping to build a latrine trench," Dolinger remembers, "this 5th Army officer . . . showed up and told my captain, John Evans, that he wanted me to be a correspondent for Division Artillery on special assignment and relieved of all other duties. Evans, who didn't know me since I was new to his outfit, demurred, saying I was 'too valuable.' (Apparently I dug a better latrine than I imagined.)" But the 5th Army officer insisted, and Dolinger was recruited: "Our job was to fan out and visit GIs in their units on the front lines and in rest areas, interview them, take notes, then go back to our movable office to write those interviews." After they had been checked by Delaney and the 5th Army censors, "The stories were sent to the hometown newspapers of the soldiers who had been interviewed. There was one rule we absolutely had to adhere to: Every story we wrote had to say, at the very beginning: ON GENERAL MARK CLARK'S FIFTH ARMY FRONT IN ITALY. Those stories were great morale-builders, reassuring the folks back home with news of their family members and a source of pride among the GIs when a clipping from home came in the mail."

In the absence of any real ideological motivation, the troops were to be persuaded that their actions would receive this sort of "credit" thanks to the help of the immense public relations machine that Clark insisted on for 5th Army. Most of the public relations men had been advertising or public relations executives, or, like Milton Dolinger, trained journalists. As Dolinger says, "We also tried to influence those civilian correspondents covering our units to write about us." Every time the army or division was mentioned back home, it was believed, the men fighting in Italy would be given a boost. So important was this considered by Clark that it would even influence the way he handled his forces in the field, as shall be seen.

It was considered particularly vital that men should have pride in their particular outfit. Dolinger considers his PR unit's greatest success to be the invention of the name "Blue Devils" for the 88th Division. The troops of the division wore a blue shoulder patch of crossed eights in the manner of a cloverleaf. "Jack [Delaney] had an inspiration, in which we all joined," says Dolinger. "One of the interpreters in the division had loosely reported that some captured German POWs had described our troops as fighting like blue devils. Jack took that and ran with it and persuaded the brass—and the media—that henceforth we would call ourselves the 88th 'Blue Devil' Division."

For the men in the front line, life was very different from that described in the heroic and romantic stories printed for hometown consumption. When the 88th took over from the British, there were dead bodies everywhere. One group lay where a headlong charge had carried them, still facing the enemy, a veteran remembers. Another "grim group of dead, in a sangar on the very front lines where some of our men crouched each day, was a ghostly complement to our strength . . . one still held the receiver of a telephone in his partially decomposed hand, and his head rested grotesquely against a rock which pierced the rotting flesh of his cheek." All the corpses were covered with flies and other insects.

Although the sector was officially "quiet," there were steady casualties— 99 dead, 252 wounded, and 36 missing by the end of March. Dr. Klaus Huebner saw his first battalion casualty on the second day: "A deserted building near the battalion command post is our morgue. I venture to it cautiously, curious to inspect the mortal damage of mortars. I slowly open the creaking front door of the house; lying on the cement floor is a GI, his legs deformed by compound fractures, his skull fractured and brain exposed. A brown rat is feeding on the spilled brain and never stirs. One brief glance is enough; I close the door and walk away." Huebner also comments on the continued presence of Italian civilians in the area. If they were caught between the lines, they were very likely to step on a mine. If they ventured toward either the German or American positions, they would be shot by the other side, concerned that they might communicate positions to the enemy. But Huebner, like the other "green" troops before him, soon grew accustomed to the noise of the battlefield: "We fire heavy artillery all night— twenty shells to Jerry's one—and the sound is music in our ears. Shells no longer disturb my sleep—only scabies, fleas and cockroaches do."

As the date of the great offensive came closer, more and more armor and artillery was moved into the Garigliano bridgehead. As elsewhere all along the front, secrecy was paramount. Shortly before 11 May, Huebner was "strolling over small paths and through neglected grottoes" when he made a surprising discovery: "I stumble upon tanks, cannons, and halftracks. They have all been so well hidden and camouflaged that I do not see them until I am practically upon them. The buildup of weapons has truly been tremendous during the past month. The entire valley is loaded with death-dealing armor, all hidden and silent, ready to spit fire and death on command, but now just waiting, waiting for the big day, the day on which everyone can prove his worth . . . It will be soon."

As the moment for the offensive neared, the saying became "Rome and

Home." Thirty-eight-year-old New Yorker mess sergeant Arthur Schick, like everybody else, felt the tension. "The cooks are jittery," he wrote to his wife, Liz, and eight-year-old daughter, Barbara, on 26 April. "They're not like me—I'm scared." He was living in an abandoned farmhouse under sporadic shellfire. Clearly the Italian owners of the farm had buried everything they could not carry away: "The boys are digging all kinds of stuff out of haystacks and the earth. Some fun, especially when we come across bottles of wine . . . One squad dug up some bottled tomato sauce and tomato paste and some Italian sausage." But between cheery tales about the improving weather and the men eating artichokes, Schick's letters contain the usual loneliness and anxiety about loved ones: "I haven't received a letter from you for several weeks now and am becoming worried. Is there anything wrong at home? . . . Are you mad at something I've written?"

On 3 May the division was visited by Gen. Mark Clark, who ended his speech, "I promise you it will be soon." The next day Schick wrote home: "We have been bothered with Generals again inspecting and awarding medals . . . everyone gets excited and starts cleaning up the area and I get bothered and hot in my kitchen and get a bit riled." More important to him, though, was the fact that he had just received four letters from his wife: "I had a gang of a time all nite and day reading and re-reading your letters. You're swell, you're sweet, you're divine." He then goes on to suggest a second honeymoon when he gets home. "I will be with you every day. I can't help it. I love you so much. I always will . . . After this let the Hitlers and the Mussolinis rant and rave and I will laugh at them all from my nice snug home with you and Bab by my side."

Just before the attack was due to be launched, one of the division's regiments—the 350th—got a new commander, Col. J. C. Fry. In his candid account of his time in combat, Fry describes the days preceding 11 May: "The effect of this tense period of waiting for the attack was to be seen and felt everywhere. Tempers were more easily turned into sharp and caustic words and there were those who found the danger and interminable waiting intolerable. Occasionally some of the men made violent efforts to escape from the impending danger. The usual method was to shoot themselves through the foot. There were far more cases of this nature than I care to remember."

———

The French were positioned between Castelforte and the Liri River in front of the bleak Aurunci Mountains, terrain so difficult that the Germans were barely bothering to hold it. Juin had four divisions—the 3rd Algerian, the 2nd and 4th Moroccan, and the 1st Division de Marche—with which to carry out his bold plan to advance from the northern end of the Garigliano bridgehead across rugged, roadless mountains to Ausonia and thence up the Ausente valley to the Liri at Pontecorvo, one of the strong points on the Hitler Line.

The Free French Division de Marche on the right was to attack along the west bank of the Garigliano towards the Liri valley; to their left, the 2nd Moroccan Division was to capture the high ground to the right of the Ausente valley. Clearance of the lower valley of the Ausente was the responsibility of the 4th Moroccan Mountain Division and the 4RTT, which had taken such a battering on Belvedere, and were now asked to complete the conquest of Monte Damiano and the heavily fortified village of Castelforte, persistently attacked back in mid-January, without ultimate success, by the British 56th Division.

"The waiting was agonizing," says Jean Murat, who had survived the month on Monte Castellone, and after a short break had returned to the front with his 1st Battalion of the 4RTT on 6 May. "The forty-eight hours of waiting before the attack, which are spent observing the position which we were going to attack, were grueling, until the time that the moment arrived." His battalion was temporarily attached to the 4th Moroccan Division. Murat's instructions were daunting: "My company will link up, on the right, with the 2nd Moroccans and on the left with the 2nd Company of the battalion [1/4RTT]. The 3rd Company will be in reserve behind the two forward units. My captain has determined that I should assume the command of the three forward sections. He would stay in the second echelon with a support section and a section of heavy machine guns, to provide reinforcement."

For Murat, the six days of waiting were strangely peaceful, but also full of dread. "From a forward observation point, I have the opportunity to examine the panorama," he writes. "The terrain mounts in a gentle slope for several hundred meters. It then descends toward the village of Castelforte, invisible from this position because of a long, rounded crest running parallel and separated by a ravine cut deep into the hillside. The terrain is covered with a few fruit trees. The ground is so rocky that it will be impossible to dig out even the slightest shelter if the need arises. The sky is a deep blue. The heat has already set in. Shirts are removed. How calm it all is, we are tasting our last days of tranquility."

Opposite the Liri valley, where the British XIII Corps of the 8th Army was to attack, the overwhelming priority was to avoid the disaster that had befallen the US 36th Division back in January. The three key factors that had doomed the Texans were identified as uncleared minefields, poor approach roads to the river, and the failure to construct bridges over the Rapido that could take tanks. All these were the responsibility of the Engineer Corps, which now had a crucial role in preparing for the offensive.

The British 4th Division's 7th Field Engineering Company had been in the Garigliano bridgehead from 18 March, clearing mines and improving jeep tracks. Also attached to the division were the 59th and 225th companies. Each company contained, at full strength, some 245 men organized into four platoons. All three units would distinguish themselves in one of the key actions of the fourth battle.

One of the 59th Company sappers was Frank Sellwood, a twenty-four-year-old former trainee carpenter who was a veteran of North Africa and had cleared "thousands of mines" before he even reached Italy. His subsection of eight men had been together throughout their time in Africa. Along with the other 4th Division engineering companies, from the beginning of April he was detailed to clear mines from the Rapido River approaches and would work at night improving the approach roads to the designated crossing points. One of the jobs was to pull apart the railway, laying the sleepers on top of the tracks, so that it looked from the monastery as if the railway were still there. On raised ground above the boggy valley, this was to be one of the key approach roads to the river. At the end of the night's work, all newly prepared tracks had to be covered by brushwood at first light.

Arriving opposite the remains of the monastery at Cassino was, Sellwood recalls, "A bit of a shocker. There were still American bodies lying around there, on the ground, near where we had our little camp waiting for the big business to start." On a number of occasions Sellwood was ordered into the town and had to run the gauntlet of the single approach road. "Clambering around, you'd see these bodies lying on the ground, in the town and coming up to the town." One such corpse made a particularly strong impression. "One of them was a lady news reporter in the American Services. She was lying on a stretcher there. Obviously she was being carried out at the time and they must have dropped her and run for it. She was still there. She had a blue uniform with striped pieces around the corners."

The most meticulous preparation went into identifying and examining potential bridging sites. In the 4th Division's sector there were to be three, each of which was the responsibility of one of the division's engineer companies. From north to south they were code-named Amazon, Blackwater, and Congo. At each site the engineers were to build a Bailey bridge and two ferries.

As early as 17 April detailed reports were circulating concerning the crossing sites, and by 5 May a comprehensive plan had been drawn up. It took into account the smallest detail, including exact timing for every bulldozer task. It was a huge contrast to the rushed and pessimistic engineer reports that had been carried out for the 36th Division back in January. But gathering information at the river's edge had been a difficult and risky business. Major Tony Daniell, commanding officer of the 59th Company, had to reconnoiter the site for the Blackwater bridge. With Lieutenants Boston (whose platoon was to build the bridge) and Chubb (whose platoon was to improve the approach and exit) and a Sergeant Cox, Daniell went to the site on the evening of 27 April. There he met Maj. Michael Low, commanding officer of 7th Company. "We arranged a rendezvous at the HQ of the Indian battalion who were then holding the river . . . We were given the password ('Rice,' then 'Pudding') and told the Indians where we were going and that we intended to be back in about an hour," wrote Daniell. "The river was noman's-land, but was freely patrolled by both British and Boche alike. From there we made our way in single file down the approach track to the river. It was rather light with a half moon, very quiet and extremely eerie. The river had a flood bank of shingle which had at some time been dredged out of it. There was still plenty of American equipment lying about and some very unpleasant smells."

They surveyed the river as Chubb kept a lookout. They had planned to swim across to measure it, but Daniell thought it was too light. Then Chubb rolled down to them to say there were four Germans on the other side, carrying spades, only eighty feet away. Daniell was itching to shoot but didn't want to give away his interest in the bridging site. Having checked the approach roads, they headed back to their positions behind the lines.

There were plenty of volunteer swimmers to measure the width a few nights later, and Lieutenant Boston's driver, McTighe, was chosen. It was cloudy as they crept along the riverbank, and, while Cox and Daniell kept watch with Tommy guns, Boston and McTighe prepared to measure the river. The latter, wearing canvas shoes, dark bathing pants, and Daniell's brown pullover to hide the white of his body, waded in, then swam across with white tape. Just as he was making his way under the far bank to stand opposite Boston, two loud explosions went off above his head. Either he had activated a tripwire or someone had heard him and lobbed a couple of grenades. He was untouched, though, and swam the sixty-odd feet back "as fast as he had ever swum in his life."

There followed ten days of intensive rehearsals on the Volturno River, during which the men managed to reduce the bridging time from four hours to just under two. "Morale was very, very good," says Sgt. Jack Stamper of 7th Company. "We'd done a lot of training and Major Low had put us through our paces. Of course, conditions weren't the same."

On 11 May the enforced inactivity during the afternoon stretched everyone's nerves. Sergeant Tommy Riordan, a twenty-three-year-old in the 7th Company, recalled, "There was time to write letters home without mentioning what was on everyone's mind." Then the last meals were served from the cookhouse, vehicles and uniforms were cleared of all divisional and tactical markings, lights and horns were disconnected, and the move began down to Trocchio. All around, the men could see gunners starting to chop down trees in front of their carefully concealed guns. Nightingales were singing, Riordan remembers, and "swarms of fire flies hugged the water meadows leading to the river line."

The British 4th Division's plan was to attack with two brigades—28th and 10th—forward, crossing the Rapido on a narrow front between Cassino and Sant' Angelo. To their left, on either side of Sant' Angelo, was the 8th Indian Division, which had recently been pulled across from the Adriatic. Like the 4th Indian, its three brigades each contained one British and two Indian battalions. The 1st Royal Fusiliers were in the 17th Brigade, and one of its troops was nineteen-year-old Frederick Beacham. Bristol-born, Beacham had worked in various jobs—in a biscuit factory and at Temple Meads railway station—before being conscripted at eighteen in late 1942. Even before he joined the army, the war had made a great impression on him: it seemed that everything in his life—the factory where he worked, his church, his old school, even his local chip shop—had been destroyed by the bombing that devastated the important port of Bristol between 1940 and 1942. The First World War had already left its scars on his family. Both his uncle and his father had fought at the Somme, his uncle being "blown to pieces." "My father was gassed, and had a scar on his upper lip," says Beacham. "I saw him suffer psychologically. When he had a few drinks he had to be restrained. If he had a few more, he burst into tears."

Beacham vividly remembers the journey across Italy: "It was long, tiring and, at times, very frightening. The trucks were being driven by Indians and their standard of driving around some of the winding and hairpin bends made our hair stand on end. Many times on the journey, we banged on the rear of the cab and in unison called out, 'Steady on, Johnny, we don't want to get killed before we get there.' We did pass the odd truck or two that had gone over the edge and, in the end, we slumped down on the bed of the truck and hoped for the best."

The Fusiliers arrived in the Cassino sector around midday on 5 May and were addressed that afternoon by Lieutenant General Leese, "during a Montgomery-style meeting . . . Standing on a jeep, he told us that we were going to be part of the battle to take Monte Cassino," says Beacham. "The talk filled us with confidence as he outlined the fact that over 1,600 guns of all types would saturate the enemy positions in the form of a creeping barrage of artillery fire and all we apparently had to do was to cross the river in the rubber boats and following behind the barrage more or less mop up any resistance that was left (if any). Tanks would soon cross the river in our support and plenty of aircraft would be available . . . I must confess the way he spelt it out, I felt that nothing could go wrong and everything would, to use today's jargon, be a piece of cake. How wrong could one be?"

———————

Perhaps the hardest task of all had been taken on by the Polish Corps, commanded by Lt. Gen. Wladyslaw Anders. The 3rd Carpathian Rifle and 5th Kresowa Infantry divisions, supported by the Polish 2nd Armored Brigade, were to isolate the monastery by capturing the adjacent heights and then push down into the Liri valley to make contact with the advancing British XIII Corps. After that, they were to thrust through the mountains behind the monastery to Piedimonte, a hilltop town on the Hitler Line, which the Germans were hoping would become a "mini-Cassino."

The Poles have a special place in the Cassino story. The corps numbered about fifty thousand, all of whom had a long and dangerous journey behind them. Following the occupation of eastern Poland by Stalin in 1939, the

Russians had set about "beheading" the local community to eliminate all potential resistance. Anyone of property or education was liable to be rounded up, together with their family, and put aboard a train to the Soviet Union. Józef Pankiewicz, who fought at Cassino with the Carpathian Division, was fourteen when the war started and was living in Lvov, then part of Poland and the nation's third largest town. Lvov surrendered to the Germans on 19 September, but three days later the Germans withdrew and the Russians arrived. Pankiewicz remembers, "They were a sorry sight; badly dressed, ill-equipped and full of lice . . . vastly different to the Germans." In February 1940 the family was awakened by three Ukrainian militiamen and told to pack up and report to the village school. The men of the family went into hiding as there were rumors that all males over the age of sixteen were being rounded up as slave labor. The others, including young Józef, reported as requested and were taken to the railway station. "There was a long train waiting for us," he says. "The wagons were converted goods wagons—no seats—just bunks made of rough planks, a small stove and a hole cut in the floor for a toilet. We were loaded forty people to each wagon and given buckets of water . . . then the nightmare journey began." Nobody knew why or where they were being taken, and soon the food they had with them ran out. For a week, as the train rumbled eastward, they were given nothing; then they were allowed water and a heavy, sticky bread, two slices per person. "We tried to maintain some sort of dignity and held up a blanket whenever someone wanted to use the toilet," says Pankiewicz. "Mother was busy writing notes and pushing them out of the little window—she wanted people to know about us."

The oldest and youngest among them started dying first. "Across the wagon was a young woman with a tiny baby and a small boy. She became unable to feed the baby and tried mixing crumbs of bread in water. Of course, it was impossible. It cried a lot for a day or so and, to my shame, I remember wishing it would stop and was relieved when it became quiet. At fourteen, I had no idea what it foretold. It just slept peacefully for a day or so and then slipped quietly away. The guards took the tiny baby away and everybody became very quiet and depressed. Nobody wanted to talk and we were of little comfort to the poor mother. Her other child climbed on to her lap, not understanding any of it. I have never forgotten them."

As they headed deeper into the Soviet Union, the temperature dropped and the Poles became ever weaker and shakier through lack of food. After traveling for four weeks, they were dropped off in the Ural Mountains, where they were given saws and told to build themselves huts. For the next year, Pankiewicz worked in various gold mines, surviving only through good fortune, the kindness of local Russians, and by stealing food. Many did not survive the hunger, exposure, and continual hard labor. "Every day people were getting a sort of blindness," says Pankiewicz. "The Russians called it chicken blindness. It is caused by lack of vitamins. Those that could see had to lead them to work. Then came the swollen bellies and later they looked like skeletons. When it went too far, they became unable to eat—the old and young succumbed to this first." At one point typhus struck the camp, and even more were carried off.

Pankiewicz's story is far from unique. In all some 1.5 million Poles were deported to Siberia, along with 200,000 ex-Polish soldiers. Four thousand of the Polish army's officers were shot by the Soviets in the Katyn Forest; for the rest there was hard labor with no concern if they died. But for those who survived that Siberian winter, their fortunes changed on 22 June 1941, when Hitler invaded the Soviet Union.

On 14 August 1941 the Polish government-in-exile in London signed an agreement with the USSR that arranged for independent Polish fighting forces to be formed from these prisoners of war and deportees. Their commander was to be Lt. Gen. Wladyslaw Anders. Anders was born in Warsaw in 1892 and served in the Russian army in the First World War. He fought against the Red Army in the Polish–Soviet war of 1919–20, when Poland's leaders tried to take advantage of the Russian civil war to reclaim "historic lands." In 1939 he was commander of a cavalry brigade. In the face of German air and armored attacks, Anders frantically maneuvered his troops for the first few days of the war, with some local successes, only to hear on 17 September of the Soviet attack from the east. He tried to evacuate his troops through Hungary but was prevented by the Russians. He was wounded, separated from his force, and eventually captured and sent to Lvov. While in the hospital there, Anders was in touch with the newly forming Polish underground and was able to get a message to General Sikorski, the Polish commander in chief, but then fell into the hands of the NKVD, Stalin's secret police. Despite his wounds he was imprisoned in Lvov in dreadful conditions, became frostbitten, and was subjected to interrogations and a trial. He was close to death when, in March 1940, he was transferred to the Lubianka in Moscow, a prison "reserved for people of special interest to the Central Office of the NKVD." At first he was interrogated continuously, and then kept in solitary confinement for six months, but after September this ceased. Around mid-July 1941, his treatment improved and he was told of the German attack on Russia and the Anglo-Soviet treaty that provided for an amnesty for Poles in Russia, and the formation of a Polish army there under his command. He was then freed and given a flat, two servants, and a huge supply of vodka. He was still on crutches.

The Katyn massacre had already taken place, and Anders was initially suspicious because of the few officers who presented themselves to join his army. Eventually, however, the numbers swelled enough for Anders to obtain, "with great difficulty," permission to organize two divisions and a reserve regiment (as well as a women's auxiliary service and a chaplains' service). An Enrollment Commission was sent to some of the prisoner-of-war camps to recruit more.

The new army, made up of weakened and destitute men, spent the winter of 1941–42 in tented camps in the steppes of Central Asia, with temperatures dropping to minus fifty degrees Celsius. Many froze to death. Finally, in July 1942, Stalin allowed the evacuation to Iran of 40,000 soldiers along with 26,000 women and children. Leaving their Soviet "hosts" was a great moment for the Polish soldiers and civilians: "I didn't believe it, I thought I had died in Russia, and now I was in heaven," one Cassino veteran remembers. The British in Iran immediately destroyed the soldiers' lice-ridden uniforms and gave them sustenance and medical treatment. Many died, so unaccustomed were they to normal food, and many more needed treatment for malaria. The men were moved to Iraq and formed into two divisions, the 5th Kresowa and the 3rd Carpathian. The latter also included men from the Brigada Karpacka, which had been in Palestine for two years, its soldiers having made their way there from Poland through Hungary and Romania, and who distinguished themselves during the fighting for Tobruk.

In April 1943 the Germans discovered the bodies of the Polish officers in the Katyn Forest and broadcast the news immediately. The Polish government-in-exile asked the Red Cross to investigate, upon which the Soviets broke off relations with them. It was now obvious that the Poles were entirely dependent on the goodwill of the Western Allies to regain any sort of independence after the war. This issue was extensively chewed on during the summer, with assurances from Churchill and Roosevelt; but Sikorski was killed in an air accident in July. Anders believed this deprived Poland of a crucial defender of its interests later. "What was clear," he wrote after the war, "was that the Allies still feared that Russia might make a separate peace."

In the month of Sikorski's death, the army was moved to Gaza in Palestine for further training, and in mid-December 1943 the 3rd Carpathian Division arrived in Taranto and entered the line on the Adriatic coast as part of the British 8th Army. The rest of the army had followed by the end of February. For the Poles it was a miracle that they were back in Europe after their epic journeys.

To the British, the Poles were a curiosity. Sapper Richard Eke recorded his impressions of the latest of many nationalities to arrive in Italy: "We met the men of the Polish Division for the first time when they paused at our snow post ... They were strange soldiers, clean and smart and smelling of perfume. They smoked their cigarettes through long holders, and had taken the trouble to learn perfect Italian. They treated the local women with great charm, and the *signorinas* were most impressed with such gracious treatment. For all their apparent softness, the Poles were reckless and brave, as they were to prove in the next few weeks."

On 22 February, Churchill made a statement in the Commons outlining what had been agreed at the Tehran Conference the previous November: that the Soviets would take over prewar Polish territory in the east, and Poland would be compensated by being given German territory to the west. This, Anders wrote, "greatly depressed our soldiers, most of whom had homes and families east of that line." But at this point, Anders still hoped that it was a "political maneuver," and ordered his corps to continue the fight against the Germans. On 3 March (the day the Polish troops first came under fire) he made a broadcast, saying, "We shall fight the Germans without respite because we all know that without defeating Germany there will be no Poland. We cannot accept ... that any of our enemies will be able to take away even a small part of Poland. We trust that our great Allies and friends—Great Britain and the US ... will assist us to make Poland rise again free and independent ... Poland is not yet lost."

The line on the Adriatic side of Italy was relatively quiet, but in mid-March 1944, the 8th Army's commander, Lieutenant General Leese, briefed Anders on a possible role for the Polish Corps in the next offensive. "[Leese suggested that] the Polish II Army Corps should carry out the most difficult of the initial tasks, the capturing of the Monte Cassino heights and then of the Piedimonte," Anders wrote. "It was a great moment for me. The difficulty of the task assigned to the Corps was obvious, and, indeed, General Leese made it clear that he well understood all that was involved . . . I realized that the cost in lives must be heavy, but I realized too the importance of the capture of Monte Cassino to the Allied cause, and most of all to that of Poland, for it would answer once and for all the Soviet lie that the Poles did not want to fight the Germans. Victory would give new courage to the resistance movement in Poland and would cover Polish arms with glory. After a moment's reflection I answered that I would undertake the task."

The Polish HQ was moved to within view of the monastery, screened by camouflage, and on 6 May, Leese briefed all of Anders's officers down to battalion commanders on the forthcoming attack, handing out pipes to all attending. An incident back in February illustrates the difference between Leese and Anders. The latter had complained that *8th Army News* relied on Soviet sources, and thereby "slandered" his soldiers. Leese responded, telling Anders "how superfluous it is for a Corps Commander to express in public any opinions concerning the political situation." For the unideological British, who saw themselves as "just doing a job," this may have held true, but it was nonsense to Anders, whose corps had a political importance far in excess of their military usefulness. Similar culture clashes occurred at every level between the Poles and the British. The Poles had taken over on the massif from British soldiers of the 78th Division in mid-April. Fred Majdalany, the Lancashire Fusilier, comments that "At times their seriousness seemed to contrast noticeably with the apparent casualness of their British comrades in the Eighth Army." The Poles, he says, "thought we were far too casual about everything because we didn't breathe blind hate all the time." The British in turn were concerned that the ardor of the Poles, shown by their impatience to get into the attack and their disregard for personal safety, might prejudice their mission. Majdalany "wondered whether the intensity of the Poles might not sometimes be their undoing and cost them many lives. For modern war is a skill as well as a test of courage, and bravery is not enough. Assault had to be cunning as well as fanatical." Another officer gave his impressions with a similar note of admiration and caution: "Their motives were as clear as they were simple. They wished only to kill Germans, and they did not bother at all about the usual refinements when they took over our posts. They just walked in with their weapons and that was that."

Although it was supposed to be a secret, as the Poles entered the line, the Germans started broadcasting in Polish four times a day from a transmitter

in Rome. "They would say, 'Come on Polish boys, the Russians are coming,' "
one veteran remembers, "but it was good music and everyone sang Lili Mar-
lene." Nevertheless, the Russians *were* coming. By the beginning of May they
had crossed the prewar Polish border. Eighty percent of the Polish soldiers
at Cassino had been in Soviet labor camps, and they had good reason to
worry about their relatives left behind. They also learned that the Soviets
were busy setting up a Polish Committee of National Liberation, staffed by
compliant communists. To Anders's men, it now seemed, they *were* Free
Poland, its only hope. Only by distinguishing themselves in the violence to
come, they believed, could they assure the continued existence of their
country. Anders's order of the day, issued just before the battle, gives a good
indication of the mixture of piety, nationalism, and vengefulness that char-
acterized the approach of the Poles: "Soldiers! The moment for battle has arrived. We have long awaited the moment for revenge and retribution over
our hereditary enemy . . . Trusting in the Justice of Divine Providence we go
forward with the sacred slogan in our hearts: God, Honor, Country."

All across the front the men listened to their generals' words of encouragement as the time ticked down to the opening of the offensive. "Throughout
the past winter you have fought hard and valiantly and killed many Germans," Alexander's order of the day informed them. "Perhaps you are disappointed that we have been unable to advance faster and further, but I, and
those who know, realize full well how magnificently you fought among these
almost insurmountable obstacles of rocky, trackless mountains, deep snow
and in valleys blocked by rivers and mud against a stubborn foe." After prais-
ing the men for drawing into Italy and "mauling" many of the Germans'
finest divisions, he went on, "Today the bad times are behind us, and tomorrow we can see victory ahead . . . From east and west, from north and
south, blows are about to fall which will result in the final destruction of the
Nazis and bring freedom once again to Europe and hasten peace for us all.
To us in Italy has been given the honor to strike the first blow. We are going
to destroy the German armies in Italy . . . You will be supported by overwhelming air forces, and in guns and tanks we far outnumber the Germans.
No armies have entered battle before with a more just and righteous cause.
So, with God's help and blessing, we take the field—confident of victory."

Fred Majdalany, listening with his fellow Fusiliers, remembers that "while the order was being read out the men stood with their mess-tins in their hands under the trees, and watching their faces you could see that it was getting right home. Though all they said, as they moved away in little groups to get their tea, was: 'Oh well, it won't be long now.' " "It was a very impressive order," says Pioneer officer F. G. Sutton, whose 4th Division battalion would be in the first wave attacking across the Rapido. "But what immediately struck us were his words: 'To us has fallen the honor to strike the first blow.' Alex meant his armies in Italy, and that the invasion of France would follow later. But our only concern was that we were, personally, to strike the first blow of the attack on Cassino, and we would not have objected had this 'honor' gone to another unit." On his way to his assembly point near Monte Trocchio, Sutton talked with two of his closest friends in the battalion. "The thought occurred to me that one of us, most likely, would not survive this battle. It did not disturb me that the one might be I; one is more scared of wounds than of death. Not for a moment did I think that I would be the sole survivor of the three, which, in fact, I am." Before the attack, the battalion's padre went from company to company conducting short prayers. "It was the most moving service to which I had ever been," says Sutton. "We all thought it might be our last, but nobody showed it . . . The cooks had prepared a nice meal of roast beef and 'Burma Road' [rice pudding]. Then we slowly put on our equipment and got ready to go."

"Before an attack fear is universal," a British subaltern has said of waiting to go into combat. "The popular belief that in battle there are two kinds of person—the sensitive, who suffers torment, and the unimaginative few who know no fear and go blithely on—is a fallacy. Everyone was as scared as the next man, for no imagination was needed to foresee the possibility of death or mutilation. It was just that some managed to conceal their fear better than others. Officers could not afford to show their feelings as openly as the men; they had more need to dissemble. In a big battle a subaltern had little or no influence over the fate of his platoon—it was the plaything of the gods. His role was essentially histrionic. He had to feign a casual and cheerful optimism to create an illusion of normality and make it seem as if there was nothing in the least strange about the outrageous things one was asked to do. Only in this way could he ease the tension, quell any panic and convince his men that everything would come out right in the end."

Jack Meek, a twenty-year-old gunner in a Sherman tank of the 17/21st Lancers, was among the force detailed to be the first across the Amazon bridge. He remembers being a "bundle of nerves" as he waited for the fighting to start. "As was my wont before any sort of battle, I became morbid and tense. Other chaps have different ways of preparing themselves for battle, some talk unceasingly and try to joke but the laughter is hollow, meaningless, and false. Some try to read but the words don't register, their minds are too full of more sinister thoughts. Me, I just lay thinking, all the while trying not to think, trying to make my mind a vacuum, but it was never possible, for at every glance around me there was a reminder of war, and of death. Death, how I loathed that word, but how often it kept recurring in my thoughts. It seemed as if there was a battle going on inside my brain, the subconscious hammering incessantly the thought of death, and the conscious struggling to reject it, to think of more pleasant things, of things living, and breathing, enjoying life to the full. All the time the two extremes were flashing through my mind, living and dying, happy laughter and mournful weeping. God, how I tormented myself on that occasion. Every sound, every smell, everything I looked at, they all had a different significance—for this was the end, of that I was sure."

Another tank man from the same unit, H. Buckle, describes how, as dusk fell and they moved up, American engineers appeared in their vehicle park and began erecting dummy tanks and vehicles made of wood and canvas or constructed of light alloy frames and inflated rubber. He was as nervous as Jack Meek. "This was to be my first action in a tank and I was a little apprehensive. So too I felt was Bob [Nutland, the driver] but neither of us said much that night as we drove up in the dark." The final briefing they had just received from their commanding officer was still ringing in their ears. "From my point of view it was as good as a laxative," says Buckle, "and I remember more than once running off into the bushes with a shovel."

In the artillery lines, too, tension was mounting. For gunner Lee Harvey, the final hour from ten to eleven was "the longest of my life . . . The gun crews checked and re-checked all the gun mechanisms and ammunition a dozen times or more, mainly because it gave them something to do, but all the same it did not seem to make the time go any quicker."

16

Break-In

During the night before the attack, Frederick Beacham and his fellow Royal Fusiliers from the 8th Indian Division had carried their rubber boats down a narrow track to the Rapido River to their starting point, about three-quarters of a mile east of Sant' Angelo. There the Fusiliers concealed the boats with bushes and branches before they retired to their daylight position in a vineyard about a mile from the river. Extra camouflage nets had been draped over the vines to hide the men from the all-seeing monastery. "Movement of any kind was strictly forbidden during the whole of that day, which was hot," says Beacham, "and we were only too glad to catch up on some sleep, play cards in small groups and to seek the now welcome shade of the grapevines."

For Beacham, dusk seemed to come quickly, and as it darkened the men were given some hardtack to eat, a tin of bully beef, and a small tin of rations. Their water bottles were checked and then they were ready to go. Beacham was his platoon's machine gunner, so after receiving a rum ration, he and his number two, Bill Balsdon, made their way forward to the crossing point and took up a position to cover the river. "I selected a point about twenty-five yards or so to the right of the actual crossing," Beacham writes. "We lay on the edge of the fairly fast-flowing river, and I set the sights to fire at around six hundred yards. Bill got his ammunition magazines ready and by that time, as it was about ten minutes to the start, I got out a bar of chocolate, which I shared with him, and in the almost complete silence, broken only by the buzzing of the insects and the sound of the crickets, we waited for it to start."

Throughout the evening of 11 May the Allied artillery had kept up its usual shelling of the German positions; it was imperative that nothing out of the ordinary be suspected. At around 10 P.M. the firing died away and, at the same time, the German artillery also ceased. Concerns arose that the Germans might have realized that a great attack was imminent, but they were simply performing a relief that night and didn't want to provoke the Allied guns. An uncanny silence fell on the battlefield, overlooked, as always, by the monastery, shattered but still a brooding presence on the hilltop. In the Allied lines, plans were checked and rechecked, and nerves became stretched as the men waited. Then, as the BBC pips sounded eleven o'clock, the darkness and silence were shattered by an earsplitting roar: sixteen hundred guns along the length of the twenty-mile front opened fire simultaneously on every known German battery and defensive position.

That enormous opening barrage has remained vividly imprinted on the memories of all who witnessed it. One artillery observation officer describes it as "the most exciting and exhilarating experience I have ever had." "The roar of the guns is so deafening that you can shout at the man standing next to you and still not be heard," wrote the US 88th Division doctor, Klaus Huebner. "I venture outside the house and see sheets of flame spring from behind every bush." For German paratrooper Robert Frettlöhr, in his dugout opposite Castle Hill, it was "as if someone had switched on the lights." Even for an experienced soldier like Frederick Beacham, waiting by the riverbank with his Bren gun, the barrage was "awe-inspiring . . . The entire sky as far as the eye could see erupted in light and sound as the guns fired. The shells approached us from the rear like a hundred express trains running past us at a hundred or more miles an hour and the far bank erupted to the sound and sight of orange flame as the shells struck." It is said that such was the continuous nature of the gun flashes that it was possible to read a newspaper five miles away. For forty minutes the guns pounded the German batteries behind the lines before switching to batter the attacking infantry's first objectives. The US 88th Division's publicist Milton Dolinger remembers, "Artillerymen worked like automatons. Ammunition, accumulating for weeks, dwindled into nothingness only to be replaced by ever-rising mounds of shell casings."

First off were the two American divisions on the left flank of the Allied line, the 88th and the 85th; forty minutes later the four French divisions jumped off in their attempt to drive into the heart of the Aurunci Mountains. Five minutes after that, the first assault boats of the 8th Indian and 4th British divisions on the right of the French splashed into the fast-flowing current of the Rapido. Soon after one o'clock the Polish Corps launched its attack on the high ground around the monastery. Two hours after the barrage had started, the entire front for twenty miles was locked in combat.

At 11:30 P.M., Frederick Beacham's riflemen comrades left their forming-up place and started moving toward the river, guided by white tapes and tracer fire. Nineteen-year-old Harry Courcha, a fusilier in the battalion's A Company, in his first battle, remembers that as they picked up their boats, the Germans opened fire: "The bullets started whizzing around our heads and we just kept stumbling forward to the sound of the river. Some people were already dead. We could hear the water a long way down in the dark, running very fast . . . Many of our blokes pitched over the bank and drowned as they had full battle kit on. I heard a voice down below, but I couldn't see a boat. Well, I was hanging on to the bank and kicking out with my feet and someone dragged me in to the boat and we went across. Many of the boats were just swept away because the river was so fast. We eventually made it and found that the fire was even heavier than before."

"The amount of artillery being fired now by both sides was tremendous," says Frederick Beacham, "and a gradual mist and smoke began to envelop the battlefield." Unable to fire from his position without hitting his comrades, and anxious that a mortar bomb might land smack on top of them at any moment, Beacham and his companion took cover a short distance from the river. "While we were in this shellhole," says Beacham, "we heard a cry for help coming from somewhere to our right. It was a plaintive cry repeating over and over again, 'Help me, I've been hit.' We had orders not to stop in the event of anyone getting wounded as they would be dealt with by the stretcher bearers. We did not go to the aid of this person and it may well be that he was killed in the continuing enemy bombardment for, after a few more minutes, the cries stopped."

After a short time, Beacham and his companion made their way to the crossing point, almost falling into shellholes as the smoke from the barrage mixed with mist to create a thick fog. Sliding down the bank to the river, they joined others in a boat and were soon clambering out onto the far bank. By now visibility was down to about two yards. Beacham was glad he

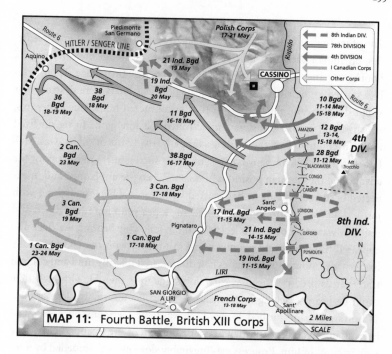

MAP 11: Fourth Battle, British XIII Corps

couldn't be seen by the German machine gunners, but to carry out the operation virtually blind called on all their expertise and training. "After a short while we were given the whispered order to catch hold of the bayonet scabbard of the man in front and we started to move off in slow motion, it seemed to me, and at times I felt that we were going around in a circle. After a short distance, not more than about thirty yards, we stumbled into what later turned out to be an irrigation furrow. This was about two feet wide and about a foot deep and we went no further. We again received orders whispered from man to man, to get into the furrows, and this we did, lying full length in it."

The whole battalion was across in two and a half hours, but already enough time had been lost for the troops to have failed to keep up with the artillery barrage, which advanced at a hundred yards every six minutes. The thick fog helped shield the men from direct German observation, but it caused considerable confusion and disorganization. At 4 A.M. the battalion commander ordered the leading companies to halt and remain where they were, pinned down only yards from the riverbank.

The other leading battalion of the brigade was the 1/12th Frontier Force Rifles, an Indian battalion, that was attacking downstream of Sant' Angelo, hoping, together with the Royal Fusiliers, to encircle the village. Their troubles started at the river, where all but two of their boats were destroyed or swept downstream. Finally across, they encountered numerous trip-wires, which set off smoke canisters and activated machine guns firing on fixed lines. In command of the leading company, made up of Sikhs, was Maj. David Wilson. "A Company having got across successfully formed up for the advance on the German positions," he says. "Then the unplanned and unexpected occurred. The night had started with reasonably clear weather with just a mild mist at ground level. Suddenly a pea soup fog came down and visibility was reduced to two feet." For those following behind, the river disappeared from view and many got lost. An officer with the HQ Company has written, "White guiding tapes had disappeared into the mud and colored tracer shells fired overhead as direction signs were invisible although they could be heard cracking and screaming past uncomfortably close ahead." Wilson's company pushed forward, "toward the Germans on a compass bearing in single file, each man grasping the butt of the weapon held by the man in front of him. Progress was inevitably slow and was impeded by a series of irrigation ditches about two feet deep into which men stumbled in the darkness and fog." Eventually the Sikhs reached the German defensive wire at the foot of the bank, which was the company's objective. A gap was found in the wire, and the men pushed forward leaving the forward German defensive line behind them, and dug in. "Three very frightened German youths ran into the middle of us and were taken prisoner," Wilson says. "They were clearly petrified at the sight of the Sikhs who were appearing very wild in somewhat disheveled beards and turbans."

For the rest of the battalion, and for the division's 19th Brigade attacking to 17th Brigade's left, the opening offensive was similarly thrown off balance by the fog and pinned down under heavy German fire. "The confused night continued," wrote the officer from the Sikhs' HQ Company, "sometimes just damp and dark and eerily quiet for a few moments—but most of the time rather nasty and noisy. Every minor move forward was meeting resistance and no one seemed to be quite sure where they were—or, for that matter, where they should be . . . Our own artillery concentrations had by now moved away from the river faster than we had and enemy pockets that had survived the stonks were still active."

As dawn broke, Frederick Beacham and the Fusiliers were in exactly the same position. With restored visibility came heavier enemy fire. Having been unable to attack because of lack of visibility, the battalion was now pinned down in daylight between Sant'Angelo and high ground on their right. "The sun came up in all its glory and there we were stretched head to toe as in a massive long open grave, unable to move at all without the risk of being shot down," says Beacham. "What in the hell had gone wrong during the night that we found ourselves in this position, only yards from the river and unable to advance? I felt a sense of anger and fear, especially as several shells started to come down on our position. The sun grew hot and beat down on our backs. We drank a little from our water bottles and occasionally I even drifted off into a semiconscious state. I didn't feel hungry and even if I had, I think that I would have been afraid to reach into the pack on my back to get it as I felt I would probably have gotten my hand blown off."

At around eleven o'clock there was a sustained burst of enemy machine gun fire, and a few minutes later a sergeant crawled by, blood streaming from a head wound. "This incident prompted the man whose studded boots were near my head to ask me if I was married and I told him I wasn't," says Beacham. "He then asked me if I would look after a photograph of a girl-friend in case he got killed as he wouldn't want his wife to know about it if it was sent home with his possessions. I said I would and he handed me a small photograph of an ATS girl in full uniform. I cannot remember who the soldier was and I have never seen him since that battle. I still have the photograph and many times over the years, I have wondered who she was, where she lived and what happened to that man."

For the whole of 12 May, Beacham's Fusilier company remained lying head-to-toe, facedown in the shallow ditch while all along the front the battle raged around them. "The day passed ever so slowly," he says. "That evening and the fading light seemed as if it would never arrive, and when it did, it brought no comfort to us. The enemy machine guns opened up at intervals and kept us firmly in our places. The night dragged on and the next day found us no further on, totally pinned down by machine gun fire." But during the night a whispered order had circulated that the Fusiliers were to make a frontal assault on the enemy positions at 11 A.M. "It was explained that the company's 2-inch mortars were to fire at the enemy positions from the flanks and we were to rush the positions while they did so," says Beacham. "I couldn't help but wonder what good would the 2-inch mortars be against a well-dug-in and virtually unseen enemy when a barrage of a thousand guns had failed to achieve the same result. My stomach turned over at the prospect."

The fog had added to the difficulties of constructing the three bridges that were planned for the 8th Indian Division's sector, but it also provided some cover for the engineers. Although the bridge which was to have facilitated tank support from Canadian squadrons for Beacham's battalion had to be abandoned, and another was hit by a German shell only an hour after it was completed, one on the left side of the division's front was ready for use by dawn. Four squadrons of tanks crossed during the morning, and although many became immediately bogged down, others reached the forward troops of the Indian forces to the southwest of Sant'Angelo. "At about 8 A.M. the fog lifted almost as suddenly as it had fallen and it became broad daylight," remembers David Wilson. "Our relief was immense when we looked toward the river and saw a completed bridge and Canadian tanks crossing over and coming toward us. I contacted the leading tank commander and suggested positions he might like to take up to support and protect us."

In the American sector nearest to the coast, the 85th Division managed to secure only one of its objectives while the rest of their attacking companies were either pinned down or surrounded and taken prisoner. On 88th Division's front, two battalions of the 350th Regiment, commanded by Col. J. C. Fry, made good progress on the first night, capturing the southern part of Monte Damiano, but the 351st Regiment's attack against the village of Santa Maria Infante encountered difficulties from the outset as the 2nd Battalion tried to advance on either side of the road from Minturno, which was guarded by two hillocks. Because of the failure of the 85th Division troops to clear high ground on their left flank, they came under heavy machine gun and mortar fire and, in the darkness and mist, control broke down as company commanders were killed or wounded. At this point the battalion's commanding officer, Lt. Col. Raymond Kendall, decided to go forward to try to reorganize his men. With his headquarters company was twenty-three-year-old Joseph Menditto, an Italian-American from New Britain, Connecticut. For him it was "a day never to be forgotten . . . The colonel's command group was advancing forward, ducking the machine guns and mortar fire. The Germans kept firing parachute flares into the sky . . . and barrages of artillery and mortar fire deafening our ears and deadly machine gunners blasting away . . . The colonel kept looking back to see if his group was keeping pace with him. He was moving aggressively and we kept seeing casualties and no leadership in the forward movement. E Company's commander must have been hit." E Company was on the right-hand side of the road, but stalled behind some sheltering walls.

Kendall decided to call for armored support to this position and instructed his radio operator to pass back the message. "Shortly, perhaps twenty minutes after the battle started, we got a call from our second battalion," says signaler Richard Barrows, also from New Britain, who received the message. "Our 2nd Battalion said 'Send up the buffaloes.' " Unfortunately neither Barrows nor the officer with him, a major, knew what this meant. "There was a hesitation, we didn't know what to do, so I called back the radio number and asked them for identification," Barrows continues. "At that particular time, I heard someone shouting and yelling 'Give me the phone!' " Unknown to Barrows, this was Kendall. "Then someone started shouting at me, 'We asked for the buffaloes, send them up, don't question us.' And then he got off the radio again. So, consequently, the major was still upset. He didn't know who the person was. So he said: 'Call them back, ask for identification,' which I did. The person on the other end was furious. He said: 'If you don't know how to operate that blankety-blank radio, get the hell off that radio, and put someone on who knows how to operate it. Roger out.' We learned a lot that night," says Barrows. "We learned for one thing to discard a lot of the rules that had been set up while we were training in the United States, particularly in radio language transmission."

A thoroughly angry and frustrated Colonel Kendall then moved to the front of the sheltering troops and, according to Menditto, "yelled and screamed at them, telling them to use their weapons and fire at the enemy." Having identified a nearby farm building as hiding a machine gun nest, Kendall personally led an attack, "firing his 45 pistol until it ran out of ammo and then [grabbing] a GI's carbine and fir[ing] its full load of ammo," says Menditto. "Then he grabbed the bazooka man's gun and told him to load it and fired at the building. The back blast of the bazooka burned the ammo bearer, rear of the gun." Menditto was with the colonel's jeep driver, Frankie, following behind, firing all the time. "As we advanced the colonel fell in front of me. I knew he was hit and I yelled to Frankie that the colonel was down. Frank and I took off his bullet-struck helmet and then we took the first-aid kit off his belt and tried to wrap the bandage around his bleeding head. But he was bleeding profusely and then his brains were oozing from his left temple. We knew then he was gone. We passed the word around that the colonel was dead and told everyone to hold what we had until we had an officer in charge. We were all told to be prepared and alert for a possible counterattack."

More troops were pushed forward, and on the left-hand side of the road F Company made good progress, but then became cut off. E Company on the right captured their hillock objective but was unable to advance further in spite of being reinforced. At dusk it was decided to cease all attacks until the next day. "During the night after the colonel was killed both sides were exchanging gunfire," says Menditto. "We waited all night in fear." The next morning his unit was spotted by the battalion's reserve company. "They were at the bottom of the hill and couldn't identify us readily and, believing us to be German soldiers, started small-arms fire at us. We now had to respond quickly. We took our helmets and stuck them on our rifles and held them high in the air and started yelling, 'We're Americans, we're Americans.' Seeing this, G Company then realized we were part of the forward element, shouted for us to withdraw down the hill while giving us overhead protection. As we were retreating down the slope the Germans saw us out in the open and began throwing everything at us: artillery, mortar and heavy machine gun fire. No matter in what direction we ran we were running into exploding shells. But the hand of God was on us and we made it to the bottom of the hill. There we scouted the area and found a deserted German machine gun bunker. We made sure there were no booby traps in there and we stayed in it."

In spite of receiving lavish air support during daylight, it had been a poor first thirty-six hours in offensive combat for the "Blue Devils" of the 88th Division. When officers had fallen, the inexperienced troops had frozen. There had also been many casualties in frontline and support troops. Among those lost was the mess sergeant Arthur Schick, killed when an artillery shell landed directly on his dugout.

Twenty-one-year-old ambulance driver Solange Cuvillier was with the 2nd Moroccan Division north of Castelforte when the barrage began: "Five . . . four . . . three . . . two . . . ONE and hell breaks loose," she writes. "A flood of shells serve as openers for the army on the attack. The telephone lines sizzle at the Command Post of the Medical Battalion. 'We need ambulances!' Already? The battle's only been waging for three minutes. We rattle along the riverbank in the smoke, among tanks and other armored vehicles, lightning flashes from the mouths of the artillery spewing fire that sets the mountain alight in an apocalyptic glow. Our bodies, our vehicles vibrate with the pounding shells."

The French, to the immediate right of the Americans, had more initial successes. There was a particularly heavy bombardment to support their attacks, and in the mountains the acoustic effect of the shelling alone was devastating to the Germans, who also had severe casualties inflicted on reserves and guns behind the lines as well as disruption to communication and supply lines. Just after midnight a Moroccan battalion captured the heights of Monte Faito, a key early objective that gave vital artillery observation to its holder. They were much helped by a French Alsatian deserter from the German army, who guided them through a minefield on the approach to the summit.

Elsewhere, though, minefields and heavy fire from well-constructed and -situated pillboxes broke up many of the attacks, or gains were lost during the course of the night. As the British had found fighting in the same mountains in January and February, the failure to capture one mountain would mean failure all along the front as the intact defensive positions brought down fire on movement on its flanks. Minefields and a breakdown in radio communication hampered Juin's armored thrust along the west bank of the Garigliano. "The advanced surgical units are quickly overwhelmed," writes Solange Cuvillier. "We spend the whole night going back and forth on the long, snaking tracks whose 30-degree incline dizzies us. We are living in another dimension which allows us to resist sleep, hunger, thirst. Only coffee keeps us going, 30 a day when we're under attack."

Jean Murat's company of Tunisians was not due to attack until sunrise on 12 May, extending the "agonizing" wait. "From 1 A.M. on 12 May, the battalion has taken position at the base camp," he writes. "And the wait begins under a flood of fire that passes over our heads. I look at my watch nonstop. For now, time can't go fast enough. At four o'clock, the battalion sustains its first casualties. They belong to a patrol who made up the advance party. The wait is becoming more and more cruel. Faces are tensed. The men are by now completely at-the-ready even though the attack won't start for another hour. The preliminary shots are still passing over us with great intensity. Minus five minutes. A pale day is dawning. The leaders give their final instructions. Oh that this day will end!"

Like many, Murat found that once on the move he was liberated from the tension and apprehension of waiting to start. After that, he says, "There was no time to be frightened, I had so much to do! I have come to believe that faced with the same risk, it is easier for a leader to be brave than someone following orders." His three sections left the base camp, moving very quickly in line. "Now the company goes into attack formation. Two sections in the forward section, the third behind. The men line up to fire. I position myself just behind the first scouts in order best to lead the procession. Slightly stooped, weapons held with both hands at stomach level, we advance without running but at a very rapid pace." After a few moments, the men heard the crack of gunfire. Murat's first thought was that men behind were shooting them in the back. Then he worked out that it was covering fire going over their heads from heavy machine guns. After "the momentary confusion" the men moved forward again. "The Company has now advanced a good kilometer and is ready to descend toward Castelforte. Absolutely no reaction from the enemy. Have the Germans retreated?! I can already see myself in the streets of the village—the conqueror who never fought. I'm still in my daydream when a burst of machine gun fire kills our frontline soldiers at short range. In just a few seconds the Company sustains a few dead and wounded."

Murat moved his men back, out of the field of fire of the enemy position, and decided to outflank the German bunkers. "A section starts to push from the right where the ground, a bit more wooded, lends itself to the possibility of infiltration. The infantrymen proceed with caution but as soon as they reach the opposite slope, they encounter extremely heavy automatic gunfire. Men fall. The section retreats dragging the wounded towards the back when it can." Another section tried a similar maneuver on the other side but met with the same result. "I must face the facts, the Company has exhausted all the possibilities for advancement. It is stopped in front of a line of buried pillboxes which are built one next to the other. These blockhouses, built on a counter slope, don't allow for a wide range of fire (less than fifty meters) but that distance appears to be impenetrable as long as the bunkers haven't been destroyed."

During the fighting, on Murat's left some tanks managed to penetrate to the center of Castelforte, but the day's other major gain, Monte Faito, came under fierce barrage and counterattack during the afternoon. The situation became critical, and Juin himself went forward to direct operations and rally the troops. Faito was held, but elsewhere gains were meager or nonexistent. At midday, Murat's company commander came forward and directed him to take up defensive positions and send out patrols. Wounded and dead were evacuated and new supplies of ammunition handed out. "The men build themselves small stone walls," says Murat. "For the moment, the commander has no means of dealing with the corpses. Even though I didn't give any orders to do so, the section has gathered all their dead near my shelter. Due to the intense heat, the dead take on a waxy look. They're everywhere. With a glance I can perceive the extent of our failure. And I know at the same time that other [corpses] still under fire have not been recovered from behind enemy lines. The afternoon brings no improvement. The commander, surprised by the turn of events, constantly demands reports on the resistance, which necessitates sending out patrols. The commander perhaps has good reasons to hope for a German retreat, but for us, pressed up against the pillbox or the cadavers, knowing nothing of the overall situation, that eventually seems quite improbable."

Murat later discovers that the battalion suffered 158 casualties on that first day, the 1st and 2nd Companies losing more than 40 percent of their fighting force. "Night falls," he writes. "The situation hasn't progressed. The first day is a failure, a bitter failure. The exultation of the battle is followed by a profound depression. Faces are sad and grave. The news is all bad and we don't talk about the wounded and the dead."

"Night gives way to day," writes Solange Cuvillier. "Around 400 wounded have already passed through our company. The scene before us brings tears to the eye: shattered houses, twisted metal, mutilated mules, and the unbearable stench of burned flesh that permeates the front. It's horrific."

Corporal Zbigniew Fleszar, with the 1st Battalion of the Polish Carpathian Division, was making his way along Snakeshead Ridge when the Allied barrage started. "A whistling shell flew low overhead—and another, and another," he remembers. "I felt as if a bridge of iron was being erected overhead, and wondered how it was that shells did not collide . . . The noise reverberated over the mountains. One could pick out whistles, crying and

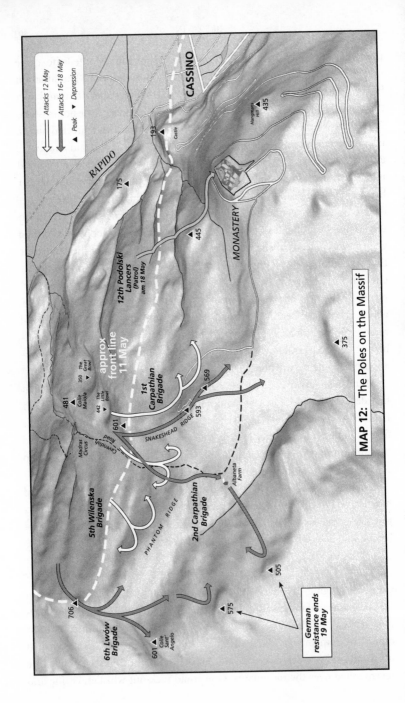

MAP 12: The Poles on the Massif

RAPIDO

CASSINO

Castle

193

175 ▲

12th Podolski
Lancers
(Patrol)
am 18 May

445 ▲

MONASTERY

Hangmans ▲
Hill ▲ 435

approx
front line
11 May

481 ▲ Colle
Maiola

350 ▲ The
Great
Bowl

442 ▲ The
Little
Bowl

Madras
Circus

Cavendish
Road

601 ▲

SNAKESHEAD RIDGE

593 ▲

569 ▲

1st Carpathian
Brigade

375 ▲

PHANTOM RIDGE

5th Wilenska
Brigade

Albaneta
Farm

2nd Carpathian
Brigade

706 ▲

6th Lwów
Brigade

601 ▲ Colle
Sant' Angelo

575 ▲

505 ▲

German
resistance ends
19 May

Attacks 12 May
Attacks 16–18 May
▲ Peak   ▼ Depression

sobbing and roaring of shells." At 11:40 P.M. the fire switched from the German artillery batteries to their forward positions, the Poles' objectives. "Then it all changed. The Phantom Hill in front of us was suddenly on fire. There was an explosion every split second. The mountain trembled."

The general attack was due to start at 1 A.M., Fleszar's battalion advancing along the gorge running between the Snakeshead and Phantom Ridges as part of Anders's plan to take on all of the key German positions simultaneously. Previous attacks on Point 593 had failed, Anders reasoned, because the Germans had been able to use flanking fire from Phantom Ridge and Colle Sant'Angelo. So the Carpathian Division was sent against Point 593 as well as along the gorge while the Kresowa Division attacked the strong points at the end of Phantom Ridge. With these cleared, the way to the Liri valley behind the monastery would be open and the abbey itself isolated.

Edward Rynkiewicz, a commander of a Pioneer platoon in the 2nd Battalion of the Carpathian Division, was waiting close to the front line as the artillery barrage continued. His group was to go forward to clear mines as part of the battalion's attack on the dreaded Point 593. "Shells from our own artillery were screaming over our heads in sporadic bursts," he says. "The Germans were blasting away, too . . . We could feel the ground trembling and were conscious of the quivering air. I personally was very aware of the thumping of my heart . . . Tension, as might be supposed, was inexorably mounting. Zero hour was rapidly approaching, but my men, with one notable exception, were not afraid. The only man whose nerve broke was a young corporal who begged me to leave him behind. I understood exactly how he was feeling, so I granted his request."

As Cpl. Zbigniew Fleszar's unit struggled up the steep slope to their start position for the attack through the gorge—"sweat running down into our eyes, battledress wet, chests like smithies' bellows"—the German artillery responded: "All Hell broke loose . . . The heavy shells started breaking among us . . . The explosions sounded like an enormous giant clearing his throat. I had an extraordinary wish—to be one of the smallest pebbles under one of the biggest rocks."

At 1:30 A.M. on 12 May the leading units advanced, as close to the barrage as they could, in the hope that the Germans would not have time to reoccupy their forward positions, having taken shelter on the reverse slopes. The Poles arrived on the top of Point 593 first and pushed ahead along the saddle of rock that led toward the monastery. In front of them was a heavily fortified hillock, Point 569. This the Germans had reoccupied, and the attackers were pinned down.

Edward Rynkiewicz's unit followed along the ridge close behind the leading elements. "We surged forward . . . Many of us had lost our bearings and there was a great deal of confusion. None of us was certain of our whereabouts, but every man felt that the rise in front just had to be the beginning of Hill 593. The enemy fire increased in volume and intensity with each yard we gained and we were showered with myriad fragments of splintered rocks."

He reached the summit of Point 593 at about 2:30 A.M., passing through formidable rolls of barbed wire that had been displaced by the artillery bombardment. Severe problems were now being encountered in communicating with commanders to the rear. Telephone lines were cut by explosive fire almost as soon as they were laid, and radios had been knocked out or their operators killed. "If only we could have seen clearly what was happening we should have felt better," says Rynkiewicz. Instead, the forward troops had to rely on word-of-mouth, and soon rumors of who was dead and who was still alive were shouted about. "Meanwhile the German guns blasted us so effectively that we were obliged to throw ourselves flat and crawl around looking for cover. It was practically nonexistent, since all the sizable boulders had been blown to bits by our own artillery." Rynkiewicz eventually found cover in a shellhole filled with men "all sprawled on top of each other." Burrowing down into the mostly lifeless bodies, he could see unsuccessful attacks being carried out on Point 569, but by now he was "mentally blank, stupefied, exhausted . . . We no longer knew where to shoot or whom to aim at." For the rest of the night Rynkiewicz remained huddled in a small hole he had found, aware that the attackers' numbers were being depleted. He decided that to pull back to his own lines in daylight would be suicidal, and with a small group of stragglers found shelter in a cave, together with three or four wounded German prisoners.

In the gorge between the Snakeshead and Phantom Ridges, the advancing infantry had come under murderous machine gun and mortar fire, and the burned-out hulks of the tanks left behind after the disastrous assault up the "Cavendish Road" during the third battle now provided excellent cover for snipers. There had been high hopes for the tanks attached to this battalion, but newly sown antitank mines as well as artillery had knocked most of them out before they got anywhere near the gorge. Eighteen of the twenty engineers working with the tanks to clear mines were killed or wounded during the failed push.

To the right of the gorge, the Kresowa Division's attack had also been hampered by German artillery fire and minefields. The Poles reached the top of the ridge and engaged the Germans in intense hand-to-hand fighting, but were unable to advance more than halfway to their objective at the end of the ridge. At first light they were counterattacked and also had to contend with Germans emerging undaunted from intact bunkers and caves in their rear. As elsewhere, communication broke down, and senior commanders were unable to tell where reserves or supporting fire were needed. Daylight saw the attackers from both divisions exposed, and four times the indomitable German paratroopers counterattacked Point 593, eventually succeeding on their fifth attempt in driving off the last of the Poles still standing, an officer and seven men. Both divisions had by then sustained heavy casualties, and Anders had no alternative but to call off the attack and order the men back to their starting lines.

Soon the cave in which Edward Rynkiewicz was sheltering came to the attention of Germans, and one man who leaned out to have a look around was killed instantly by a mortar shell. Unaware of what was going on outside, Rynkiewicz was still hoping that the Poles had control of the hill above them. During the day the situation became desperate in the cave as ammunition ran out and more sniper bullets ricocheted around the entrance. Anyone who tried to make a dash outside was cut down by a German machine gun now trained on the entrance.

"When darkness fell the Germans moved in on us with guns," says Rynkiewicz. "Six or seven of them came into the cave and formally announced that we were their prisoners. It was gratifying to see that they were as exhausted as we were." The captors settled down beside the prisoners and "together we passed a sleepless night, listening to the thunder of the artillery." The next morning they were moved about one hundred yards down a steep slope and then were halted alongside a hole in the hillside. "Skillfully hidden by camouflage, this hole was no more than three feet in diameter and only the luckiest of shots would have found such a target. Anyway, we crawled through a passage which led into a vast cavern divided by canvas partitions into three large rooms, all excellently lit." Inside were wounded Germans and a doctor, who approached the Poles apologetically, asking for their medical kits. "When we saw that the wounded Germans had been bandaged with nothing but paper, we willingly gave [them to] him," says Rynkiewicz.

Anders was distraught at the failure of the attack. The slopes and gullies, already choked with the dead of several countries, were now littered with new Polish casualties. Men who had endured and survived the harshest of Russian labor camps had now been destroyed, and there was nothing to show for it. Just eight hundred Germans had succeeded in driving off attacks by two divisions. Monte Cassino seemed as impregnable as ever. Neither did Anders have a source of reserves to replace the losses. His analysis of what went wrong would have sounded unhappily familiar to the US 34th Division and the 4th Indian Division, which had attacked in the same area. "Enemy reserves would suddenly emerge from concealment in caves to make a series of powerful counterattacks, which were supported by accurate fire from guns," Anders writes. "Our troops, on the other hand, could get little support from our artillery, partly because these latter themselves suffered heavy losses and partly because of the complex nature of the ground . . . It soon became clear that it was easier to capture some objectives than to hold them."

At the end of 12 May, 8th Army commander Lieutenant General Leese visited Anders and, looking for consolation for the awful losses, praised the Polish Corps for tying up enemy forces, particularly artillery, and preventing them from being employed against the British and Indian troops down in the valley. The 8th Indian Division, as has been seen, had established only precarious bridgeheads either side of Sant'Angelo. But the 4th British Division had struggled even more.

————

In spite of the efforts of the Poles, in the 4th Division's sector between the town and the 8th Division on their left, there had been particularly heavy artillery fire from German batteries behind Cassino. The division attacked with two brigades, the 28th and 10th. On the left, 28th Brigade's assaulting battalions arrived half an hour late at the crossing site and found German fire already coming in. The thick fog caused great confusion, boats were destroyed and when some of the men eventually made it across, there were numerous casualties from mines. Battalion commanders were killed and communications lost with the rear. Some men returned over the river on an "alleged order" and by morning the brigade had only 250 men on the German side of the river. Out of 40 boats, 35 had been knocked out by 8 A.M. on the twelfth and the other five had been lost by midday. The men, under fierce fire once the morning mist lifted, were on their own. On the right, 10th Brigade had fared a little better. By morning they had parts of all three of their battalions across and had captured some of their initial objectives. As elsewhere, however, there were considerable casualties and many boats were lost during the course of the night.

Pioneer officer F. G. Sutton's 2nd Beds and Herts Battalion had advanced only half a mile before digging in. "The enemy counterattacked seven times during darkness," he says, "but they were beaten back each time with help from the gun barrage." Work by an imperturbable forward observation officer, "pulling the chain" to call down a "stonk" (a barrage on an area) or a "murder" (a barrage on a specific spot), protected the British soldiers. It was now of crucial importance that the engineers succeed in constructing bridges for tanks and antitank guns. Without them, the forward troops would be unable to withstand a greater German counterattack.

Tommy Riordan's 7th Field Company reached the site of the Congo bridge soon after the first troops of 28th Brigade had at last got across. There had already been some casualties from shellfire on the way to the river. "The smoke was building up, it became more and more difficult to see ahead," wrote Riordan. "River mist, dust from gunfire, all contributed to make a thick fog, and the enemy added to this unexpectedly; smoke canisters had been set in the riverbanks with trip wires, when tripped the canisters emitted a thick black smoke, indicating a crossing point, giving watching observers the targets they were looking for to shoot into, which they did with great fury." "When we got to the site the smoke had thickened up and there was a heavy river mist," says fellow 7th Company engineer Jack Stamper. "We were all taped together so that we got to the site in one party. I think we got one bridging lorry unloaded and then the enemy started shelling. It was the worst shelling I experienced during the war." At that moment gunfire started sweeping the site from out of the fog on the other side of the river. Clearly German machine gunners had moved up to the river's edge as the creeping barrage passed behind them. The engineers did have a small section of infantry with them, but they were unable to return fire as they could see no targets. "It was clear that unless the infantry cleared a few hundred yards of the far bank and held it, work would be difficult if not impossible on the site," says Riordan. But the men of 28th Brigade were in a state of utter confusion and were struggling to hold on in small numbers on the other side of the river. Casualties among the sappers continued to rise, and before daybreak the CO, Michael Low, ordered the men to return to their starting position. Once back, "Nobody said anything, we were all a bit shaken," says engineer Robert Lister. "You've no idea what it's like to be on the receiving end of shells and mortars. We were only young kids, I was only twenty-one years and eight months old. We were all very shaken and disoriented."

In spite of the greater success of the 4th Division's 10th Brigade on the right of the front, 225th Company experienced the same difficulties at the Amazon bridge site, and work there never proceeded beyond starting the preparation of the near bank. At 59th Company's Blackwater site, the noise produced by the bulldozer on the near bank attracted fire immediately, and each time it was restarted a hail of bullets arrived. Commanding officer Tony Daniell looked around for a junior officer to attack the machine guns, but could find only "dejected parties of infantry milling around." "There were people coming across and bumping into you, asking, 'Which way are you going, which way is the river?' " remembers sapper Frank Sellwood. "It was about four or five individuals at a time, not sections or big groups. They were cussing, frustrated, saying, 'What are we going to do? We can't see anything. No one can see anything.' "

Just before dawn, Lt. Peter Boston swam the river, attached a rope, and also found an infantry officer. But his party soon returned, having got hopelessly lost in the fog. By now, although no work on the bridge itself had started, 20 out of the 32 trucks carrying equipment had arrived and started piling up at the top of the track. "The Boche must have sensed our concentration of vehicles at the top of the track, for suddenly he started shelling," says Tony Daniell. Several men were wounded in this "jam of struggling vehicles" when the Germans opened up with *Nebelwerfers*, and Daniell reluctantly ordered the abandonment of the bridge. "Our tails could not have been lower," he says.

17

Amazon Bridge

With not a single bridge built to take tank and antitank support over to the forward troops, the situation for the British 4th Division on the Rapido on the morning of 12 May was desperate. Pioneer officer F. G. Sutton remembers that as dawn came, the fog cleared and the men in the shallow bridgehead were in full view of the monastery. Immediately the Allied artillery started firing smoke shells at Monastery Hill, and soon, Sutton says, "It looked as if the whole big mountain was steaming." In 10th Brigade's sector, only one boat was left by 12:30 P.M., and, just like 28th Brigade on their left, they were effectively stranded. "We had no tanks or antitank guns on our side of the river," says Sutton. "We could not have withstood a well-organized counterattack with tanks that day."

For the moment, though, luck held for the British. The much-feared counterattack failed to materialize. The smoke and fog meant the Germans did not know where to concentrate their main effort, but, more to the point, they themselves were reeling from the onslaught of the first night and its fearsome barrage. As Kesselring writes: "As I saw for myself on the morning of 12 May, both the 10th Army and XIV Corps headquarters had almost ceased to function; both had lost their commanders and their deputies were doing their best to carry on."

The situation across the whole twenty-mile front was not happy for the

Allies—there had been setbacks and failures in all the attacking sectors—but the assault had achieved surprise. The German reinforcements were far away, guarding against an amphibious landing that they still considered to be imminent, and the fact that the Allies had attacked on such a broad front meant that this time the Germans were unable to move local reinforcements to threatened sectors as they had done with such success in the previous Cassino battles. For the moment all they could do was launch piecemeal attacks and pour as much mortar and shellfire as they could into the shallow Rapido bridgeheads.

Nevertheless, it was clear that the surprise and violence of the initial attack had won only breathing space. If the disaster of the US 36th Division was going to be avoided, it was imperative that at least one bridge should be constructed so that reinforcements and tanks could reach the Rapido bridgehead. "The order was sent out," 4th Division's war diary records, "giving details of regrouping for the night—which based its whole plan on the construction of Amazon Bridge and the passing through of 12th Brigade and its supporting tanks [from 17/21st Lancers] to push on." The bridge was to be built "at all costs." All three 4th Division engineering companies would now work together in shifts on just one bridge, which would be supported by a special artillery program as well as a heavy smokescreen covering the site. No rafts or ferries would be built. It was Amazon bridge or nothing.

At 2:30 P.M., Michael Low, commanding officer of 7th Company, held an order group for officers and NCOs and explained the plan. The work would be started by 225th Company, then the 7th would take over, followed by the 59th. "Do you think this is a good thing?" Low asked the assembled men. There was a slight pause, then the answer came back: "No, we don't think this is a good thing, but we are going to build this bridge." It was decided that only volunteers would go on the job, but, in the event, all of those who had survived unscathed the work on the failed Congo bridge the previous night were to be back in action.

At 5 P.M., work on the near bank and approach was started by 225th Company. The activity was seen by F. G. Sutton. "The sapper on the bulldozer seemed either to have a complete disregard for danger, or else a safe charm," he says. "He was continually sniped by a Boche spandau post within our perimeter, which we had not yet been able to wipe out. Once, the sapper got off his machine and started tinkering with the engine; just then I could see the spandau bullets tear a pattern into the backrest of his seat." The British troops on the German side of the river did what they could to deal with this machine gunner, but they were themselves under heavy *Nebelwerfer* fire, and they were unsuccessful. The work continued under fire, with the men periodically taking cover in foxholes but always then resuming.

Meanwhile, the senior officers of 7th Company were leading a recce (reconnaissance) party to the bridge. "It was a bright, clear evening," Tommy Riordan remembers, "and the monastery was in full view, too conspicuous for comfort. There was time while trotting to look around to give the monastery the 'Two finger sign' . . . there was little evidence of [the promised] smoke." The instruction was given that the recce officer, Lt. John Barnes, should bring the rest of 7th Company forward to the lying-up area.

At 6:30 P.M., officers and NCOs of the 7th gathered at the temporary company headquarters, itself under sporadic mortar fire. According to twenty-three-year-old section leader Lt. Bert Hobson, the atmosphere was tense. On top of the news that Major Low had been badly wounded in the leg while on the recce, it became apparent as the meeting was breaking up that the acting commanding officer, Lt. Michael Sharland, was also seriously wounded. He had been hit while on the bridge site, taking instructions from 225th Company. Lieutenant Hobson, who had been commissioned only six months previously, was now the senior company officer.

By 7 P.M. the company was sheltering in an area behind the railway cutting. According to Hobson, everyone was thinking, "Bloody hell, we're on next!" Three-quarters of an hour later, part of the company moved down to the bridge site to help the 225th men unload the bridging equipment. The first job, now that the bank was more or less ready, was to lay the rollers on which the bridge would be slid across the river on to the far bank. "They had to be level or at least as near level as you could get them," says Hobson. "If you are scurrying around on rough ground, with people shelling you and firing at you, it's a bit awkward, to say the least."

At 9 P.M. most of 225th Company left the site and Hobson was now the bridge site commander. All but two of the trucks were unloaded, but the larger of the two bulldozers was out of action, having had its elevating gear hit by machine gun fire. By this time, 59th Company had come forward and was waiting to be called to the site, hoping, according to Frank Sellwood, "that they wouldn't be needed and that the other two companies would finish the job." But at 9:45 they were told to go to the site to help finish the unloading of the final trucks.

Now heavy fire from snipers and mortars was coming in, and efforts to get across the river to prepare the other bank were unsuccessful. Among those hit was Sgt. Jack Stamper. "A brilliant blue flash appeared at my right-hand side, quite close," he says. "I never heard anything, but of course there was a lot of noise. My first impression was that I'd stood on a *Schümine* that hadn't been lifted. I was very relieved to find that my foot was intact, so it wasn't a *Schümine*, but I felt suddenly pain in my shoulder and my buttocks and then I went stiff. I just seemed to be paralyzed . . . and a couple of the chaps took me to the aid post." As the steady stream of casualties mounted, the number of men available to work on the bridge diminished. "The trouble was that for every one wounded, at least two people were needed to get him back to the first-aid post," says Hobson. "You had more volunteers for getting people away than hanging about."

At midnight, Lt. Peter Boston from 59th Company took over from Hobson on the site. The latter stayed on in spite of being exhausted. At this point it was hoped that the bridge would be completed by 2 A.M., but it was not to be. Shelling and mortaring intensified and gained accuracy. The Germans also started firing flares behind the site to silhouette the men and provide easy targets for snipers. When this happened, everybody had to freeze until the light died away.

At 1 A.M., Sherman tanks of the 17/21st Lancers were heard coming up the road. Tony Daniell, who had been in the nearby temporary bridge head-quarters, ran down the track and stopped the first tank about two hundred yards off, but the damage was done. The noise attracted renewed fire, and at 2 A.M., a three-ton truck carrying smoke canisters was hit on the road next to bridge HQ. This caught fire and blazed furiously for two hours, attracting yet more shells. It was too hot to get near to put out, and haystacks at the top of the field were also hit and caught fire, "adding to the conflagration."

Sheltering in a slit trench only a few feet from the waiting tanks was twenty-three-year-old Stan Goold, a Welshman with the 18th Field Park Company. He and two companions had the unenviable task of driving the remaining small bulldozer in turns. He had been busy trying to level the ground on the approach to the crossing site. The noise the bulldozer made attracted fire and prevented the driver from hearing incoming shells, making it a particularly hazardous job. The exposed driver was also vulnerable to sniper fire, and the men wore bulletproof vests, although they found them cumbersome. Goold vividly recalls the scene at the Amazon site: "It was like

Dante's inferno, like nothing any of us had really experienced before," he says. "There was such a rain of fire from the enemy and a tremendous noise." He also saw "three or four engineers mentally affected being evacuated. Some were laughing, some were crying, some were talking gibberish."

Rumors started circulating that the Germans had crossed the river north of the bridging site. According to one engineer from 7th Company, "Everyone downed tools and ran. They were reprimanded by Lieutenant Barnes and hauled back to the bridge."

There were further delays. At about 2:30 A.M., with men working on the assembly of the bridge itself, a machine gun fired down the center. "It was very disconcerting when bullets started hitting the Bailey panels," Hobson remembers. Only the officers and NCOs were armed, and they now took up defensive positions on the bank. Without leaders, the work slowed even more. According to Tony Daniell, the time of completion was amended to 3 A.M., "and later, out of sheer desperation, to 0500 hours."

At 4 A.M., the process started of pushing the bridge forward on its rollers, using the small bulldozer and the brute strength of the engineers. Other sappers used crowbars, heaving the bridge just a little this way, a little that way, to keep it on the runners. A mortar bomb landed in the water right next to the bridge, soaking everyone but causing no casualties.

At this point a small party was dispatched across the river. This consisted of Frank Sellwood's eight-man subsection from 59th Company: "We carried a canvas boat folded up, to clear antitank and antipersonnel mines on the opposite bank. Each of us was carrying a pickaxe, shovel or mine-detecting equipment. We had a tool in one hand and were hanging on to a piece of the boat in the other. We had just got to the bank and were about to slide the boat into the water when there was a bang. This mortar landed just to the side of us and knocked all eight of us out. It may have dropped right in the middle of us, but I'm pretty sure there was a bright flash alongside of me. I came around with the smoke still around me, so I couldn't have been out for very long. There wasn't a thing from the rest of them apart from someone groaning. It was John: 'Where have you got it?' 'In the leg,' I replied. 'Where have you got it?' 'In the stomach,' he said. Then someone shouted, 'Stretcher bearer!' " Four of the eight men were killed outright and the others all had terrible wounds. Sellwood was quickly evacuated.

On the bridge, all was going well until, with twenty feet to go, the bulldozer seized up. Both radiator and sump had been punctured by bullets some time earlier. "This was a major disaster, as the bridge could not be pushed by hand alone," says Tony Daniell. "Then we suddenly remembered the tanks." Peter Boston ran to the leading Sherman waiting some distance down the track. After knocking for some time on the hull, the turret opened and the leader of 2nd Troop, C Squadron, 17/21st Lancers, Lt. M. H. M. Wayne, appeared. Boston persuaded him to bring his tank forward and use it to push the bridge. "The enemy took extreme exception to this," says Daniell, "and put down a number of well-aimed mortar rounds causing several casualties. It was decided not to bother jacking down, but to push the bridge clean off the rollers on to the ground. It did in fact fall nicely on the base plates . . . and the ramps were quickly built." Lieutenant Barnes and two others ran to the end to bed down the bridge. Suddenly Barnes noticed that he was lifting a base plate normally carried by four men. "I can only conclude that the occasion had produced considerable adrenalin in all of us," he says.

It had indeed been a superhuman effort. At a quarter to five, Wayne led his troop of tanks across the makeshift bridge and it held. Lieutenant Barnes tells of how he returned to the nearby advanced dressing station, where the party took their first rest. Like Hobson, Barnes had been at the site, under fire, for ten hours. "Someone offered me a cup of tea," he says. "For the moment I was overcome; such is the effect of a release of tension brought about by an act of kindness." After a moment's rest, he made his way to the headquarters that controlled the movement of men and tanks across the bridge. "I found there a formally mannered major," Barnes remembers. "Saluting, I said, 'Amazon bridge is now open.' 'Will it take tanks?' came the reply. This was no moment to explain the possibilities: 'Yes,' I said, and that was all there was to it."

Early that morning, F. G. Sutton was leading a file of wounded back toward the river. "I had already heard the noise of tanks," he says. "Now one of them loomed up in the dark straight ahead of us. Hastily we got an antitank projector aimed, when the turret opened and a voice said, 'Are you the Bedfords?' Amazon bridge had just been completed and his was the first tank over, a Sherman tank of 17/21st Lancers."

The opening of the bridge was the turning point of the battle opposite the Liri valley, and arguably of the whole Cassino offensive. It had cost the engineers 83 casualties out of the 200 men involved, but, with the bridge open, the British were able to send through tanks and infantry reinforcements.

"Then we saw infantry crossing the bridge at the double," says Sutton. "We heard bagpipes and our faces brightened. We had only one Scottish battalion in 4th Division, the 6th Black Watch. They were in 12th Brigade, which had been divisional reserve."

Charlie Framp was one of the Black Watch crossing the bridge. "We raced by a Bren carrier, it was on fire, its cargo of small-arms ammunition exploded in all directions," he writes. "We passed by a number of bodies, their faces, where visible, were already taking on a waxen appearance. The bridge was hidden by smoke but the Germans knew, roughly, its whereabouts; they deluged the area with fire. We ran a gauntlet of bursting shells, then we were on the bridge. As we raced off, at the other end, we passed through a number of bodies lying scattered on the ground . . . I felt an iron band of fear clamp itself tightly around my chest." The Black Watch immediately attacked a group of smashed buildings near Amazon bridge. Framp, with the HQ company, watched from a ditch: "I saw the bright gleam of polished steel, describing the movement from scabbards to rifle muzzles, all along the ditch, as the platoons on either side of us fixed bayonets . . . The British barrage on the German positions before us abruptly lifted. I saw the platoon men scramble, 1916 fashion, from the ditches and move forward, in extended line with rifles held at high port . . . Despite the British shelling, a gathering storm of small-arms fire shot out from the German positions. I gazed after our lads, their outlines were blurred in the mist and smoke of the battle, I couldn't tell who was who but they all looked equally magnificent as they walked steadily forward into the German fire . . . No one who has ever witnessed such a sight as the one I witnessed then could fail to be deeply impressed by it; it was a truly magnificent display of courage and discipline. I felt proud to be one of them."

As 12th Brigade pushed forward, shielded by a thick morning mist, Sutton's 10th Brigade wheeled northward toward Route 6. Now the Germans were beginning to surrender. "There were more prisoners, all paratroopers," says Sutton. "Our boys were hot after their pistols, for which the American gunners on Monte Trocchio had promised to pay twenty pounds. They also took off their watches, binoculars, cameras and fountain pens."

The objective for the tanks was the Cassino–Pignataro road, but a large number got bogged down in the soft ground near the river. H. Buckle's tank was the sixth one over. It advanced a few yards before getting stuck and staying in the same place for the next four days. Jack Meek's tank had more luck, but he remembers the horror of crossing the bridge under fire and finding at the other end that it was almost impossible to proceed without running over one of the many British dead that littered the German side. "There were bodies all over the place," he remembers. "They had just been mown down. It was just horrible." For the next five days he had very little idea what was going on. "It was very messy, it was easy to get lost . . . there were all sorts of incidents taking place, you might be getting shelled, someone might be machine gunning, we were firing face to face. It was just confusion, mayhem . . . all you do is try to press on best as you can."

The mist on the morning of 13 May added to the confusion, but also prevented German antitank guns from finding targets. By the end of the next day, 12th Brigade had established a bridgehead of three thousand yards, and was precariously on the Pignataro road. At the same time, Leese was preparing to send in his 78th Battleaxe Division to make the breakthrough to Route 6.

––––––

The night of 12 May passed very slowly for Fusilier Frederick Beacham, pinned down in the irrigation ditch to the left of Sant' Angelo, downstream from 4th Division's sector. At eleven o'clock the company was to attack the high ground in front of them in support of a midday strike against Sant' Angelo by the 8th Indian Division's Gurkha battalion. "About half past three [in the morning], the enemy started to shell our positions with the largest caliber shells that I had heard from their side," says Beacham. "I virtually shrank into the ground with fear. One shell burst no more than five yards away, vibrating the ground and sending clods of earth in all directions, which fell down upon us like rain." As the time of the attack neared, he tried to relax his stiff muscles and prepared the Bren gun. Then the whistles sounded, and the Fusiliers rose and began to run forward. "The machine guns opened up at once and the crack of the bullets as they sometimes passed close by my ears almost made one deaf. I had no idea what was happening on either side of me. As I ran I knew that Bill was still with me, and looking ahead I saw that the ground was flat except for these irrigation furrows which ran parallel with the river for a distance of about four hundred yards. Then the ground sloped gently upward to where the enemy was dug in. I don't think we had covered more than a hundred yards or so when, with no orders being given, I and the rest of the company dropped into another of these irrigation furrows (thank God they were there). Puffing and panting with exertion and fear, we tried to get our breath back. The enemy kept up a constant stream of machine gun fire and we pressed against the dirt on the side nearest to the enemy. We were in a much worse position than before and wondering what to do about it when, after a few minutes, the order was whispered from man to man that we were to make our way, in our own time, back to our original start line." As soon as they had got their breath back, Beacham and Bill made a frantic dash to their original position, expecting at any moment to feel bullets "ripping" into their backs. Beacham anticipated an instant German counterattack and thought that they would stand little chance, unable as they were even to put their heads over the rim of the irrigation furrow. Then he heard the sound of tanks in front of him and thought it was the end. But they were Canadian tanks, advancing from the other side of Sant' Angelo. The attack by the Gurkhas had succeeded, albeit at a high cost. When those Germans who had been keeping the Fusiliers pinned down saw the stronghold of Sant' Angelo fall, they surrendered or retreated through crawl trenches.

"I stood up and looked around me for the first time since the battle had started," says Beacham. "I looked to my right and there, lying facedown and obviously dead, was our company commander. I started to walk forward and had gone only a few yards when I recoiled as I nearly stepped on the bodies of four dead Fusiliers. The furrow that they had been sheltering in was slightly wider than the one I had been in and they were lying in pairs rather than singly, as we had been. I could see no sign of injury to their bodies, but it was obvious that the large shell that had slammed into their furrow about one yard away from the heads of the first two had sucked the breath from their lungs, causing instant collapse and death . . . Further to my right, I saw two more Fusiliers lying out in the open. One was dead, lying facedown, still clutching his rifle. He had received a burst of machine gun fire on the left side of his head and, as a result, the whole of that side of his brain had slipped out on to the grass. As I went nearer, a swarm of flies rose from him."

As far as Beacham was concerned the attack had been a fiasco. "To be asked to charge unseen German machine gunners firing at 1,500 rounds per minute, entrenched on raised ground, in an area we hadn't seen before, was madness, absolute madness. I could get quite cross about how we were treated . . . I'm a bit contemptuous of the officers. I lost so many of my mates."

But with Sant' Angelo in Allied hands, the Germans, although still counterattacking, started to fall back. On the night of the thirteenth the first units of the 78th Division entered the line in the 4th Division sector, while the 8th Indian Division's reserve brigade joined the fighting behind Sant' Angelo. It was now a battle of attrition, as the British used their superior numbers—in other words, their ability to take more casualties and keep bringing up fresh troops—to batter their way forward up the Liri valley. The Germans fought superbly, and even the Luftwaffe made a rare appearance, attacking the growing number of bridges over the river and dive-bombing and strafing British infantrymen.

The fighting during this week is remembered by the individual soldiers for its confusion, fear, extreme discomfort, and physical and mental exhaustion. A lieutenant in the 1/6th Surreys, who had taken over command of the battalion when all of his superiors were killed or wounded, describes how "in [seven days] my command managed to advance a total of three-quarters of a mile to a culvert on the Cassino–Rome road . . . For the whole of the seven days it was impossible to stand upright and stay alive. We crawled, rolled, slithered and dragged ourselves about on our bellies, occasionally enjoying the luxury of sitting upright in a slit trench that had been dug deeper than the norm before the attack began."

"We've attacked, attacked, attacked from the beginning," Cpl. Walter Robson wrote to his wife, "with numbers dwindling all the time . . . We sat in holes and trembled. Hicky cracked the day before, now Gordon did . . . he scrambled in head first, crying 'I can't stand it, I can't stand it. My head, my head.' And he clutched his head and wept. I wiped his forehead, neck and ears with a wet handkerchief and sang to him . . . When, when, when is this insanity going to stop?"

Early on the morning of 13 May, the US 88th Division doctor, Klaus Huebner, received an order to move up the road toward Santa Maria Infante. After the setbacks of the day before, every effort was now to be made by the Americans to capture the village and clear the high ground to its north. At noon, Huebner's column ground to a halt, and he set up a temporary aid post in a gully near the road. His vague instructions were to wait for a guide to take him to the advanced dressing station. At around 4 P.M., the soldiers with him had moved forward. "I hear abundant small-arms fire," Huebner writes, "and know they must have met resistance."

For the renewed attack, the commander of the 351st Regiment, Colonel

Champeny, went forward to take personal charge of the 1st Battalion. "It was magnificent," says the divisional history, written by none other than Jack Delaney, the wartime head of the 88th's public relations unit. "We wanted to lie down and stay there, but with the Old Man standing up like a rock you couldn't stay down. Something about him just brought you right to your feet. The guys saw him, too. They figured that if the Old Man could do it so could they. And when the time came they got up off the ground and started on again to Santa Maria." With the colonel was radio operator Richard Barrows, whose account has a rather different tone. "We dug in in an old German sump hole full of garbage and other trash. The noise was terrific. To this day, I cannot believe that I was not frightened to death. The German machine gun fire was coming from several locations. Also, the German shellfire was intense. We were taking quite a pounding. To say that we did not know what was going on would be a major understatement."

Later in the afternoon, the colonel himself approached Barrows's dugout. "Sergeant, call the rear and have them send up the buffaloes," said Champeny. "Here we go again with the buffaloes," Barrows remembers thinking. He called the rear, passed on the message, and was told to identify himself. "Of course, I didn't know what to say," he remembers. "We had no plans, no code letters or code names or anything. I was totally bewildered." Then he had an idea, and called back, saying, "We want the buffaloes up here and I am the Corbin Screw Corporation calling." This was a big factory in Barrows's home town. "The captain in the rear said: 'Wait.' Then he came back on and said: 'OK, the tanks are coming up.' I must have told someone in the rear where I had worked and they knew it was me calling. Within a few minutes we heard the tanks coming up and the German artillery fire became very intense. It was really frightening. We were going to get up and move but something made us stop . . . We heard the tanks come up. The first one hit a land mine and blew up. The second one followed and so did a third. The tank crews were running around crazily because they didn't know where they were. One came running right at us and, like an idiot, I yelled: 'Halt.' Of course, if he had been a German, I would probably still be over there in Italy. But, as it turned out, he was more frightened than me. He turned around and ran back the other way."

A short distance behind the front line, the road next to Klaus Huebner's temporary aid station was now clogged with vehicles. "The tanks are slowly rumbling over the road at twenty-yard intervals," he writes, "and the supply jeeps weave back and forth between them. Foot troops can no longer use the road, it is so crowded with vehicles." At 5 P.M. the traffic on the road ground to a halt. "The Germans must have been waiting for this moment," writes Huebner. "The Germans' artillery, which has been silent all day, has now opened up with everything at its command. One shell falls directly into the open turret of a tank, and the vehicle explodes in flames. All occupants are killed. Tank after tank is disabled; they are jammed too close in formation to dodge the incoming shells. A passing jeep receives a direct hit and disintegrates in a cloud of smoke and dust. Whining shrapnel fills the air, and chunks of hot metal land in my gully. We are swamped with casualties occurring directly in front of us. Wounded jump out of burning vehicles and run to us. Others crawl along the road to reach us . . . I am really in a hot spot and have no business here. Where in the hell is my guide? . . . I can't sweat this murderous fire out much longer." Eventually the guide arrived. "He is not very helpful. The poor fellow is shell shocked, shakes all over, sobs, and is in a severe state of anxiety." But the guide managed to pull himself together enough to take Huebner to the forward command post. "At 1 A.M. I dig my slit trench and practically fall into it from sheer exhaustion. My first day of actual fighting lies behind me. I shall never forget it . . . Another session like yesterday, and I doubt if I shall last."

The American attack had been poorly coordinated, and an entire company cut off the previous day was now forced to surrender. Santa Maria Infante remained in German hands. Again, the inexperience of the soldiers and their commanders resulted in heavy losses. By the evening of the thirteenth, the men were also becoming exhausted. Colonel Fry, the commander of the 350th Regiment, writes how his staff kept going by taking the amphetamine Benzedrine. Fry hadn't slept since the night of 10 May and, he says, "had to call on a doctor to give me a hypodermic injection to keep me awake." His account is very different from the heroic narratives of the French and, to a lesser extent, the Poles, and he is very candid about two of his company commanders who "failed." "The only descriptive word I know is cowardice," he writes. "Instead of demonstrating the leadership for which he had been trained, he faked a sudden illness that upset the entire company staff. Ultimately, he went to the rear and reported himself to an aid station for imaginary injuries. Along with others he disappeared into the administrative limbo in the rear and was never heard from again. Unknown to me at the time a company commander in the second battalion had also failed miserably under that first violent introduction to combat."

The French had also suffered setbacks on the first day of the offensive, and Juin was determined to renew the attack the following day. The main thrust was to exploit the solitary success of the previous day by driving on from Monte Faito to Monte Maio, the heights of which commanded the southern part of the Liri valley. After a ferocious artillery bombardment, Juin's Moroccans moved forward and, bunker by bunker, drove back the Germans. As successive heights between Faito and Maio fell to the French, the brittle nature of the German defenses in this sector became apparent. Here alone there was no defense in depth and insufficient German troops to launch their trademark counterattacks. As the whole of the German line began to fall back, the summit of Maio was reached. Soon artillery observers were on the peak, directing fire on the retreating Germans. Meanwhile, a large tricolor measuring twelve-by-twenty-five feet was erected on the summit, from where it could be seen from ten miles around.

Down in the Garigliano valley, Jean Murat had received orders that the pillboxes that had held him up the previous day had to be cleared at all costs. Extra machine guns and rocket launchers were brought up. "All at once, all our arms open fire on the embrasures of the fortifications," writes Murat. "Long bursts are punctuated by the explosions of the rockets hitting the sides of the bunkers. The men take the opportunity to rush forward. The enemy is completely neutralized since the team advances without one shot . . . Knocked out, the enemy still doesn't react. The team is now on the bunker. The incident should now be over, but, contrary to our plans, the embrasures of the fortification are too narrow to allow the grenades to penetrate. The [leader of the team] just allows himself to shoot long bursts through embrasures of the fortification and then comes back toward us indicating that the pillbox is no longer occupied."

On 14 May, the previous day's rumors of the French successes in the mountains were confirmed. "The Gustav Line has been cracked," Murat writes. "The Germans are retreating. Castelforte has fallen . . . These bunkers which caused so many losses to the company are no longer occupied. The company gets the order to go back to Castelforte where our battalion, the most exhausted of the three, will get reinforcement, will reorganize and will rest for three days. The company hasn't yet taken in the victory. It is busy crossing the bunker zone which is riddled with mines. In single file, we follow a mule trail. A specialist proceeds to de-mine with an instrument, a kind of a frying pan which 'oinks' incessantly since the ground is so packed with spent shell fragments. My captain then took the decision to do without it. The man in front advanced very slowly then everyone put their feet in the footprints left by the person ahead. A deadly silence engulfs the operation." When it seemed that the company had passed the danger zone, the pace returned to normal. "We're less short of breath and can talk among ourselves," Murat continues. "On the way, we see a white flag flying from a hut. Around twenty Germans appear. We push past each other to see them. We take their arms and machine guns. This white flag which waves in front of us suddenly makes me realize the success of our troops and our success. The blood rushes to my head. I feel knots in my throat and my eyes fill with tears. An intense emotion comes over me. It's a cocktail of jubilation to be alive, pride to have won and to be part of an elite army, the happiness to see for the first time a German soldier surrender, pride and contentment to have been up to the task."

Once Maio had fallen, the French advanced all along their front and, instead of consolidating in the British way, kept pushing forward, refusing to allow the Germans time to recover. On 14 May, Juin unleashed his mountain troops, which included his Moroccan Goumier irregulars. Moving through the trackless mountains, they drove the French advance forward at an astonishing speed, leaving the entire right flank of the German forces in disarray. A letter found on the battlefield from a German officer to his wife gives some indication of what was being experienced by the retreating troops, now out in the open. "You can have no idea of the brutality and the horror of this retreat," he writes. "We aren't letting ourselves be killed, but the men are tired, for three days they've had nothing to eat . . . Our adversaries, the Free French and Moroccans, are incredibly good. My heart bleeds when I see my beautiful battalion, after five days: 150 men lost . . . the trail of destruction is long, three reconnaissance vehicles in pieces, my armored car and all the radio material—all have been destroyed by a French armored tank . . . Arms, food, paper, completely gone since 26 April . . . *auf Wiedersehen*, I hope in better times."

On the morning of 14 May the Americans found that the Germans facing them on the high ground around Santa Maria Infante had gone, having retreated in order to keep contact with their left flank, which was reeling from the French attacks. After that they pressed forward through the mountains and had only rear guards, mines, and booby traps to face. On their right flank were the Goumiers, and the Americans were instructed to wear adhesive tape on the backs of their helmets to avoid being mistaken for Germans if they ran into the North Africans during the night.

American machine gunner Len Dziabas was attached to a unit of Goumiers and recounts how when they reached Spigno, "All of a sudden we could hear firing and screaming coming from the village and we couldn't figure out what was going on. Someone said, 'I think they're raping those women.' One of the sergeants asked whether they should do something about it. The lieutenant replied, 'We are under their command, we must wait for their orders.' " The French nurse Solange Cuvillier supports this story, writing in her memoir: "Unfortunately, the rapes carried out by certain North African soldiers threw a veil over our triumphs. In Spigno . . . we heard the screams of women through the sounds of the war, which plunged us into despair. The French (military) Command, not pardoning these crimes, straightaway executed a certain number of the guilty. In this sector I had to evacuate a woman of about thirty in a straitjacket. A male nurse sat vigil over her while we wandered through the night searching for an Italian asylum that would admit her. This incident remains the only moment of shame throughout my war experience."

In military terms, the French had much to be proud of. Juin's audacious attack through the mountains had smashed the southwestern flank of the Gustav Line, and the speed of the subsequent attacks prevented the Germans from holding the Hitler Line in the coastal sector. It also made the German position in the Liri valley much more difficult. The British were aware of this, and late on 16 May, 8th Army commander Lieutenant General Leese ordered the 78th Division to cut Route 6 behind Cassino. At the same time the Polish Corps, which had taken such a battering on the opening day of the attack, was to try again at the dreaded monastery.

18

The Monastery

Ever since the failed attack on 12 May, a continuous artillery program had blasted away at the German positions in and around the monastery. The German artillery observer Kurt Langelüddecke vividly remembers the "pounding fire . . . We sat there for five days with incessant fire. Shell on shell—boom, boom, boom, boom—everything full of dust. Our contingent became always smaller and smaller." As the British, reinforced from 16 May by two Canadian divisions, made slow but significant progress in the valley below, increasing numbers of the monastery's defenders were moved down to try to stop the advance, and only about two hundred paratroopers remained in the monastery area by 17 May. Those few were now in dire straits. The hot sun made the smell of the dead intolerable, and those still alive took to wearing gas masks. The continual smoke shells fired at the monastery to prevent observation of the troops below added to the choking atmosphere. A German major in the monastery noted at the time, "Impossible to get wounded away . . . enveloped in a smokescreen. Great number of dead on the slopes—stench—no water—no sleep for three nights—amputations being carried out at battle headquarters . . ."

When the smoke cleared enough to allow a view of the Liri valley below, "What they saw boded nothing but evil," reported a paratroop officer. "An unbroken stream of Allied tanks and vehicles was flowing westward. Battery followed battery in endless array. It was a superb spectacle of material power, and for the first time the German private soldier caught a comprehensive glimpse of the immense material wealth of the Allies. How, they wondered, could anyone stand up to such odds? Very soon the British would close the gates in their rear, and here on the Cassino front Heidrich's Division was sitting in a trap."

Once the advance up the Liri valley was underway, the abbey could be bypassed or contained. If the fresh Polish assault was necessary, it was for psychological or political rather than strictly operational reasons. When they attacked on the evening of 16 May, they were surprised by how the defenders had thinned out. By morning, much of Colle Sant'Angelo had been captured by the Kresowa Division, and the next day the Carpathians moved again against Point 593 and the high ground behind the monastery, aiming to cut off the strong point and join up with British soldiers of the 78th Division down on Route 6. Heavily laden with extra ammunition, the Poles struggled up the slopes of 593 and engaged the German defenders with grenades and small-arms fire. Soon men became separated from their platoons and fought on using their own initiative. The position was taken, and then counterattacked, but by 11:30 A.M. most of the hill was in Polish hands. Still the diminishing number of German paratroopers fought on, counterattacking Sant'Angelo, where many positions changed hands several times. At one point the leading companies of the Poles found themselves cut off from their supplies and running out of ammunition. The German artillery and mortars that had escaped the attentions of Allied fighter-bombers continued to pour fire on to those exposed on the hillside and losses mounted again. "It was more than nerves could stand and mass hysteria began to grip the men," an eyewitness Polish account reads. "One soldier slowly gets to his feet and then sits down cross-legged, as though he were in the park. A shot rings out and he is killed. Others, cowering helplessly, begin to throw stones at the Germans. And then, incredibly, someone begins to sing the Polish national anthem: 'Poland will not surrender, not yet . . .' All the soldiers join in the chorus, on the summit of Colle Sant'Angelo, the mountain of death."

Behind the Polish lines, new units were frantically scraped together from drivers, cooks, and other noncombatants, and sent forward. At dusk, the contact was reestablished with the forward units, and the men advanced again, reoccupying the summit of the mountain, but at debilitating cost. To their left, the capture of 593 had been as far as the Carpathians could get, and the end of the day saw their progress blocked both toward the monastery and down to the Liri valley. One unit of the 6th Battalion forced its way toward the high ground on the other side of the gorge, only to be pinned down by "vicious crossfire from small arms and machine guns . . . We stayed where we were and sought the best cover we could find or contrive," reports Cadet-Officer Pihut. "We hung on grimly . . . [It] was something out of another world. We lived in a shifting murk of drifting smoke, heavy with the pestilential reek of death."

Both sides were now utterly exhausted. By the evening of 17 May, one German company was down to only three men fit to fight—one officer, one NCO, and a single soldier. At the same time, units of the British 4th Division had at last crossed Route 6 near the town and approached the southern slopes of Monastery Hill, while the 78th Division, having fought off numerous counterattacks, had cut the route further up the Liri valley. Monte Cassino, although still unconquered, was now almost surrounded. On the German right flank, Juin's mountain fighters were entering the Liri valley from the southwest, threatening to isolate the German forces still fighting hard against the British in the valley. Late on this day, the following conversation took place between Kesselring and his 10th Army commander, von Vietinghoff:

> Kesselring: ". . . I consider withdrawal to the Senger position necessary."
> Vietinghoff: "Then it will be necessary to begin the withdrawal north of the Liri. Tanks have broken through here . . ."
> Kesselring: "Then we have to give up Cassino."
> Vietinghoff: "Yes."

The order was passed forward, with the instruction that a bombing raid on Cassino station at midnight would be the signal to leave the monastery and the town. "The 1st Parachute Division did not dream of surrendering 'its' Monte Cassino," Kesselring wrote. "In order to maintain contact with the XIV Panzer Corps I had personally to order these last, recalcitrant as they were, to retire." In the monastery Kurt Langelüddecke received the radiogram confirming the order: "Cassino will be given up. Retreat on the Senger Riegel. Monte Cassino remained held. Long live the Führer."

"We intercepted [a] message in German," says Colonel Lakinski, artillery commander of the Polish Carpathian Division. "This time to the effect that the defenders were ordered to withdraw from the Abbey. I arranged a steady fire on all exit routes."

Only a very narrow corridor now remained open for the Germans as an escape route. A handful of paratroopers was ordered to stay behind as rear guards, and about a hundred left the monastery southward, clearly preferring to surrender to the British rather than the Poles. Kurt Langelüddecke, however, was determined to avoid capture: "I went to Captain Beyer, who was one of our Paratroopers, who had just earned a Knight's Cross." Beyer had been injured in the legs and was sheltering in St. Benedict's crypt. "He had alcohol there and said, 'Oh, this is so over for us. We can wait here until we end up being taken as prisoners of war. We have only a few people left anyway . . . I called them all back and told them not to shoot anymore. Makes no sense, you can't see anything anyway. It's the middle of the night. You know, Herr Langelüddecke, we're going to play cards and wait here for the Amis [Americans].' He was captain and I was captain," Langelüddecke continues. "We knew each other. 'Herr Beyer,' I said. 'Not me. I'm recently married—since November. I am not going into a prisoner-of-war camp.' " Langelüddecke turned to those around him, saying, "Men, I'm breaking through. I'm going back to the troop, home. I can't stay here. Who's coming with me?"

Twenty-eight men accompanied Langelüddecke. "After three or four days, we were over the mountain, so beautiful that Monte Cairo," says Langelüddecke. "Beneath us there was movement, the Amis. We somehow made it through. When we came back, we were twenty-four. Four fell, nobody was wounded. We finally arrived and we had our helmets on our rifles so our troops could recognize that we were Germans. Then the general spoke with me and we were in sunshine, sitting on the steps in a village. An officer from my own troop approached us—an older guy. He introduced himself to the general, and then he did the same with me. 'Are you crazy? You know me,' I said. 'Captain?' he asked. He hadn't recognized me. I had changed so much: pale, overtired, ripped uniform. I might as well have been a stranger to him."

The order to pull out was also received by paratrooper Robert Frettlöhr, still in his machine gun position near the castle, who then headed up toward the monastery. He reached a grotto near its base where other paratroopers were waiting for a pause in the shelling to dash around the corner of the monastery. When his turn came, he ran out with another man and almost at once there was a "big flash." Frettlöhr was hit and went down. After a few moments of unconsciousness, he woke up to find his leg "black and blue with the skin falling off" and swollen "like a big balloon." He then crawled the remaining couple of hundred yards to reach the safety of the monastery. His leg was bandaged in the first-aid post in St. Benedict's crypt. He was told, "That's it; you're not going back." When the last of the remaining paratroopers pulled out, Frettlöhr gave them a letter to send to his parents, telling them what had happened. He knew he was going to be a prisoner of war.

Werner Eggert had spent the first week of May in Cassino town in the large cave that had sheltered paratroopers during the carpet bombing back in March. "Our combat strength had melted away," he says. Early on 17 May, he heard a voice coming from loudspeakers that the British had set up in the town: "Paratroopers, your hour has come," went the message. "Leave the city, waving a white cloth, to the east!" "Each man had to operate on his own," says Eggert. "He had a map and should figure out how to make it out. Suddenly we were all awake, wide awake. Our boys, to a large extent aged between eighteen and twenty-five, packed their most necessary items while hits roared over the entire mountain. Starting at 7 P.M., they disappeared from our good old cave, one after the other. Surrounded by fifty or more burning candles, I sat like a chaplain in a solemnly decorated chapel. I waited. At about 10 P.M. somebody squeezed himself in and announced he was the last. All positions were vacated. He took his backpack, crawled through the side cave up to the road . . . and I was alone."

As quickly as he could, Eggert wired up a delayed-action fuse to blow up the cache of arms and explosives in the cave, then prepared himself for his escape. "Understanding that I was on my own from this point on, something started to tickle in me. First there was a kind of stubbornness not to give up now as one of the few who had made it through three months of Cassino. The other driving force was trivial: a certain curiosity whether I would make it. Not for people and native country, no, it was a very private thing." With a group of about ten people, Eggert stumbled out to Route 6. "Suddenly we got MG fire from ahead on the road," he says. "We pushed ourselves to the right into the ditch and squeezed through the remainders of a dried hedge on to a field. While we ran to the foot of the mountain, firing hissed over and beside us. And then we heard the voice of an Allied soldier who was following us. 'Stop! You won't go ahead!' The voice was not far behind me. I threw myself to the ground, got two rifle grenades out and threw them blindly behind me. They cracked twice and suddenly there was peace. I jumped up and reached the dirt road at the foot of the mountain with the others."

Eggert and three other men started to climb the steep terraces toward the monastery. Machine gun fire was flying over the entire slope. "As soon as the impacts in the stone walls came closer, we threw ourselves to the ground," Eggert continues. "One guy was hardly able to breathe and said he had to take a rest. The other two weren't wounded, but completely out of breath. I heard a rush coming closer, three impacts directly over us, then three others beside us, stone splitters. We continued to climb. Maybe I was too fast, so when I turned around I was alone. I took a rest. Somewhat further below I heard people moving along the slope. I reached a portion of the old road leading to the monastery and followed it up to the next zigzag curve. Somewhat higher I heard a few voices. In front of me, short-fire bursts from submachine guns were coming down from the cliff.

"The sky was completely clear. Whether we had moonlight or not, one could see easily a hundred meters ahead. On the top right the monastery ruin gleamed in the pale gray light. My watch showed ten minutes before midnight. I reached the saddle above the second cliff. The monastery seemed so close you could touch it." As Eggert paused to consider his best route, artillery shells started flying over his head into the valley behind the abbey. Then the shells started landing just in front of him. "I threw myself to the ground and collected every stone I was able to get my hands on. With the next series [of explosions], I was lying right in the middle of it. It seemed to me like a hand lofted me and dropped me again. Feverishly, I reached for a few more stones to put around my open grave. After I don't know how many shells, I could not bear it any more. I jumped up and rushed toward the monastery."

Eggert found the carrier path to the abbey as the shelling subsided. As he was getting his breath back, he "heard rattling metal and a few indistinct voices; five shadowy figures pushed themselves down the trampling path. They carried helmets, but I was not able to determine whether they were our comrades or from the other side. I waited about a quarter of an hour and when no others came up, I followed them. My legs were shaking. The path was hardly recognizable. From time to time distant MG fire came up from below. I reached a place where in former times there had been a small forest. The black trunks stood out in the gray vapor over the valley. In the middle of the path, and at the right and the left, twenty or thirty dead people lay scattered around. While I was climbing over them, shaking some and calling them in vain, I thought of the heavy lumps flying over me into the ravine a while ago."

Half an hour later Eggert reached a medical camp and at last he was safe, one of the few paratroopers to escape from the town or monastery. "I got rid of my gun and backpack and headed on the way to Roccasecca with two radio operators of the neighboring company," he says. "The dirt road went parallel to Via Casilina. The area plowed by shells soon changed into juicy green. Flowers, poppies, scattered everywhere, a mild morning breeze and no sound as far as you could hear, only our tired steps."

Early in the morning of 18 May, a tattered white flag was hoisted over what remained of the monastery of Monte Cassino. Polish artillery officer Colonel Lakinski spotted it from his observation post and contacted the Carpathian Division's brigade commander to give him the news. "At first he refused to believe the Germans had surrendered," says Lakinski. "When I had finally convinced him, I asked for a patrol to be sent to the Monastery with our national flag, but was told that the infantry were too exhausted. I then got in touch with our cavalry regiment . . . and bade them send somebody up to Monte Cassino."

At about 8 A.M., twenty-six-year-old Lt. Kazimierz Gurbiel of the 1st Squadron, 12th Podolski Lancers Regiment received an order to lead a patrol to the ruins. With twelve other men, he approached the monastery through the minefields. No shots were fired. At the foot of the hill Gurbiel left six men on guard with a machine gun and took the others on the steep climb to the monastery. "The stink of decay hung over the hill and the light breeze made it even more unbearable," Gurbiel reported. As they reached the mighty ruined walls at about 9:30 A.M., Sergeant Wadas climbed onto a comrade's shoulders and clambered into the abbey, where he was confronted by the beheaded statue of St. Benedict. At its foot a German soldier lay half buried in the rubble. The others were given the sign to enter the abbey, and Wadas ran to a half-opened door and shouted, "*Hände hoch, oder ich schiesse!*" After a while, with their hands up, the German paratroopers started to emerge, about seventeen in all, "in bandages and rags, unshaven, filthy," says Gurbiel. "When they noticed the Polish Eagles on the uniforms, they turned white with fear. I told them through Wadas not to be afraid. Then one of my lancers said, 'Lieutenant, here is a hole.' " Gurbiel went down some steps and found himself in St. Benedict's crypt. "The Germans organized here a small field hospital," says Gurbiel. "What I saw—in the light of two wax candles—was macabre! Near the altar—among the boxes filled with corpses, on golden chasubles—three severely wounded young para-chutists were lying. Almost boys . . . Their comrades left them bread, water, and tinned food. Sacks and rucksacks were filled with corpses or remnants of corpses of the German soldiers who could not be buried during the fight-ing. There was an intense stench from decaying bodies. The wounded para-chutists were looking at the Poles with fear in their eyes and uncertainty about their fate."

One of the three wounded men was Robert Frettlöhr. "It was ten o'clock in the morning when the Poles came into the monastery," he says. "I don't know what we were expecting—a grenade to be tossed in, maybe." Gurbiel quickly reassured the three men. "I said, through my [German-speaking] Silesian, 'Don't worry, boys, nothing will happen to you.' " Gurbiel quickly left the crypt to be in the fresher air and sent a soldier for stretcher bearers in order to remove the three men.

No one had been able to find a Polish flag, but at 9:50 A.M., Gurbiel stuck up a branch displaying a 12th Podolski Lancers Regiment pennant hastily cobbled together from parts of a Red Cross flag and a blue handkerchief. "After all that fighting, all those months," he says, "the monastery was cap-tured without a shot being fired." Shortly afterward, Section Leader Czech played the *Krakow Hejnal,* a medieval Polish military signal, on the bugle. Section Leader Choma recalled the moment: "There was a lump in my throat as, through the echo of the cannon's roar, the notes of the *Hejnal* rang out from the abbey . . . These soldiers, hardened by numerous battles, only too well acquainted with the shocking wastefulness of death on the slopes of Monte Cassino, cried like children, as, after years of wandering, they heard not from the radio, but from the previously invincible German fortress, the voice of Poland, the melody of the *Hejnal.*"

The Battle of Monte Cassino was at an end.

―――――――

That morning, messages flashed around the Allied armies telling of the cap-ture of the monastery as continued fighting drove the German rear guards from their last positions on the Cassino Massif. Brick Lorimer, whose 19th Armoured Regiment was one of the few New Zealand units still operating in the Liri valley, remembers the message from his commanding officer to New

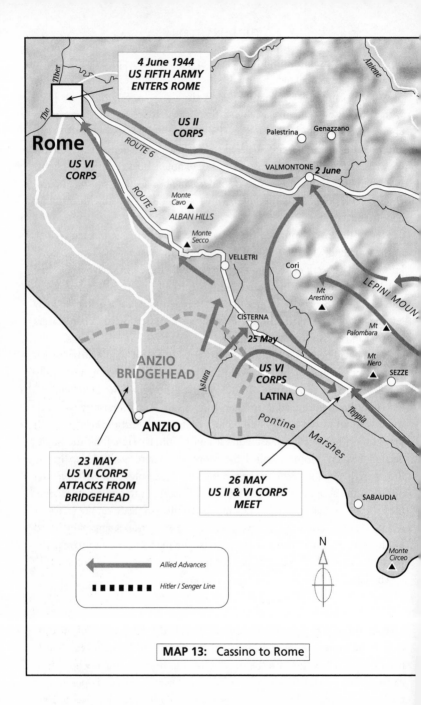

4 June 1944
US FIFTH ARMY ENTERS ROME

Palestrina Genazzano

US II CORPS

Rome

US VI CORPS

ROUTE 6

VALMONTONE **2 June**

ROUTE 7

Monte Cavo ▲
ALBAN HILLS

Monte Secco ▲

VELLETRI

Cori

LEPINI MOUN...

Mt Arestino ▲

CISTERNA

25 May

Mt Palombara ▲

ANZIO BRIDGEHEAD

Astura

US VI CORPS

LATINA

Mt Nero ▲ SEZZE

Teppia

ANZIO

Pontine Marshes

23 MAY
US VI CORPS ATTACKS FROM BRIDGEHEAD

26 MAY
US II & VI CORPS MEET

SABAUDIA

N

Monte Circeo ▲

Allied Advances

Hitler / Senger Line

MAP 13: Cassino to Rome

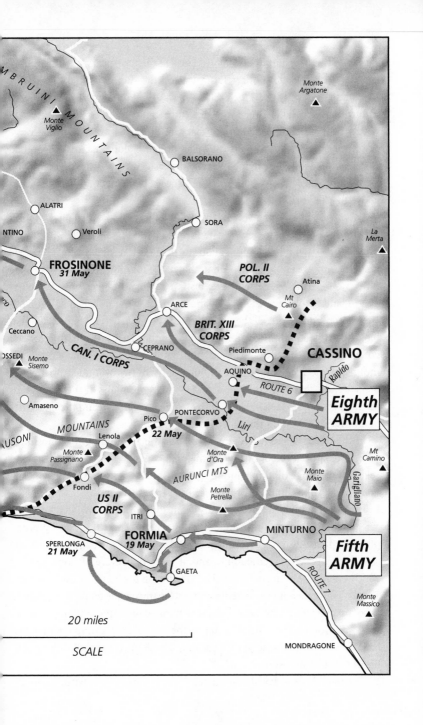

Zealand HQ: "Cassino in our hands. Poles in the monastery. Regiment in at the kill." Polish Cadet-Officer Pihut was on the slopes of Phantom Ridge: "We hung on grimly until the exciting news arrived that the Monastery was in our hands. I shall never forget the pure joy of that moment. We could hardly believe that at long last our task was done. We were all on the verge of complete nervous and physical collapse." For Colonel Lakinski, who had first seen the white flag flying over the monastery, "it was the most moving sight of the whole campaign to see the Lancers' pennant stirring in the wind above the silent ruins."

Soon the abbey was overrun by senior officers and journalists. Robert Frettlöhr was waiting to be evacuated when he was approached by an American reporter "who knew more about us than we knew about ourselves. He knew all our officers. We had been in that battle for months on end. We were filthy, we were full of lice. We were unshaven. We must have looked a hell of a sight, and he came in there with an American white trenchcoat, immaculately clean, and he put all these questions to us. Well, I could have killed that bloke; he rubbed salt into the wounds. What they have and what we haven't got and all this, that and the other." In the afternoon he was taken down the mountain and picked up by an ambulance. With two wounded British soldiers, he was then driven to an American field hospital. On the way, he remembers being amazed by the wealth of vehicles and men and the huge piles of ammunition behind the Allied lines.

In the town, where British guardsmen had been holding their positions while the battle raged about them, the men could at last leave their squalid cellars and emerge blinking into the glorious sunshine. Small groups of Germans were still coming down the hill to surrender, and patrols from the British 4th Division entered the city from the south. "By midday," reports a regimental history, "the Company found its position overrun by press-photographers, war correspondents and a whole crowd of enthusiastic sightseers who wandered happily, and, it seemed, irreverently, over ground which only a few hours before had been firmly in the hands of the Germans. To the Guardsmen it was incredible that so many people could be interested in so disagreeable a place; the 'swanners' thinned out rapidly after two pressmen had trodden on a mine. Later in the day when S Company marched back down the Mad Mile in unaccustomed daylight, it left the stinking rubble of Cassino almost deserted."

The next day the Polish commander Anders visited the battle scene together with his senior officers. On his instruction, a Polish flag and a Union Jack were hoisted atop the ruins of the monastery. "The battlefield presented a dreary sight," he wrote. "There were enormous dumps of unused ammunition and here and there heaps of landmines. Corpses of Polish and German soldiers, sometimes entangled in a deathly embrace, lay everywhere, and the air was full of the stench of rotting bodies. There were overturned tanks with broken caterpillars and others standing as if ready for an attack, with their guns still pointing toward the monastery. The slopes of the hills, particularly where the fire had been less intense, were covered with poppies in incredible number, their red flowers weirdly appropriate to the scene . . . Crater after crater pitted the sides of the hills, and scattered over them were fragments of uniforms and tin helmets, Tommy guns, Spandaus, Schmeissers and hand grenades. Of the monastery itself there remained only an enormous heap of ruins and rubble, with here and there some broken columns. Only the western wall, over which the two flags flew, was still standing. A cracked church bell lay on the ground next to an unexploded shell of the heaviest caliber, and on shattered walls and ceilings fragments of paintings and frescoes could be seen. Priceless works of art, sculpture, pictures, and books lay in the dust and broken plaster." Colonel Lakinski describes how, inside the monastery, they found the results of their shelling in the form of smashed and mutilated German corpses and in one part of the ruins "they came across a long corridor lined with chests of huge drawers, normally used for the storing of liturgical clothes. When they pulled open the drawers, they saw that they had been stuffed with corpses."

Over the next two weeks the Allies pushed forward all along the front line, while German rear guards sought to delay the advance sufficiently to allow themselves to occupy the Hitler Line. On the Allies' left flank, the French moved forward so quickly that they had to wait for the British 8th Army on their right to catch up, much to Juin's fury. On 23 May, the Anzio breakout was launched as Canadian troops, after fierce fighting, pushed through the Hitler Line between Aquino and Pontecorvo.

The offensive at Anzio was successful but, in a controversial move, on 25 May, Gen. Mark Clark diverted men away from closing the trap on the retreating German 10th Army in order that his men could be the first to enter Rome. By this stage Clark's Anglophobia had reached neurotic proportions, and he was convinced that he was going to be tricked out of his prize, along with the resulting publicity and "credit" for his men of the 5th Army. He even said he would have his troops fire on the British 8th Army if they tried to get to Rome ahead of him. But the first Allied soldiers to reach the city were men of the US 88th Blue Devils Division on 4 June. The result was that Clark was able to make a triumphant entry on 5 June, and the German 10th Army escaped Alexander's trap and retreated in good order up the Italian peninsula. The Allied soldiers would learn to their disgust that they would have to fight the same soldiers again and again as they advanced northward.

On 5 June, BBC journalist Godfrey Talbot reached Rome. "Went in at dawn," he wrote in his diary that day. "Amazing scenes—mobbed and kissed and buried in flowers as we went in in my jeep. Thousands of Romans in Sunday best throng streets and squares and almost prevent us from moving. One time 12 on my jeep. Clapping, waving, cheering, crying . . . Lovely city—with streets and fine buildings and trees under moon. Warm and beautiful. Contrast with battle almost indecent. We dumb and silent with it."

For Clark, it was his moment of glory, and he had a large "Roma" sign taken down and shipped home as a memento of his triumph. Many others found it more difficult to believe that the victory had been worth the cost. Soon after its capture, Fusilier Frederick Beacham made a visit to Rome, which he describes as something of an anticlimax: "The city had not then got back to normal trading and apart from the odd restaurant, there was not much in the way of entertainment," he says. "At midday we, as a group, the remains of B Company, did have a walk around the Colosseum, but little else as I recall. So ended our trip to Rome for which so many men had died. There were to be many more engagements with a superb enemy for more than a year before the war finished and lots more Royal Fusiliers were destined to die. It's as well that no one knew who it was to be."

Walter Robson wrote to his wife, Margaret, soon after the fall of the monastery on 18 May: "Don't expect normal letters from me because I won't be normal for some time . . . The papers are no doubt crowing about us and our achievements, but we aren't. We're bitter, for we've had a hell of a time . . . Everybody is out on their feet and one bundle of nerves . . . none of us feel any elation."

The judgment of historians of the Italian campaign in general and the Cassino battles in particular has not been sympathetic. J. F. C. Fuller, in his

Second World War, called it "a campaign which for lack of strategic sense and tactical imagination is unique in military history." For Fuller, the blame lay most firmly on the architect of the attack on the so-called soft underbelly of Europe, Winston Churchill. John Ellis, in his superbly detailed account of the Cassino fighting (to which I am much indebted), called it a "hollow victory." Interviewed for a postwar film about the battles, Alexander's chief of staff, Gen. A. F. Harding, defended his boss, saying, "There were those people who thought the campaign should never have been started. There were others who thought that it should have been curtailed at a certain point in time. There were others who were anxious to take away various of the resources in terms of troops and matériel and so on. This led to uncertainty and misunderstanding at times, the withdrawal of resources at critical moments. And indecision. And all these things created a situation that added very greatly to the problems and difficulties of General Alexander in conducting the campaign."

But, with the exception of the successful deception plan at the beginning of the fourth battle, and the great achievements of the French Expeditionary Force, there is little positive to take from the conduct of the campaign by the Allied leaders. At Cassino the Allies had eventually triumphed as much as anything through sheer weight of men and material. By May the Allies had 2,000 tanks to Kesselring's 450. One German prisoner captured late that month, a hardened veteran, was asked by the young American guarding him, "If you're so tough, how come you're a prisoner and I'm guarding you?" The German described how he had been in charge of six 88mm guns against approaching American tanks. The Americans kept sending tanks down the road, and the Germans kept knocking them out. "Eventually," the German explained, "we ran out of ammunition and the Americans didn't run out of tanks."

Although it has been argued that the fighting in Italy kept elite German divisions—and brilliant German generals—away from the Normandy invasion that was launched the day after Clark's entry into Rome, it is hard to reconcile the appalling cost of this "diversion." After the fall of Rome, the Italian campaign limped on, rarely on the front pages, but always hard and bloody. Operation Anvil, the largely irrelevant invasion of southern France in August 1944, took the best divisions away from the 5th Army and put an end to Alexander's and Churchill's hopes of "turning right" once the Po valley had been reached, and heading for the Ljubljana Gap to reach Vienna before the Russians. Instead, the Allied armies would be held at the Gothic

Line, another series of mountain fortresses north of Florence, from August 1944 until April 1945.

————————

After the grudging German retreat from the monastery of Monte Cassino, the victors took possession of a field of battle that, after six months' fighting, was a vision of hell. For the Italians sheltering in their caves in the mountains, it would be many months before they could return to rebuild their town of Cassino, now a hideous mass grave where malaria and other diseases were rampant and half a million mines remained to be cleared. In the days and weeks after the final battle, thousands of Allied soldiers rumbled through the town along the hastily cleared Route 6. One was rifleman Alex Bowlby: "In the late afternoon we passed through the outskirts of Cassino. Tanks and carriers lay around like burnt tins on a rubbish heap. A row of black crosses, topped with coal-scuttle helmets, snatched our pity. The smell—the sour-sweet stench of rotting flesh—cut it short. Instinctively I realized I was smelling my own kind, and not animals. I understood what they must feel in a slaughterhouse. These dead were under the rubble. If we could have seen their bodies it would have helped. The unseen, unconsecrated dead assumed a most terrifying power. Their protest filled the truck. We avoided one another's eyes."

Surviving the Peace

The soldiers shrug, "C'est la guerre." That's all. Our senses and sympathies can't comprehend too much. They were numbed a long time ago, I suppose ... There's a great deal more than homes and cities for us to reconstruct.

—Walter Robson, October 1944

The rank stench of those bodies haunts me still,
And I remember things I'd best forget.

—Siegfried Sassoon

New Zealand artilleryman John Blythe was on a train back to his home town of Dunedin when it halted for a few minutes outside Burnham military camp. Looking out of the window, he saw "three small figures in battle-dress ... standing at the edge of the distant trees." Suddenly, one broke away, "long hair flying as she ran to meet one of our passengers galloping toward her. They met in the middle with such force they both reeled back before embracing to hold each other and remained locked together. The whole troop train to a man cheered and whistled." Later that night the train at last pulled into the familiar platform of Dunedin railway station. On spotting John Blythe, his mother and sisters rushed forward. They embraced, and, tripping over Blythe's kitbag, "nearly all fell on a huddle on the platform. But who cared?" On the way home in a taxi, a crowd of people cheered the returning hero. When he finally went to bed, he found it far too comfortable and spent his first night at home sleeping on the floor.

At the end of the war with Germany, engineer Matthew Salmon made a long train journey from northern Italy through Switzerland and France to the coast. He had not been home for three and a half years. "We arrived at Folkestone," he says, "and saw the white cliffs—it felt like a dream. There had been times when I thought I would never return home, but now I felt that God had been watching over me and keeping me safe." Yet another train journey took him to London Victoria. He remembers his pleasure at hearing everybody speaking his language. From Victoria he caught a bus to Dalston Junction in East London and, while waiting for another bus to take him home, one came along driven by his father. "I shouted to him but he obviously hadn't recognized me," says Salmon. "I suppose I had changed a lot during the years I had been away. I continued to attract his attention, and then all of a sudden his face lit up. He jumped down from the cab and ran around the bus to grab hold of me. There were tears in his eyes, and I don't know what the people on the bus thought, but we were beyond caring." Leaving his father, he made his way to his parents' house. "As I started to walk down the road that I had played in as a child everything seemed very small. I had memories of things being much bigger and the road being much longer. All the houses seemed very close together . . . I rang the bell and waited for the door to open. Suddenly there was my mother. I said, 'Got a room for a soldier?' I thought she was going to faint on me."

But for some of the survivors of Cassino, there was to be no homecoming. Following their occupation of the monastery of Monte Cassino, congratulations had poured in to the Polish headquarters from Leese, Clark, the newly promoted Field Marshal Alexander, the Polish authorities in London, the underground army in Poland, and the Italian royal family. On the walls of many towns in occupied Poland the inscription "Monte Cassino" started appearing. Anders was decorated by the British and the Americans and given command on the Adriatic front, with several British brigades under his control. An audience with the pope followed. But much of the rest of his account of the war records the progressive abandonment of the Polish cause by the Allies, his chapter headings giving a reliable feel: The Sin of Tehran . . . , The Battle of Warsaw . . . , A City Sacrificed . . . , Bad News From Yalta . . . , No V-Day for Poland . . . , The Homeless Million . . . , An Army Fades Away . . . , Old Comrades Cold-Shouldered. In his last chapter he gives the figures for the members of his corps who eventually accepted repatriation to Poland after the war: seven officers and 14,200 men out of

112,000. Of these, 8,700 had joined after the end of the war. Only 310 of those whom Anders had originally brought out from Russia returned at the end of the war to a Poland now firmly under Soviet control.

So the army made out of those forcibly removed from their homes in eastern Poland remained in exile. Many emigrated to Canada, Australia, or the United States, and still more made their homes in Britain. Józef Pankiewicz, who as a teenager had survived the mines of the Urals, ended up living in Colchester in Essex. "In 1946 I came to England," he says, "where I have remained, and, although I now visit Poland quite often, I regard England as my home. The International Red Cross found my family after the war. They were resettled in the west of Poland, which used to be Germany. My mother always wanted to go back to Lvov and never came to terms with living, as she called it, in Germany. She could never forget being hungry, and she always dried every bit of spare bread and insisted on having some warm clothes and food packed. She lived until she was ninety-one and, right to the end, always said she would be ready if the Russians came again. Who could blame her after all the hardships we endured? . . . I can never forget some of the horrors I have seen and hope my children and grandchildren never witness such things."

Even for those who returned to a hero's welcome in Britain, the United States, Canada, or New Zealand, the initial euphoria often gave way to difficulties in readjusting to civilian life. Matthew Salmon admits he struggled and began to drink heavily. "My mother did not like this lifestyle and, looking back, I know that I wasn't nice to know during this period," he says. "My mental outlook had been altered by the war, and I somehow thought the world owed me a living." Salmon refused to attend army reunions or Remembrance Day parades, preferring to shut it all out of his mind: "When I heard or saw items on the radio or television about events in the Second World War, I would go down the garden into my shed and cry."

Cartoonist Bill Mauldin, writing as the war was coming to an end, sought to reassure those at home in the United States who were concerned that the infantrymen would be returning as "social problems": "This feeling has been so strong in some places that veteran combat men are looked at askance by worried and peaceable citizens. That's a sad thing for a guy who was sent off to war with a blare of patriotic music, and it's really not necessary. There will be a few problems, undoubtedly . . . But the vast majority of combat men are going to be no problem at all." He goes on to appeal for "bosses who will give them a little time to adjust . . . friends and families who stay by them until they are the same guys who left years ago . . . it is very important that these people know and understand combat men." But later he contradicts himself, saying, "Perhaps he [the combat soldier] will change back again when he returns, but never completely." Furthermore, it was as difficult for those at home to "understand combat men" as it was for the returning soldiers to communicate their experiences to those who had not seen battle.

New Zealander Jack Cocker ended the war in Trieste. "It was a strange time for us. Once the war ended we were sort of at a loose end and didn't know quite how to handle it," he says. "I got into some trouble but luckily our company commander was a good bloke and he was understanding." On the way home he met a woman in Fremantle, Australia, with whom he had first hooked up on the way out. They married but, once home, he found it hard to "stabilize": "I was only twenty-one, but from the age of eighteen I'd seen more than most people see in a lifetime and a lot of it not very nice . . . I'd go out with a group of people my age and they were so bloody childish as far as I was concerned. They didn't have any idea of what we'd been through and you were on a different plane to them altogether. What they used to speak about was so frivolous that you'd think, Oh, it's not worth bothering about.

"After a fairly tumultuous couple of years my wife and I parted and I returned to the best place I could think of—the army. It was amazing the number of chaps from broken marriages who were there. I think it was a sign of the times: we were still very young and what we'd been through didn't fit us for civilian life. Let alone having to cope with all the trauma of married life. Our respective fuses were somewhat short and I think we missed the male company . . . There were so many of us that couldn't make it go away properly and so we went back to Momma. That's what it seemed like."

Fellow New Zealander Brick Lorimer had a similar experience on returning home: "We were completely lost," he says. "We'd been out of circulation for so many years that we didn't have anything in common with the civilians. We couldn't communicate at all. All we had known was war service for some years. We didn't have any conversation. It was a difficult time and the result was many broken marriages and homes. We troops tended to congregate. I used to meet up with my fellas and naturally we spent a fair amount of time in the different bars. It took me a long time to settle down. I couldn't just drop back into civilian life very easily. I don't think I did for years. I've come out of it, of course—I've been very fortunate. But some fellas never did. Their whole life had gone, they couldn't pick up the threads again at all. You cannot begin to communicate to your nearest and dearest what you've seen and what you've been through."

Even the most articulate of those who had seen war close up were often forced to admit that ultimately the horror was impossible to communicate. "These articles are in no way adequate descriptions of the indescribable misery of war," the brilliant US war correspondent Martha Gellhorn wrote in an introduction to a collection of her pieces. "War was always worse than I knew how to say—always."

There were other reasons, too, why what had happened could not, or should not, be told to those at home. Essex Regiment infantryman Ken Bond returned to Cassino soon after the end of the fighting there, "to look for our own casualties. No one knew who had died, who had been taken prisoner. No one knew what had happened to the chappies what disappeared. We had to draw lots for it. I was lucky, or unlucky as you want to call it, and I was in the party that went back from the battalion and we went up beyond the castle. I personally found two chappies from our own lot. They were just lying there all those months after, among many more, including Germans obviously. There were wires everywhere. It was very grisly—maggots and flies going in and out of the bodies. I took dog tags off these two, and brought them back to the company. One was a Bristolian, the other from more up the country in Gloucestershire. I wrote to their mothers, and neither of them had heard a word about what had happened to their sons until I wrote. And they were most, most grateful." When Bond's address was published with his marriage notice shortly after the end of the war, one of the mothers came around to ask him what he could tell her about her son. Bond was unwilling and unable to tell her the truth of what he'd found on the hillside: "that he'd had his head blown off. You couldn't say that, could you?"

Years spent in the army, particularly for those who fought in the abattoir of Cassino, altered men in ways that they could not, and did not want to communicate to their families at home. On a trivial level, men in the army had used language that most would never countenance at home. Then there were the episodes of heavy drinking, whoring, and looting that were facts of life for some in Italy. All this was part of a general suppression of morals and deadening of sensibilities. In an interesting coda to his account of the action at Santa Maria Infante, Blue Devil radio operator Richard Barrows wrote to me saying: "One thing I did not put in, and I hesitate to do right now, shows how callous people in war can become. Right on the edge of Minturno and Santa Maria Infante was a little bridge to cover a small brook. On the Minturno side, right by the little bridge, was part of the body of a dead German who had been run over many times by vehicles. It was a gruesome sight but, being in combat, we chose to make jokes instead of showing our true feelings, including compassion for human beings. But that is the very nature of combat."

We have seen how, to the dismay of the army authorities, many men were reluctant to use their weapons and few had the necessary "hate" to kill face-to-face. This was, of course, the greatest moral somersault the men were required to undertake. Back in a civilian world where killing was once again murder and a cardinal sin, there was inevitable confusion, regret, and self-disgust. For Fusilier Frederick Beacham, the nightmare of being pinned down for two days in a shallow ditch and then seeing friends with fatal battlefield injuries will always stay with him. Even worse for him, though, was an incident two days later when, having heard that a friend in England had been killed, he "pumped a whole magazine into the prone body of a German soldier" before downing three more as they ran for safety. At the time he was triumphant, cutting notches into the butt of his Bren gun, but over the following sixty years the incident has caused him indescribable anguish. The American Clare Cunningham says that, when killing someone, there were no regrets as "you're kind of angry and it made up for them killing our guys. But afterward it gets working on you. For years I'd wake up at night dreaming of those things." New Zealander Alf Voss, who was decorated at Cassino and went on to have a distinguished army career, told the story of a visit he made to an ex-comrade called Bill, who saved his life in Italy by bayoneting a German who was on the point of shooting Voss: "It took me eighteen years to catch up with Bill. I was distressed to find that he had not got over the fact that he had killed someone by bayoneting him at close quarters. He had not understood that he had saved my life, and he also had this idea that he had somehow let the show down . . . After talking about the incident, his wife told me that he felt a lot better about his life."

Few at home were able, or wanted, to deal with this issue. One Canadian returning serviceman, wounded three times, got off the boat to find "nice, smiling Red Cross girls . . . They give us a little bag and it had a couple of chocolate bars in it and a comic book. We had gone overseas not much more than children but we were coming back, sure, let's face it, as killers. And they were still treating us as children. Candy and comic books."

———————

In April 1945, US ordnance officer Tom Kindre found himself on a boat together with men being sent home. In his diary, he notes, "There is no wild exuberance, strangely enough, on the part of these officers and men on their way home. They are for the most part quiet, tired, perhaps a bit dazed at the tremendous thought of going home . . . There is no loud talk, no boasting of the 'First thing I'm going to do when I hit New York.' They talk mostly of the ship, the voyage and their battle experiences, which they review with a sense of awe at their own luck in coming through everything unscathed or at least undamaged." British novelist Evelyn Waugh reported similar sentiments, writing in his diary on 31 March 1945: "Everyone expects the end within a few weeks but without elation." Five days later he wrote: "No exhilaration anywhere at the end of the war."

Each veteran has his own relationship with his war experiences depending on a huge range of factors. Nevertheless, it is striking that for most Italian campaign veterans the personal horrors of what they experienced overwhelms any pride they might have in what they achieved at Cassino or, indeed, in the wider war. In some cases there was pride in their own unit, but hardly any in being on the right side in a "good war." Perhaps this was taken as read; maybe it is down to the natural modesty of this generation. In the case of Cassino, it must have something to do with the general feeling that there were no real victors in these bloody and Pyrrhic battles.

Of the hundreds of people who have contributed to this book, all but two viewed the fighting at Cassino as the most intense moments of the war and, indeed, of their lives. A small number recall this intensity with an almost fond nostalgia. They tend to be the volunteers, the officers, those who remained in the army after the war was over. The majority remember Cassino with anger, disgust, and grief. Much of this is pity for many comrades who died or were maimed, but it's evidently also for themselves: for the years in the army lost that should have been spent with wives and young children; for the things they saw and did that no one should have been asked to see and do.

Strikingly, nearly all of the octogenarians interviewed for this book were wounded at some point during their service. Truly, for the frontline infantryman, the only way home was through serious injury, mental breakdown, or death. Bill Hartung, who fought in the disastrous US 36th Division Rapido crossing, says, "I also managed to survive Anzio and Rome, the invasion of southern France, and the Battle of the Bulge, then the war got the best of me." During the Ardennes Offensive, he says "I folded up . . . I still have problems today and have a hundred percent service-connected disability. The nightmares make it seem like it all happened yesterday, not sixty years ago." Fusilier Frederick Beacham has also suffered sixty years of nightmares connected to his wartime service. "I became so psychologically damaged by fear of shells in particular," he says. "I shouldn't be here, don't know if I'm still here really, or if it's all a bad dream."

The American medic Robert Koloski was wounded at Cassino when he was hit by a mortar fragment. A practicing Catholic as a young man, "After the war," he says, "I decided that Christianity had nothing going for it as far as I was concerned. Let's face it, the Germans had a belt buckle with *Gott Mit Uns* on it, so if He was with them, and also with us, what the heck was going on? I won't say I was irreligious in any sense during the war but certainly afterward. I mean, it just doesn't make sense."

For many there were simpler, inescapable, and irreversible changes to their lives. Clare Cunningham, who lost a leg on Monte Castellone, tells of the screaming and crying on the boat home with other amputees: "One guy on the ship from Naples to Africa said, 'I don't want to go home this way. Keep me here.' He just kept saying that over and over. It was kind of demoralizing to the rest of us." Both Cunningham and Frank Sellwood, who lost a leg during the building of the Amazon bridge, have coped with their losses with impressive bravery, going on to have families and fulfilling careers. Others, understandably, fared less well. "Some of them just never got over it," says Cunningham. "They were still mad at the army or the Germans. Drinking themselves to death, that was rather common, you know."

At least at the end of the Second World War, the American veterans returned as victors and into a booming postwar economy. In his letters home, artilleryman Ivar Awes often discussed the future and anticipated that he would have difficulties returning to civilian life. In the event, thanks to the GI Bill, which provided funds for all returning US soldiers to further their education, he went to college and then on to a successful career in insurance.

"When I first got back, it's funny, but I never thought about it much," he says. "I just blanked it out, tucked it away." But driving past a cemetery one day nearly sixty years after the end of the war, he found himself remembering Tony Yablonski: "He was an eighteen-year-old newly drafted replacement who died as I was applying a tourniquet close to the shoulder of an arm that was hanging on by a shred of tissue. I will never forget his plea that I not leave him just before he died. I began to sob, which really alarmed [my wife] Lois." Soon afterward he was diagnosed with post-traumatic stress disorder (PTSD). A leaflet published by the US Veterans' Association explains why so many men who had successfully buried their wartime traumas later encountered problems: "Many [initially] had disturbing memories or nightmares, difficulty with work pressure or close relationships, and problems with anger or nervousness, but few sought treatment for their symptoms or discussed the emotional effects of their wartime experiences . . . But as they grew older, and went through changes in the pattern of their lives—retirement, the death of spouse or friends, deteriorating health, and declining physical vigor—many experienced more difficulty with war memories or stress reactions and some had enough trouble to be considered a 'delayed onset' of PTSD symptoms, sometimes with other disorders like depression and alcohol abuse."

"In the summer 2002," says Awes, "the kids said to me, 'Dad, you are drinking an awful lot.' They were measuring off the bottles. It seemed like I could handle it then I discovered I was just drinking an awful lot and getting meaner than hell." After talking to a psychiatrist, who made the diagnosis of PTSD, Awes took medication and entered therapy with a group of Second World War veterans, most of whom had been bomber pilots. "I will probably be on happy pills for the rest of my days," says Awes. "Coverage of the [Iraq war] in the spring of 2003 has been very hard on me," Awes adds, "as well as the other seven octogenarians in my group therapy. The therapist told us to watch the Disney Channel instead."

Jean Murat remained in the French army, ultimately being promoted to general. Ten months after Cassino, of the seventeen young officers who graduated with him from the military academy and joined the 4RTT, he was the only one left. "I still now feel an immense pride," he says, "to have participated in this campaign which, perhaps because of the lack of strategic results, remains unknown, but which allowed the French army to reclaim its former reputation and permitted France to take back its place among its allies." In France itself, few are aware of the exploits of the FEC. A recent scholarly book on the subject has as its subtitle *Les victoires oubliées de la France*.

For the Gurkha troops, there was a choice of whether to join the Indian army, the Pakistani, or remain with the British. Of those who stayed, many were subsequently sent to Malaya. Kharkabahadur Thapa of the 1/2nd Gurkhas did not get home until 1956. In gratitude to the Indian troops who had fought so hard in the Mediterranean, there was a short-lived scheme that financed trips to England. A ballot was arranged, and the "lucky" few were taken on a curious itinerary that started with Whipsnade Zoo and included the Ford Motor Works, ice hockey, and football. Once consulted, Indian participants successfully pressed for the inclusion of three days in Scotland. A favorite refrain of the Indian soldiers who fought in the Cassino battles was:

> *Oh, bury me at Cassino*
> *My duty to England is done.*
> *And when you get back to Blighty,*
> *And you are drinking your whisky and rum,*
> *Remember that old Indian soldier,*
> *When the war that he fought has been won!*

Among the Germans interviewed for this book, there is a divergence of opinion about the war. Werner Eggert, who emigrated to Australia in 1951, ends one e-mail: "War: today more than ever—stupid, dirty, dreadful." Directly after the war, he says, he had six months of nightmares, but then came out of it: "I coped astonishingly well with these moments. Years later, however, I had to ask myself under which star all these strains and blood sacrifices had stood, all these indescribable events that brought our country to the eternal demise. As long as I live, I must live with the insight to have been fooled together with a lot of other people."

At the end of the war, Joseph Klein was, he says, "in complete shock. It took a quarter of a year to come out of this lethargy. The world broke down for me. After this, in Egypt, comrades pulled me slowly out of it, so I was my old self again. It wasn't National Socialism for which I cried a tear . . . I missed the *Volksbewusstsein*—that one stands up for the other man." Most of his friends, Klein says, don't want to hear about the war. Klein himself now runs the Monte Cassino Veterans' Association in Germany. "I want to say that it was a fortunate thing," he insists. "Because of Hitler, Europe did not become communist."

Artillery observer Kurt Langelüddecke was taken prisoner by the Americans three days after the end of the war in Europe. "The Amis with fifty tanks corralled us," he says. "The tanks surrounding us were our camp. They also taped a white band around us. And for three weeks they didn't give us anything to eat. I don't want to exaggerate, but there were certainly five hundred of us German officers. And what grows in May? Grass and such things. So we ate that. We had a couple of horses and we slaughtered them—the Americans had nothing against that. But the Amis also wanted to protect us from the Czechs because they expected that if we fled, the Czechs would have really slaughtered us. The Amis knew that, and let all of us officers keep our pistols. We were five hundred prisoners with pistols. We didn't shoot an Ami and we didn't shoot a Czech. There was a brook for water, and we got dysentery from that. But you can go hungry for a long time."

After three weeks, the Americans erected a few tents and started screening the German officers. "We were checked to make sure we weren't SS," says Langelüddecke. "Then they looked through our things; we each had a suitcase or so. Mostly they spoke English but there were German Jews in uniform—you could tell by their German. They asked questions and the doctor checked us and took our fingerprints and with this certificate we were let go. In my suitcase there was a copy of *Mein Kampf* that everyone got from the marriage office when you got married. A friendly Ami told me to open my case so he could check it, and he gave me a strange look when he saw this book with the famous picture of Adolf on the cover. I thought, Now it's settled, but it turned out OK." Like millions of Germans who had lived in East Prussia, Langelüddecke and his wife now had no home. They survived because of Langelüddecke's stonecarving skill, much in demand by the Russians for the string of memorials to the Red Army being erected in East Germany.

Robert Frettlöhr also found himself an exile from his home. Having been taken prisoner in the monastery by Kazimierz Gurbiel, he was patched up and sailed to the United States, where he worked while a prisoner of war as a lumberjack. At the end of the war he was shipped back to Europe, having been told he would be repatriated. But the temptation to use the cheap labor that the prisoners offered was too much for the British, who set him to work as an electrician under POW status. He subsequently visited his hometown of Duisburg, by then "a pile of stones," but returned to England, married, and settled in North Yorkshire.

In March 1983 a television program broadcast in West Germany alleged that the Polish patrol that captured the monastery had murdered three wounded German paratroopers. The accusation caused a scandal. Two years later, Frettlöhr heard of it and contacted a Polish veterans' association in Huddersfield, near where he lived, and made a sworn statement denying the allegations. From this, he made contact with Gurbiel, who had lost a leg fighting on the Adriatic coast three months after Cassino, and later married and settled in Glasgow, before finally returning to Poland. A correspondence and friendship thus began. Frettlöhr wrote: "My dear Kazimierz: during sleepless nights my thoughts turn often to Monte Cassino . . . we took part in the greatest battle of the last war in which many young Germans and Poles lost their lives. And we survived. Why this senseless war? My heart aches when I think of those boys killed there, at Monte Cassino. In the cause of what? The generals, far from the field of the battle, were giving their orders and we had to obey and die . . . let it never be again that Germans and Poles shoot at each other."

Gurbiel replied: "Dear Robert, I thank you from my heart for your defense of the honor and dignity of the soldiers from my patrol, unjustifiably accused of committing a multiple murder . . . Myself, although I ended the war mutilated, I do not feel hatred to Germans. This feeling is foreign to me because it is impossible to build the future on hate. Therefore I propose to you a soldierly friendship, whose foundations will be deeper than the foundations of the monastery at Monte Cassino. They will be deeper because they are in the heart of man."

On 18 May 1989, exactly forty-five years after their first encounter, the two men met again at Monte Cassino as part of a commemoration. Wreaths were laid at the German and Polish cemeteries, and Frettlöhr and Gurbiel promised to meet again five years later. It was not to be, as Gurbiel died in 1992. The funeral in Przemysl, Poland, was modest: there was no orchestra, no farewell salvo. Such was the departure of the commanding officer whose men were the first Allied soldiers to enter the monastery of Monte Cassino.

The abbot Gregorio Diamare returned to Cassino in 1944, but died the next year of the malaria that was still rife. Both the monastery and the town were rebuilt in the years after the war. There is now not a single building in the town that predates the carpet bombing of 15 March 1944. Tony Pittaccio, who had played in the streets and around the castle as a boy, returned three years after the end of the war and, he says, "It was not the elegant, friendly town we once knew. I felt like a complete foreigner."

Visiting Cassino now, it is hard to equate its bustling modernity with the ghastly events of sixty years ago. Cars belch out their smoke, horns blare, and well-dressed young Italians shop in the main streets. Above the town towers the monastery, its sheer prominence and height above the valley startling, however many photographs one has seen. It still holds the menace that so many of those who fought there described: some sort of evil, brooding presence, seeming to watch your every move. Certainly, returning veterans feel this. Cyril Harte, whose Grenadier Guards battalion held the ruins of the town in April 1944, revisited fifty years later: "Of course it wasn't the Cassino I knew and left behind in 1944. Instead of one large heap of rubble, a new town had been built. Then that heartbreak mountain, which had cost the lives of so many infantrymen of all nations, came into view. Just for a moment, my heart stopped beating. That hasn't changed. It still loomed forbiddingly and I chilled at the thought of the enemy who looked down on us."

The veterans, along with the families of the deceased, make frequent pilgrimages to Cassino. Another is planned for the sixtieth anniversary in May 2004. The dwindling number of survivors don't go to see the modern town, of course. Rather, they are there to pay their respects at the military cemeteries that crowd around its edges. For, at Cassino, the dead far outnumber the living.

The most prominent is the Polish cemetery, built into the hillside between Point 445 and the monastery, where men from many nations laid down their lives in attacks on the almost impregnable positions. Of all the cemeteries, this is the grandest, the most deliberately symbolic. A visitor here will, at any time around the key date of 18 May, encounter busloads of visitors, almost all far too young to have been participants, accompanied by priests in full vestments and guitarists singing Polish songs. Monte Cassino has been for a long time a rallying point for and symbol of Polish nationalism and freedom from external oppressors, be they Nazi or Soviet. But the sacrifice made in the name of that symbolism was high: the Poles suffered nearly 4,000 casualties, nearly 50 percent of their force, in bloody attacks, according to John Ellis, "devoid of any real strategic rationale."

Behind it, up the now thickly wooded slope, is Point 593, Monte Calvary.

Atop this summit, which commands a panoramic view over the Liri valley, there is a stone monument topped with a cross. On it is written:

> *We Polish soldiers*
> *For our freedom and yours*
> *Have given our souls to God*
> *Our bodies to the soil of Italy*
> *And our hearts to Poland.*

This epitomizes the sadness of Cassino: men fighting for a country that was already lost to them, in attacks that should never have been ordered in the first place but were nevertheless carried out with an enthusiasm born of desperation and hatred.

The German cemetery, wrapped around a hill above the village of Caira, is less grand, but much larger, containing over twenty thousand graves. Small, white stone crosses circle the steep slope on terraces. The dead are buried three to a grave. There are many stones inscribed with no more than *Ein Deutscher Soldat* repeated three times. The high number of unidentified Germans was due in part to the Allied soldiers' habit of "souveniring" leather identity tags from dead German troops.

Here, nationhood cannot be invoked to excuse or justify the slaughter, and God is represented by a stark iron cross, which stands flanked by tall, gloomy firs. The entrance hall contains a metal sculpture of two figures, clearly parents. The father stands upright, staring into the middle distance, his hand resting on the shoulder of the mother who is seated, stooped and shattered by grief.

Nearest to the town is the British Commonwealth cemetery, down a small scruffy road overlooked by the monastery. It is all clean white stone and neat rows of graves: British, New Zealanders, and Canadians at the front; the Indians and Gurkhas at the back. It is immaculately maintained, and most gravestones have the dead man's regimental badge meticulously carved at the top. Uniquely for Cassino, at the bottom of many of the graves, half-hidden by the brightly colored flowers, appear epitaphs which betray the names of those left behind: "A dear husband and son, / Your life for your country / You nobly gave—Wife Edith and baby Graham"; "His courage and devotion / Held ever in fond memory / by Suze and Roxie Anne"; "Darling husband of Ruth / Daddy of Heather."

Reading these, one understands that the regimental symbols so carefully carved, the wider war, the heroic purpose of it all, meant nothing compared to the personal loss, the individual catastrophe that each grave represents. In August 1944, Walter Robson received a letter from the young wife of a friend in his unit who had been killed. "I am being brave," she wrote. "No one ever broke their hearts with less fuss before. You wouldn't guess my world was in ruins when I discuss the good war news with people. You would never think that as far as I am concerned it can go on for ever and ever now."

On 20 July 1944, Barbara Schick, by then nine years old, received a letter from a padre who had served with her father, the US 88th Division mess sergeant Arthur Schick, killed on 12 May:

Dear Barbara

I am anxious to get to New York and to meet the daughter of my very good friend, your "Dad." Many times I stopped by the kitchen that he ran and had coffee and doughnuts or cookies with him . . . I have missed those stop-ins since he is no longer with us. You see some of us just won't return from this war and your "Dad" is one of those who won't return . . . The men and officers miss him a lot.

Now we want you to be a brave "little girl" and know that your "Dad" did not suffer any at all, and that he wants you to carry on just as if he were going to be there to go with you all of the way . . . He told me quite a lot about you and showed me your pictures so I feel like I know you. Just remember that he wants you to be a brave girl.

Read the 23rd Psalm.

Sincerely
Day B. Werts
Regimental Chaplain

Perhaps, though, the greatest sympathy should be for the dead fathers, the "Poor devils, well out of it," those whose worst fear was leaving behind their loved ones, the people who needed them.

ACKNOWLEDGMENTS

My first and greatest debt of gratitude is to the veterans who have allowed me to talk to them and use the interviews in this book. I am also grateful to all those with whom I have been in touch via letter, phone, or e-mail and those who sent me letters, photos, diaries, and unpublished memoirs. It has, of course, been impossible to include in the final version of this book more than a tiny fraction of the material gathered, but all has been useful in building a picture of the events in Italy in early 1944. I am also particularly grateful to Louise Osborne, Jane Martens, Katja Elias, and my father, David Parker, who have provided additional research.

An enormous number of people have contributed to the research and writing of this book—more than it is possible to list here. However, I would especially like to thank: Colin Bowler, GeoInnovations; Maj. E. L. Christian, Honorary Secretary, Royal Sussex Regimental Association; John Clarke, Monte Cassino Veterans Association; Alan Collinson, GeoInnovations; John Cross; Ivar Cutler, Italy Star Association; Lindsay Davies; Milton Dolinger; Grant Dyson; Ben and Louise Edwards; Werner Eggert; Patrick Emerson of the Indian Army Association; K. Erdmann, Bundesarchiv, Freiburg; Bettina Ferrand, German Embassy, London; Jerry Gordon; Gavin Edgerley-Harris, Assistant Curator, Gurkha Museum; Sandra Stewart Holyoak, Director of Rutgers Oral History Archives of WWII; Marc Jeanneteau; Windsor Jones, Curator, Army Museum, Waiouru; Barbara Schick Kardas; Dr. Peter Liddle, The Second World War Experience, Leeds; Fred Lincoln, Membership Chairman, 88th Infantry Division Association; Karen McGlone; Tom Mc-Gregor; Sheila Parker; Stan Pearson; Evan Powell-Jones, Gurkha Welfare Trust; Dr. Christopher Pugsley, RMA Sandhurst; Cameron Pulsifer, Canadian War Museum; Alan Readman, County Archivist, West Sussex Record Office; Carol Reid, Canadian War Museum; John Rout, Secretary, New Zealand Permanent Forces Old Comrades Association; Maggie Roxburgh,

Royal Engineers Museum, Chatham; Herb Schaper; Dr Robin J. Sellers, Director, Reichelt Program for Oral History, Florida State University; Dr Gary Sheffield; Ben Shephard; Rajindar Singh, Indian Ex-Servicemen Association; Pat Skelly; Lesley Stephenson; Heather Stone, Curator, Auckland War Museum; Carl and Eleanor Strom; Anne and Paul Swain; Jerry Taylor, Vice-President, 88th Infantry Division Association; John Taylor, Rajputana Rifles Association; Michelle Tessler, Carlyle & Co., New York; Harold Tonks, Italy Star Association; Richard Van Emden; Alan Winson, Grand Island Films.

I am also grateful to the staff of all the archives and libraries I have used, in particular the Imperial War Museum, London, and the London Library. I have been lucky to have the most enthusiastic and professional publishing teams, in particular Heather Holden Brown, Lorraine Jerram, and Wendy McCance in London, and Adam Bellow and Jenny Choi in New York. I am also grateful to my agent Julian Alexander for his calming advice and help, and to Philip Parr for his expert copy-edit. Thanks go to Nigel de Lee of Royal Military Academy, Sandhurst, for his careful checking of the manuscript. All errors remain, of course, my own.

I am also indebted for their support and forebearance to my children, Ollie and Tom, and to Hannah, to whom this book is dedicated.

I would like to thank the following for permission to quote from published works: Peter Liddle, Director, The Second World War Experience Centre, Leeds, England (*Everyone's War* magazine); Marshall Cavendish (*Images of War* magazine); the *New Statesman* (the poem 'Lest we Forget' by Y. Alibhai); the estate of Sheila Dickinson (Patric Dickinson's 'War'); Pen and Sword Books (Peter Hart's *The Heat of Battle*); Alex Bowlby (his *Recollections of Rifleman Bowlby*); Eland Books (Norman Davis' *Naples 44*); George Sassoon (Siegfried Sassoon's 'The rank stench of those bodies haunts me still'); André Deutsch (John Blythe's *Soldiering On* and Roy Fuller's 'Virtue'); Mrs J. Smith (E. D. Smith's *Even the Brave Falter, Cassino*, personal diary); Texas A&M University Press (Klaus Huebner's *Long Walk Through War*); Weidenfeld and Nicolson, the estate of Laura Waugh and Peters, Fraser & Dunlop Ltd (*The Diaries of Evelyn Waugh* edited by Michael Davie); A. M. Heath & Co. Ltd (Fred Majdalany's *The Monastery*); Pollinger Limited (Alan Moorehead's *Eclipse*); Faber and Faber (W. S. Robson's *Letters from a Soldier*); Spike Milligan Productions Limited (his *Mussolini: His Part in my Downfall*); Simon & Schuster Adult Publishing Group (Joseph Heller's *Catch-22*); the estate of Bill Mauldin and the Watkins/Loomis Agency (Mauldin's *Up Front*); and the Scripps Howard Foundation (Ernie Pyle's *Brave Men*).

APPENDIX 1

A Typical British Infantry Battalion, 1943–44

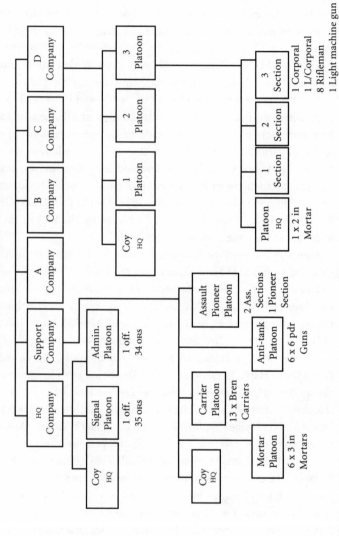

Orders of Battle

This is necessarily a simplified version, particularly with regard to the German formations, which changed during the course of the fighting. I have also not included the artillery regiments, anti-aircraft units, engineering and field park companies, nor additional recce, cavalry, and machine gun units.

FIRST BATTLE

BRITISH X CORPS (US FIFTH ARMY)

5th Division
> 13 Bgd.
>> 2 Cameron Highlanders
>> 2 Inniskilling Fusiliers
>> 2 Wiltshires
>
> 15 Bgd.
>> 1 Green Howards
>> 1 King's Own Yorkshire Light Infantry
>> 1 York and Lancs
>
> 17 Bgd.
>> 2 Royal Scots Fusiliers
>> 2 Northants
>> 6 Seaforth Highlanders

46th Division
> 128 Bgd.
>> 2 Hampshires
>> 1/4 Hampshires
>> 5 Hampshires

138 Bgd.
   6 Lincolns
   2/4 King's Own Yorkshire Light Infantry
   6 York and Lancs

139 Bgd.
   2/5 Leicesters
   5 Sherwood Foresters
   16 Durham Light Infantry

56th Division
167 Bgd.
   8 Royal Fusiliers
   9 Royal Fusiliers
   7 Oxford and Buckinghamshire Light Infantry

168 Bgd.
   1 London Scottish
   1 London Irish
   10 Royal Berkshires

169 Bgd.
   2/5 Queen's
   2/6 Queen's
   2/7 Queen's

201 Guards Bgd.
   6 Grenadier
   3 Coldstream
   2 Scots

US II Corps (US 5th Army)

34th Division
   133 Regt.
   135 Regt.
   168 Regt.

36th Division
   141 Regt.
   142 Regt.
   143 Regt.

1st Armored Division

French Expeditionary Corps (US 5th Army)

2nd Moroccan Infantry Division
   4 RTM [Régiment de Tirailleurs marocains]
   5 RTM
   8 RTM

3rd Algerian Infantry Division
    3 RTA [Régiment de Tirailleurs algériens]
    4 RTT [Régiment de Tirailleurs tunisiens]
    7 RTA

GERMAN 10TH ARMY

XIV Panzer Corps
    44th Infantry Division
    3rd Panzer Grenadier (PG) Division
    71st Infantry Division
    15th PG Division
    94th Infantry Division
    29th PG Division
    5th Mountain Division
    90th PG Division

SECOND AND THIRD BATTLES

NEW ZEALAND CORPS (FEBRUARY–MARCH 1944) (US 5TH ARMY)

2nd New Zealand Division
    5 Bgd.
        21 Battalion (Auckland)
        23 (South Island)
        28 (Maori)

    6 Bgd.
        24 (Auckland)
        25 (Wellington)
        26 (South Island)

    4 Armoured Bgd.
        18 Armoured Regt. (Auckland)
        19 (Wellington)
        20 (South Island)
        22 Motorized Battalion

4th Indian Division
    5 Bgd.
        1/4 Essex
        1/6 Rajputana Rifles
        1/9 Gurkha Rifles

    7 Bgd.
        1 Royal Sussex
        4/16 Punjab
        1/2 Gurkha Rifles

11 Bgd.
    2 Cameron Highlanders
    4/6 Rajputana Rifles
    2/7 Gurkha Rifles

78th Division (from 17 February)

11 Bgd.
    2 Lancashire Fusiliers
    1 Surrey
    5 Northants

36 Bgd.
    6 Royal West Kents
    5 Buffs
    8 Argyll and Sutherland Highlanders

38 Bgd.
    2 London Irish
    1 Royal Irish Fusiliers
    6 Inniskilling Fusiliers

FOURTH BATTLE

XIII British Corps (British 8th Army)

4th Division

10 Bgd.
    2 Bedford and Herts
    2 Duke of Cornwall's Light Infantry
    1/6 Surreys

12 Bgd.
    2 Royal Fusiliers
    6 Black Watch
    1 Royal West Kents

28 Bgd.
    2 Somerset Light Infantry
    2 King's
    2/4 Hampshires

6th Armoured Division

1 Guards Bgd.
    3 Grenadiers
    2 Coldstream
    3 Welsh

26 Armoured Bgd.
    16/5 Lancers
    17/21 Lancers
    2 Lothian and Border Horse

8th Indian Division

17 Bgd.
- 1 Royal Fusiliers
- 1/12 Frontier Force
- 1/5 Gurkha Rifles

19 Bgd.
- 1/5 Essex
- 3/8 Punjab
- 6/13 Frontier Force Rifles

21 Bgd.
- 5 Royal West Kents
- 1/5 Mahratta Light Infantry
- 3/15 Punjab

I CANADIAN CORPS (BRITISH 8TH ARMY)

1st Canadian Infantry Division

- 1 Bgd.
- 2 Bgd.
- 3 Bgd.

5th Canadian Armoured Division

- 11 Bgd.
- 5 Armoured Bgd.

POLISH CORPS (BRITISH 8TH ARMY)

3rd Carpathian Infantry Division

- 1 Bgd.
- 2 Bgd.

5th Kresowa Infantry Division

- 5 Wilkeńska Bgd.
- 6 Lwów Bgd.

2 Polish Armored Bgd.

- 1 and 2 Polish Armored Regts.
- 6 Kresowa Armored Regt.

6 South African Armoured Division (in reserve)

US II CORPS (US 5TH ARMY)

85th Division

- 337 Regt.
- 338 Regt.
- 339 Regt.

88th Division
349 Regt.
350 Regt.
351 Regt.

FRENCH EXPEDITIONARY CORPS (US 5TH ARMY)

2nd Moroccan Infantry Division—as above
3rd Algerian Infantry Division—as above
1st Division de Marche (formerly 1st Division Française Libre, then 1st Division
    d'Infanterie Motorisée)
1 Bgd.
2 Bgd.
4 Bgd.

4th Moroccan Mountain Division
1 Regt.
2 Regt.
6 Regt.

Goumiers
1 Tabor Group
3 Tabor Group
4 Tabor Group

GERMAN 10TH ARMY (MAY 1944)

XIV Panzer Corps
71st Infantry Division
94th Infantry Division
29th PG Division (from 21 May)
90th PG Division (from 14 May)
305th Infantry Division (from 21 May)
334th Infantry Division (from 26 May)
26th PG Division (from 18 May)

LI Mountain Corps
44th Infantry Division
15th PG Division
5th Mountain Division
1st Parachute Division
114th Jäger Division

NOTES

Foreword

p. ix   They are saying, "The Generals . . ." Michael Davie, ed., *The Diaries of Evelyn Waugh* (Weidenfeld & Nicolson, 1976), pp. 448–49, quoted in Paul Fussell, *Wartime* (New York: OUP, 1989; paperback, 1990), p. 4. Reproduced by permission of Weidenfeld & Nicolson and PFD on behalf of the estate of Laura Waugh.

p. x   one American artilleryman at Cassino . . . Francis J. Vojta (151st Field Artillery Battalion, US 34th Division) *The Gopher Gunners: A History of Minnesota's 151st Field Artillery* (Burgess Publishing, 1995), p. 216.

Introduction: The Monastery and the Gustav Line

p. xvi   "Impregnable mountains . . ." D. H. Deane (2nd Scots Guards, 201st Guards Brigade, British 56th Division) Papers, Imperial War Museum, London (IWM).

Part One: Sicily to Cassino

p. 1   David L. Thompson, *Battles and Leaders of the Civil War*, quoted in Terry Copp and Bill McAndrew, *Battle Exhaustion* (Montreal: McGill–Queens University Press, 1990), p. 62.

1: The Casablanca Conference and the Invasion of Sicily

p. 3   whose "easy, smiling grace . . ." W. Churchill, *The Second World War* (Cassell, 1964), vol. 6, p. 606.

p. 3   "I have never seen him in finer form . . ." quoted in Martin Gilbert, *The Road to Victory* (Heinemann, 1986; paperback, 1989), p. 306.

p. 4   "led down the garden path . . ." Brooke diary entry, 18 May 1943; Field Marshal Lord Alanbrooke, *War Diaries, 1939–45* (Weidenfeld & Nicolson, 2001), p. 405.

p. 6   "soft, green, and quite untrained . . ." Alexander to Alanbrooke, 3 April 1943; Alanbrooke papers, quoted in Carlo D'Este, *Fatal Decision* (HarperCollins, 1991), pp. 16–17.

p. 7   "In Africa," he wrote, "we learned . . ." Omar Bradley, *A General's Life* (New York: Simon & Schuster, 1983), p. 159; quoted in D'Este, *Fatal Decision*, p. 17.

p. 7   "We have fired our last cartridge . . ." quoted in Gilbert, *Road to Victory*, p. 404.

p. 8   Notes made by an Allied cameraman; at the IWM Film Archive.

p. 8   "an overwhelming force against us . . ." quoted in Gilbert, *Road to Victory*, p. 534.

p. 9   "very slender indeed . . ." Eisenhower to Marshall, 9 July 1943; quoted in M. Blumenson, *Salerno to Cassino* (US Government Printing Office, 1969), p. 15.

p. 9   "Marshall absolutely fails . . ." Alanbrooke, *War Diaries*, p. 433.

p. 10   "at the water's edge . . ." quoted in D'Este, *Fatal Decision*, p. 22.

p. 11   "still felt himself firmly in the saddle . . ." Albert Kesselring, *The Memoirs* (William Kimber, 1953), p. 168.

p. 11   "believed in an immediate danger for the regime . . ." Ibid., p. 168.

p. 11   the German Embassy in Rome . . . Gerhard L. Weinberg, *A World at Arms* (Cambridge University Press, 1994), p. 596n.

p. 11   "I understood his spontaneous delight . . ." Kesselring, *Memoirs*, p. 168.

p. 11   "chilly, reticent, and insincere" Ibid., p. 169.

p. 12   "My audience at the palace . . ." Ibid., p. 170.

p. 12   "They say they'll fight, but that's treachery!" quoted in D'Este, *Fatal Decision*, p. 31.

p. 12   over 100,000 Italian soldiers were captured (nearly 35,000 deserted during the campaign) . . . Brian R. Sullivan, "The Italian Soldier in Combat, June 1940–September 1943: Myths, Realities, and Explanations," in Paul Addison and Angus Calder, eds., *Time to Kill: The Soldier's Experience of War in the West, 1939–45* (Pimlico, 1997), p. 203.

p. 12   and nearly 40,000 German troops and over 10,000 vehicles were successfully evacuated . . . Dominick Graham and Shelford Bidwell, *Tug of War* (Hodder & Stoughton, 1986), p. 21n.

p. 13   "What's wrong with you, soldier?" quoted in Ben Shephard, *War of Nerves: Soldiers and Psychiatrists, 1914–1994* (Jonathan Cape, 2000), p. 219.

p. 14   "I never again expect to witness such scenes of sheer joy . . ." Maj. Warren A. Thrasher, quoted in Blumenson, *Salerno to Cassino*, p. 55.

2: THE INVASION OF ITALY

p. 15   The artillery alone fired four hundred tons of ammunition . . . Graham, *Tug of War*, p. 15.

p. 15   "It was night, and we could see little . . ." Alan Moorehead, *Eclipse* (Hamish Hamilton, 1945), p. 24.

p. 15   In the back were ten thousand cigarettes . . . Ibid., p. 27.

p. 16   In the city, Italian forces matched the Germans in numbers . . . Sullivan, "Italian Soldier," p. 204.

p. 16   "The raid was illuminating . . ." Kesselring, *Memoirs*, p. 176.

p. 16   "We're going somewhere to do an invasion . . ." Geoffrey Smith (172nd Field Artillery Regiment, British 46th Division) interview, 15 September 2002.

p. 17   "The sea is like a mill pond . . ." quoted in Blumenson, *Salerno to Cassino*, p. 3.

p. 18   "I was not certain that Mark Clark was the best choice . . ." quoted in Lee Smith, *A River Swift and Deadly* (Eakin Press, 1997), p. 104.

p. 18   "going to be a kind of walk in . . ." Clare Cunningham (1st Battalion, 142nd Regiment, US 36th Division) interview, 24 February 2003.

p. 19   described by a subordinate . . . F. Von Senger und Etterlin, *Neither Fear Nor Hope* (Macdonald, 1963), p. 181.

p. 20   situated in a great barn . . . Moorehead, *Eclipse*, p. 36.

p. 20   Major General Dawley, who had been considered impressive . . . Blumenson, *Salerno to Cassino*, p. 350.

p. 20   "We got pushed back out of Altavilla . . ." Cunningham interview, 24 February 2003.

p. 20   As *The Times* (London) reported on 15 September . . . quoted in J. Piekalkiewicz, *Cassino: Anatomy of a Battle* (Orbis, 1980), p. 28.

p. 20   "evade the effective shelling from warships" Kesselring, *Memoirs*, p. 187.

p. 21   In all, 716,000 Italian troops were rounded up by the Germans . . . Marco Pluviano and Irene Guerrini, "The Italian Home Front: The Price Paid for an Illusion," in *Everyone's War: The Journal of the Second World War Experience Centre, Leeds* no. 6 (autumn/winter 2002), p. 40.

p. 21   "Italian soldiers who had walked away from the war . . ." Norman Lewis, *Naples '44* (Collins, 1978; Eland Press, 1983), p. 14.

p. 21   "What I shall never understand . . ." Ibid., p. 18.

p. 22   "Several of these lay near, or in, tremendous craters . . ." Ibid., pp. 20–21.

p. 22   "I doubt very much . . ." Walker diary, 24 September 1943, quoted in Blumenson, *Salerno to Cassino*, p. 146.

p. 22   "greatly depressed at the complete destruction . . ." Walker diary entry, 1 October 1943, quoted in Ibid., p. 146.

p. 22   had suffered nearly nine thousand casualties . . . Graham, *Tug of War*, pp. 91–92.

p. 22   "Everyone knew someone that was killed . . ." Cunningham interview, 24 February 2003.

p. 23   "feather duster . . ." Graham, *Tug of War*, p. 92.

p. 23   "peanut . . ." D'Este, *Fatal Decision*, p. 62.

p. 23   Clark insisted he would be photographed only on his good side . . . Ibid., p. 58.

p. 23   "his reading of Clausewitz's famous dictum . . ." quoted in Fussell, *Wartime*, p. 161.

p. 23   Even so, the episode . . . Saul David, *Mutiny at Salerno* (Brassey's, 1995).

p. 24   "I had full confidence . . ." Kesselring, *Memoirs*, p. 187.

p. 25   "Everyone treated us kindly, it was all in good fun . . ." Tony Pittaccio interview, 12 August 2002.

p. 25   "most people were not happy about it . . ." Gemma Jaconelli (née Notarianni) interview, 15 September 2002.

p. 27   "Little did we dream . . ." e-mail from Tony Pittaccio, 24 December 2002.

p. 28   Twenty-five-year-old Terence Milligan . . . (19th Battery, 56th Heavy Regiment of 7.2-inch howitzers, attached to British X Corps)

p. 28   "I'm writing this in a hole in the ground . . ." Spike Milligan, *Mussolini: His Part in My Downfall* (Michael Joseph, 1978; Penguin paperback, 1980), p. 7.

p. 28   the American 45th Division needed twenty-five new bridges . . . Graham, *Tug of War*, p. 110.

p. 29   "There was no weapon more valuable than the engineer bulldozer . . ." L. K. Truscott, *Command Missions* (Dutton, 1954), pp. 255–59.

p. 29   "depended on the nerve and skill of relatively few men . . ." Graham, *Tug of War*, p. 111.

p. 29   Twenty-three-year-old Matthew Salmon . . . (220th Field Engineers Company, British 56th Division) material from interview, 22 October 2002, and from his book *Oh to Be a Sapper!* (privately published, 1984).

p. 31   The cost of the operation . . . Blumenson, *Salerno to Cassino*, p. 166.

p. 31   "On the outskirts of Naples itself . . ." Moorehead, *Eclipse*, p. 62.

p. 31   a baby manatee, was kept for a welcome dinner for Mark Clark . . . Lewis, *Naples '44*, p. 61.

p. 32   "In the grand manner of conquerors . . ." quoted in M. Blumenson, *Mark Clark* (New York: Congdon & Weed, 1984), p. 146.

p. 32   "hundreds, possibly thousands of Italians, most of them women and children . . ." Lewis, *Naples '44*, p. 30.

p. 32   "Cor Naples, eh? . . ." Milligan, *Mussolini*, p. 27.

p. 32   "The docks had suffered . . ." T. M. Powell, unpublished diary.

p. 32   "I hope . . . by the end of the month or thereabouts . . ." Prime Minister's personal telegram T.1481, Churchill Papers 20/119, quoted in Gilbert, *Road to Victory*, p. 520.

p. 32   twenty thousand tons a day . . . Rudolf Böhmler, *Monte Cassino* (Cassell, 1964), p. 17.

p. 33   "The roads are so deep in mud . . ." quoted in M. Blumenson, *Salerno to Cassino*, p. 194.

3: The Gustav Line

p. 34   "because they had nothing left to lose . . ." Lewis, *Naples '44*, p. 116.

p. 34   "He lectured us . . ." Bhaktabahadur Limbu (2/7th Gurkha Rifles, 11th Brigade, 4th Indian Division) interview by J. P. Cross and Buddhiman Gurung, Tape 29. Cross and Gurung's interviews with ex-Gurkhas in Nepal are available at the Gurkha Museum, Winchester. Used here with kind permission of John Cross.

p. 35   "our new friends . . ." Pittaccio interview, 12 August 2002.

p. 35   "when we saw Flying Fortresses . . ." from *Images of War* 27, vol. 3 (Marshall Cavendish, 1990), p. 748.

p. 36   At the Notariannis' shack . . . Jaconelli (née Notarianni) interview, 15 August 2002.

p. 36   all they could do was take him to a German field hospital . . . Pittaccio e-mail, 24 December 2002.

p. 37   "Oh, Monte Cassino will protect us . . ." Pittaccio interview, 12 August 2002.

p. 37   Most of the eighty monks also left at this time . . . David Colvin and Richard Hodges, "Tempting Providence: The Bombing of Monte Cassino," *History Today* 44, issue 2 (Feb. 1994), p. 13.

p. 37   "What they are doing there is extraordinary . . ." Pittaccio interview, 12 August 2002.

p. 38   Near their shepherd's shack . . . Gemma Jaconelli (née Notarianni) interview, 15 September 2002.

p. 38   "Our troops were living in almost inconceivable misery . . ." Ernie Pyle, *Brave Men* (Henry Holt, 1944: University of Nebraska paperback, 2001), p. 151. Pyle was killed by a sniper's bullet on 18 April 1945 on the small island of Ie Shima off Okinawa.

p. 39 "Soldiers become exhausted in mind and in soul . . ." Ibid., p. 89.

p. 41 "The seemingly unending succession of mountain ranges . . ." Alexander of Tunis, *Alexander Memoirs, 1940–45* (Cassell, 1962), p. xiii.

p. 41 "full of blunders . . ." and "irritations . . ." Bill Mauldin, *Up Front*, © 1945 by Henry Holt and Co., Inc. Facsimile edition published by W. W. Norton & Co., 1995. Reprinted by permission of the Estate of Bill Mauldin and the Watkins/Loomis Agency. (University of Nebraska ed, 2000), p. 5.

p. 41 "Not all colonels and generals and lieutenants are good . . ." Ibid., p. 16.

p. 42 "more out of loneliness . . ." J. M. Lee Harvey, *D-Day Dodger* (Kimber, 1979), pp. 13–18.

p. 42 "a cynicism bordering on the misanthropic . . ." Ibid., p. 39.

p. 43 "The way these guys lived was sort of appalling . . ." Thomas A. Kindre (34th Division, ordnance company) interview conducted by G. Kurt Piehler, 28 June 1994, for the Rutgers Oral History Archives of World War II.

p. 43 "usual practice for British commanders . . ." M. Clark, *Calculated Risk* (Harrap, 1951), p. 252.

p. 44 "the substitute for hierarchy . . ." Theodore A. Wilson, "Who Fought and Why? The Assignment of American Soldiers to Combat," in Addison, *Time to Kill*, p. 309.

p. 44 it took a mere eighty-eight days . . . Leo Balestri, "Combat Command: US Frontline Officers in Europe: 1942–45," *History 411: War and Society*, Princeton, May 1992, quoted in Ibid., p. 310.

p. 44 "The normal tendency is to attempt to stress his ability in the attack . . ." "Lessons Learned in Combat 8 November 1942 to 1 September 1944," Charles L. Bolte Papers, Box 6, US Army Military History Institute Library, Carlisle Barracks, PA.

p. 44 "His company of green, inexperienced troops . . ." E. D. Smith (2/7th Gurkha Rifles, 11th Brigade, 4th Indian Division) *Even the Brave Falter* (Robert Hale, 1978; Allborough Press ed., 1990), p. 6.

p. 45 "Rightly or wrongly, I led from the front whenever possible . . ." Lt. Russell Collins (16th Durham Light Infantry, 139th Brigade, British 46th Division) quoted in Peter Hart, *The Heat of Battle* (Leo Cooper, 1999), p. 82.

p. 45 "A man forgets to be afraid if you can get him to start firing . . ." John V. Pendergast (135th Regiment, US 34th Division), quoted in "Lessons Learned in Combat."

p. 45 "The Germans fired two shots . . ." Alex Bowlby, *The Recollections of Rifleman Bowlby* (Leo Cooper, 1969), p. 115.

p. 45 Bill Mauldin satirizes it in one cartoon drawn in January 1944 . . . Mauldin, *Up Front*, p. 225.

p. 46 "integral part of state and society in the Third Reich . . ." Jürgen Förster, "Motivation and Indoctrination in the Wehrmacht, 1933–45," in Addison, *Time to Kill*, p. 264.

p. 46 "I was in the Hitler Youth . . ." Robert Frettlöhr (15th [Pioneer] Company, 4th Regiment, 1st Parachute Division) interview, 15 September 2002.

p. 46 "we were being prepared to be soldiers . . ." Robert Frettlöhr telephone interview, 17 March 2003.

p. 46 "We saw the men marching . . ." *Everyone's War* 5 (spring/summer 2002), p. 20.

p. 46 "I was—at that time—a true Nazi . . ." Joseph Klein (3rd Regiment, 1st Parachute Division) interview, 1 February 2003.

p. 48 "Europe was not talked about a great deal . . ." Robert Koloski (135th Regiment, US 34th Division) interview, 25 February 2003.

p. 48 "No one [in the United States] ever shouted or sang 'Remember Poland' . . ." Fussell, *Wartime*, p. 138.

p. 48 playwright Arthur Miller . . . Ibid., p. 138.

p. 48 "By the time we got to Italy . . ." Koloski interview, 25 February 2003.

p. 48 "Some say morale is sky-high at the front . . ." Mauldin, *Up Front*, p. 13.

p. 48 "Who the hell dies for King and Country anymore . . ." Barry Broadfoot, *Six War Years* (Toronto: Doubleday, 1974), p. 19; quoted in Fussell, *Wartime*, p. 131.

p. 48 "He was there, quite simply, because he was there . . ." Charles Framp (6th Black Watch, 12th Brigade, British 4th Division) *The Littlest Victory*, privately published, n.d., p. 3.

p. 49 "For most of the troops . . ." Fussell, *Wartime*, p. 129.

p. 49 "no matter how cold the mountains, or how wet the snow . . ." Pyle, *Brave Men*, p. 152.

p. 49 fewer than 10 percent said they would "really like" to kill a German soldier . . . Theodore A. Wilson, "Who Fought and Why?: The Assignment of American Soldiers to Combat," in Addison, *Time to Kill*, p. 313.

p. 49 "I spoke a little German but I didn't interrogate them . . ." Kindre interview, 28 June 1994.

p. 50 "The tastes and morals of the individual fighting men . . ." J. B. Tomlinson (214th Engineering Company, British 78th Division) Papers, IWM.

p. 50 "You don't become a killer . . ." Mauldin, *Up Front*, p. 14.

p. 50 "It was in the first week . . ." Werner Eggert (2nd Battalion, 4th Regiment, 1st Parachute Division), unpublished memoir and written answers to questions, 20 March 2003. All translations from German by Katja Elias.

p. 51 "[He] had been living in Coventry," says Beckett . . . Denis Beckett (C Company, 1/4th Essex, 5th Brigade, 4th Indian Division) interview, 9 September 2002.

p. 51 "Slightly mad and brave . . ." Richard Eke (754th Field Engineering Company) Papers, IWM, p. 83.

p. 51 "We had learned our first lesson . . ." Ibid., p. 44.

p. 52 "Major Smith, our commanding officer . . ." Matthew Salmon interview, 22 October 2002.

p. 52 As had been pointed out, he said little about the frequent casualties . . . by G. Kurt Piehler, in his introduction to University of Nebraska Press ed. of *Brave Men*, p. xi.

p. 52 "I don't know what it is that impels some men . . ." Pyle, *Brave Men*, p. 75.

p. 52 "an ever smaller number of strivers . . ." Richard Holmes lecture at Armouries Museum, Leeds, 12 November 2002.

p. 52–53 "commanders and staff were alarmed . . ." quoted in Shephard, *War of Nerves*, p. 240.

p. 53 a report for the War Office in late 1944 . . . Ibid., p. 240.

p. 53 The British 56th Division official historian . . . David Williams, *The Black Cats at War* (IWM, 1995).

p. 53 "saw many men being tried for misbehavior . . ." e-mail from Tom Kindre, 2 January 2003.

p. 54   What they found there amazed them . . . Shephard, *War of Nerves*, p. 221.

p. 54   no such thing as "getting used to combat . . ." Ibid., p. 245.

p. 54   "viewed the matter as an affront . . ." Copp, *Battle Exhaustion*, p. 68.

p. 54   "Persons who are not exposed . . ." Ibid., p. 70.

p. 55   "We travel north along a tree-lined road . . ." Milligan, *Mussolini*, p. 66.

p. 55   as the American official historian complained . . . Blumenson, *Salerno to Cassino*, p. 175.

p. 55   about the "limitations of Marshall's brain . . ." Alanbrooke, *War Diaries*, p. 465.

p. 56   "Enemy gains constituted no great threat . . ." quoted in Blumenson, *Salerno to Cassino*, p. 232.

p. 56   "There is no doubt that the Italians are paying a stiff price . . ." Mauldin, *Up Front*, p. 65.

p. 56   "You can usually tell . . ." Ibid., pp. 74–76.

p. 57   "Feeling very nervous . . ." Milligan, *Mussolini*, p. 78.

p. 57   "badly shelled and bombed . . ." Ibid., p. 80.

p. 57   "We end up in village for the night . . ." S. C. Brooks (6th Cheshires, attached to 167th Brigade, British 56th Division) Papers, IWM, p. 61.

p. 57   "The doggie knows where his next meal is coming from . . ." Mauldin, *Up Front*, pp. 67–68.

p. 58   "It was without doubt the most squalid area inhabited by humanity . . ." Lee Harvey, *D-Day Dodger*, p. 74.

p. 58   "Those of us who have spent a long time in Sicily and Italy . . ." Mauldin, *Up Front*, p. 64.

p. 58   peasants "for whom we had all so quickly developed a great respect . . ." Lee Harvey, *D-Day Dodger*, p. 78.

p. 58   "Everybody is hungry here . . ." Public Records Office (PRO) WO 204/985.

p. 59   "Armistice Day. Ha ha ha . . ." Milligan, *Mussolini*, pp. 108–9.

p. 59   and had its contents "float under the tent flaps . . ." Ibid., p. 117.

p. 59   "Ammunition is being dumped by the guns . . ." Ibid., p. 168.

p. 59   "It was awful . . ." Lance Cpl. William Virr (16th Durham Light Infantry, 139th Brigade, British 46th Division) quoted in Hart, *Heat of Battle*, pp. 78–79.

p. 60   "of an intensity such as I had not witnessed . . ." Von Senger, *Neither Fear*, p. 186.

p. 60   "a wayside bath in a tin . . ." Milligan, *Mussolini*, p. 177–78.

p. 61   Over 300 civilians . . . Blumenson, *Salerno to Cassino*, p. 285n.

p. 61   "It was very demoralizing losing so many men . . ." Cunningham interview, 24 February 2003.

p. 62   "I regret the hardships they must suffer tonight . . ." quoted in Blumenson, *Salerno to Cassino*, p. 286.

p. 62   "The stagnation of the whole campaign . . ." quoted in Gilbert, *Road to Victory*, p. 611.

p. 62   "While driving toward the Abbey . . ." Von Senger, *Neither Fear*, p. 188.

4: INTO THE GUSTAV LINE

p. 63   "High winds [and] bitter cold . . ." Tom Kindre unpublished diary 29 December 1943; 31 December 1943; 9 January 1944.

p. 64   "one of the original in-for-a-year, $25-a-month gang . . ." Donald Hoagland (3rd Battalion, 135th Regiment, US 34th Division) interview, 26 February 2003.

p. 64   "We marched in, and we were wearing the old helmets . . ." Ivar Awes (151st Field Artillery, US 34th Division) interview, 22 February 2003.

p. 64   "we trained physically hard . . ." Hoagland interview, 26 Feb. 2003.

p. 64   quickly renamed the Belgravia Riding Academy . . . Vojta, *Gopher Gunners*, p. 141.

p. 64   "We had a very capable cadre of British artillery officers . . ." Awes interview, 22 Feb. 2003.

p. 64   "My, we are the elite, we have been chosen . . ." Koloski interview, 25 Feb. 2003.

p. 65   "After you got whipped . . ." Hoagland interview, 26 Feb. 2003.

p. 65   commanders and staff watching from the other side of the river . . . Blumenson, *Salerno to Cassino*, p. 222.

p. 65   to drive flocks of sheep or goats . . . Ibid., p. 231.

p. 65   "My company commander had his brother as shop foreman . . ." Kindre interview, 28 June 1994.

p. 66   "wise and worn, like a much-read book . . ." Pyle, *Brave Men*, p. 193.

p. 66   "There were old timers . . ." Kindre interview, 28 June 1994.

p. 66   "I'd certainly like to be home . . ." Awes letter to his parents, 13 April 1944.

p. 66   "It's raining like mad . . ." Awes letter, 8 November 1943.

p. 66   "The news broadcasts . . ." Awes letter, 13 November 1943.

p. 66   "I hope they break internally . . ." Awes letter, 11 November 1943.

p. 67   "vino . . . really rough red wine . . ." Ken Bartlett (2nd Hampshires, 128th Brigade, British 46th Division) interview, 20 Nov. 2002.

p. 67   "In no time at all [Rusch] was producing a product . . ." Homer R. Ankrum (133rd Regiment, US 34th Division) *Dog Faces who Smiled through Tears* (Graphic Publishing, 1987), pp. 371–72.

p. 68   "With the heights seized . . ." Ibid., p. 391.

p. 68   "When we moved up I was leading my battery . . ." Awes interview, 22 Feb. 2003.

p. 69   "It would appear doubtful if the enemy can hold . . ." quoted in E. D. Smith, *The Battles for Cassino* (Ian Allan, 1975), p. 27.

p. 70   only 20 percent of the Vichy army . . . John Ellis, *Cassino: The Hollow Victory* (André Deutsch, 1984), p. 41.

p. 70   "My instructions were to take my group . . ." Vern Onstad (3rd Battalion, 135th Regiment, US 34th Division) interview, 22 Feb. 2003.

p. 71   "The wealth of ammunition was remarkable . . ." Jean Murat (4RTT, 3rd Algerian Division) interview, 12 Feb. 2003. All translations from French by Jane Martens and Mark Jeanneteau.

p. 72   A typical FEC unit in Italy . . . Ellis, *Cassino*, p. 43n.

p. 72   North Africans fought for the "chance of proving . . ." Richard Holmes, "Five Armies in Italy," in Addison, *Time to Kill*, p. 212.

p. 72   "exploded at the suggestion . . ." quoted in Blumenson, *Salerno to Cassino*, pp. 254–55.

p. 73   "The column stretches over many kilometers . . ." Solange Cuvillier, *Tribulations d'une Femme dans L'Armée Française* (Lettres du Monde, 1991), p. 21.

p. 75   "It was a tough assignment . . ." A. Juin, *Mémoires Alger, Tunis, Rome* (Librairie Arthème Fayard, 1959), p. 31.

p. 75 But before they even set off, disaster struck . . . Capitaine Heurgon, *La Victoire sous la Signe des Trois Croissants* (Editions Pierre Voilon, 1946), p. 32.

p. 75 "The section under Sous-lieutenant Vétillard is in front . . ." Ibid., pp. 56–57.

p. 76 "The . . . young officers . . ." quoted in Ellis, *Cassino*, p. 57.

p. 76 troops "pushed on into the night . . ." Ibid., p. 56.

p. 76 "Here and also later on . . ." Von Senger, *Neither Fear*, p. 189.

p. 77 "I had the occasion to move forward . . ." quoted in Heurgon, *La Victoire*, p. 38.

p. 77 "Constantly on alert. Morale is dropping . . ." quoted in Ellis, *Cassino*, p. 61.

p. 77 "With an extra division, perhaps it could have been possible . . ." Juin, *Mémoires*, p. 55.

p. 78 "We knew which shells were . . ." Jaconelli (née Notarianni) interview, 15 Sept. 2002.

p. 78 "On the 16th and again on the 17th our patrols had to cross . . ." Heurgon, *La Victoire*, pp. 58–61.

p. 78 "We thought that once we were behind Allied lines . . ." Jaconelli (née Notarianni) interview, 15 Sept. 2002.

p. 79 "We could hear the artillery . . ." Pittaccio interview, 12 Aug. 2002, and e-mail, 3 Feb. 2003.

PART TWO: THE FIRST BATTLE

p. 81 " 'I'm afraid . . .' " taken from Joseph Heller, *Catch-22*. Copyright © 1955, 1961 by Joseph Heller. Copyright renewed © 1989 by Joseph Heller. Reprinted with permission of Simon & Schuster Adult Publishing Group.

p. 81 "Those who occupied the lower level were up to their knees . . ." quoted in Tony Williams, *Cassino: New Zealand Soldiers in the Battle for Italy* (Penguin, 2002), p. 142.

5: BRITISH X CORPS ON THE GARIGLIANO: THE LEFT HOOK

p. 83 The 9th Fusiliers had lost 25 officers . . . E. Linklater, *The Campaign in Italy* (HMSO, 1951), p. 134.

p. 83 "I was a bit naïve . . ." Len Bradshaw (9th Royal Fusiliers, 167th Brigade, British 56th Division) interview, 11 Oct. 2002.

p. 83 "It was an extraordinary existence . . ." quoted in D. Williams, *Black Cats*, p. 71.

p. 84 many of them had been subsequently bought by the Americans . . . Ibid., p. 75.

p. 84 "We had a fire, and a rum ration in the evening . . ." Bradshaw interview, 11 Oct. 2002.

p. 84 "so that at least the men could have with them the badge . . ." quoted in D. Williams, *Black Cats*, p. 73.

p. 84 "receive men from the units within the Division . . ." Ibid., pp. 76–77.

p. 84 "These few lines to let you know I am still alive and well . . ." letter home from Glyn Edwards (8th Royal Fusiliers, 167th Brigade, British 56th Division), 3 January 1944.

p. 84 "pitch black cold, and a howling gale . . ." Milligan, *Mussolini*, p. 248.

p. 87 "The smell inside the prison was hell . . ." Ibid., p. 251.

p. 87 "It's going to be a big 'Do' . . ." Ibid., p. 263.

p. 87   "I had a terrible foreboding of death . . ." Ibid., p. 264.

p. 87   mines, some 24,000 of them . . . Blumenson, *Salerno to Cassino*, p. 316.

p. 87   "We didn't know what was going on . . ." Bradshaw interview, 11 Oct. 2002.

p. 88   "Well before dawn we were at the foot of the mountain . . ." Gilbert Allnutt (8th Royal Fusiliers, 167th Brigade, British 56th Division) Papers, IWM.

p. 89   "These few lines to let you know I am still alive and well . . ." letter home from Glyn Edwards, 24 January 1944.

p. 89   "We were quite depleted . . ." Len Bradshaw interview, 11 Oct. 2002.

p. 90   "It was difficult and unpleasant, mines were a very real danger . . ." PRO WO170/1411, quoted in Ellis, *Cassino*, p. 75.

p. 90   "At last the river itself could be seen . . ." quoted in Jim Stockman, *Seaforth Highlanders, 1939–45* (Crecy Books, 1987), p. 142.

p. 90   to use amphibious craft at the mouth of the river to land troops . . . of 2nd Royal Scots Fusiliers, 17th Brigade, 5th Division.

p. 91   One company's boat went so far out . . . George Aris, *The Fifth British Division* (5th Division Benevolent Fund, 1959), p. 180.

p. 91   "At that point it wasn't too bad, because Jerry hadn't been alerted . . ." Jack Williams (2nd Inniskilling Fusiliers, 13th Brigade, British 5th Division) interview, 12 Sept. 2002.

p. 93   The engineer Matthew Salmon . . . Salmon interview, 22 Oct. 2002.

p. 94   "Barrages all day . . ." PRO WO204/985. The unnamed German soldier died of his wounds in a Canadian dressing station, just after his nineteenth birthday.

p. 94   "On the way to Company HQ . . ." quoted in Ellis, *Cassino*, p. 86.

p. 94   "I am done. The artillery fire is driving me crazy . . ." PRO WO204/985.

p. 95   "hung by a slender thread . . ." Kesselring, *Memoirs*, p. 192.

p. 95   "No bridge across the river yet . . ." Brooks Papers, IWM.

p. 95   "People were getting edgier with each other . . ." Matthew Salmon interview, 22 Oct. 2002.

p. 95   "it appeared to make no difference to them . . ." Aris, *Fifth British Division*, p. 193.

p. 95   The company advanced with two platoons forward . . . VC citation and background from D. Williams, *The Black Cats at War*, pp. 80–81 and John Laffin, *British VCs of the Second World War* (Sutton, 1997), pp. 106–8.

p. 96   "God made gentle people as well as strong ones . . ." Milligan, *Mussolini*, p. 288.

p. 97   The next day one of the forward observers returned to the battery . . . Ibid., pp. 274–85.

p. 98   "I suppose in World War I . . ." In the First World War, Britain executed 346 soldiers for cowardice or desertion.

p. 99   By the end of January, the corps had suffered over four thousand casualties . . . Clark, *Calculated Risk*, p. 256.

p. 99   "Transport brought supplies . . ." George Pringle (175th Pioneer Regiment, X Corps) written account and telephone interview, 11 Nov. 2002.

p. 100   David Cormack was originally a tankman . . . David Cormack interview, 18 Sept. 2002.

p. 100   "Spent day making two trips up hill . . ." Cormack diary entry, 8 February 1944.

p. 101   only one company . . . of 2nd Hampshires, 128 Brigade.

p. 101   "mental reservations . . ." Clark diary entry, 19 January 1944, quoted in Blumenson, *Salerno to Cassino*, p. 320.

p. 101 "His failure makes it tough for my men . . ." Walker diary entry, 20 January 1944, quoted in ibid., p. 328.

p. 101 "little chance of success . . ." Clark diary entry, 19 January 1944, quoted in ibid., pp. 320–21.

6: BLOODY RIVER

p. 102 "combat-wise platoon sergeants . . ." *Yank* (May 1944).

p. 103 twenty-three-year-old Carl Strom (1st Battalion, 141st Regiment, US 36th Division) interview, 24 Feb. 2003.

p. 104 His report to Walker . . . quoted in L. Smith, *A River Swift*, p. 17.

p. 104 "muddy bottleneck . . ." Ibid., p. 18.

p. 106 he still told Clark on 18 January . . . Blumenson, *Salerno to Cassino*, p. 327.

p. 106 "We might succeed but I do not see how we can . . ." Ibid., p. 332.

p. 107 "I drew the high card so I had the lead platoon . . ." Strom interview, 24 Feb. 2003.

p. 108 "At the river they slid the first boat . . ." C. P. "Buddy" Autrey (1st Battalion, 141st Regiment, US 36th Division) quoted in Smith, *A River Swift*, p. 38.

p. 108 "I remember talking to my guys . . ." Bill Everett (1st Battalion, 141st Regiment, US 36th Division) interview by David Gregory, 16 Feb. 2000, for the Reichelt Program for Oral History, Florida State University; telephone interview, 25 Feb. 2003.

p. 110 "Strong enemy assault detachments . . ." quoted in Blumenson, *Salerno to Cassino*, p. 339.

p. 110 "I stuck my head up . . ." Strom interview, 24 Feb. 2003.

p. 110 "who complain and try to return to the rear . . ." quoted in Blumenson, *Salerno to Cassino*, p. 340.

p. 111 "I expect this attack to be a fizzle . . ." Ibid., p. 340.

p. 111 Bill Hartung, a twenty-one-year-old scout . . . Bill Hartung (2nd Battalion, 143rd Regiment, US 36th Division) telephone interview, 3 June 2003.

p. 111 "We went down a little horse and wagon road . . ." Hartung account from *36th Division Historical Quarterly* XIII, no. 3 (fall 1993): pp. 40–42.

p. 112 "The officers were noticeably nervous . . ." Robert Spencer (2nd Battalion, 143rd Regiment, US 36th Division) account from 36th Division Library, online at www.kwanah.com/36Division, last accessed 28 May 2003.

p. 115 "This German came to our side . . ." Zeb Sunday (1st Battalion, 143rd Regiment, US 36th Division) quoted in L. Smith, *A River Swift*, p. 91.

p. 115 "At the river Germans and Americans labored side by side . . ." R. L. Wagner, *The Texas Army* (Wagner, 1972), pp. 122–23.

p.115 "When I saw my regimental commander . . ." quoted in ibid., p. 92.

p. 115 "Nothing was right except the courage . . ." Howard Kippenberger, *Infantry Brigadier* (OUP, 1949), p. 350.

p. 116 "found wanting . . ." Ellis, *Cassino*, p. 102.

p. 116 "Guys disappeared . . ." Everett interview, 16 Feb. 2000.

7: ANZIO AND CASSINO

p. 117   he had countermanded the order . . . Kesselring, *Memoirs*, p. 193.

p. 117   "His opinion of the enemy's amphibious intentions . . ." quoted in Blumenson, *Salerno to Cassino*, p. 319.

p. 118   "Don't stick your neck out, Johnny . . ." quoted in D'Este, *Fatal Decision*, p. 119.

p. 118   "we were hurling a wildcat . . ." quoted in Gilbert, *Road to Victory*, p. 667.

p. 118   "How many of our men are driving . . ." quoted in Fred Majdalany (2nd Lancashire Fusiliers, 11th Brigade, British 78th Division), *Cassino: Portrait of a Battle* (Longmans, Green, 1957; Cassell Military paperback ed., 1999), p. 77.

p. 118   "This whole affair had a strong odor of Gallipoli . . ." Lucas diary entry, 10 January 1944, quoted in D'Este, *Fatal Decision*, p. 107.

p. 118   outside the scope of this book . . . The story of Anzio has been well told by Blumenson, Trevelyan, D'Este, and others.

p. 119   "We could have had one night in Rome . . ." Penney Papers, quoted in D'Este, *Fatal Decision*, p. 7.

p. 119   "We have a great need to keep continually engaging them . . ." quoted in Gilbert, *Road to Victory*, p. 670.

p. 121   "enough barbed wire . . ." quoted in Ankrum, *Dog Faces*, p. 389.

p. 121   "At Cassino this appearance . . ." C. J. C. Molony, *The Mediterranean and the Middle East*, vol. 5 (HMSO, 1973), pp. 694–95.

p. 122   "You felt so bad for the infantry . . ." Awes interview, 22 Feb. 2003.

p. 122   "As I see it, there were three main functions performed by the tanks . . ." "Lessons Learned in Combat."

p. 123   "As he did so," the official history reports . . . Blumenson, *Salerno to Cassino*, p. 371.

p. 123   "Storm Belvedere? . . ." General Monsabert, quoted in Ellis, *Cassino*, p. 135.

p. 123   "I was asked to carry out a mission . . ." Juin, *Mémoires*, p. 269.

p. 124   "[The engineers] built a small provisional bridge which was destroyed by German fire . . ." René Martin (3rd Battalion, 4RTT, 3rd Algerian Division) interview, 26 Nov. 2002.

p. 125   "The battalion is physically and mentally ready . . ." quoted in R. Chambe, *Le Bataillon du Belvedere* (Flammarion Press, 1953), p. 80.

p. 125   "His forearm has been shot off by a shell . . ." Heurgon, *La Victoire*, p. 83.

p. 125   "the slope of the gorge was so steep . . ." Chambe, *Le Bataillon*, p. 70.

p. 127   "The climb became a nightmare . . ." Ibid., p. 91.

p. 128   "a warrant officer suddenly shouted . . ." Martin interview, 26 Nov. 2002.

p. 128   "Our hearts overflowing . . ." Juin, *Mémoires*, p. 274.

p. 129   "The 3rd Algerian Division has carried out . . ." Ibid., pp. 273–74.

p. 129   One US officer, returning from the hospital . . . Ankrum, *Dog Faces*, p. 399.

p. 130   "Every day Cassino is reported taken . . ." Tom Kindre diary entry, 30 January 1944.

p. 130   "Gun emplacements were also camouflaged . . ." "Lessons Learned in Combat."

8: The Cassino Massif

p. 132   "Initially we were in reserve . . ." Hoagland interview, 26 Feb. 2003.

p. 133   "Present indications . . ." quoted in Blumenson, *Salerno to Cassino*, p. 377.

p. 133   "There was never a time that we were free of intermittent or heavy mortar fire . . ." Hoagland interview, 26 Feb. 2003.

p. 134   "In deep snowbanks . . ." Gordon Gammack in the *Minneapolis Morning Tribune*, 11 March 1944.

p. 134   "a farm outbuilding, with only a partial roof . . ." Koloski interview, 25 Feb. 2003.

p. 135   "Mortars are more accurate . . ." Klaus H. Huebner (3rd Battalion, 349th Regiment, US 88th Division) *Long Walk through War* (Texas A&M University Press, 1987), p. 49. Reprinted by permission of the Texas A&M University Press. © 1987 Klaus Huebner.

p. 135   "Sometimes a bullet can go clear through a man . . ." Pyle, *Brave Men*, p. 58.

p. 136   "If there was blood pumping out of an artery . . ." Koloski interview, 25 Feb. 2003.

p. 137   "It seemed like we were under observation . . ." Cunningham interview, 24 Feb. 2003.

p. 137   "The first sergeant came round . . ." John Johnstone (1st Battalion, 168 Regiment, US 34th Division) interview, 22 November 2002.

p. 139   "after about a week there were several times . . ." Hoagland interview, 26 February 2003.

p. 139   "the American infantry was worn out . . ." Kippenberger, *Infantry Brigadier*, p. 351.

p. 139   "found morale progressively worse . . ." quoted in Ellis, *Cassino*, pp. 130–31.

p. 139   "For two weeks we have been in action . . ." PRO WO 204/985.

p. 140   "located about 1,000 yards from the abbey . . ." C. N. "Red" Morgan (3rd Battalion, 141st Regiment, US 36th Division) account from 36th Division Library, online at www.kwanah.com/36Division, last accessed 28 May 2003.

p. 140   "We started up the trail in a blinding rain . . ." Everett interview, 16 February 2000.

p. 141   "attacked several times. They came up the hill . . ." Strom interview, 24 February 2003.

p. 141   "Confusion reigned that day . . ." Morgan account, 36th Division Library online.

p. 141   "At about 1700 February 11 . . ." Ibid.

p. 142   "My ass was dragging . . ." Hoagland interview, 26 February 2003.

p. 142   "This gave me the opportunity to study the faces . . ." M. Bourke-White, *Purple Heart Valley* (Simon & Schuster, 1944), pp. 79–80.

p. 142   "Katula and I got hit before daylight . . ." Cunningham interview, 24 February 2003.

p. 143   "It didn't smell so good after firing a couple of hours . . ." Sergeant Haliburton (142nd Regiment), quoted in *Yank* (May 1944).

p. 143   the American chosen to administer it was Lt. Col. Hal Reese . . . Reese wrote an account in the spring of 1944 of his part in the truce, now in 36th Division Records in the Texas State Archives. He was killed on 1 June 1944 near Velletri. The story is told in David Hapgood and David Richardson, *Monte Cassino* (Congdon & Weed, 1984, Da Capo Press ed., 2002), pp. 186ff.

p. 144   "It was snowing part of the time . . ." Strom interview, 24 February 2003.

p. 144   "in real bad shape when we pulled back . . ." Everett interview, 16 February 2000.

PART THREE: THE SECOND BATTLE

p. 147   "Cold are the stones . . ." Patric Dickenson, "War," in Robin Skelton, ed., *Poetry of the Forties* (Penguin, 1968), p. 123.

p. 147   "In these old hackneyed melodies . . ." Roy Fuller, "Virtue," in Ibid., p. 223.

9: THE DESTRUCTION OF THE MONASTERY

p. 149   John Lardner in *Newsweek* . . . 28 February 1944, p. 27, quoted in Hapgood, *Monte Cassino*, p. 202.

p. 149   "the finest weapons in the whole of Alexander's armory . . ." Böhmler, *Monte Cassino*, p. 155.

p. 149   The Indian component . . . Gerard Douds, "Matters of Honour," in Addison, *Time to Kill*, p. 115ff.

p. 150   Nepal at this time . . . J. P. Cross and Buddhiman Gurung, eds., *Gurkhas at War: The Gurkha Experience in Their Own Words, World War II to the Present* (Greenhill Press, 2002), p. 25.

p. 150   "poverty, privations, drudgery and weariness . . ." Ibid., p. 16.

p. 150   in some cases village headmen . . . Tahalsing Rana (2/8th Gurkha Rifles): "The village headman had orders from Kathmandu for all men between sixteen and sixty years of age to be sent away for enlistment—so I went . . ." Cross Tape 228.

p. 150   "I joined the army for money and honor . . ." Pahalman Pun (2/4th Gurkha Rifles) interview, Cross Tape 116.

p. 151   "I went to Dehra Dun for ten months' recruit training . . ." Balbahadur Katuwal (1/9th Gurkha Rifles, 5th Brigade, 4th Indian Division) interview, Cross Tape 157.

p. 151   "Our NCOs punished our mistakes . . ." Jumparsad Gurung (1/2nd Gurkhas, 7th Brigade, 4th Indian Division) interview, Cross Tape 202.

p. 151   "Then it was time to go overseas . . ." Katuwal interview.

p. 151   "I was enlisted on 19 November 1940 . . ." Kharkabahadur Thapa (1/2nd Gurkhas, 7th Brigade, 4th Indian Division) interview, Cross Tapes 67 and 68.

p. 152   "We didn't speak to the girls . . ." Dilbahadur Rai (2/7th Gurkhas, 11th Brigade, 4th Indian Division) interview, Cross Tape 102.

p. 152   "I came across some Gurkha soldiers . . ." Maj. E. G. Cox (5th Buffs, 36 Brigade, British 78th Division) unpublished memoir, p. 37.

p. 152   "In transit, the various battalions and companies made an odd-looking convoy . . ." B. Smith (signaler attached to 4/16th Punjab, 7th Brigade, 4th Indian Division) account, IWM.

p. 153   "Both with gratitude for the past . . ." quoted in T. Williams, *Cassino*, pp. 24–25.

p. 153   this would be a war of survival for New Zealand as well . . . I am indebted to Dr. Christopher Pugsley of RMA Sandhurst for advice on the New Zealand background material.

p. 154   there were 5,000 volunteers . . . T. Williams, *Cassino*, p. 25.

p. 154   "It was just after I'd turned twenty-one . . ." telephone interview with Ian McNeur (23rd Battalion, 5th Brigade, 2nd New Zealand Division), 11 December 2002.

p. 154   "A few hardy souls rushed to enlist . . ." Clem Hollies (21st Battalion, 5th Brigade, 2nd New Zealand Division) Papers, IWM.

p. 155   "casualty conscious . . ." Alanbrooke, *War Diaries*, p. 536.

p. 155   "duly . . . jabbed and stabbed . . ." Jack Cocker (27th Machine Gun Battalion, 2nd New Zealand Division) telephone interview, 15 December 2002.

p. 155   "It took us a while to acclimatize . . ." Jack Cocker memoir taped December 1998.

p. 156   4,600 vehicles . . . T. Williams, *Cassino*, p. 61.

p. 156   "This 'secret' move was ridiculous . . ." Hollies Papers, IWM.

p. 156   "During the day's travel, Italian civilians . . ." J. B. McKinney, *Medical Units of 2 NZEF in Middle East and Italy* (Wellington: Department of Internal Affairs, 1952), p. 336.

p. 157   "These are dominion troops . . ." Clark diary entry, 4 February 1944, quoted in Blumenson, *Salerno to Cassino*, p. 402.

p. 157   "And thus I was about to agree with Napoleon's conclusion . . ." quoted in E. D. Smith, *Cassino*, p. 67.

p. 157   "At the end of the Sangro campaign . . ." quoted in Lawrence Watt, *Mates and Mayhem* (HarperCollins New Zealand, 1996), p. 122.

p. 157   "We arrived at the platoon headquarters . . ." Cocker interview, 15 December 2002, and taped memoir.

p. 158   "Although still winter, it seemed almost autumnal . . ." John Blythe, *Soldiering On* (Sphere, 1968), p. 30.

p. 158   "We were depicted by the propaganda as savages . . ." Brick Lorimer (19th Battalion, 4th Armored Brigade, 2nd New Zealand Division) telephone interview, 17 December 2002.

p. 158   "Daily I could see their faces losing the strained look . . ." Kippenberger, *Infantry Brigadier*, p. 349.

p. 158   "a great laugh . . ." Cocker interview, 15 December 2002.

p. 158   "They told us all about the terrain and what it was like . . ." Ibid.

p. 158   "unfamiliar green combat jackets . . ." Blythe, *Soldiering On*, pp. 130–31.

p. 159   "New Zealanders are a law unto themselves . . ." Hugh MacKenzie (25th Battalion, 6th Brigade, 2nd New Zealand Division) interview, 16 December 2002.

p. 159   "Your chaps don't salute, do they?" quoted in Hapgood, *Monte Cassino*, p. 149, among other places.

p. 159   "New Zealand is such a small place . . ." MacKenzie interview, 16 December 2002.

p. 159   "The whole area around Cassino had an ominous air . . ." Hollies Papers, IWM.

p. 159   "The regiment started advancing to the front . . ." Blythe, *Soldiering On*, p. 131.

p. 160   "We are undoubtedly facing one of the most difficult operations . . ." quoted in E. D. Smith, *Cassino*, p. 66.

p. 161   "General Tuker apparently has a flare-up of chronic sinusitis . . ." John David letter, 6 February 1944.

p. 161   An Italian from Cassino has since described it . . . Granada television documentary, directed by Ken Grieve, produced by Nick Skidman, broadcast 1985.

p. 161   Clark's headquarters had stressed the need to preserve the building . . . Blumenson, *Salerno to Cassino*, p. 397.

p. 161   "Today we are fighting in a country . . ." 29 December 1943, quoted in Hapgood, *Monte Cassino*, p. 158 and elsewhere.

p. 162   "Consideration for the safety of such areas . . ." 9 January 1944, quoted in Blumenson, *Salerno to Cassino*, p. 399.

p. 162   In early February a debate in the House of Lords . . . quoted in R. Trevelyan, *Rome '44* (Secker & Warburg, 1981), p. 128.

p. 162 A diary kept by the abbot's secretary, Don Martino Matronola . . . Colvin and Hodges, "Tempting Providence," pp. 13ff.

p. 163 "an ominous change . . ." David diary entry, 6 February 1944, IWM.

p. 163 "The main gate has massive timber branches . . ." quoted in Majdalany, *Cassino*, pp. 114–15.

p. 163 the monastery might have to be "blown down" . . . Blumenson, *Salerno to Cassino*, p. 402.

p. 163 "I want it bombed . . ." Ibid., p. 404.

p. 163 "probably enhance its value as a military obstacle . . ." Ibid., p. 405.

p. 163 "in view of General Freyberg's position . . ." Ibid., p. 405.

p. 163 "When soldiers are fighting for a just cause . . ." Alexander, *Alexander Memoirs*, p. 121.

p. 164 "irrefutable evidence . . ." Blumenson, *Salerno to Cassino*, p. 408.

p. 164 "Whether the monastery is now occupied . . ." quoted in Majdalany, *Cassino*, p. 115.

p. 164 "Opinion at NZ Corps HQ . . ." quoted in Ibid., p. 121.

p. 165 "necessary more for the effect it would have on the morale . . ." Alexander, *Alexander Memoirs*, p. 121.

p. 165 "the all-seeing eye . . ." J. B. Tomlinson Papers, IWM, p. 114.

p. 165 "As the road became less crowded . . ." Fred Majdalany, *The Monastery* (Bodley Head, 1945), p. 17. © Fred Majdalany.

p. 165 "Bloody monastery gazing down at you . . ." Cormack interview, 19 September 2002.

p. 165 "If you let me use the whole of our bomber force . . ." quoted in E. D. Smith, *Cassino*, p. 68.

p. 165 "Italian friends . . ." quoted in Blumenson, *Salerno to Cassino*, p. 409 and elsewhere.

p. 166 "to intimidate and for propaganda purposes . . ." Colvin and Hodges, "Tempting Providence."

p. 167 "were the grimmest of my army career . . ." Douglas Hawtin (Royal Corps of Signals, attached to 1st Royal Sussex, 7th Brigade, 4th Indian Division) unpublished memoir and interview, 19 September 2002.

p. 168 "We had no reserve rations . . ." quoted in E. D. Smith, *Cassino*, p. 77.

p. 168 "a string of flares lit the whole valley . . ." B. Smith Papers, IWM.

p. 170 "Let the boys have another crack at it . . ." David diary entry, 14 February 1944, IWM.

p. 170 "[There were] live, or just about alive, Yankee soldiers . . ." Hawtin unpublished memoir.

p. 170 "You had to build sangars from the boulders . . ." John Buckeridge (1st Royal Sussex, 7th Brigade, 4th Indian Division) account from Royal Sussex Tercentenary video, 2001. Royal Sussex Regiment Museum/South East Film & Video Archive. Used with permission.

p. 171 "It was like a cemetery up there . . ." Granada program.

p. 171 "There were a number of dead GIs lying around . . ." B. Smith Papers, IWM.

p. 171 "flew in perfect formation . . ." quoted in Colvin and Hodges, "Tempting Providence," and elsewhere.

p. 172   "As wave after wave came in . . ." Blythe, *Soldiering On*, p. 143.

p. 172   "We heard the planes coming then huge explosions . . ." Granada program.

p. 172   "The whole mountain was alight . . ." Ibid.

p. 172   "Target cabbaged real good . . ." quoted in Hapgood, *Monte Cassino*, p. 208.

p. 172   "as if the mountain had disintegrated . . ." quoted in Ellis, *Cassino*, p. 183.

p. 173   "The sight that confronted us . . ." private papers, Wales.

p. 173   "It was a tremendous spectacle . . ." quoted in Blumenson, *Salerno to Cassino*, p. 411.

p. 173   "I remember the actual bombing . . ." Gellhorn quoted in Hapgood, *Monte Cassino*, p. 212.

p. 173   "soul destroying to watch . . ." Lorimer interview, 17 December 2002.

p. 173   "The Allied air forces bomb the monastery . . ." *Daily Mail*, 21 May 1994.

p. 173   "As for Monte Cassino, whereas the military may have felt . . ." Pittaccio interview, 12 August 2002.

p. 174   His diary entry concludes . . . Colvin and Hodges, "Tempting Providence."

p. 174   "the weary old man was dragged off . . ." Von Senger, *Neither Fear*, p. 203.

p. 174   "Without a single adjective . . ." Iris Origo, *The War in the Val D'Orcia* (London, 1947); quoted by Colvin and Hodges, "Tempting Providence."

p. 174   "In the senseless lust of destruction . . ." quoted in Ibid., Trevelyan, *Rome '44*, p. 138, and elsewhere.

p. 175   "[It] was turned into a fortress by the German army . . ." NMV 769–1, IWM Film Archive.

p. 175   "a baseless invention . . ." quoted in Ellis, *Cassino*, p. 171.

10: SNAKESHEAD RIDGE

p. 176   "Everyone, including the monks and the enemy . . ." quoted in Majdalany, *Cassino*, p. 142.

p. 176   "We went to the door of the Command post . . ." quoted in E. D. Smith, *Cassino*, p. 79.

p. 177   "I could see hordes of Flying Fortresses in groups . . ." Royal Sussex Tercentenary video.

p. 177   "We were to attack and take Point 593 . . ." Ibid.

p. 179   "It was fierce close-quarter fighting . . ." Hawtin interview, 19 September 2002.

p. 179   "Suddenly a whistling came at us . . ." Werner Eggert interview, 20 March 2003, unpublished memoir and written answers to questions.

p. 180   "We got on with it because . . ." quoted in E. D. Smith, *Cassino*, p. 83.

p. 181   the Sussex had suffered over 50 percent casualties . . . Ellis, *Cassino*, p. 188.

p. 182   "had little to do with patriotic duty . . ." Wira Gardiner, *The Story of the Maori Battalion* (Reed, 1992), p. 29.

p. 182   "When you know people from way back . . ." George Pomana (28th Battalion, 5th Brigade, 2nd New Zealand Division) telephone interview, 16 January 2003.

p. 182   "full of tricks. Inimitable jokers . . ." Lorimer interview, 17 December 2002.

p. 182   "My 12 Platoon on the right . . ." quoted in J. F. Cody, *28 (Maori) Battalion* (Department of Internal Affairs, 1958), p. 359.

p. 183   "The Germans put up flares, unusually short-lived . . ." Peter Cochrane (2nd Cameron Highlanders, 11th Brigade, 4th Indian Division), *Charlie Company* (Chatto & Windus, 1977), p. 133.

p. 184 "We also opened fire from time to time . . ." Thapa interview, Cross Tapes 67 and 68.

p. 184 "He said that we had had heavy casualties . . ." John ffrench, unpublished account.

p. 185 "The battalion, which had contained many veterans . . ." quoted in E. D. Smith, *Cassino*, p. 90.

p. 185 "It was typical of this hopelessly disorganized battle . . ." Cochrane, *Charlie Company*, p. 114.

p. 185 "Very eventful day for me today . . ." David diary entry, 19 February 1944, IWM.

p. 186 "It was just possible that the enemy . . ." Kippenberger, *Infantry Brigadier*, p. 357.

p. 186 "like walking a tightrope in a shooting gallery . . ." quoted in N. C. Phillips, *The Sangro to Cassino* (Department of Internal Affairs, 1957), p. 240.

p. 186 "During the afternoon he came at us . . ." Granada program.

p. 187 Six weeks later, in the hope of recovering their dead . . . Gardiner, *Story of the Maori Battalion*, p. 154.

p. 188 "given the New Zealanders a bloody nose . . ." quoted in Ellis, *Cassino*, p. 191.

11: LULL AT CASSINO, COUNTERATTACK AT ANZIO

p.190 "I couldn't understand it . . ." Salmon interview, 22 October 2002, and his book, *op. cit.*

p. 192 "A rugged-looking man with a broken nose . . ." Milligan, *Mussolini*, p. 286.

p. 192 the way he talked about "cowardice" . . . Shephard, *War of Nerves*, pp. 217–18.

p. 192 "About two-thirds were under drugs . . ." Milligan, *Mussolini*, p. 286.

p. 192 "questioning me over and over again . . ." Salmon interview, 22 October 2002.

p. 193 "Essex people very fed up . . ." David diary entry, 18 February 1944, IWM.

p. 193 One such was Ken Bond . . . Ken Bond (1/4th Essex, 5th Brigade, 4th Indian Division) interview, 10 August 2002.

p. 194 "It rained as only it can in southern Italy . . ." quoted in T. A. Martin, *The Essex Regiment, 1929–50*, privately published, 1952, p. 307.

p. 195 "We were laid up in what was a dry ditch . . ." Ted Hazle (1/4th Essex, 5th Brigade, 4th Indian Division) interview, 15 July 2002.

p. 195 "a strangely unreal situation . . ." Beckett interview, 9 September 2002.

p. 195 "Again it rained nearly all day . . ." Charlie Fraser (signaler attached to 5th Brigade, 4th Indian Division) unpublished diary entry, 27 February 1944.

p. 195 "I was soaking wet . . ." Bond interview, 10 August 2002.

p. 195 "I never drew pictures about 'screaming meemies' . . ." Mauldin, *Up Front*, p. 98.

p. 195 "The gun didn't go off with a roar . . ." Pyle, *Brave Men*, p. 205.

p. 196 "like someone sitting violently . . ." Majdalany, *Monastery*, p. 161.

p. 196 but on 3 March at another conference . . . Martin, *Essex Regiment*, p. 307.

p. 196 "The Essex are said to be getting the honor . . ." David diary entry, 13 February 1944, IWM.

p. 196 "Just when our morale was sadly needing a fillip . . ." quoted in Martin, *Essex Regiment*, p. 307.

p. 196 "A report both misleading and untrue!" Tomlinson Papers, IWM.

p. 196 "On many nights we heard the odd crack . . ." B. Smith Papers, IWM.

p. 196 In all, 7th Brigade was losing sixty men a day . . . Ellis, *Cassino*, p. 214.

p. 197 "I did not undress at all for two months . . ." Hawtin interview, 19 September 2002.

p. 197 "Our troubles now begin in earnest . . ." David diary entries, 25–27 February 1944, IWM.

p. 198 "Went out with fifty mules . . ." Cormack diary entry, 28 February 1944.

p. 198 "I had to tell what I had seen . . ." Kurt Langelüddecke (Heavy Artillery Troop 602, attached to 3rd Battalion, 1st Parachute Division) interview, 7 March 2003.

p. 199 "Day passed slowly. Few odd jobs . . ." *Daily Mail*, 21 May 1994.

p. 199 "tired, disheveled, many of them wounded . . ." E. D. Smith, *Even the Brave*, p. 7.

p. 199 "He was a different man . . ." Ibid., p. 8.

p. 199 "Have we been condemned to live forever . . ." *Daily Mail*, 21 May 1994.

p. 199 "I left the farmhouse where I was in the last letter . . ." David letter, 10 March 1944, IWM.

p. 199 "Rain has been falling for several hours . . ." Jean Murat unpublished diary account entitled "Campagne d'Italie 1st Compagnie du 4ème Regiment de Tirailleurs Tunisiens, 1944," and interview, 12 February 2003.

p. 200 "I've been in the line for several days now . . ." AFHQ G-2 Intelligence Notes No. 57, 2 May 1944, p. C7; PRO WO204/986.

p. 201 "The weather did not improve . . ." F. G. Sutton (2nd Beds and Herts Battalion, 10th Brigade, British 4th Division) Papers, IWM.

p. 201 "The only paths were goat tracks . . ." Framp, *Littlest Victory*, p. 71.

p. 201 "a curiously hole-and-corner life . . ." Bernard Fergusson, *The Black Watch and the King's Enemies* (Collins, 1950), p. 202.

p. 201 "It was bitterly cold, blizzards were frequent . . ." Framp, *Littlest Victory*, p. 72.

p. 202 German snipers would always target . . . R. J. Bubb (2nd Coldstream Guards, 1st Guards Brigade, British 6th Armoured Division) letter from son.

p. 202 "We were spotted . . ." Sgt.-Maj. Les Thornton (16th Durham Light Infantry, 139 Brigade, British 46th Division), quoted in Hart, *Heat of Battle*, pp. 98–99.

p. 202 "Almost our whole marriage . . ." Walter Robson, (1st Royal West Kents, 12 Brigade, British 4th Division) *Letters from a Soldier* (Faber & Faber, 1960), p. 12.

p. 202 "In Cairo I saw a newsreel showing our boys in Italy . . ." Ibid., p. 73.

p. 202 "chap, tin hat, overcoat, leather jerkin . . ." Ibid., p. 77.

p. 203 "I would I think, be haunted all my life . . ." Ibid., p. 87.

p. 203 "Jerry hadn't started his nightly bout of shelling . . ." Ibid., p. 81.

p. 203 "There was a lot of sickness . . ." Lorimer interview, 17 December 2002.

p. 203 "lined up for chow . . ." Cocker interview, 15 December 2002.

p. 203 "People appeared subdued . . ." Blythe, *Soldiering On*, p. 144.

p. 204 "There was a lot of booze . . ." Vojta interview, 25 February 2003.

p. 204 The comedian Tommy Trinder . . . Allnutt Papers, IWM, p. 52.

p. 204 "a plague of telephone-wire cutting . . ." Lewis, *Naples '44*, p. 72.

p. 205 "The first great city of German Europe . . ." Moorehead, *Eclipse*, pp. 62–64.

p. 205 "a vision of a den of iniquity . . ." Murat interview, 12 December 2003.

p. 205 "Nothing had been too large or too small . . ." Lewis, *Naples '44*, p. 86.

p. 205 65 percent of Neapolitans' per capita income . . . Ibid., p. 119.

p. 206 "The victims who fall . . ." Ibid., p. 99.

p. 206   "Whenever you went on leave, especially to a place like Naples . . ." Cocker interview, 15 December 2002.

p. 206   "The impudence of the black market . . ." Lewis, *Naples '44*, pp. 134–35.

p. 206   where "the same international society, a little diminished . . ." Moorehead, *Eclipse*, p. 65.

p. 207   "rather bad form . . ." Christopher Buckley, *The Road to Rome* (Hodder & Stoughton, 1945), pp. 251, 253.

p. 207   they had wanted to buy food and clothes . . . Moorehead, *Eclipse*, p. 63.

p. 207   "Six-year-old boys . . ." Ibid., p. 63.

p. 207   "Nine out of ten girls have lost their menfolk . . ." Lewis, *Naples '44*, p. 115.

p. 207   who "just couldn't stay away from the prostitutes . . ." Kindre interview, 28 June 1994.

p. 207   "Not all of the men participated . . ." Vojta interview, 25 February 2003.

p. 208   "It was totally liberating . . ." Kindre interview, 28 June 1994.

p. 208   "They all feel a certain freedom . . ." Mauldin, *Up Front*, p. 73.

p. 208   "helping themselves to whatever they could lay their hands on . . ." Lewis, *Naples '44*, pp. 25–26.

p. 208   "was do whatever you want to . . ." Kindre interview, 28 June 1994.

p. 209   with several hundred new cases every week . . . Moorehead, *Eclipse*, p. 66.

p. 209   "to all intents and purpose were reintroduced . . ." Lewis, *Naples '44*, p. 95.

p. 209   "It begins, 'I am not interested in your syphilitic sister' . . ." Ibid., p. 101.

p. 209   "the temptation is very great . . ." Ibid., pp. 192–93.

p. 210   "I departed with the others in a somewhat funny mood . . ." Blythe, *Soldiering* pp. 145–48.

PART FOUR: THE THIRD BATTLE

p. 213   "I only know what we see . . ." Newspaper article quoted in Hollies Papers.

p. 213   "What I saw took me back . . ." Von Senger, *Neither Fear*, p. 215.

12: THE BATTLE FOR CASSINO TOWN

p. 215   "after the first bombs fell there were a few seconds . . ." MacKenzie interview, December 2002.

p. 215   "The impressive spectacle . . ." E. Puttick, *25 Battalion* (Department of Internal Affairs, 1958), p. 392.

p. 216   "None who saw it will forget . . ." quoted in Phillips, *Sangro to Cassino*, pp. 267–

p. 216   "Mitchells in a long column . . ." Robin Kay, *27 Machine-Gun Battalion* (Department of Internal Affairs, 1958), p. 394.

p. 216   Jack Cocker's 27th Battalion . . . Cocker taped memoir, and ibid., p. 395.

p. 216   "Just back to camp, when Americans . . ." Cormack diary entry, 16 March 1944.

p. 216   One bomb killed twenty-two of their friends . . . Jaconelli (née Notarianni) interview, 15 September 2002.

p. 216   "When four or five bombs had landed . . ." E. D. Smith, *Even the Brave*, p. 12.

p. 217   "Tensely we waited in our holes . . ." quoted in Böhmler, *Monte Cassino*, 210–11.

p. 217   "The first wave dropped most of its load . . ." quoted in Trevelyan, *Rome '44*, p. 199.

p. 217   "More and more sticks of bombs fell . . ." quoted in J. Piekalkiewicz, *Cassino: Anatomy of a Battle* (Orbis, 1980), p. 130.

p. 217   "The crash of bursting bombs . . ." quoted in Böhmler, *Monte Cassino*, p. 211.

p. 218   a thousand tons of shells, the equivalent of 275 truckloads . . . Piekalkiewicz, *Cassino*, p. 133.

p. 218   "We have fumigated Cassino . . ." Lt. Gen. Ira C. Eaker, commander of the Mediterranean Allied Air Force, quoted in Ellis, *Cassino*, p. 222.

p. 218   "Today hell is let loose at Cassino . . ." PRO WO 204/986.

p. 218   "Entering Cassino was a vision . . ." quoted in Trevelyan, *Rome '44*, p. 201.

p. 220   "There was no way the tanks . . ." Lorimer interview, 17 December 2002.

p. 221   "thankful that at last we were engaged . . ." Roger Smith, *Up the Blue* (Ngaio Press, 2000), p. 193.

p. 222   "consistency of dough . . ." New Zealand report, quoted in Ellis, *Cassino*, p. 234; PRO WO204/8287.

p. 222   "in a thick grey slime . . ." R. Smith, *Up the Blue*, p. 195.

p. 222   "As Bill and I came to the edge of the rock . . ." quoted in Puttick, *25 Battalion*, p. 401.

p. 223   "Darkness brought the rain . . ." Bill Humble (signaler attached to 4th Indian Division), unpublished diary.

p. 223   "It was raining and we started to climb . . ." Bill Hawkins (1/4th Essex, 5th Brigade, 4th Indian Division) interview, 15 August 2002.

p. 223   "The damage caused by the bombing . . ." Beckett, quoted in E. D. Smith, *Cassino*, p. 109, and interview, 9 September 2002.

p. 223   "It seemed to be neverending . . ." Hawkins interview, 15 August 2002.

p. 224   "The prearranged plan . . ." Hawkins interview, 15 August 2002.

p. 225   "no longer an effective battalion . . ." Fraser diary entry, 17 March 1944.

p. 225   "At lunchtime the Raj. Rif. Officers began to come in . . ." David diary entry, 17 March 1944.

p. 226   "Just as we prepared to move off . . ." Tom Simpson (4/6th Rajputana Rifles, 11th Brigade, 4th Indian Division) personal account.

p. 227   "I was left with no food, nothing . . ." Hazle interview, 15 July 2002.

p. 227   "down the side. You never saw them again . . ." Bond interview, 10 August 2002.

p. 227   "Getting through was difficult . . ." Lorimer interview, 17 December 2002.

p. 227   "morass of liquid mud . . ." Puttick, *25 Battalion*, p. 409.

p. 228   "shared a house with the enemy . . ." Ibid., p. 405.

p. 228   "Town literally full of enemy snipers . . ." quoted in John Crawford, *North from Taranto: New Zealand and the Liberation of Italy, 1943–45* (New Zealand Defence Force, 1994), p. 39.

p. 228   "the consternation that greeted Hannibal's elephants . . ." Majdalany, *Cassino*, p. 187.

13: CASTLE HILL

p. 229   "We were in a pretty fair state of chaos . . ." Beckett interview, 9 September 2002.

p. 230   "nothing less than the last phase of a medieval siege . . ." Ellis, *Cassino*, p. 250.

p. 230 "We could not use artillery defensive fire . . ." Beckett interview, 9 September 20[ ] and his written account.

p. 231 "Fighting at times was at very close quarters . . ." Hawkins interview, 15 Aug[ ] 2002.

p. 231 "I had never done a truce . . ." Beckett interview, 9 September 2002.

p. 232 "It's the jackpot for us . . ." *Daily Mail*, 21 May 1994, and E. D. Smith, *Even Brave*, p. 13.

p. 232 "We moved into the town . . ." E. D. Smith, *Even the Brave*, p. 14.

p. 232 "The scene inside the Castle . . ." Ibid., pp. 16–17.

p. 232 "I was convinced," he says . . . Beckett interview, 9 September 2002.

p. 232 "One way you get shot . . ." E. D. Smith, *Even the Brave*, pp. 18–19.

p. 234 "[The Germans] were abusing him . . ." Pomana interview, 16 January 2003.

p. 235 "as the door crashed open they were framed . . ." R. Smith, *Up the Blue*, p. 205.

p. 235 "Suddenly we heard tank noises . . ." Eggert unpublished memoir.

p. 236 "Once again one fist struck . . ." G. R. Stevens, *Fourth Indian Division* (McCla[ ] and Sons, 1949), p. 306.

p. 236 "shredded trees, all splintered . . ." Bond interview, 10 August 2002.

p. 236 "Jerry was shooting at us . . ." Hazle interview, 15 July 2002.

p. 237 "just as difficult as coming up . . ." Hawkins interview, 15 August 2002.

p. 237 "We were taken forward by a truck . . ." Hollies Papers, IWM.

p. 238 "an unearthly place . . ." quoted in Watt, *Mates and Mayhem*, pp. 127–29.

p. 239 "could see no rifle or other flash . . ." A. Ross, *23 Battalion* (Department of Int[ ] nal Affairs, 1957), p. 329.

p. 239 "Our local war had reached a stalemate . . ." Hollies Papers, IWM.

p. 239 "The air in the town [was] heavy with smoke . . ." quoted in T. Williams, *Cassi[ ]* p. 178.

p. 239 "You'd be down in your gun pit . . ." Cocker interview, 15 December 2002.

p. 239 "Our four days and nights . . ." Hollies Papers, IWM.

p. 239 "There seems little doubt that the conditions . . ." Crawford, *North from Taranto* 41.

p. 240 "come to the end of its tether . . ." quoted in Phillips, *Sangro to Cassino*, p. 328.

p. 240 "ultimate quintessence of war . . ." quoted in Trevelyan, *Rome '44*, p. 205.

p. 240 "infantry from Cassino showed signs of prolonged strain . . ." McKinney, *Med[ ] Units*, pp. 351–52.

p. 240 "If we weren't altogether happy . . ." quoted in Stevens, *Fourth Indian Division*, 307.

p. 241 "There was no one to give us instruction . . ." Bond interview, 10 August 2002.

p. 241 "Chappatis by parachute . . ." Pathé news report, INR 62, IWM Film Archive.

p. 241 "You had to scramble out . . ." Bond interview, 10 August 2002.

p. 241 The Essex Battalion historian tells the story . . . Martin, *Essex Regiment*, p. 317.

p. 241 "It was our own smoke . . ." Hazle interview, 15 July 2002.

p. 241 "Canisters, shell cases, and base plugs . . ." Lt. Col. G. S. Nangle (1/9th Gurkhas, 5[ ] Brigade, 4th Indian Division) quoted in Stevens, *Fourth Indian Division*, p. 307.

p. 242 "Tiredness was the worst . . ." Hazle interview, 15 July 2002.

p. 242 "What growth that was left . . ." Granada program, and others.

p. 242 "The fire was so heavy . . ." Balbahadur Khanka (1/9th Gurkhas, 5th Brigade, 4[ ] Indian Division) interview, Cross Tape 116.

p. 242 "For a week we were not resupplied . . ." Katuwal interview, Cross Tape 157.

p. 242 "We had virtually no food or drink . . ." Gumansing Chhetri (1/9th Gurkhas, 5th Brigade, 4th Indian Division), interview, Cross Tape 234.

p. 242 "My battalion is One Nine GR . . ." Dalbahadur Chhetri (1/9th Gurkhas, 5th Brigade, 4th Indian Division), Cross Tape 167.

p. 242 "One young officer came up . . ." Hazle interview, 15 July 2002.

p. 243 The Germans later counted 165 dead Gurkhas . . . Böhmler, *Monte Cassino*, p. 217.

p. 243 "fourteen different holes in me . . ." quoted in Martin, *Essex Regiment*, p. 318.

p. 243 "When we reached them . . ." McKinney, *Medical Units*, pp. 352–53.

p. 244 "I was so delighted . . ." quoted in Martin, *Essex Regiment*, p. 320.

p. 244 the number of New Zealand admissions . . . McKinney, *Medical Units*, p. 354.

p. 244 "I noticed that there was a different approach to battle . . ." Hollies Papers, IWM.

p. 244 "Great guys, kind-hearted . . ." Pittaccio interview, 12 August 2002.

p. 245 "For most of the time in the front line . . ." E. D. Smith, *Even the Brave*, p. 26.

p. 245 "4th Division lost more than a battle . . ." quoted in E. D. Smith, *Cassino*, p. 140.

p. 245 "steak, chips and tomatoes . . ." Hazle interview 15 July 2002.

p. 245 "the 1/4th Essex left the 5th Army . . ." Ibid., p. 320.

p. 245 twice the losses . . . Ibid., p. 340.

p. 245 "After Cassino we had lost quite a lot of our offensive spirit . . ." Beckett interview, 9 September 2002.

p. 245 "Before Cassino you had the blokes . . ." Hawkins interview, 15 August 2002.

p. 246 "There was terrible fear . . ." Granada program.

14: THE GREEN DEVILS OF CASSINO

p. 247 "I had to go to Brussels to see the chief psychiatrist . . ." Klein interview, 1 February 2003.

p. 248 "You start at six o'clock in the morning . . ." quoted in *Images of War*, p. 751.

p. 248 "There were people who got so worn out . . ." Klein interview, 1 February 2003.

p. 249 "Unfortunately we are fighting the best soldiers . . ." quoted in Ellis, *Cassino*, p. 263.

p. 249 "Even after those casualties they were still fighting hard . . ." quoted in Watt, *Mates and Mayhem*, p. 128.

p. 249 "bold and determined . . ." *The Times*, 23 March 1944.

p. 249 Naples radio reported on 21 March . . . quoted in Böhmler, *Monte Cassino*, p. 242.

p. 249 "We are there for each other . . ." Klein interview, 1 February 2003.

p. 249 "so-called heroic acts . . ." Eggert interview, 20 March 2003.

p. 250 whipped "black and blue" . . . Klein interview, 1 February 2003.

p. 250 "The progress of the fighting in Italy . . ." quoted in Piekalkiewicz, *Cassino*, p. 145.

p. 250 "blotting out all enemy resistance . . ." Air Marshal Sir John Slessor, quoted in Ellis, *Cassino*, p. 234.

p. 251 "one of the most perplexing operations of the war . . ." quoted in E. D. Smith, *Cassino*, p. 100.

p. 251 "These Italians are funny people . . ." Awes letter, 24 March 1944.

p. 252 "I saw one woman with a little girl . . ." Awes interview, 22 February 2003.

p. 252 "The Germans flooded . . ." Pittaccio interview, 12 August 2002.

p. 252 "They would not give us food . . ." Jaconelli (née Notarianni) interview, 15 September 2002.

p. 252   "The ones we could have done without . . ." Pittaccio e-mail, 21 November 2002.

p. 253   "the French colonial troops are on the rampage . . ." Lewis, *Naples '44*, pp. 143–44.

p. 253   banning Allied "colored" troops . . . Owen Chadwick, *Britain and the Vatican during the Second World War* (Cambridge University Press, 1987), p. 290.

p. 253   "the Goums have become a legend . . ." Marsland Gander, quoted in Jean-Christophe Notin, *La Campagne d'Italie* (Librarie Académique Perrin, 2002), p. 500.

p. 253   "I myself witnessed a most dangerous incident . . ." Pittaccio e-mail, 21 Nov. 2002.

p. 254   "we lost several fellas looking for loot . . ." Cocker interview, 15 Dec. 2002.

p. 254   "We shouted at them to come out . . ." Lt. Russell Collins, quoted in Hart, *Heat of Battle*, pp. 82–83.

p. 254   "we souvenired his plane's compass . . ." Alf Voss (21st Battalion, 5th Brigade, 2nd New Zealand Division), quoted in Watt, *Mates, and Mayhem*, p. 115.

p. 254   in some instances cutting off the finger . . . Joseph Menditto (2nd Battalion, 351st Regiment, US 88th Division) interview, 22 Feb. 2003.

p. 254   "We are back in the hills behind Cassino . . ." quoted in AFHQ Intelligence Notes, No. 57; PRO WO204/986.

p. 255   "a lifeline to sanity . . ." Bennett J. Palmer, (1st Battalion, 143rd Regiment, US 36th Division), *The Hunter and the Hunted*, privately published 1992, p. 55.

p. 255   "I've had no letters . . ." Robson, *Letters*, p. 92.

p. 255   One American veteran sent five hundred . . . Joseph Menditto is the soldier in question.

p. 255   "A few magazines and books . . ." Ronald Blythe, quoted in Fussell, *Wartime*, p. 212.

p. 256   "Soldiers at the front read K-ration labels . . ." Mauldin, *Up Front*, p. 25.

p. 256   Nineteen-year-old Colin O'Shaughnessy, a private . . . in the 5th Northants, 11 Brigade, British 78th Division.

p. 256   "I don't want to write . . ." Robson, *Letters*, pp. 31–33.

p. 256   "It's hard to compose a letter . . ." Mauldin, *Up Front*, p. 24.

p. 256   "It's a rotten shame . . ." O'Shaughnessy letter, n.d.

p. 256   "I should write gay *triviata* but I can't . . ." Robson, *Letters*, p. 87.

p. 256   "One day I am going to send you a letter packed . . ." Ibid., p. 17.

p. 256   "the feeling that you can't keep on going up these mountains . . ." Ibid., p. 85.

p. 257   "Poor devil, he's well out of it . . ." Ibid., p. 83.

p. 257   "You always had that just-before-the-race feeling . . ." Majdalany, *Monastery*, pp. 13–14.

p. 257   "rusty and hideous . . ." Ibid., p. 17.

p. 257   "You thought of a clean hospital bed . . ." Ibid., p. 19.

p. 257   "We eventually reached the Gurkha battalion HQ . . ." J. MacKenzie, (2nd Lancashire Fusiliers, 11th Brigade, British 78th Division), privately published memoir, 1997, p. 33.

p. 258   "As we approached Snakeshead . . ." Majdalany, *Monastery*, p. 20.

p. 258   "The forward defensive layout . . ." MacKenzie memoir, p. 37.

p. 258   "you would see small groups of bare hindquarters . . ." Majdalany, *Monastery*, p. 24.

p. 258   "The lines in your hand ingrained with dirt . . ." Ivor Cutler (5th Northants, 11th Brigade, British 78th Division), interview, 11 Sept. 2002.

p. 259   "in an advanced state of decomposition . . ." Majdalany, *Monastery*, p. 25.

p. 259   "A state of utter timelessness set in . . ." Ibid., p. 77.

p. 259   "Our potable water supply was delicate . . ." Eggert unpublished memoir.

p. 260   "They were shelling us all the time . . ." Robert Frettlöhr, quoted in *Images of War*, p. 751.

p. 260   "It wasn't a pleasant time up there . . ." Robert Frettlöhr, quoted in *Everyone's War* 6, p. 22.

p. 260   "It was obvious the French were very good soldiers . . ." Sutton Papers, IWM.

p. 261   "Did you know that the British troops . . ." Service Historique de l'Armée de Terre (SHAT) 10P39, quoted in Notin, *La Campagne*, p. 344.

p. 261   "Boys of the NZEF . . ." quoted in T. Williams, *Cassino*, p. 41.

p. 261   "TO INDIAN TROOPS . . ." PRO WO 204/986.

p. 261   "While you are away . . ." propaganda leaflet shown to the author by Mr. R. Hornsby, RASC.

p. 262   "No American boys will be sacrificed . . ." Ibid.

p. 262   "In spite of all that, Winston had a great affection . . ." propaganda leaflet shown to the author by Mr. G. E. Stevens (2nd Lancashire Fusiliers, 11th Brigade, British 78th Division).

p. 262   The mobile press could turn out four-by-six-inch leaflets . . . Hapgood, *Monte Cassino*, p. 190.

p. 262   "Those of you who are lucky enough . . ." PRO WO 204/986.

p. 263   "Take a laxative . . ." leaflet shown to the author by Mr. L. Bradshaw.

p. 263   "as if this was a regular service . . ." "Experiences of an Interrogator 46th Division"; PRO WO 204/985.

p. 263   a special radio station near Cassino . . . PRO WO 204/986.

p. 263   "We always used to listen to the German propaganda . . ." Henry McRae (21st Battalion, 5th Brigade, 2nd New Zealand Division), quoted in T. Williams, *Cassino*, p. 38.

p. 264   "When you now return home . . ." translation of an information leaflet issued to a member of 134th PG Regiment prior to his returning to Germany on furlough; PRO WO 204/985.

p. 264   "About two-thirds said . . ." "Impressions of an Escapee from a Camp for Allied PWs in Italy"; PRO WO 204/985.

p. 264   "despite the immense casualties . . ." Intelligence report, 21 October 1943, 15th Army Group Intelligence; PRO WO 106/3918.

p. 265   "a very dangerous place . . ." Cocker taped memoir.

p. 266   "I was overawed by what I saw . . ." Cyril Harte (3rd Grenadiers, 1st Guards Brigade, British 6th Armoured Division), article in *Northampton Chronicle and Echo*, 9 May 1994, and interview, 19 Sept. 2002.

p. 266   "Can't wash, the water's rationed . . ." Robson, *Letters*, pp. 101–2.

p. 266   "There was a big German outside . . ." George Holme (attached to 2nd Coldstream Guards, 1st Guards Brigade, British 6th Armoured Division), interview, 13 Sept. 2002.

p. 266   "During the hours of daylight we looked out . . ." Framp, *Littlest Victory*, p. 84.

p. 266   "The sentry, in the blackness of the interior . . ." Robson, *Letters*, p. 93.

p. 267   "And above the entrance to our cellar . . ." Framp, *Littlest Victory*, p. 83.

p. 267   "I remember being sent to collect dead bodies . . ." quoted in Trevelyan, *Rome '44*, p. 209.

p. 267   "extraordinary obsession . . ." quoted by E. D. Smith, *Cassino*, p. 144.

p. 268   "We sat under the olive trees . . ." Klein interview, 1 Feb. 2003.

PART FIVE: THE FOURTH BATTLE

p. 269   "He knew that the essence of war . . ." Macaulay, "Essay on Lord Nugent's Memorials of Hampden," 1831.

p. 269   "I was at Stalingrad . . ." quoted in Ellis, *Cassino*, p. 356.

15: DECEPTION

p. 272   "There is nothing special going on . . ." quoted in Ellis, *Cassino*, p. 277.

p. 272   "Four unknown factors . . ." Kesselring, *Memoirs*, p. 200.

p. 274   57 battalions to face the 108 Allied . . . Ellis, *Cassino*, p. 267n.

p. 274   "Only numbers can annihilate . . ." quoted in Majdalany, *Cassino*, p. 221.

p. 275   "truly sorry for GI Joe . . ." Klaus H. Huebner, *Long Walk through War* (Texas A&M University Press, 1987), p. 11.

p. 275   "I don't quite understand exactly . . ." Ibid., p. 18.

p. 275   "As we entered combat . . ." Len Dziabas (2nd Battalion, 351st Regiment, US 88th Division), personal account.

p. 275   "The sounds of war are still new . . ." Huebner, *Long Walk*, p. 42.

p. 275   "publicity hound . . ." Milton Dolinger telephone interview, 3 April 2003.

p. 276   "One day while helping to build a latrine trench . . ." Milton Dolinger, "The 88th Infantry Division's Public Relations Section," *The Blue Devil* newsletter (2001).

p. 276   "credit . . ." Fussell, *Wartime*, p. 153.

p. 276   "Jack [Delaney] had an inspiration . . ." Dolinger, "88th Infantry."

p. 277   "grim group of dead, in a sangar . . ." John Delaney, *The Blue Devils in Italy* (Infantry Journal Press, 1947), p. 45.

p. 277   99 dead, 252 wounded . . . Ibid., p. 47.

p. 277   "A deserted building near the battalion command post . . ." Huebner, *Long Walk*, p. 49.

p. 277   "We fire heavy artillery all night . . ." Ibid., p. 53.

p. 277   "strolling over small paths . . ." Ibid., p. 61.

p. 278   "The cooks are jittery . . ." Arthur Schick (3rd Battalion, 351st Regiment, US 88th Division), letter, 26 April 1944.

p. 278   "I haven't received a letter from you . . ." Schick letter, 28 April 1944.

p. 278   "I promise you it will be soon . . ." Delaney, *Blue Devils*, p. 58.

p. 278   "We have been bothered with Generals again . . ." Schick letter, 4 May 1944.

p. 278   "The effect of this tense period of waiting . . ." James C. Fry (350th Regiment, US 88th Division) *Combat Soldier* (National Press Inc., 1968), p. 11.

p. 279   "The waiting was agonizing . . ." Murat unpublished diary.

p. 280   "thousands of mines . . ." Frank Sellwood (225th Field Engineering Company, British 4th Division), interview, 12 Aug. 2002.

p. 281   "We arranged a rendezvous . . ." A. P. de T. Daniell (59th Field Engineering Company, British 4th Division), "The Battle for Cassino May 1944," in *Royal Engineers Journal* (1951): p. 287.

p. 282   "as fast as he had ever swum . . ." Ibid., p. 293.

p. 282   "Morale was very, very good . . ." Royal Engineers video "Amazon (Crossing the Rapido)," RSME G309, 1988, © Royal Engineers Library, Chatham. Used with permission.

p. 282   "There was time to write letters home . . ." Thomas M. J. Riordan (7th Field Engineering Company, British 4th Division), *A History of the 7th Field Company RE*, privately published, 1984, p. 139.

p. 282   "swarms of fire flies hugged . . ." Ibid., p. 140.

p. 283   "My father was gassed . . ." Frederick Beacham (1st Royal Fusiliers, 17th Brigade, 8th Indian Division), interview, 5 Aug. 2002.

p. 283   "It was long, tiring and, at times, very frightening . . ." Beacham written account, IWM 67/384/1.

p. 284   "They were a sorry sight . . ." Józef Pankiewicz (2nd Brigade, 3rd Carpathian Division), interview, 7 Aug. 2003, and his written account.

p. 286   "I didn't believe it, I thought I had died . . ." Piotr Sulek (7th Horse Artillery Regiment, Polish Corps), interview, 16 Sept. 2002.

p. 287   "What was clear . . ." W. Anders, *An Army in Exile* (Macmillan, 1949), p. 149.

p. 287   "We met the men of the Polish Division . . ." Eke, Papers, IWM, p. 94.

p. 287   "greatly depressed our soldiers . . ." Anders, *Army in Exile*, p. 159.

p. 287   "We shall fight the Germans without respite . . ." Ibid., p. 161.

p. 287   "the Polish II Army Corps should carry out . . ." Ibid., p. 163.

p. 288   "At times their seriousness . . ." Majdalany, *Cassino*, p. 234.

p. 288   "thought we were far too casual . . ." Majdalany, *Monastery*, p. 105.

p. 288   "wondered whether the intensity . . ." Majdalany, *Cassino*, p. 234.

p. 288   "Their motives were as clear . . ." John Horsfall, *Fling our Banner to the Wind* (Kineton, 1978), p. 33.

p. 289   "They would say, 'Come on Polish boys, the Russians are coming,' . . ." Zbigniew Budzynksi (5th Kresowa Infantry Division), quoted in Diana M. Henderson, ed., *The Lion and the Eagle* (Cualann Press, 2001), pp. 34–35.

p. 289   "Soldiers! The moment for battle . . ." quoted in C. Connell, *Monte Cassino* (Elek, 1963), pp. 125–26.

p. 289   "Throughout the past winter . . ." quoted in ibid., p. 124.

p. 289   "while the order was being read out . . ." Majdalany, *Monastery*, p. 125.

p. 290   "It was a very impressive order . . ." Sutton Papers, IWM.

p. 290   "Before an attack fear is universal . . ." quoted in Copp and McAndrew, *Battle Exhaustion*, p. 75.

p. 291   "bundle of nerves . . ." Jack Meek (17/21st Lancers, British 6th Armoured Division), interview, 11 Sept. 2002.

p. 291   "As was my wont before any sort of battle . . ." Jack Meek account, written 1946.

p. 291   "This was to be my first action . . ." H. Buckle (17/21st Lancers, British 6th Armoured Division) Papers, IWM, p. 85.

p. 291   "the longest of my life . . ." Lee Harvey, *D-Day Dodger*, p. 112.

16: Break-In

p. 292   "Movement of any kind was strictly forbidden . . ." Beacham account.

p. 293   "the most exciting and exhilarating experience . . ." John Williams (328th Battery, 99th Light AA, Royal Artillery, attached to British XIII Corps), letter, 15 Dec. 2002.

p. 293   "The roar of the guns is so deafening . . ." Huebner, *Long Walk*, p. 62.

p. 293   "as if someone had switched on the lights . . ." Frettlöhr interview, 15 Sept. 2002.

p. 293   "awe-inspiring . . ." Beacham account.

p. 293   "Artillerymen worked like automatons . . ." Milton Dolinger, "With the 88th Division Artillery, Rome," written June 1944, *The Blue Devil* (1991).

p. 294   "The bullets started whizzing . . ." quoted in *Images of War*, p. 745.

p. 294   "The amount of artillery being fired . . ." Beacham account.

p. 296   "A Company having got across successfully . . ." David Wilson (1/12th Frontier Force Regiment, 17th Brigade, 8th Indian Division), personal account.

p. 296   "White guiding tapes had disappeared . . ." A. F. Chown (1/12th Frontier Force Regiment, 17th Brigade, 8th Indian Division), personal account.

p. 296   "toward the Germans on a compass bearing . . ." Wilson account.

p. 296   "The confused night continued . . ." Chown account.

p. 297   "The sun came up in all its glory . . ." Beacham account.

p. 298   "At about 8 A.M. the fog lifted . . ." Wilson account.

p. 298   "a day never to be forgotten . . ." Menditto interview, 22 Feb. 2003.

p. 299   "Shortly, perhaps twenty minutes . . ." Richard Barrows (HQ Company, 351st Regiment, US 88th Division), account and written answers to questions.

p. 299   "yelled and screamed at them . . ." Menditto interview, 22 Feb. 2003.

p. 300   "Five . . . four . . ." Cuvillier, *Tribulations*, p. 33.

p. 301   "The advanced surgical units . . ." Ibid., p. 34.

p. 301   "From 1 A.M. on 12 May, the battalion . . ." Murat unpublished diary.

p. 302   "There was no time to be frightened . . ." Murat interview, 12 Feb. 2003.

p. 302   "Now the company goes into attack formation . . ." Murat unpublished diary.

p. 303   "Night gives way to day . . ." Cuvillier, *Tribulations*, p. 34.

p. 303   "A whistling shell flew low overhead . . ." Zbigniew Fleszar (1st Battalion, 1st Brigade, 3rd Carpathian Division), quoted in *Images of War*, p. 749.

p. 305   "Shells from our own artillery . . ." Edward Rynkiewicz (2nd Battalion, 1st Brigade, 3rd Carpathian Division), quoted in Connell, *Monte Cassino*, p. 180.

p. 305   "sweat running down into our eyes . . ." quoted in *Images of War*, p. 749.

p. 306   "We surged forward . . ." Connell, *Monte Cassino*, p. 179ff.

p. 306   Eighteen of the twenty engineers working with the tanks . . . Piekalkiewicz, *Cassino*, p. 170.

p. 307   "When darkness fell the Germans . . ." Connell, *Monte Cassino*, p. 189.

p. 307   "When we saw that the wounded Germans . . ." Ibid., p. 191.

p. 308   "Enemy reserves would suddenly emerge . . ." Anders, *Army in Exile*, p. 176.

p. 308   Some men returned over the river on an "alleged order" . . . Ellis, *Cassino*, p. 300.

p. 309   "The smoke was building up . . ." Riordan, *A History*, p. 142.

p. 309   "When we got to the site . . ." Royal Engineers video.

p. 309   "It was clear that unless the infantry cleared . . ." Riordan, *A History*, p. 143.

p. 310   "Nobody said anything . . ." Robert Lister (7th Field Engineering Company, British 4th Division), interview, 24 Oct. 2002.

p. 310   "dejected parties of infantry . . ." Daniell, "Battle of Cassino," p. 294.

p. 310   "There were people coming across . . ." Sellwood interview, 12 Aug. 2002.

p. 310   "The Boche must have sensed . . ." Daniell, "Battle of Cassino," p. 294.

17: Amazon Bridge

p. 311   "It looked as if the whole big mountain . . ." Sutton Papers, IWM.

p. 311   "As I saw for myself on the morning of 12 May . . ." Kesselring, *Memoirs*, p. 200.

p. 312   "giving details of regrouping for the night . . ." War Diary 4 Division, 20.00, 12 May 1944, quoted in Ellis, *Cassino*, p. 302.

p. 312   "Do you think this is a good thing? . . . " quoted in Riordan, *A History*, p. 145.

p. 312   "The sapper on the bulldozer . . ." Sutton Papers, IWM.

p. 313   "It was a bright, clear evening . . ." Riordan, *A History*, p. 147.

p. 313   "Bloody hell, we're on next! . . . " Bert Hobson (7th Field Engineering Company, British 4th Division), interview, 12 Sept. 2002.

p. 313   "that they wouldn't be needed . . ." Sellwood interview, 12 Aug. 2002.

p. 314   "A brilliant blue flash appeared . . ." Royal Engineers video.

p. 314   "The trouble was that for every one wounded . . ." Hobson interview, 12 Sept. 2002.

p. 314   "adding to the conflagration . . ." Daniell, "Battle of Cassino," p. 298.

p. 314   "It was like Dante's inferno . . ." Stan Goold (18th Field Park Company, British 4th Division), telephone interview, 6 Dec. 2002.

p. 315   "Everyone downed tools and ran . . ." Jo Gileard (7th Field Engineering Company, British 4th Division), telephone interview, 5 Nov. 2002.

p. 315   "It was very disconcerting . . ." Hobson interview, 12 Sept. 2002.

p. 315   "and later, out of sheer desperation . . ." Daniell, "Battle of Cassino," p. 299.

p. 315   "We carried a canvas boat folded up . . ." Sellwood interview, 12 Aug. 2002.

p. 316   "This was a major disaster . . ." Daniell, "Battle of Cassino," p. 300.

p. 316   "I can only conclude that the occasion . . ." quoted in Riordan, *A History*, p. 165.

p. 316   At a quarter to five, Wayne . . . R. L. V. ffrench Blake, *History of the 17/21 Lancers, 1922–59* (Macmillan, 1962), pp. 160–61.

p. 316   "Someone offered me a cup of tea . . ." quoted in Riordan, *A History*, pp. 165–66.

p. 316   "I had already heard the noise of tanks . . ." Sutton Papers, IWM.

p. 317   "We raced by a Bren carrier . . ." Framp, *Littlest Victory*, pp. 103–4.

p. 317   "I saw the bright gleam of polished steel . . ." Ibid., pp. 105–6.

p. 317   "There were more prisoners . . ." Sutton Papers, IWM.

p. 318   "There were bodies all over the place . . ." Meek interview, 11 Sept. 2002.

p. 318   "About half past three . . ." Beacham account.

p. 319   "To be asked to charge . . ." Beacham interview, 2 Aug. 2002.

p. 320   "in [seven days] my command managed . . ." H. G. Harris (1/6th Surreys, 10th Brigade, British 4th Division) Papers, IWM.

p. 320   "We've attacked, attacked, attacked . . ." Robson, *Letters*, p. 97.

p. 320   "I hear abundant small-arms fire . . ." Huebner, *Long Walk*, p. 65.

p. 321   "It was magnificent . . ." Delaney, *Blue Devils*, p. 70.

p. 321   "We dug in in an old German sump hole . . ." Barrows personal account.

p. 321   "The tanks are slowly rumbling . . ." Huebner, *Long Walk*, p. 68.

p. 322   "had to call on a doctor . . ." Fry, *Combat Soldier*, p. 35.

p. 322   "The only descriptive word I know is cowardice . . ." Ibid., p. 29.

p. 323   "All at once, all our arms open fire . . ." Murat unpublished diary.

p. 324   "You can have no idea of the brutality and the horror . . ." SHAT 1K475, 18 May
          1944, quoted in Notin, *La Campagne*, p. 382.

p. 325   to avoid being mistaken for Germans . . . Huebner, *Long Walk*, p. 76.

p. 325   "All of a sudden we could hear firing and screaming . . ." Len Dziabas telephone in-
          terview, 2 April 2003.

p. 325   "Unfortunately, the rapes carried out . . ." Cuvillier, *Tribulations*, pp. 45–46.

18: THE MONASTERY

p. 326   "pounding fire . . . We sat there for five days . . ." Langelüddecke interview, 7
          March 2003.

p. 326   "Impossible to get wounded away . . ." Major Veth, quoted in Böhmler, *Monte
          Cassino*, p. 266.

p. 326   "What they saw boded nothing but evil . . ." Ibid., p. 266.

p. 327   "It was more than nerves could stand . . ." quoted in Ellis, *Cassino*, p. 334.

p. 328   "vicious crossfire from small arms . . ." Cadet-Officer Pihut (6th Battalion, 2nd
          Brigade, 3rd Carpathian Division), quoted in Connell, *Monte Cassino*, p. 162.

p. 328   one German company was down to only three men . . . Böhmler, *Monte Cassino*, p.
          268.

p. 328   "I consider withdrawal to the Senger position necessary . . ." quoted in Ellis,
          Cassino, p. 311.

p. 328   "The 1st Parachute Division did not dream of surrendering . . ." Kesselring, *Mem-
          oirs*, p. 202.

p. 328   "Cassino will be given up . . ." Langelüddecke interview, 7 March 2003.

p. 328   "We intercepted [a] message in German . . ." Colonel Lakinski (3rd Carpathian Di-
          vision), quoted in Connell, *Monte Cassino*, p. 172.

p. 329   "I went to Captain Beyer . . ." Langelüddecke interview, 7 March 2003.

p. 329   "big flash . . ." Frettlöhr interview, 15 Sept. 2002.

p. 330   "Our combat strength had melted away . . ." Eggert account and interview, 20
          March 2003.

p. 332   "At first he refused to believe . . ." Connell, *Monte Cassino*, p. 172.

p. 332   "The stink of decay hung over the hill . . ." quoted in Piekalkiewicz, *Cassino*, p. 181.

p. 332   "in bandages and rags, unshaven, filthy . . ." Kazimierz Gurbiel (1st Squadron, 12th
          Podolski Lancers, 3rd Carpathian Division), quoted in Zenon Andrzejewski, un-
          published interview with Gurbiel.

p. 333   "It was ten o'clock in the morning when the Poles came . . ." quoted in *Images of
          War*, p. 751.

p. 333   "I said, through my [German-speaking] Silesian . . ." quoted in Andrzejewski, in-
          terview.

p. 333   "After all that fighting . . ." *Images of War*, p. 749.

p. 333   "There was a lump in my throat . . ." quoted in Piekalkiewicz, *Cassino*, p. 181.

p. 336   "Cassino in our hands . . ." Lorimer interview, 17 Dec. 2002.

p. 336   "We hung on grimly . . ." quoted in Connell, *Monte Cassino*, p. 162.

p. 336   "it was the most moving sight . . ." quoted in ibid., p. 172.

p. 336   "who knew more about us . . ." *Everyone's War* 6, p. 23.

p. 336 he remembers being amazed . . . Frettlöhr interview, 15 Sept. 2002.

p. 336 "By midday . . ." D. Erskine, *The Scots Guards, 1919–55* (Clowes, 1956), p. 234.

p. 337 "The battlefield presented a dreary sight . . ." Anders, *Army in Exile*, p. 179.

p. 337 "they came across a long corridor . . ." Connell, *Monte Cassino*, p. 151.

p. 338 "Went in at dawn . . ." quoted in *Everyone's War* 5, p. 40.

p. 338 "The city had not then got back to normal trading . . ." Beacham account.

p. 338 "Don't expect normal letters . . ." Robson, *Letters*, p. 96.

p. 339 "a campaign which for lack of strategic sense . . ." J. F. C. Fuller, *The Second World War* (Eyre & Spottiswoode, 1948), p. 261.

p. 339 "There were those people who thought the campaign . . ." *Battle for Cassino*, Big Little Picture Company video, BLP110 (1996).

p. 339 "If you're so tough, how come you're a prisoner . . ." quoted in Ellis, *Cassino*, p. 464.

p. 340 "In the late afternoon . . ." Bowlby, *Recollections*, p. 20.

POSTSCRIPT: SURVIVING THE PEACE

p. 341 "The soldiers shrug . . ." Robson, *Letters*, pp. 139–40.

p. 341 "The rank stench of those bodies . . ." copyright Siegfried Sassoon, by kind permission of George Sassoon.

p. 341 "three small figures in battledress . . ." Blythe, *Soldiering On*, p. 184.

p. 342 "We arrived at Folkestone . . ." Salmon, *Oh to Be a Sapper!*, p. 84.

p. 342 seven officers and 14,200 men . . . Anders, *Army in Exile*, p. 299.

p. 343 "In 1946 I came to England . . ." Pankiewicz personal account.

p. 343 "My mother did not like this lifestyle . . ." Salmon, *Oh to Be a Sapper!*, p. 95.

p. 343 "This feeling has been so strong . . ." Mauldin, *Up Front*, p. 19.

p. 344 "Perhaps he [the combat soldier] will change . . ." Ibid., p. 34.

p. 344 "It was a strange time for us . . ." Cocker interview, 15 Dec. 2002.

p. 344 "We were completely lost . . ." Lorimer interview, 17 Dec. 2002.

p. 345 "These articles are in no way adequate . . ." Martha Gellhorn, *The Face of War* (Hart Davies, 1959; Granta ed., 1998), p. 96.

p. 345 "to look for our own casualties . . ." Bond Interview, 10 Aug. 2002.

p. 346 "One thing I did not put in . . ." Barrows e-mail, 12 Dec. 2002.

p. 346 "pumped a whole magazine . . ." Beacham interview, 5 Aug. 2002.

p. 346 "you're kind of angry . . ." Cunningham interview, 24 Feb. 2003.

p. 346 "It took me eighteen years to catch up with Bill . . ." quoted in Watt, *Mates and Mayhem*, p. 141.

p. 346 "nice, smiling Red Cross girls . . ." quoted in Fussell, *Wartime*, p. 288.

p. 347 "There is no wild exuberance . . ." Kindre diary entry, 11 April 1944.

p. 347 "Everyone expects the end . . ." Davie, *Diaries of Evelyn Waugh*, pp. 623–24, quoted in Fussell, *Wartime*, p. 137.

p. 348 "I also managed to survive Anzio and Rome . . ." Hartung interview, p. 42.

p. 348 "I folded up . . ." Hartung interview, 3 June 2003.

p. 348 "I became so psychologically damaged . . ." Beacham interview, 5 Aug. 2002.

p. 348 "After the war . . ." Koloski interview, 25 Feb. 2003.

p. 348 "One guy on the ship from Naples to Africa . . ." Cunningham interview, 24 Feb. 2003.

p. 349 "When I first got back . . ." Awes interview, 22 Feb. 2003.

p. 349 "Many [initially] had disturbing memories . . ." VA leaflet, www.dartmouth.edu/dms/ptsk/FS_Older_Veterans.html, accessed 2 Aug. 1999.

p. 349 "In the summer 2002 . . ." Awes interview, 22 Feb. 2003.

p. 349 "has been very hard on me . . ." Awes e-mail, 7 April 2003.

p. 349 "I still now feel an immense pride . . ." Murat interview, 12 Feb. 2003.

p. 350 "Les victoires oubliées de la France . . ." Notin, La Campagne.

p. 350 A ballot was arranged . . . Douds, "Matters of Honour," p. 128.

p. 350 "Oh, bury me at Cassino . . ." Y. Alibhai, "Lest we forget," first appeared in New Statesman, 21 June 1991, p. 16; quoted in Douds, "Matters of Honour," p. 128.

p. 350 "War: today more than ever . . ." Eggert e-mail, 12 March 2003.

p. 350 "I coped astonishingly well . . ." Eggert interview, 20 March 2003.

p. 350 "in complete shock . . ." Klein interview, 1 Feb. 2003.

p. 351 "The Amis with fifty tanks . . ." Langelüddecke interview, 7 March 2003.

p. 352 "My dear Kazimierz . . ." letters provided by Frettlöhr.

p. 353 "It was not the elegant, friendly town . . ." Pittaccio telephone interview, 8 April 2003.

p. 353 "Of course it wasn't the Cassino . . ." Cyril Harte article in Northampton Chronicle and Echo, 30 May 1994.

p. 353 "devoid of any real strategic rationale . . ." Ellis, Cassino, p. xv.

p. 354 "souveniring" leather identity tags . . . Awes interview, 22 Feb. 2003.

p. 355 "I am being brave . . ." Robson, Letters, p. 130.

p. 355 "Dear Barbara . . ." letter to Barbara Schick, 20 July 1944.

p. 355 "Poor devils, well out of it . . ." Robson, Letters, p. 83.

Select Bibliography

Addison, Paul, and Angus Calder, eds. *Time to Kill: The Soldier's Experience of War in the West, 1939–45.* Pimlico, 1997.

Alanbrooke, Field Marshal Lord. *War Diaries, 1939–45.* Weidenfeld & Nicolson, 2001.

Alexander of Tunis. *Alexander Memoirs, 1940–45.* Cassell, 1962.

Anders, W. *An Army in Exile.* Macmillan, 1949.

Ankrum, Homer R. *Dog Faces who Smiled through Tears.* Graphic Publishing, 1987.

Anon. *The Tiger Triumphs.* HMSO, 1946.

Aris, George. *The Fifth British Division.* 5th Division Benevolent Fund, 1959.

Barclay, C. N. *The History of the Sherwood Foresters.* Clowes, 1959.

———. *The London Scottish in the Second World War.* Clowes, 1952.

Blumenson, M. *Bloody River.* Allen & Unwin, 1970.

———. *Salerno to Cassino.* Government Printing Office, 1969.

———. *Mark Clark.* Congdon & Weed, 1984.

Blythe, John. *Soldiering On.* Sphere, 1968.

Blythe, Ronald. *Private Words, Letters, and Diaries from the Second World War.* Viking, 1991.

Böhmler, Rudolf. *Monte Cassino.* Cassell, 1964.

Bond, H. L. *Return to Cassino.* Doubleday, 1964.

Bourke-White, M. *Purple Heart Valley.* Simon & Schuster, 1944.

Bowlby, Alex. *The Recollections of Rifleman Bowlby.* Leo Cooper, 1969.

Broadfoot, Barry. *Six War Years.* Doubleday, 1974.

Brutton, Philip. *Ensign in Italy.* Leo Cooper, 1992.

Bryan, Sir Paul. *Wool, War, and Westminster.* Tom Donovan, 1993.

Buckley, Christopher. *The Road to Rome.* Hodder & Stoughton, 1945.

Carver, Field Marshal Lord. *The Imperial War Museum Book of the War in Italy.* Sidgwick & Jackson, 2001.

Chadwick, Owen. *Britain and the Vatican during the Second World War.* Cambridge University Press, 1987.

Chambe, R. *Le Bataillon du Belvedere.* Flammarion Press, 1953.

Chaplin, H. D. *The Queen's Own Regiment, 1920–50.* Michael Joseph, 1954.

Churchill, W. *The Second World War.* Cassell, 1964.

Clark, M. *Calculated Risk.* Harrap, 1951.

Cochrane, Peter. *Charlie Company.* Chatto & Windus, 1977.

Cody, J. F. *21 Battalion.* Department of Internal Affairs, 1953.

———. *28 (Maori) Battalion.* Department of Internal Affairs, 1958.

Connell, C. *Monte Cassino.* Elek, 1963.

Copp, Terry, and Bill McAndrew. *Battle Exhaustion.* McGill-Queens University Press, 1990.

Crawford, John. *North from Taranto: New Zealand and the Liberation of Italy, 1943–45.* New Zealand Defence Force, 1994.

Cross, J. P., and Buddhiman Gurung, eds. *Gurkhas at War: The Gurkha Experience in Their Own Words, World War II to the Present.* Greenhill Press, 2002.

Cuvillier, Solange. *Tribulations d'une Femme dans l'Armée Française.* Lettres du Monde, 1991.

Daniell, A. P. de T. "The Battle for Cassino, May 1944," *Royal Engineers Journal,* 1951.

———. *Mediterranean Safari.* Orphans Press, 1990.

David, Saul. *Mutiny at Salerno.* Brassey's, 1995.

Delaney, John. *The Blue Devils in Italy.* Infantry Journal Press, 1947.

D'Este, Carlo. *Fatal Decision.* HarperCollins, 1991.

Doherty, Richard. *Clear the Way! A History of the Irish Brigade, 1941–1947.* Irish Academic Press, 1993.

Ellis, John. *Cassino: The Hollow Victory.* André Deutsch, 1984.

Erskine, D. *The Scots Guards, 1919–55.* Clowes, 1956.

Fergusson, Bernard. *The Black Watch and the King's Enemies.* Collins, 1950.

Fisher, E. J. *Cassino to the Alps.* Government Printing Office, 1977.

Ford, Ken. *BattleAxe Division.* Sutton, 1999.

Fox, F. *The Royal Inniskilling Fusiliers in the Second World War.* Gale and Polden, 1951.

Framp, Charles. *The Littlest Victory.* Privately published, n.d. (in the IWM).

ffrench, R. L. V. B. *History of the 17/21 Lancers, 1922–59.* Macmillan, 1962.

Fry, James C. *Combat Soldier.* National Press, 1968.

Fuller, J. F. C. *The Second World War.* Eyre & Spottiswoode, 1948.

Fussell, Paul. *Wartime.* Oxford University Press, 1989.

Gardiner, Wira. *The Story of the Maori Battalion.* Reed, 1992.

Gellhorn, Martha. *The Face of War.* Hart Davies, 1959 (quotes from Granta ed., 1998).

Gilbert, Martin. *The Road to Victory.* Heinemann, 1986 (quotes from paperback ed., 1989)

Godfrey, E. G. *The History of the Duke of Cornwall's Light Infantry.* Images Publishing, 1994

Gooch, John, ed. *Decisive Campaigns of World War Two.* Frank Cass, 1990.

Graham, Dominick. *Cassino.* Ballantine Books, 1971.

Graham, Dominick, and Shelford Bidwell. *Tug of War.* Hodder & Stoughton, 1986.

Hapgood, David, and David Richardson. *Monte Cassino.* Congdon & Weed, 1984 (quote from Da Capo Press ed., 2002).

Hart, Peter. *The Heat of Battle.* Leo Cooper, 1999.

Heller, Joseph. *Catch-22.* Jonathan Cape, 1962.

Henderson, Diana, ed. *The Lion and the Eagle.* Cualann Press, 2001.

Heurgon, Capitaine. *La Victorie sous la Signe des Trois Croissants.* Editions Pierre Voilon 1946.

Hinsley, F. H. *British Intelligence.* Vol. 3. HMSO, 1984.

Horsfall, John. *Fling our Banner to the Wind.* Kineton, 1978.

Huebner, Klaus H. *Long Walk through War.* Texas A&M University Press, 1987.

Jackson, W. G. F. *The Battle for Rome.* Batsford, 1969.

Juin, A. *Mémoires Alger, Tunis, Rome.* Librairie Arthème Fayard, 1959.

Kay, Robin. *27 Machine-Gun Battalion.* Department of Internal Affairs, 1958.

Keegan, John. *The Second World War.* Century Hutchinson, 1989.

Kesselring, Albert. *The Memoirs.* William Kimber, 1953.

Kippenberger, Howard. *Infantry Brigadier.* OUP, 1949.

Laffin, John. *British VCs of the Second World War.* Sutton, 1997.

Lee Harvey, J. M. *D-Day Dodger.* Kimber, 1979.

Lewis, N. *Naples '44.* Collins, 1978 (quotes from Eland Press ed., 1983).

Linklater, E. *The Campaign in Italy.* HMSO, 1951.

Lutter, Horst. *Das War Monte Cassino.* Wilhelm Heyne Verlag, 1960.

Madden, B. J. G. *The History of the 6th Battalion the Black Watch, 1939–45.* Leslie, 1948.

Majdalany, Fred. *The Monastery.* Bodley Head, 1945.

———. *Cassino, Portrait of a Battle.* Longmans, Green, 1957 (quotes from Cassel Military paperback ed., 1999).

Martin, T. A. *The Essex Regiment, 1929–50.* Privately published, 1952.

Mauldin, Bill. *Up Front.* Henry Holt, 1945 (quotes from University of Nebraska ed., 2000).

McKinney, J. B. *Medical Units of 2 NZEF in Middle East and Italy.* Department of Internal Affairs, 1952.

Milligan, Spike. *Mussolini: His Part in My Downfall.* Michael Joseph, 1978 (quotes from Penguin paperback ed., 1980).

Molony, C. J. C. *The Mediterranean and the Middle East.* Vol. 5. HMSO, 1973.

Moorehead, Alan. *Eclipse.* Hamish Hamilton, 1945.

Morris, Eric. *Circles of Hell.* Hutchinson, 1993.

Nicolson, N. *Alex.* Weidenfeld & Nicolson, 1973.

Norton, F. D. *26 Battalion.* Department of Internal Affairs, 1952.

Notin, Jean-Christophe. *La Campagne d'Italie.* Librarie Académique Perrin, 2002.

Origo, Iris. *The War in the Val D'Orcia.* David R. Godine, 1947.

Overy, Richard. *Why the Allies Won.* Jonathan Cape, 1995.

Palmer, Bennett J. *The Hunter and the Hunted.* Privately published, 1992.

Parkinson, C. N. *Always a Fusilier.* Sampson Low, 1949.

Phillips, N. C. *The Sangro to Cassino.* Department of Internal Affairs, 1957 (republished Battery Press).

Piekalkiewicz, J. *Cassino: Anatomy of a Battle.* Orbis, 1980.

Puttick, E. *25 Battalion.* Department of Internal Affairs, 1958.

Pyle, Ernie. *Brave Men.* Henry Holt, 1944 (quotes from University of Nebraska paperback ed., 2001).

Ray, C. *Algiers to Austria: The History of the 78th Division in World War II.* Eyre & Spottis-woode, 1952.

Riordan, Thomas M. J. *A History of the 7th Field Company RE.* Privately published, 1984.

Robson, Walter. *Letters from a Soldier.* Faber & Faber, 1960.

Rock, George. *The History of the American Field Service, 1920–1955.* American Field Service, 1956.

Ross, A. *23 Battalion.* Department of Internal Affairs, 1957.

Shephard, Ben. *War of Nerves: Soldiers and Psychiatrists, 1914–1994.* Jonathan Cape, 2000.

Sinclair, D. W. *19 Battalion and Armoured Regiment.* Department of Internal Affairs, 1954.

Smith, E. D. *Even the Brave Falter.* Robert Hale, 1978 (quotes from Allborough Press ed., 1990).

———. *The Battles for Cassino.* Ian Allan, 1975.

Smith, Lee. *A River Swift and Deadly.* Eakin Press, 1997.

Smith, Roger. *Up the Blue.* Ngaio Press, 2000.

Stevens, G. R. *Fourth Indian Division.* McClaren and Sons, 1949.

Stockman, Jim. *Seaforth Highlanders, 1939–45.* Crecy Books, 1987.

Sym, J. *Seaforth Highlanders.* Gale & Polden, 1962.

Trevelyan, R. *Rome '44.* Secker & Warburg, 1981.

Truscott, L. K. *Command Missions.* Dutton, 1954.

Vojta, Francis J. *The Gopher Gunners: A History of Minnesota's 151st Field Artillery.* Burgess Publishing, 1995.

Von Senger und Etterlin, F. *Neither Fear Nor Hope.* Macdonald, 1963.

Wagner, R. L. *The Texas Army.* Wagner, 1972.

Walker, Fred L. *From Texas to Rome: A General's Journal.* Taylor Publishing Company, 1969.

Watt, Lawrence. *Mates and Mayhem.* HarperCollins, 1996.

Weinberg, Gerhard L. *A World at Arms.* Cambridge University Press, 1994.

Westphal, S. *The German Army in the West.* Cassell, 1951.

Williams, David. *The Black Cats at War.* IWM, 1995.

Williams, Tony. *Cassino—New Zealand Soldiers in the Battle for Italy.* Penguin, 2002.

Wright, Robert. *'Strewth so Help me God.* Privately published, 1994.

INDEX

(Page numbers in italics refer to maps)